SHARED HISTORIES

SHARED HISTORIES

A Palestinian-Israeli Dialogue

Editors

Paul Scham, Walid Salem, Benjamin Pogrund

Left Coast Press Inc.

Walnut Creek, California

LEFT COAST PRESS, INC.
1630 North Main Street, #400
Walnut Creek, CA 94596
www.LCoastPress.com

Copyright © 2005 by Paul Scham, Walid Salem, Benjamin Pogrund

*Originally published by the Palestinian Center for the Dissemination of Democracy &
Community Development (Panorama) and the Yakar Center for Social Concern, 2005*

ISBN 1-59874-012-1 hardcover
ISBN 1-59874-013-X paperback

Library of Congress Control Number: 2005928677

Printed in the United States of America

The paper used in this publication meets the minimum requirements of American National Standard for Information Sciences—Permanence of Paper for
Printed Library Materials, ANSI/NISO Z39.48–1992.

09 10 11   5 4 3

CONTENTS

FOREWORD

"SHARED HISTORIES" is the title and leitmotiv of this book and of the project behind it. Thanks to the courageous, untiring, and persistent collaboration of Israelis and Palestinians, this project has been implemented over some years and I have had the honour and pleasure to be part of it.

In this conflict-ridden world and especially in that country that needs peace so desperately but that still seems to be so far removed from it, the commitment and the attitude of the Israeli and Palestinian authors and, above all, of the publishers, Benjamin Pogrund, Walid Salem and Paul Scham, are particularly note-worthy. I am filled with confidence that the descriptions of a specific period in the history of Palestine, which have previously been developed and discussed here and are now represented, will contribute to the process of ending the conflict, which is, hopefully, regaining momentum, and to the longed-for peace between Israelis and Palestinians.

"Shared history" is also "common history" endured together, which can simultaneously be the basis and point of departure of dialogue, respect, and understanding for the other side, in each case.

Rabbi Michael Rosen, head of the Yakar Center in Jerusalem, says: "History is a means of self-understanding. Unless one is prepared to be self-critical and objective about oneself, there can be no real development. Without history one can neither understand oneself, nor the world around."

Furthermore, it is impossible without an understanding of history to discover the present or indeed to predict future developments. And history consists of narratives, in the first place. Here, too, various sources were selected, analyzed, interpreted, and finally published as narratives. In Palestine and Israel, in particular, there are very different points of view and evaluations of the historical facts.

By the nature of things, in the 100-year-long conflict between the Jewish and Palestinian populations, it is particularly difficult to acknowledge the history of the other partner to the conflict, in addition to one's own viewpoint and description of history, never mind accepting it as being of equal worth. That is why presenting factually honest historical descriptions from both sides of a given period is highly commendable, in the face of all the adversity that the conflict has generated in recent years.

History has involved both sides with their own particular stories in such a way that it is possible to talk of both a "common" and a "shared" history. The claim being made, in the project represented and in the contributions collected, is that it is a factually and politically honest search for a fair description of proved historical facts, which is both the basis of the understanding of the attitude of the other side in each case and an evaluation of it. Movements toward peace start with growing reciprocal knowledge. This knowledge alone produces self-knowledge and understanding of the point of view and attitude of the other side and only in this way will understanding finally be attained.

The "Truth Commissions" in South Africa or in Central America are good examples of the necessity of gaining comprehensive knowledge of the development; the actors and the victims in the conflicts, preparing the way for processes of understanding and for peace. The work of the German-French and German-Polish "Schoolbook Commissions" is another impressive demonstration of how historical narratives, analyzed and evaluated through dialogue, can contribute to understanding between peoples who were former war-time enemies.

As supporter and moderator, I have had the opportunity to accompany this project for part of the way, particularly at an important conference in Cyprus, and I share the conviction of the publishers and authors that peace is possible in Israel and Palestine and that the reciprocal propagation of the knowledge of the common, shared history will make quite a considerable contribution to it. In this respect, I wish for this publication to attract considerable attention and be widely distributed and I wish the project much continued success.

Burckhard Michael Blanke
Bonn, January 2005

ACKNOWLEDGMENTS

WE would like to thank the generous financial benefactors who made this Shared Histories project possible: David and Elaine Potter and Michael Polonsky of the David and Elaine Potter Charitable Foundation in Britain who supported us from the start, and the Friedrich Naumann Foundation in Germany whose Jerusalem Director, Dr. Burckhard Michael Blanke, shepherded the project through his organization; we invited him, as a historian and impartial observer of the Middle East scene, to chair the discussion sessions which he did with authority and sensitivity. On his departure from his posting in Jerusalem, Anne Koehler, also from the Friedrich Naumann Foundation, ably took over. The current Director, Dr. Rene Klaff, has continued to give us unstinting support and it is through his efforts that the Friedrich Naumann Foundation has made this book possible. Suleiman Abu-Dayyeh at the Foundation has been a helpful friend throughout.

We thank Dima Bazbaz of Panorama for her constant help, Isabelle Klebanow for her accurate transcription of the discussions, Lama Habal for her assistance in editing, and Hannah Sholl for preparing the texts for printing. Paul Scham expresses his thanks to his current colleagues at the Middle East Institute and at George Washington University, both in Washington, D.C., for their support and encouragement in the long process of preparing this work for publication.

All three of us express our deep gratitude to the Palestinians and Israelis who agreed to take part in the Shared Histories project and were willing to cross the lines of division to share their knowledge and ideas. We hope that their efforts and the publication of this book will contribute to ending the divisions.

Editing of the text has been a cooperative Palestinian-Israeli operation. It has worked well but has opened the way to some variations in spellings of names and places, which are in any event often problematic. Certainly, the experience of the three of us—who have worked together harmoniously and determinedly as originators, organizers, and editors—in overcoming one obstacle after the other to bring this project to a successful conclusion, is a practical example of what can be achieved in Israeli-Palestinian relations.

P.S.
W.S.
B.P.

*Words marked * at first mention in the text
are described alphabetically in the
Glossary on Page 277*

INTRODUCTION

WHAT do Palestinian and Israeli historical narratives have to do with peace between the two sides? Aren't the issues those clear and tangible problems – settlements, borders, refugees, "right of return", self-government, security, water, holy sites, etc. – which are invariably the stuff of every failed set of Israeli-Palestinian negotiations? Compared to this, aren't Israeli and Palestinian "narratives" primarily of academic, or simply parochial, interest?

On the contrary. It is the premise of this book that how the two sides understand – and misunderstand – their own and the "other's" history has a profound influence on their ability – and inability – to make peace. In other words, like the invisible "dark matter" that cosmologists tell us makes up 90 percent of our universe, the intangibles in the conflict, largely based on history that is "remembered, recovered, invented" (as Bernard Lewis once entitled a book), profoundly influence the willingness of the two sides to make peace, or to continue with war. Without some understanding of the historical experience of the other side, and how that other side views its own history, Israeli-Palestinian peacemaking may be doomed to further rounds of violent and pointless failure. What is worse, peacemaking failures can significantly aggravate the situation rather than ameliorating it, as was the case with the Camp David summit of 2000. Camp David II not only failed to make peace; its failure added a new element to the narratives of both sides, and a new hurdle which those who still think peace is possible must clear.

This volume is based on the premise that the intangible elements, especially the historical narrative of the two sides, make a difference in both *peace-making* (prior to an agreement) and *peace-building* (after an agreement is reached). While its three editors – who designed and carried out the project on which it is based – fully recognize and advocate the need for compromise of the tangible issues that divide their societies, we also believe that history is ignored at one's peril.

This point may seem unexceptional. In fact, however, the conventional wisdom of Palestinian-Israeli peace-making regards discussions of history as counter-productive.[1] This point may well be valid for ice-breaking negotiations. But, after that ice has been broken, as it was between Israeli and Palestinian negotiators in the early Oslo negotiations in 1993, the continued ignorance of historical narratives, whether by negotiators or the two publics, poses a significant danger to the success of the whole process. A crucial reason for the collapse of the Camp David negotiations was the failure of public education, by both sides, to create public understanding of the "red-line" issues for both sides. As long as the two sides see the other in terms of stereotypes handed down through more than 100

1

years of conflict, that understanding, and thus the ability to create peace between the two societies, will continue to be lacking.

Recognizing that narratives matter acknowledges that the societies themselves have a deep stake in both the continuation and the ending of the conflict. It implies that the two societies have to recognize – not ignore – each other, and squarely face each other's deepest beliefs. In order to do this, there must be a willingness to listen to the other side, not necessarily to agree, but to try to understand what the enemy is saying. This recognition helps to move the conflict from the realm of exchanging pieces of territory under near-compulsion to a relationship that encompasses the human history of each side, as understood and experienced by the protagonists.

We, and many (though not necessarily all) of the participants in this project, still accept the now-unpopular view that understanding is not only possible but attainable between Palestinians and Israelis. Partly this is because of our own experiences in working with each other and with many other members of the "other" side in this and other projects to create understanding. This hands-on activity has helped us to reject as self-indulgent and self-serving some of the conventional logic of peacemaking, especially the notion that the only way that Israelis and Palestinians can get along is to stay apart.

Genesis of this book
This project was conceived and carried out through three Jerusalem-based institutions, The Truman Institute for the Advancement of Peace of the Hebrew University of Jerusalem (Paul Scham), Panorama (The Palestinian Center for the Dissemination of Democracy and Community Development) (Walid Salem), and Yakar's Center for Social Concern (Benjamin Pogrund). In the spring and summer of 2002, after three years of fundraising and preparation, Palestinian and Israeli historians, as well as geographers, journalists, translators, and others, met for a series of discussions in Cyprus and Jerusalem to share their views on what happened in Israeli and Palestinian history. Seven topics were chosen from the period 1882-1949, and a Palestinian and an Israeli prepared a short paper intended to present an "Israeli" or "Palestinian" view of that subject. Those papers, edited, appear in this book.

The discussions, one 2-3 hour session for each topic, were transcribed edited for length and intelligibility. They are a major part of this book, and the interplay between the participants, both professional historians and laypersons, shows how the process of understanding can proceed.

Unlike negotiations, no agreement was sought or expected. Rather, it is precisely the disagreements, expressed in this case verbally rather than violently, that are of particular interest in trying to bring to a wider audience a greater understanding of the elusiveness of peace between the two sides.

We chose the period from 1882 to 1949 because that can be termed the "classical" period of Israeli and Palestinian history. It covers the beginning of modern Jewish settlement and ends with the establishment of the State of Israel, which the Palestinians term al-Nakba (the Catastrophe). The elements of the conflict have all emerged, though certainly there are many events of great interest – and controversy – both before and after this period. Archaeology is itself in great dispute between the two sides, as is the Six Day/June War of 1967; both of which are integral to the sides' view of themselves. We hope to cover further issues in a subsequent volume.

It should be noted that conditions of life in the Holy Land do not spare scholars any more than anyone else. While those Palestinians living in Jerusalem were able to travel through Ben Gurion Airport to Cyprus, those in the Palestinian Authority were not able to enter Jerusalem or reach Ben Gurion Airport. Some were able to make the difficult journey to Amman and thence to Cyprus; Issam Nassar could not and his paper was presented by Ata Qaymari. Later, Salim Tamari could not enter Jerusalem and his paper was given by Bernard Sabella.

'Shared History'

As noted, this project developed out of a belief that Palestinians and Israelis cannot attain a durable peace between them without some degree of understanding – on a societal, not simply an academic level – of each other's historical narrative. By historical narrative, we mean how a society understands itself and others through history – how it came into being, how it fits into the world, how it relates to its enemies and friends. The historical narrative is truly the property of a nation as a whole; in fact, possession of an historical narrative is one definition of a nation.

We called the project "Shared History", but a participant later pointed out that it is more truly "Shared Histories", as our premise is that there are two basic narratives of the past. This is not to eliminate the notion that a truly shared narrative may be possible, but that is not our assumption. We believe that the two narratives both can and must be enriched by a knowledge and understanding of the "other".

On the other hand, it can be truly maintained that there is not just one narrative on either side. Each historian, each writer, each statesman, each teacher weaves his or her own narrative. However, we believe that this adds up to a general narrative, that helps each people collectively explain its place in the world.

Academic history is not in itself the historical narrative of a people, though it is usually a significant component and, normally, maintains a continual dialogue with the narrative. That narrative is transmitted through primary and secondary education, politicians and statesmen, the media (of all sorts) and, to a great extent, personal experiences. Every time a Palestinian talks of his suffering in an Israeli prison, or an Israeli grandfather relates his combat experiences, they are

3

participating in the transmission of the historical narrative. While textbooks, media, and political statements play a crucial role, they can sometimes be dwarfed when, as in this case, both populations are continually involved in the ongoing conflict, and have been so for more than half a century.

However, academic history has a major role in the unearthing of new sources of information, and in changing the narrative. While the term "academic" is often pejorative in common usage, its debates do bring out new viewpoints and perspectives. And, it is usually the ultimate source for the other aspects of historical narratives, as comparatively few non-professional historians will spend years unearthing records and grounding themselves in the innumerable secondary sources.

Israeli and Palestinian historical narratives come out of the struggle between the two peoples, and thus reflect its power asymmetries, as well as each side's ambivalence about the other's national existence. While Israel and the Palestine Liberation Organization (PLO) formally recognized each other as part of the Declaration of Principles signed on the White House Lawn in 1993, a century of ideological as well as military conflict was not, of course, wiped away by the stroke of a pen. Unfortunately, most ordinary people, as well as informed observers on both sides, underestimated by orders of magnitude the work that remained in dealing with the accumulated historical debris. Understanding the reason for this sheds light on the importance of historical narratives in making peace.

First, and most important, each side was caught up in its own narrative without realizing it. For Israelis, "Oslo" (which we will use as a shorthand for the 1993-95 series of agreements between Palestinians) represented a recognition of Israel by its enemies and a promised end to violence against the state and its citizens. Of course, Israelis, both in the street and at policy-making levels, understood that recognition of the PLO was a fundamental shift of *policy*, but Israelis by no means recognized that the Palestinian *narrative*, encompassing such sticky issues as Israeli responsibility for the events of 1948 and Palestinian suffering, continued. On the contrary. Since most Israelis consider the "right of return" by Palestinians a euphemism for the destruction of the Jewish state, they believed that recognition of Israel's existence necessarily involved dropping the demand for return. Since very few Israelis, including those in policy-making positions, had a true understanding of the importance of the idea of "return" as a component of Palestinian identity and narrative, they assumed that it could simply be dropped. When it (inevitably) returned as part of final status discussions in the late 1990s, Israelis were genuinely shocked and saw it as clear evidence of bad faith.

For Palestinians, peace without some recognition of their suffering in 1948 and since was inconceivable and, likewise, a clear indication of bad faith on Israel's part. While many Palestinian moderates have long recognized (at last privately) that there was no possibility of Israel accepting a blanket right of return, they were genuinely astonished that even many left-wing Israelis, who had long been part of the "Peace Camp," were intransigent on any recognition of the right of return, however diluted, or even acceptance of some degree of responsibility for the events of 1948. They did not comprehend that, according to the Israeli narrative, any flexibility on this issue constituted a frontal attack on Israel's legitimacy.

It should be noted that there have been important and significant efforts to push past this barrier. At the Taba negotiations of December 2000-January 2001, specific numbers of Palestinians were suggested, apart from which no return would be allowed. Other initiatives, notably the Geneva Accord, have come up with other solutions.

Historical narratives are equally central to the role of Jerusalem. Many moderates on both sides were genuinely astonished to hear, as the Camp David negotiations were going on in the United States, of the central role of Jerusalem in the historical narrative and national identity of the other side. They were even more astonished, not to mention furious, to hear how their own attachment to Jerusalem was denigrated and even ridiculed by the other side. Since this centrality to their own side was so obvious, and the importance to the other side was so poorly understood, it was deemed as bad faith and prima facie evidence of unwillingness to make peace by both sides.

As in the case of the "Right of Return," various creative solutions have been proposed, including "God's sovereignty," dividing up the Old City of Jerusalem, or making it one unit policed by both Israelis and Palestinians. However, without a sense of the legitimacy of the "other" as a partner in the enterprise, such solutions have not yet received majority support.

Thus, historical narratives are essential to the questions of legitimacy, which are literally existential issues to both sides. Both sides saw the questioning and denigration of their narrative as literal proof that their national existence was being denied.

Ironically, it was the rejectionists on both sides who had a handle on this, but their ideology precluded them from dealing with it. Some of those who believed most strongly and passionately in their own rightness understood that the other side would not easily surrender its most cherished beliefs. However, they do not accept that an acknowledgement and understanding of another's narrative is of importance in itself.

This project
As noted above, the most obvious way of dealing with two narratives is to try to merge and even reconcile them. Most non-historians – and certainly some professional historians as well – see this as necessary and desirable, perhaps in the short and certainly in the long term. However, this project is based on the

opposite assumption, which may seem counter-intuitive to many. That is, that before any attempt can be made to merge them, the separate, distinct, and in many cases contradictory narratives must be recognized, respected, and understood by both sides. As we have shown above, both sides consider respect for their national narratives tantamount to respect for their legitimacy. Since both sides consider their legitimacy under direct attack in many ways from the other side – by violence, intimidation, vilification and many other means – this respect must be demonstrated as part of a peace process.

It is essential to stress that respect by no means implies agreement. But this project – like many of the coexistence projects that all of us have been involved in for many years – provides a framework within acceptance can take place. Contact with the "other" side – on both a human and an intellectual level, can show tangible proof of acceptance. Narratives are always modified through time; contact and acceptance can help move them in directions that include a respected place for the "other." Contradictions can be softened in practice, even if they are maintained proudly in theory.

An obvious example is what has been accomplished in Christian-Jewish interfaith dialogue in the last half-century. (Of course, this is particularly relevant, since the Palestinian-Israeli conflict can touch on the same issues at times.) Taken starkly, the Christian and Jewish narratives are necessarily absolutely contradictory. Either Jesus was the Messiah, or he was not. Either he was the son of God or not. These examples can be multiplied endlessly. It is now commonplace for Christian and Jewish (and, more and more, Muslim) theologians to respect, discuss and seek to understand the theology (which can be considered a religious narrative) of the other, while remaining firmly within their own tradition. On the other hand, the controversy over Mel Gibson's movie, "The Passion of the Christ," provides a perfect illustration, if one were needed, of the power of traditional narratives, and the different and incompatible perspectives of different religious communities.

Historical narratives are as powerful as religious narratives were (and in many cases still are). One aspect of the Israeli-Palestinian conflict which this project does not discuss, but may in a later iteration, is the sacralization of modern, as well as ancient, history, thus making disagreement a matter of religion as well as politics.

The concept of 'narrative'
We begin with the premise that Palestinians and Israelis are divided conceptually from each other by a gulf mediated by their historical experience. Seeing themselves as part of that historical experience is, to a large degree, what nowadays defines an Israeli Jew or a Palestinian. While many individual Israeli Jews and Palestinians might cavil at or reject specific elements of their own collective historical narrative, the telling and retelling of that narrative has marked them, and made it difficult to accept a contrary story.

As we use the term, "narrative" is different from, though closely related to "history." The narrative of a society is how it, in the most general terms, understands its collective history. Thus, no one book, article, movie or any other creation can embody it comprehensively, though some are more reflective of it than others. How well any one work embodies it is inherently a subjective decision. And, the narrative changes over time.

History, however, in contrast, is written by individuals who make individual choices literally on every word. Their works may be more or less reflective of the collective narrative. Professional historians, who comprise many, though not all, of the participants in this project, and whose ideas are reflected both in the essays and transcripts below, may or may not follow various elements of that collective narrative.

Below, we present what is perhaps a simplified version of the respective historical narrative of Palestinians and Israelis. Nevertheless we believe that both sides will instantly recognize one part of it as representing how they learned their past, and the other as a propagandistic representation of what the other side claims to believe.

TRADITIONAL ISRAELI NARRATIVE (1882-1949)	TRADITIONAL PALESTINIAN NARRATIVE (1882-1949)
a) The legitimacy of the Zionist enterprise of returning Jews to Eretz Yisrael is based on the Jewish descent from the ancient Israelites, and the Jewish people has inherited their right to the land. This can be understood religiously, legally, and historically. Jews have always looked and prayed toward Zion (Jerusalem) and never gave up their relationship to the land, despite their expulsion. Jews were treated as foreigners and persecuted wherever they were during their long Exile.	a) Judaism is a religion of revelation, like Christianity, and has no inherent tie to a particular land. Jews are not a nation but rather a community of believers. In any case, any Israelite presence was a short period in the long history of Palestine. Ultimately, religious myths, without presence and possession, are incapable of creating an ownership right. Those Jews living in Palestine and the Muslim world before 1882 were well treated by Muslim neighbors and rulers.
b) Zionism was an authentic response to the persecution of Jews over millennia around the world. Jews did not come as colonizers, but rather as pioneers and redeemers of the land, and did not intend to disrupt the lives of the current inhabitants of the Land	b) Zionism was a European colonialist enterprise like many in the late 19th century and was a European ideology superimposed on the Middle East. Moreover, it is an ideology of expansion directed towards robbing Arabs of their ancestral land. Arabs

of Israel. All land for Jewish settlement was legally bought and paid for, often at inflated prices.

c) The Arabs of Palestine were not a national group and never had been. They were largely undifferentiated from the inhabitants of much of Syria, Lebanon and Jordan. They had no authentic tie to the Land of Israel. Many only came for economic opportunity after the Zionist movement began to make the land fruitful and the economy thrive. In all the years of Arab and Muslim control from the 7th century, Palestine was never a separate state and Jerusalem was never a capital.

d) Zionist diplomacy legitimately sought a Great Power patron since Herzl, and found one in Great Britain. Of course Britain had its own imperial agenda, but this does not detract from the righteousness of the Zionist cause. The Balfour Declaration was ratified by the League of Nations, which constituted a statement of international law approving a Jewish homeland in Palestine.

e) The riots of 1920, 1929 and 1936 were instigated by unscrupulous Arab leaders for their own nefarious purposes, particularly the Mufti of Jerusalem, Hajj Amin Al Husseini. The "Palestinian" population had increased rapidly through immigration of Arabs who were attracted by Zionist economic successes, and the Arab population's living standards rose rapidly during this period. The British frequently stood aside when Arabs murdered Jews.

were systematically expelled by Zionist settlers from the beginning.

c) The ancestors of today's Palestinians (Canaanites, Jebusites, and others mentioned in the Bible) were there before the Israelites, as shown by both biblical and archaeological evidence. Palestinians have lived continuously in the land since then. Certainly by the 1920s and likely much earlier, there was a Palestinian identity and nationality that differed fundamentally from other Levantine Arab peoples.

d) The British foisted Zionism on the Palestinians beginning with the Balfour Declaration as part of their imperial strategy, with no right whatsoever in international law, and this was illegally ratified by the League of Nations. Zionists worked hand in glove with Britain to subjugate the Palestinian people.

e) All the disturbances were justified and spontaneous revolts by the Palestinian people against the British/Zionist alliance and increasing immigration. The increasing Jewish immigration, facilitated by the British, created the resentment that led to the revolts. The British backed the Zionists, who were responsible for and had provoked the disturbances, and punished Palestinians harshly and illegitimately.

f) The British, who had been initially supportive of the Zionist enterprise through the Balfour Declaration and the early mandate, began to backtrack early, as reflected in the splitting off of Transjordan in 1922, the Passfield White Paper of 1930, and many other incidents. They definitively repudiated the Balfour Declaration with the White Paper of 1939, and were basically pro-Arab after that point.

f) The British were always pro-Zionist, except when occasionally forced otherwise by Arab pressure. They conspired with the Zionists to destroy Palestinian leadership in the 1936-39 revolt, thus making it impossible for Palestinians to prepare for the coming war with the Zionists. The White Paper of 1939 had no effect as it was not enforced. The British deliberately trained Zionist soldiers during the 1936-39 revolt and World War II.

g) The Zionist movement accepted the UN partition resolution of 1947 in good faith, albeit reluctantly, as it had the 1937 Peel Commission Report recommending partition. War was forced on the *Yishuv* (Jewish national community) by the Arabs. Solely in self-defense, the *Haganah* (later the Israeli Army) took over more land than had been allotted to it in the Partition Resolution and was justified in holding it, as it would have inevitably become a base for attacks on Israel.

g) The UN partition resolution of 1947 was illegitimate, as the UN had no right to give away the homeland of the Palestinians. The Palestinians cannot be blamed for trying to hold on to what was rightfully theirs. Compromise was out of the question. The Jewish leadership never genuinely accepted the idea of partition; in any case, expulsion (transfer) was always the plan.

h) The Yishuv was numerically vastly inferior to the combined Arab population, and it bordered on a miracle that Israeli survived the war ("the few against the many"). All Jews realized they would be massacred if they lost, and fought with absolute determination to prevent another Holocaust. Arab atrocities proved they had no other choice.

h) The Jews had planned for the war, had organized both politically and militarily, had strong support abroad and were in a much more favorable position when war came. Their armed forces outnumbered all the Arab armies. Palestinians had no infrastructure and no military training, and were attacked and massacred repeatedly by Jewish gangs. Arab "aid" consisted primarily of attempted land grabs by other Arab countries of Palestinian land.

i) The Palestinians were not expelled. They fled, in most cases, because they

i) Beginning soon after the adoption of the partition resolution in

were ordered and cajoled by their leaders and the Arab states, in order to make room for conquering Arab armies. In many cases Jewish officials pleaded with the refugees to stay. The Israeli decision to prevent refugees from returning was justified, as otherwise Israel would be destroyed by a hostile Arab internal majority. Ultimately, the responsibility and blame rests with the Arab leadership for rejecting the partition resolution	November 1947 the Zionists began to expel Palestinians from their homes, almost certainly according to a plan (Plan *Dalet*). Deir Yasin was a planned massacre that succeeded in stampeding Palestinians to leave. The Nakba was planned and carried out as ethnic cleansing. The Zionists recognized that a Jewish state could not exist until most Arabs were expelled, and history proves this was the plan that was carried out.
j) The refugee issue was artificially kept alive by the Arab states, who deliberately used the refugees as pawns against Israel. The real reason for the continuation of the conflict was the refusal of the Arab states to recognize Israeli's existence. Israel has repeatedly offered peace, but not at the price of the destruction of Israel as a Jewish state, which has been the Arab goal since 1948.	j) The Palestinian people have never ceased to protest against the illegality and immorality of their expulsion, and Palestinians continue to identify themselves as belonging to their real homes in Palestine. The Arab states have repeatedly betrayed the Palestinians, and only grudgingly gave them space in refugee camps. There can never be a settlement without Israeli recognizing its guilt and providing appropriate redress. Palestinians in other Arab countries are as much in exile as anywhere else.

Palestinian and Israeli historical writing

Modern Palestinian historical writing arose in the 1920s. Beshara Doumani's seminal article[2] identifies, only slightly tongue-in-cheek, two different trends. The first he denominates as "The Call for Battle"; the second as "Affirmation of Identity". He notes that both genres were dominated by "journalists, lawyers, politicians, and school teachers".

"Call to Battle", as its name implies, is primarily a mobilizing tool. It thus fits into the characterization of "historical narrative", as discussed above. He summarizes by noting, "As with any genre whose primary goal is to justify a nationalist struggle by mobilizing against the enemy, the 'Call to Battle' genre's primary concern is with the 'Other.' Internal contradiction, differences, and developments are glossed over."

The "Affirmation of Identity" genre moved well beyond this point, especially in pioneering the use of local archives and using them to recount the history of towns and cities where many Palestinians lived. However, he also feels that, although immense amounts of important historical information has been unearthed, the analysis of the material has tended to portray Palestinian society as too static, not recognizing its dynamic aspects. However, he feels that it has provided the basis that current and future historians, including Palestinians, Israelis, and others, can build on.

In another article, published in Arabic[3], Doumani also wrote of a third trend which he denominated the "Quest for Justice": it appeared primarily in English and was directed towards Western audiences. These emphasized principles of justice and human rights in order to mobilize foreign opinion for the Palestinian cause.

Doumani's own works, and those of other modern Palestinian historians such as Phillip Mattar, represent a more recent trend of Western-trained historians, often living in the United States, whose work is more academic and analytical and less political. They are well-read in Israeli historiography and are in contact with their Israeli colleagues, while maintaining their own narratives.

Israeli historiography comes out of very different circumstances. Jewish history flowered in the late 19th and early 20th centuries. The first Israeli university, the Hebrew University of Jerusalem, was founded in 1927. Pre-state society was both highly literate and mobilized for the cause of an independent Jewish state. After the 1948 War, Israeli historians, who almost universally saw themselves as part of the Zionist consensus, depicted Israel as a natural, if not inevitable, culmination of Jewish history. The War of 1948 was seen as forced on the Yishuv[4], and Palestinian refugees as victims of their own failed attempt to prevent partition, and of Arab leaders' power grabs.

Israeli historical writing was generally focused on building up the Land of Israel. While the struggle with Arabs/Palestinians was, of course, an integral and major part of the story, the emphasis, as with most national history, is from the inside looking out. For most of Israel's existence, little thought was given to a Palestinian narrative, which was dismissed as self-serving propaganda.

This changed in the late 1980s. A new school of younger Israeli historians, known as the "New Historians" or "Revisionists," began to present a different version of Israeli history, much closer to, though by no means identical to, the Palestinian narrative. While the perspective was not new – many of its contentions had been raised by the left-wing opposition to the Labour Party in the political wars of the 1950s - this work created a furor in Israeli society as a whole. While only some of the New Historians were linked with the concurrent "post-Zionist" movement, many Israelis, including many "Old" Historians (whatever their age), regarded the new writings as both flawed in conception and factually inaccurate. Some of these debates are reflected in the discussions in this book.

Shared History today

This project was originally conceived in early 1999. Although for those of us living in Jerusalem then, things seemed anything but peaceful, we (joined by what probably the majority of Israelis and Palestinians) believed that the conflict was on a trajectory to solution. We saw this project as assaulting a frontier of peace-building that had not yet been reached, namely the past. Palestinians and Israelis were meeting with each other, discussing joint issues, and planning for a future. We hoped and expected that a final status summit would bring an end to the fighting, and then the work of building an appreciation of peace would take priority. For this, we believed, the history that had been dropped in order to break the ice would need to be rediscovered. Our slogan was "It's time to go back to the past."

Obviously, we had misjudged the tenacity of the conflict and of those who rejected compromise solutions. The four years following the failure of the Camp David summit, and the eruption of al Aqsa Intifada in September 2000 were bleak. A mood of deep pessimism has settled over both populations. Though all three of us are engaged in a variety of joint activities we, in common with our compatriots on both sides of the conflict, had no expectations of an early solution. As of this writing, in January 2005, following the election of Mahmoud Abbas as the new Palestinian President, we are feeling new stirrings of hope. However, we continue to believe that, in order for a comprehensive peace to not only be signed, but to take hold, some degree of understanding of the narrative of the "other" is essential.

Our project has helped convince us that only a better understanding of both sides can lead to an acceptance of the basic aspirations of the "other". This is bound up in their history. Thus, we believe that, in a conflict where the two sides are fated to live together, only this knowledge and understanding can provide us with the tools to make peace.

Paul Scham
Washington, D.C.

Walid Salem
Jerusalem

Benjamin Pogrund
Jerusalem

[1] Savir, Uri. The Process: 1,100 Days that Changed the Middle East. Random House, 1998.
[2] Doumani, Beshara, Rediscovering Ottoman Palestine: Writing Palestinians into History. Journal of Palestine Studies, XXI no. 2 (Winter 1992) pp. 4-28
[3] Doumani, Beshara, Afaq Falestiniyyah (Birzeit University Research Magazine), vol. 6, (Summer 1991).

NAPOLEON TO ALLENBY: PROCESSES OF CHANGE IN PALESTINE, 1800-1918

Ruth Kark

PERIODIZATION is used as a tool in historical research and analysis. There are several possible approaches regarding periodization for the late Ottoman period in Palestine. These may be selected from the viewpoint of either Ottoman rule and reform, the Eurocentric position, which stresses the impact of the West and Westernization, the Judeo-Palestino-Centric and later Zionist angles, or more recently the Arab-Palestino-Centric angles with special focus on the inception and growth of the Palestinian national movement. In each, we may create periodizations for sub-categories of political events (e.g. wars, regime change), certain populations, or waves of immigration and settlement (the Hassidic* *Aliyah* (immigration wave) of the Jews for example in 1777, the Aliyah from North Africa in 1830, or the Lovers of Zion Aliyah in 1882 unjustifiably entitled "The First Aliyah", and the same for Arab or other sub-groups such as the wave of immigration from Egypt in the 1820s and 1830s, or the interrelations between the Greek Orthodox Patriarchate and the Community in the 19th and 20th centuries). **[See Figure 1, Page 14].**

Some examples of critical dates mentioned in the research are: the Napoleonic invasion of 1799, Muhammad 'Ali's reign (1831-40) during which the *fellahin* uprising of 1834 is considered by some scholars as the first expression of Palestinian Arab national identity, the Ottoman *Tanzimat* (reforms) period of 1839-1876, the Crimean War in 1853-56, the rule of 'Abd ul Hamid II between 1876 and 1908, and the "First" and "Second" Jewish Aliyot from 1882 to 1914.

For this paper, one should ask: (1) what is the periodization of the conflict in Palestine for the years 1800-1918? and (2) which parameters should one use for creating such a periodization, which will assist in discussing and analyzing the conflict? When examining recent research dealing with the history of Eretz Yisrael/Palestine/Israel, including the conflict between the Arab Palestinians and the Jews, the choice of terminology appears to or actually does have divergent connotations depending on the context and worldviews of the researchers. A few examples of such terminology include:

1. Colonialism/Imperialism (is Zionism part of world colonialism?)
2. Colonization/settlement
3. Post-Colonialism – the swing of the pendulum

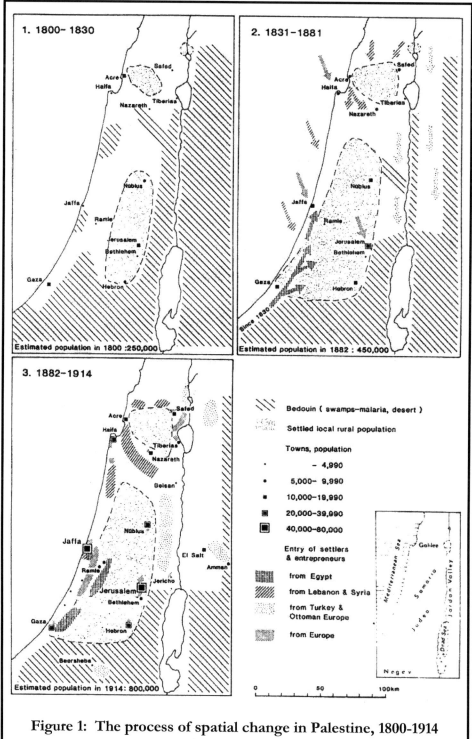

Figure 1: The process of spatial change in Palestine, 1800-1914

14

4. Orientalism, "Eurocentric Orientalism"
5. Indigenous populations (should this refer only to Arabs?)
6. Foreign populations (restricted to Europeans, or also including Circassians, Egyptians, Lebanese, Syrians, Mughrabis, Afghans, and Sudanese?)
7. Millenialism/Messianism
8. Nationalism (is it "imagined" or "real"?)
9. Zionism (is it a grassroots or an elitist movement?)
10. Post-Zionism (bad and good, black and white?) Denial of nationalism
11. "Old" and "New" History (objective? or neutral?)
12. Multiple narratives (including what Adel Manna calls the "victor's discourse")
13. Selective choice of sources (bias)

Old historians of Palestinian-Jewish interrelations and the conflict rely on empirical material based on primary documents of the period under discussion, or old (perhaps anachronistic) one-sided views based on a single narrative and influenced by the researchers' worldview.

New historians, on the other hand, rely on new (perhaps also anachronistic) research methods based on multiple narratives and scenarios evolving from not only the research subjects' own worldviews, but also and more often from the researchers' views, which are often based on a highly selective choice of sources, and whose documentation is often frail. A typical and common euphemism is the use of the term "tolerant" to characterize the attitude of Palestine's Ottoman administration and Muslim majority towards Jews and other minorities,[1] even though there is considerable evidence that suggests otherwise.

Also, some new historians, like Manna, ignore, or choose to ignore a whole body of recent research published by Israeli historical geographers on population trends, settlement processes, rural and urban developments, etc.[2] Is it not sad that Manna was unable to glean from this informative body of work anything of value that might add to his understanding of the Palestinian spatial phenomena, society, culture, economy and politics? Just one example is the salient contribution of missionary activity to the identity formation, education and health of the indigenous populations.[3]

At the comparative global level of discussion, is the case of Palestine unique, or is it similar to other examples of colonialism/imperialism, in the interaction (whether combative or cooperative) between the European invaders and the indigenous populations, and in the concept of a *terra nullius* (such as Canada, Australia, South Africa)?

Population growth and spatial distribution

Population trends
Palestine was populated by a mix of different peoples, and the division may be drawn along religious or ethnic lines. Until 1922, however, when the first comprehensive census of the area's population was conducted, information was

based on incomplete data and conflicting estimates which were not always objective. In 1800, the population stood at an estimated 250,000-300,000 (including about 5,500 Jews). Ben Arieh, basing his estimate on Western sources, placed the total population at approximately 350,000 in 700 settlements in the early 1870s, including 18,000 Jews (27,000 by 1880), in addition to about 25,000 Bedouins. According to Schmelz's estimate, Palestine had some 470,000 inhabitants in 1882 (24,000 Jews). On the eve of World War I, the population was estimated at about 800,000 according to Schmelz's new demographic study (and not 689,000, as estimated by others) of which 85,000 were Jews (60,000 according to McCarthy).[4]

The population consisted predominantly of Sunni Muslim Arabs throughout the Ottoman period. Its growth in the 19th century resulted from a slow natural growth, along with the migration of small groups of Muslims, mainly from other parts of the Ottoman Empire.[5] Part of this migration resulted from resettlement of loyal Muslim subjects who had been displaced by the loss of European territory on the fringes of the Ottoman Empire.[6] Some *metuwalis* (Shiites) lived in villages near the border with Lebanon, and a small Druze minority resided in villages on the Mount Carmel ridge and the Galilee. Under Ottoman, and later British rule, the Druze community was discriminated against, and was not recognized as a separate community. Thus it was refused juridical autonomy and was subject to Muslim court procedures. Samaritans were in the town of Nablus, and a few Karaite families resided mainly in Jerusalem. Other religious groups gained a foothold in Palestine in the 20th century, including Baha'is, in the region of Acre and Haifa, and Ahmedis in Haifa.

The Christian population was divided into a number of communities: Greek Orthodox, Roman Catholic, Maronite, Syrian Orthodox (or Jacobite), Coptic, and Ethiopian. The Ottoman regime recognized the Greek Orthodox and Armenian communities (and the Jews) as separate millets, or religious communities organized around the political-religious authority of its spiritual leader. Protestant churches entered the scene in the early 19th century, some engaging in missionary activity, mainly among other Christian sects and the Jewish population. Small groups of European and American Protestants established agricultural settlements and urban neighborhoods; most noteworthy were the German Templars who founded several successful settlements in Palestine from the late 1860s onwards. Protestant activity had a profound effect on the population of Palestine, introducing Western ideas and technologies, improving health, social, and education standards, and instituting social organizations.

The Jewish population grew from about 5,500 (2.2 percent of the total population) in 1800, to 650,000 (32 percent) in 1948. On the eve of Israel's independence, the *Yishuv* (the Jewish community in Palestine) accounted for 5.5 percent of world Jewry. Some of the determinants of change and modernization were unique to the Jewish community in Palestine, while others characterized the whole Middle East and North Africa and other Jewish and non-Jewish communities and sects. A uniqueness of the Yishuv, compared to Jewish communities in the Diaspora, was its growing internal variety of Jewish ethnic groups and communities, with Eretz Yisrael serving as the foundation of messianic yearning and Zionist national aspirations.

Waves of Jewish immigration from North Africa and the Middle East were one factor in Jewish population growth. Eastern European Jews added to the increase, some settling for traditional reasons in the Holy Land, and others as part of the *Hibbat Zion* (Love of Zion) and Zionist enterprise, after 1882.

World War I (1914-1918) had a negative effect on Palestine. The area was placed under the virtual dictatorship of Turkish General Jamal Pasha, who expelled both foreign Jewish nationals and local Muslim and Christian Arab leaders and families, and conscripted local Arabs and Jews. To the financial and economic hardships caused by the war, and aggravated by the corruption or the caprice of Turkish officials, were added the outbreak of serious epidemics among the helpless and underfed town dwellers, and further devastation inflicted by the invasion of locusts twice during the war. The war front moved through Palestine, with Jerusalem falling to the British in December 1917, and the north falling in autumn 1918.

Stages of immigration and settlement

The Jewish population, which did not exceed, as mentioned above, 5,000-6,000 in 1800, consisted of mainly Sephardic Jewish exiles and their descendants from Spain and Portugal, reaching Palestine via southern Europe, the Ottoman Empire or North Africa. European immigrants arrived in small waves. The Hasidim came during the second half of the 18th century, settling in the Galilee towns of Tiberias and Safed. A wave of *Perushim* (disciples of R. Elijah, the *Gaon* of Vilna) began to arrive at the beginning of the 19th century. Before the mid-19th century, the Jews of the "Old Yishuv" lived almost exclusively in the four "Holy Cities": Jerusalem, Hebron, Tiberias and Safed. Parfitt argues, with much justification, that between 1800 and 1880, the "Old Yishuv" played a much more central role in the creation of a Jewish entity in Palestine than had hitherto been recognized, that Jewish immigration started long before Zionism, and that many social, demographic and institutional phenomena, which were to be important later, had their beginnings during that rather neglected period.[']

The pogroms in Russia in 1881 opened a new period for Jews in Palestine. The mass exodus of Jews from Eastern Europe resulted in the immigration of some 25,000 to Palestine over the following two decades. The years 1882 to 1903 are known as the "First Aliyah,"[7] characterized as the beginning of the Jewish agricultural settlement and proto-Zionist activity in Palestine. However, the majority of the immigrants joined the Orthodox population in the towns. The "Second Aliyah" (1904-1914) saw the arrival of approximately 40,000 mainly East European immigrants. This further served to change the balance in the composition of the Jewish community, with *Ashkenazim* (European Jews) becoming the majority.

Arab Muslim immigration to Palestine continued mainly from adjoining countries – Egypt, Syria, Lebanon, and Transjordan – in pursuit of economic opportunity. Thus it can be inferred that immigration played a more important role in the increase of Palestine's Jewish community. The total population of Palestine increased by 923,000 between 1922 and 1943, with 62 percent from natural growth (reflecting an improvement in health conditions, as indicated by the reduction of the infant mortality rate), and 38 percent from net immigration. This included growth of the non-Jewish population by 503,000, with 93 percent from natural growth. The increase in the Jewish population was 75 percent due to net immigration.

Urbanization processes

Regarding the spatial distribution of the population of Palestine in 1800, it was predominately rural, with only about one-sixth of the population (54,000) living in the 12 largest towns (for example, Jerusalem had 9,000, Acre and Gaza had 8,000 each, Nablus 7,500, and Safed 5,500). By the 1870s, this urban population increased to about 120,000 (Jerusalem increased to 30,000, Gaza to 19,000, Nablus to 12,500, and Hebron and Jaffa to 10,000 each). By 1922, the population of these towns had increased to 228,600, or approximately one-third of the population.

There was also a significant nomadic population, with the Bedouins roaming the Negev, the Jordan Valley, the Jezreel Valley and the coastal plain sections. Expansion of the rural population into peripheral areas, where settlement had not been possible before, was in tandem with the partial retreat of the Bedouin population. Competition with settlers and entrepreneurs from outside Palestine served to further limit Bedouin control over sections of the country, and Ottoman authorities monitored their movement, particularly from the 1870s onward. In 1931, there were 66,553 Bedouins, two-thirds of whom were in the Negev (Beer Sheva sub-district).

On the eve of World War I, Jaffa was on its way to becoming a major city, when its population had grown to 50,000 (including 15,000 Jews), making it the second largest city in Palestine after Jerusalem (with a population of 75,000, including 53,800 Jews). In 1909, the *Ahuzat Bayit* Society's founding of a modern Jewish quarter north of Jaffa became the nucleus of the first Hebrew city in Palestine – Tel Aviv – which rapidly grew (from 1,500 in 1914, to 46,301 in 1931, reaching 250,000 in 1948) to become the center of Israel's main metropolitan region. Haifa, and Haifa Bay also developed during the 20th century into an important center, an economic base and a foreland for Britain in Palestine and the entire Middle East. During British rule, there was also an internal migration from villages to towns and cities. In 1945, 49 percent of the country's population was urban, although there were variations among the religious groups (30 percent of Muslims, 80 percent of Christians, and 74 percent of Jews were town dwellers). A number of factors promoted this process of urbanization: rural-urban migration due to increased pressures on agricultural land, the need for industrial workers in the cities, better health services, and the availability of other amenities found in the cities.

Modernization and Technological Change:
When did the modern era begin in Palestine?

According to Shimon Shamir, and unknowingly following indicators chosen by Issawi in his studies on the economic history of the Middle East, the beginning of the modern era in Palestine was in the 1830s, when the country was under Egyptian rule. Kimmerling and Migdal also determined that this same sub-period was also the beginning of a Palestinian national identity.

External versus indigenous agents of change?
Several questions may be raised for the discussion of this topic. Among them: (1) Who were the agents of change and modernization in Palestine during the late Ottoman period? and (2) Were the Europeans, including pre-Zionist and Zionist settlers, the main agents and the pioneers of modern technology, and were the "indigenous natives" the "defeated rejectionists of modernity?"[8]

The pioneers of modern technology in Palestine, beginning in the mid-19th century, were Christian and Jewish entrepreneurs, missionaries and immigrants. But the role of the indigenous population, whether from Arab (Muslim and Christian) or minority groups (Armenians, Greeks, and Jews), in local innovation and diffusion, and their role as mediators, although to a lesser extent, cannot be discounted, even though there is evidence, at least in the beginning, of some opposition from the Arab majority (cutting telegraph wires and poles (1865) for example, or damaging carriages).[9]

Land and land ownership
One of the main factors of the conflict between Jews, foreign Christians and Arabs was the issue of land and land ownership. Some of the issues to be considered are: (1) whether the land was inhabited or empty (the Zionist myth of "making the desert bloom); (2) the "fluid" inventory of available land; (3) the processes of land concentration; (4) Arab absentee landlords and entrepreneurs; and (5) the dispossession of the Palestinians.

Early land conflicts are characterized by clashes and assassinations of foreign Christians and Jewish settlers (Christians in Artas, Jaffa and Abu Shushe, Templars in Haifa and Tira, Jews in Petah Tikva, Rosh Pinah, Metula, etc.). Do these represent mere "neighborhood quarrels," or xenophobia and buds of national conflict? Manna's explanation in his contribution to this publication is a partial and an overly simplistic interpretation of the determinants of the conflict over land resources, which should be viewed at the levels of the Ottoman Empire and its local administration, the Arab urban entrepreneurial middle and upper classes, the local and foreign Jews as potential buyers of land, the Christian Churches and missions also as potential buyers of land, and at the level of local Arab fellahin and Bedouins.

At the imperial level, we need to take into consideration the legal status of land and ownership by Ottoman and foreign subjects, including the sultan, and of Ottoman land policies, including land grants and auctions. Between the Empire and the fellahin was the level of the musha' system of land holding that served as an old equalizing mechanism for holding and cultivating the land (Ottoman policies sought to abolish this institution).[10]

Local and regional Arab entrepreneurs played an important role in the privatization and concentration of large plots of land for the purposes of investment, development of modern agriculture, and prospecting, and it is they who, by selling their holdings to the Jews and foreign Christians, would later be responsible for the dispossession of the fellahin and Bedouins. The purchase contracts specified that the land was to be transferred to the buyers as vacant land, emptied of its tenants or customary users. This brought about clashes between the new owners and the previous tenants, who fought for what they perceived as their traditional (but never legal) rights.[11]

Conclusion

In order to reach a better understanding of the roots of the conflict, and the forces that drive it, an honest and dispassionate balance is required. This must take into account all the evidence, including primary sources and serious contemporary academic research by Israeli, Palestinian and international scholars. Polemics that reveal the target and draw one-sided conclusions before engaging in a serious process of compiling, weighing, synthesizing and interpreting solid data do little to contribute to an insightful or meaningful bridging of the chasm.

Appendix

The Jewish Point of View – Concepts of Land in Palestine/Eretz Yisrael, 1800-1918[12]

Examples of salient Jewish historical themes dealing with Eretz Yisrael, land rights and land "redemption:"

1. God gave Eretz Yisrael to the Jewish people as a gift.
2. The right of possession remains in the hands of God, and is transferred to the Jewish people as a collective for a period of 49 years.
3. According to the Responsa literature, Jews are obligated to settle the land of Israel, redeem it through purchase from non-Jews, and cultivate it.
4. With time, the concept of redemption took a wider and more abstract meaning, dissociated from the actual physical land.
5. From the mid-19th century on, proponents (in the Diaspora) of settling the land of Israel referred to the redemption of the land in a messianic sense (as a prerequisite to the coming of the Messiah).
6. Within the Old Yishuv in Palestine (pre- and post-1882), similar ideas emerged, forming the basis for the establishment of various agencies charged with the purchase, settlement and cultivation of the land.
7. Zionist thought regarding land was an amalgam of European and American contemporary ideas, Biblical guidelines, messianic orientation and nationalistic thought. It inspired the idea of a Jewish National Fund (created in 1902), and the demand for the nationalization of land. The people, as a collective, would replace God as landowner. The land was detached from economic considerations, and placed within the context of a nation's tie to its land.

8. With the secularization of the concept of land, the practical dimension of redemption – gaining control of land – became prominent. Settlement was necessary in order to establish holding rights, as purchase and possession of a legal title deed were insufficient. Redemption was for the sake of the people, not God; it was redemption from foreigners and from desolation, handled through land cultivation and general progress in the Western sense.

---

[1] See A. Manna's contribution to this publication.

[2] Examples of this recent research are found in Aaronsohn, Amit, Ben Artzi, Ben Arieh, Ben Yaakov, Biger, Glass, Golan, Goren, Grossman, Kark (*Land Ownership and Issues, Jaffa, Jerusalem, Including Muslim Neighborhoods, Coastal Cities, Entrepreneurship, Missionaries, Consuls, etc.*), Katz, Oren, Shiloni, Thalman, and a series of books in English edited by Ben Arieh and Kark (*Israel Studies in Historical Geography*).

[3] For more on this, see Jamal Adawi's Ph.D. thesis on the Friend's Mission in Ramallah, written at Haifa University, 2001. Also see Tibawi, Shlomit Langboim, Roland Loefler, Inger Mary Okkenberg, Paul Schmidgal, and Aharon Yaffe.

[4] See Kark, R. "Land Ownership and Spatial Changes in Nineteenth Century Palestine." Seminar on Historical Types of Spatial Organization—the Transition from Spontaneous to Regulated Spatial Organization, Warsaw, Poland, April 1983; Kark, R. and Glass, J. B. "The Jews in Eretz-Israel/Palestine, From Traditional Peripherality to Modern Centrality." Israel Affairs 5/4 (Summer 1999): 73-107. During Muhammad Ali's reign (1831-40) for example, Egyptians settled in parts of the country, as did a bit later other small groups of Muslim Bosnians, Algerians, Lebanese, Circassians and Turkomans.

[5] During Muhammad Ali's reign (1831-40) for example, Egyptians settled in parts of the country, as did a bit later other small groups of Muslim Bosnians, Algerians, Lebanese, Circassians and Turkomans.

[6] Kemal H. Karpat estimated that 1.1 million Circassians were resettled in the Ottoman Empire, mostly in Anatolia, some in Syria (including the Golan Heights) and Transjordan, and a small number in northern Palestine.

[7] During this First *Aliyah*, Jewish immigrants also arrived from Yemen and other Muslim countries.

[8] See Manna's Note 1, in his contribution to this publication.

[9] For more on this topic, see Kark's papers: "The Introduction of Modern Technology into Palestine" in T. Levi's collection; and "Transportation in 19th Century Palestine: The Reintroduction of the Wheel" in Kark (ed.), The Land That Became Israel, Yale University Press, 1990. Also see Kark and Thalman, "Technological Innovations in Palestine: The Role of the German Templers" in H. Goren and A. Cohen (eds.), Germany in the Middle East, and Kark and Glass' papers and books on Sephardic Entrepreneurs in Palestine. Gilbar also touched upon this topic in several of his publications.

[10] Kark R. and Grossman D. "The Communal (musha') Village of the Middle East and North Africa." In: Policies and Strategies in Marginal Regions, Eds. W. Leimgruber, Majoral, R. and Lee, C-W. Aldershot, UK: Ashgate, 2003, pp. 223-36.

[11] For further details, see Kark, *Land and Settlement in Eretz Yisrael, 1830-1990*, and *Selected papers by Prof. Ruth Kark*, Jerusalem, 1995.

[12] For further details see Kark, "Land-God-Man: Concepts of Land and Land Ownership in Traditional Societies and in Eretz Yisrael," in A. Baker and G. Biger (eds.), Ideology and Landscape in Historical Perspective, Cambridge University Press, Cambridge, 1992, pp. 63-82.

CONTINUITY AND CHANGE IN PALESTINE: THE LATE OTTOMAN PERIOD, 1856–1918

Adel Manna

THE victors of war and conflict write both their own history and that of the other side, and the story of the Arab-Israeli conflict, and particularly the Zionist-Palestinian conflict, is no exception. The Palestinians were the last to write their narrative, and did so long after the Eurocentric Orientalists and the Zionist settlers had. However, surprisingly enough, much of the Palestinians' historical accounts in the 20th century fall within the parameters of the victor's discourse.

Although Palestinian historians reach different conclusions and present their own value judgments, most often they use similar assumptions, paradigms and periodization methods to those of the Orientalists and Zionists.[1] This is particularly true when it comes to the history of Palestine and the beginning of the Arab-Israeli conflict during the late Ottoman era: Palestinian Arabs are portrayed as either absent or passive actors, and as victims of Ottoman administration and European colonialism; modernization is imposed from above and Palestine is radically transformed and westernized first by the Europeans, and later, after 1882, by Zionist settlers; the indigenous population is depicted simply as defeated rejectionists of modernity.[2]

The victor's dichotomous and reductionist narrative of Palestine's history since the 19th century has recently been challenged by critics both within (Israel's new radical historians and sociologists[3]) and outside its ranks (Said's Orientalism and young Palestinian historians like B. Doumani and R. Khalidi). But writing Palestinians into history remains a daunting task to undertake, and until a new generation of historians takes it on, even the best-intentioned attempts will remain within the victor's narrative.[4]

While it is beyond the scope of this paper to give a complete picture of Palestinian society during the last decades of Ottoman rule, the purpose here is to outline an alternative narrative and analysis of the formation and transformation of Arab society in Palestine during that period. Furthermore, this paper will touch upon Arab-Jewish relations before and after the early 1880s when Zionist immigration and settlement began. Finally, the paper will conclude with a comparison between the alternative narrative presented here and the Eurocentric Orientalist and Zionist one.

It is hoped that such an analysis will lead to discussions that might bridge some conceptual and factual gaps between adversaries. An acknowledgement of the Palestinian narrative and perspective might bring about a balanced and more accurate account of the past and help in reaching a better understanding of the other's perspective. Such understanding and empathy is conducive to political and cultural rapprochement between Arabs and Jews in general, and between Palestinians and Jews in particular.

1. Realities of change and continuity

Palestine witnessed a radical demographic, economic and social transformation during the 19th century. A closer look at the country's history during this period shows that the second *Tanzimat* (reforms) period, from the mid-1850s to 1878, was the critical turning point in this transformation.[5] Neither the French nor the Egyptian invasion of 1799 and 1831 respectively, nor Zionist immigration and colonization in the 1880s was as important a factor of change during this time. External powers, along with Ottoman policies, and local needs and decisions, all contributed to the accumulated process of the socio-economic and cultural transformation.[6] However, from the outset, it is important to note that the transformation process in the second half of the 19th century did not shatter the old established socio-cultural system of Palestine's indigenous Arab society, and there is a great deal of continuity alongside the forces of change and transformation. These forces, whether external or internal, were not able to change the conservative nature of Palestinian society and culture, even long after the breakup of the Ottoman Empire, after World War I. The complexity of change and continuity should be kept in mind when addressing Palestine's transformation during the second half of the 19th century.[7]

Palestine's demographic growth during the 19th century is an important indication of the socio-economic, administrative and cultural reforms. The estimated population was about 275,000 - 300,000 at the start of the century, and had doubled to about 600,000 toward its end. But this demographic growth was not evenly incremental throughout this period, the third quarter of the century being a turning point, as most historical accounts agree, when Palestine's population increased to about 470,000 by the early 1880s, from only about 350,000 in the mid 1850s.[8] Throughout the 19th century, a small Jewish minority lived in Palestine under Muslim rule, particularly during the long Ottoman period. Early in the 19th century, the Jewish community accounted for about 5,000, and except for a few families in some Galilean villages, it was traditionally concentrated in four cities: Safad, Tiberius, Jerusalem and Hebron. The Jewish community experienced demographic growth, particularly during the Tanzimat period, mostly as a result of immigration into the country. By the end of the 1870s, the Jewish community totaled about 24,000, at least half of whom lived in Jerusalem.[9]

By the early 1880s, Palestine's Jewish community was still very marginal and made up only about 5 percent of the total population, and played no important role in Palestine's transformation during this period,[10] for even after the beginning of Zionist immigration and settlement, the main factor in the demographic growth was the local population's natural growth rate, and not immigration – whether

Jewish, Arab or European. This natural demographic growth was an outcome of both Ottoman reform policies and of European influences of modernization and investment in the Holy Land.[11]

2. Modernity and early nationalism in the Holy Land

Ottoman reforms played an important role in gradually transforming Palestine into a modernized province, as was the case with the neighboring Arab provinces, as Ottoman rulers recognized the special importance of the Holy Land, particularly after its recapture from Muhammad Ali in 1840.

The second phase of Ottoman reforms (1856-1878) brought more radical changes in the day-to-day life of the people in Palestine. Deserted villages were repopulated and new ones emerged, particularly in the valleys and coastal areas. Haifa and Jaffa flourished as port cities and surpassed the inland towns of Safad, Nablus and Hebron.[12] Palestine was gradually integrated into the world market through increased exports of agricultural products, and imports of European industrial and other daily consumer products. As a result of improved security, communication, and of the standard of living, Palestine experienced, as mentioned above, an impressive demographic growth between the 1850s and the end of the 1870s, before the first Zionist wave of immigration and colonization (1882). Such historical facts are almost absent in the Zionist historiography, which continues to promote the myth of making the desert bloom since 1882. Surprisingly, not until recently did either Palestinian or other historians write much to challenge such mythical narratives.[13] The absence of an alternative Palestinian narrative allowed the Zionists to succeed in spreading this myth, not only among Jews, but also among many Europeans and Americans.

By the end of the Tanzimat (1876), Jerusalem, which had, beginning in the 1850s, experienced a demographic, political and cultural transformation, and which had seen an expansion of its administrative role, emerged as the capital of Palestine and became, in 1872, an independent *mutasarifiyya* connected to Istanbul.[14] As new neighborhoods were built by Jews, Arabs and the Europeans however, the walled Old City gradually lost its preeminence, but the old established families of the Holy City were able to strengthen their socio-political and economic bases. The Husseinis, who suffered a temporary setback during the Tanzimat period, were able to reclaim their leading political role among the local elites under Sultan 'Abd ul Hamid II's reign, emerging, after World War I, as the natural leaders in the Palestinians' struggle against Zionism.[15] The Khalidis, who had supported the reform policies, lost support during the last phase of Ottoman rule, and another Jerusalem family, the Nashashibis, appeared on the scene in the early 20th century and became the Husseinis' main competitors during the British Mandate period.

3. Muslims and Jews in Palestine before Zionism

Before addressing post-1882 Arab-Jewish relations in Palestine, it is important to briefly highlight the nature of these relations before Zionist immigration and colonization. As a minority non-Muslim community, the Jews in Palestine benefited from the relatively tolerant attitude of the Ottoman administration and

Muslim majority. This is true even in Jerusalem, where Jews were a majority over Christians and Muslims, and where, in the 1860s, they began building their own neighborhoods outside the Old City. These tolerant attitudes survived the fundamental changes in Ottoman policies and the growing European influence in the Holy Land. It is important to note that this tolerance had been the reality of Jewish-Muslim relations, until very recently, when misconceptions grew rampant because of recent events in the Arab-Israeli conflict.

Although this tolerance, both in Palestine and elsewhere in the Middle East, did not mean equality or equal status for Jews in Muslim societies, it did however mean, at the very least, that there was no deep-rooted collective Muslim hostility towards Jews.[16] The Jews of Palestine and other neighboring Arab countries suffered no persecution, as they had throughout Europe and during the Crusades. In fact, Jews and Muslims cooperated in building a flourishing culture in Muslim Spain, and when the Spaniards succeeded in re-conquering the country from its Muslim rulers, both Jews and Muslims suffered terrible persecution. On the whole, until the early 20th century, and in contrast with Christian hostility and anti-Semitism, particularly in Modern Europe, Muslim attitudes towards Jews were tolerant,[17] as they were not seen as a threat to either Muslim rule or the Muslim community in Palestine, or elsewhere in the Middle East.

Zionist ideology was born and nurtured in Europe, against the background of anti-Semitism and Western rediscovery of the Holy Land in the 19th century. Zionist activists started to immigrate to Palestine in spite of Sultan 'Abd ul Hamid's objections to each and every national enterprise. During the final years of Ottoman rule, the Jewish settlers purchased land and establish 40 new settlements, and in 1908 began building the first Jewish city in Palestine, Tel Aviv. 'Abd ul Hamid's negative response to several offers from Theodor Herzl was not backed up by fundamental steps to block the growing Zionist enterprise. Ottoman attitudes did not change much under the Young Turks who seized power in 1908 and terminated the absolutist sultan regime by restoring Parliament and the constitution.[18]

The early phase of the Zionist enterprise was not perceived by the Arabs as being a serious threat to their community. New immigrants and settlers faced only two types of sporadic, non-organized opposition. The first came in the form of local clashes between the colonizers and neighboring Arab Bedouins and fellahin. There were for example, casual clashes between the Jewish settlers of Petah Tiqva and Metula on one side, and their Arab neighbors on the other, relating mostly to different traditions for land cultivation, grazing and the like. Local conflicts over customary rights, however, were the upper layer of an encounter between two cultures and perceptions of land ownership: the absolute right of private ownership, on which European capitalism rested, and the more diffuse, but not less extensive right of usage, in practice in many pre-capitalist societies.[19]

A different type of resistance came from city elites and middle-class nationalists who expressed their opposition to Zionism in several ways. An 1891 petition, for example, sent from Jerusalem and signed by its mufti and other elites, requested that the Ottoman government stop mass Jewish immigration and settlement in the Holy City and its surroundings. Another clear voice of opposition to the Zionist venture in Palestine was expressed in an unusual private letter from Yusef Diya al Khalidi to Herzl in March 1899, wherein Al Khalidi, a former mayor of Jerusalem and one of the most prominent Arab intellectuals of his generation, while expressing sympathy for Europe's persecuted Jews, adamantly opposed the Zionist plan of establishing a Jewish State in Palestine.[20]

In the wake of the Young Turks' rise to power, and the restoration of the constitution, more and more Arab voices of opposition were heard publicly. Members of Parliament, such as Ruhi al Khalidi, Said al Husseini and Hafiz al Sa'id, demanded strict measures against Jewish immigration into Palestine.[21] In the pages of his newspaper *al Karmel*, the journalist Najib Nasser attacked the Zionist plan and exposed its dangers. Other journalists and politicians expressed their fear that the government was not doing enough to stop the Zionist colonization. Muslim and Christian Arabs were unanimously united in their rejection of the Zionist enterprise.[22]

Young nationalist activists from Palestine participated in overt and secret political clubs and societies. The relatively free press and publishing field, after 1908, made it possible for more Palestinians to express their nationalism and oppose Zionism. On parliamentary election campaign trails, candidates rushed to highlight the grave consequences of Jewish immigration and colonization in Palestine. But as long as the region was part of the Ottoman Empire, the activists believed the country was relatively safe. Most of the Palestinians relied on the government and did very little in terms of active resistance.

4. The repercussions of the Ottoman collapse on the Palestinians

On the eve of World War I, the Arabs in Palestine still made up a majority of the population. The Jews, who had dramatically increased in number during the 19th century, then represented only a little more than a tenth of the population, in spite of more than three decades of Zionist immigration. Most of the Palestinians, particularly the fellahin of the hilly regions, were not severely affected by Zionist colonization. Nationalism, whether Arab or Palestinian, was an interest to only an urban minority. These realities explain the Palestinians' weak resistance to the Zionist enterprise prior to the war.[23]

The repercussions of the war years (1914-1918) were catastrophic for the Palestinians, as the country was transformed into a military camp. Young men were conscripted into the Ottoman armies and sent to fight in far-away lands, and livestock and food products were confiscated by the government. Natural disasters, such as locusts and epidemics, also added to the suffering of the population.[24] Most of the people supported the Ottomans, but after the 1925 Arab revolt of Sharif Hussein, the Commander of the 4th Army, Jamal Pasha, and his comrades increased their repressive measures. His harsh policies antagonized many Arabs who shifted their support to the national cause. Many came to erroneously remember these war years as indicative of centuries of Ottoman repression and injustice. This misperception continued to nourish much of the national discourse about the long Ottoman rule in the Middle East.

Meanwhile, the British army succeeded in rebuffing two Ottoman attacks on the Suez Canal. The counter-attack launched in 1917 brought British soldiers into Palestine. They occupied Gaza in early November and marched toward Jerusalem the next month. Simultaneously, political decisions were being made in London, which affected the destiny of the country and its people. The British government concluded its negotiations with Zionist leaders, and issued the Balfour Declaration on 2 November 1917. The break-up and fall of the Ottoman Empire, on the one hand, and the Balfour Declaration promising the Zionists a Jewish state in Palestine, on the other, represented another major turning point in the history of Palestine. When centuries of Ottoman control in Palestine and the Arab East came to an end, a new era of colonial supremacy began, and post-war British colonial policies in Palestine were catastrophic to Palestinian national interests.

In conclusion, it is important to note that the new realities of the post-World War I years were crucial in constructing the new Palestinian identity and its new national institutions.[25] The obsessive national discourse which followed explains the attitude of Palestinian historians and politicians towards the Ottomans who bore the blame for the Arabs' predicament. This discourse was not able to create its own paradigms and judgment, but rather operated within the parameters of the Orientalist and Zionist historical narratives.

---

[1] B. Doumani, "Rediscovering Ottoman Palestine: Writing Palestinians into History." Journal of Palestine Studies, Vol. 21, No. 2, Winter 1992, pp. 5-28.

[2] Ibid.

[3] In addition to the writings of Ilan Pappé it is important to highlight the studies of Gabi Piterburg, Baruch Kimmerling and Gershon Shafir.

[4] Dozens of such encounters took place in Israel, Palestine and abroad during the 1990s.

[5] During the earlier period of the Tanzimat (1839 to 1856), most reform efforts were focused on administrative and security issues. Beirut replaced Acre as the capital of Sayda province, for example, and Jerusalem became the capital of an expanded sanjak, extending from Rafah, in the south, to the Isdraelon valley, in the north. These administrative reforms and centralization policies weakened the countryside's local elites (shaykhs), whose strongholds were destroyed by the late 1850s. For more on this, see A. Manna, "Continuity and Change in the Socio-Political Elite in Palestine During the Late Ottoman Period," in T. Philipp (ed.), The Syrian Land in the 18th and 19th Centuries, Stuttgart, 1992.

[6] B. Abu Manneh, "Jerusalem in the Tanzimat Period: The New Ottoman Administration and the Notables," in Die Welt des Islams 3a (1990) pp. 1-44.

[7] See Manna (Note 5).

[8] A. Schölch, "The Emergence of Modern Palestine 1856-1882," in Studia Islamica: Studies in Honour of C. Zurayk, Beirut, 1988.

[9] For more on the Jewish community during 1800-1882, see T. Parfitt, The Jews in Palestine 1800-1882, The Boydell Press, 1987.

[10] Ibid.

[11] A. Schölch, Palestine in Transformation 1856-1882: Studies in Social, Economic, and Political Development, Washington, 1993.

[12] Y. Ben Arieh, "The Population of the Large Towns in Palestine During the…19th Century…," in M. Ma'oz, Studies on Palestine During the Ottoman Period, Jerusalem, 1975.

[13] In addition to the cited studies of A. Schölch, it is worth mentioning the work of B. Doumani, R. Khalidi, A. Manna, M. Yazbak and M. Seikaly, among the young Palestinian historians.

[14] See Abu Manneh (Note 6).

[15] Ibid.

[16] B. Lewis, The Jews of Islam, Princeton, 1984.

[17] Ibid. See also M. Cohen, Under Crescent and Cross: The Jews in the Middle Ages, Princeton, 1994.

[18] A. Manna, The History of Palestine in the Late Ottoman Period, 1700-1918 (in Arabic) Beirut, 1999, pp. 211-237.

[19] Ibid.

[20] Ibid. See also the chapter on Y. al Khalidi in A. Scholeh's book (Note 11).

[21] N. Mandel, The Arabs and Zionism Before World War I, California Press, 1976.

[22] Ibid. See biographies of these journalists and politicians in A. Manna, The Notables of Palestine (in Arabic), Beirut, 1997.

[23] A. Manna, History of Palestine (Note 18) and N. Mandel (Note 21).

[24] Ibid.

[25] R. Khalidi, Palestinian Identity: The construction of Modern National Consciousness, New York, 1997.

DISCUSSION 1

Ruth Kark and Adel Manna

RUTH KARK: I'm going to talk first talk about periodization. We have several options for periodization, and also a series of questions that we can elaborate on later. One is the periodization of the conflict - or the shared history, if you like - of Palestine during the years 1800 to 1918, and the parameters which should be used for creating such a periodization, which will assist us in discussing and analyzing the conflict.

One periodization example divides the period into three **[Figure 1, Page 14]** and shows trends of settlers coming into the country from outside, as well as the urban growth of cities.

It is important to note the distribution and size of the population in each period. In 1800, it was an estimated 250,000; in 1882, 450,000; and in 1918, 800,000. The small cities all had less than 9,000 or 10,000 people at the beginning of the 19th century. While some cities grew by the end of the period – Gaza, Jaffa, Haifa, Nablus and Jerusalem – others were either deteriorating or growing very slowly.

The second element is the immigration of certain groups who came from outside and settled in Palestine during the 19th century. You can see the local population mainly in the mountain areas. The parallel lines show the distribution of the Bedouins. From 1831, you can already see the beginning of immigration of groups from different places. Some came from Syria and Lebanon, for example. Others came from the Ottoman Empire, Kafkaz, Circassian Bosnia and others. Still others came from Europe. Here we have to differentiate between Jews and Christians. Especially in the second period (1831-81), quite a large wave of immigrants came from Egypt and settled along the coast all the way to Wadi Ara, where you can still find their *hamoulas* today.

In the Negev as well there were Egyptians who either fled from Muhammad Ali – this was his pretext for conquering Palestine – or, for other reasons, settled around Jaffa in what we call *zaknat*, little neighborhoods of Egyptians. There are about eight of those around Jaffa, one – Abu Kbir – with an Egyptian name.

In the third period (1882-1914), you see the growth of urbanization and of the local population, the settled rural area into the coastal area, as well as in the north.

Another question, relevant to all our papers, relates to the general terminology, methodology, and research literature we are using. This comes out in the discussions about Palestine settlement, and of course, in discussions about any

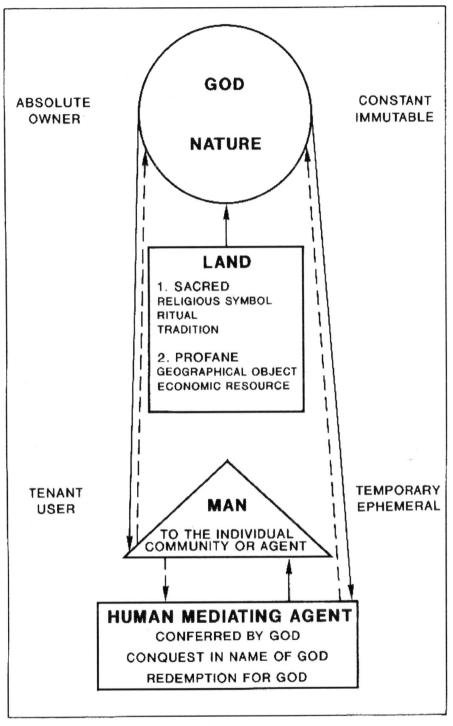

Figure 2: Some examples of human mediating agents

31

other area of the world as well, demonstrating that this is a general issue and general terminology.

One question we should ask, at the comparative global level of discussion: should we examine the uniqueness of the case of Palestine? Is it similar to other examples of colonialism-imperialism, in the interrelation (conflict-cooperation) between European invaders and indigenous populations? Does the concept of *terra nullius*, used mainly by the British in parts of the British Empire – Canada, Australia, South Africa – meaning empty lands, apply, or is this a unique case study?

I want briefly to go over the terms that Adel Manna brings up in his paper. For example: history of the victor, and that of the other side; Zionist-Palestinian or Arab-Israeli conflict; "common grounds for confrontation;" different customs concerning cultivation of land; narratives; Zionist settlers; European Orientalists; Palestinians; dichotomous and reductionist narratives of the history of Palestine; assumptions and paradigms; relatively tolerant attitudes of the Ottoman administration and the Muslim majority, and no persecution – which I have my doubts about, Adel.

You say that "modernization is imposed from above and Palestine is radically transformed and westernized first by the Europeans, and later, after 1882, by Zionist settlers" who I think were the main agents of technological innovation. In the first half of the 19th century, maybe the first two-thirds, they were the main innovators. I looked into it. If you can help me find material about Arab innovators in that period I would be very thankful, but I haven't found it yet.

BENJAMIN POGRUND: Why are there question marks after "Zionists" and "main innovators"?

RUTH KARK: I must add first that most of the innovators were Europeans and American Christians, not the Zionists.

The question marks are there because I had questions about who were the real innovators in that period. Maybe there were some that we don't know about and we haven't yet found material about. But from my findings, the first ones were principally the missionaries or settlers who came from Europe and America. For example, they brought the first oil mill to Nablus, and the first modern water pump to Jaffa.

Another thing that Adel mentions is the Zionist mythical historiography of making the desert bloom. Those historical facts are almost absent in Zionist historiography. There is very little written about that. What I think he means are facts about population trends and economic development, which are not missing. I can show you many sources in which they are discussed. There is little written by Palestinian historians or others to challenge them, even new radical historians and sociologists such as Said, Doumani and Khalidi. Very briefly, we are talking about several processes relating to the 19th century – population growth and spatial distribution, population trends, stages of immigration and settlement, urbanization processes and competition for economic benefits.

Another issue is modernization and technological change. When did the modern era begin in Palestine? We know the famous article by Shimon Shamir wherein he writes that it was during the period of Muhammad Ali. Migdal and

Kimmerling also talk about the First National Movement in that period and the revolts of 1834. And who were the agents of change? Were they external or indigenous?

Another important aspect is the issue of land and land ownership. Was Palestine a populated or empty land - again, the myth or the practice of the blooming of the desert by the Zionists since 1882? To my mind, 1882 is not a good year for dating the beginning of Zionist immigration. Even if we talk about the First Aliyah, I think it's a mistaken term because it was not the First Aliyah or the first wave of immigration of Jews into Palestine. Developments began much earlier than that.

There is also the issue of a fluid inventory of available land. There were, some empty or unsettled areas in Palestine at that time which were uncultivated and unpopulated. There is one example, from 1890-1891, of large plots of land in different areas of Palestine that were offered to various Jewish associations, mainly from Russia, who were considering, due to very special circumstances of that time, coming and buying land and settling in Palestine. This is in Turkish dunams, which are a little bit less than a metric dunam. But it's an area of over half a million Turkish dunams.

So we saw the fluid land offers to Jews. I call it fluid because it was moving from hand to hand. First it was settled by Abdul Khader and the Mughrabis, and later it was offered to Jews or to Christians. So we have a process of land concentration, mainly in the hands of Arab absentee landlords at first, and entrepreneurs.

Then there is the question of the dispossession of the Palestinians. By whom? Early land conflicts, clashes and assassinations of foreign Christians and Jews. I mention some examples in my paper. There is a process of privatization of land in Palestine beginning in 1858, when certain groups of people bought big plots of land, concentrating the lands in their hands. In the beginning, they didn't buy the land for speculation or prospecting. Eventually they thought about developing the land, but after a while they sold some of it to other groups who came to settle in the country, including Zionist Jews and Christian agencies or missions or settlers.

Finally, **Figure 2 [Page 31]** is more general and relates to the appendix to my paper. I am very interested in the concepts of land and land ownership in traditional, pre-modern and modern societies. Looking at concepts of land and land ownership in quite a few traditional societies around the world – some tribes in Africa, the aborigines in Australia, the Bible, Islam – I think that we can find a common denominator in relation to land, actually a common concept of land.

This can be presented in a triad. First there is God, or nature in some tribes, and man, with land in between. The concept of land as something legal, as an economic asset, only begins, I think, with the Greeks and the Romans. And man, who receives the land from God or nature through some kind of a human mediating agent conferred by God; conquest in the name of God; or redemption for God. If we relate this, for example, to the idea of the Jubilee in the Jewish biblical traditional, or to the Shiite or other Islamic ideologies, we find many similarities in the traditional relationship to land.

ADEL MANNA: Ruth did a good job introducing the topic and presenting options for reading and understanding the issues of periodization and historical processes. The 19th century is an important period for understanding the processes in the 20th century as well. I am not going to summarize my paper, but I would like to raise a few questions and make some points concerning this period.

One of the basic opening questions is whether it is legitimate to deal with the history of Palestine during this period separately from the history of the region. Palestine was an integral part of the Ottoman Empire. There were no borders - at least not those we know from Mandatory Palestine - for instance, between Palestine and Lebanon. In the south, we have the same borders with Egypt. In the east, the Jordan River is not a border between Palestine and Jordan. There was no Kingdom of Jordan.

This is an important point that relates to an issue Ruth raised about foreigners. Who is a foreigner? A Palestinian who moved to south Lebanon or a Lebanese who moved to Palestine - or a Syrian or a Jordanian, for that matter - is surely not a foreigner because he is part of the culture of the society of Bilad-al-Sham, or Greater Syria, where there were no borders between countries. The whole region is Arabo-Islamic. Other minorities, even though they were neither Muslim nor Arab, were nonetheless part of that Arabo-Islamic culture. Jews, for instance, spoke Arabic. The same was true for Jews living in other Arab Islamic countries. Therefore, there is a big difference between them and foreigners who came from Europe, whether Christians or Jews.

Once again, the question is whether it is legitimate to understand the history of Palestine separately from the neighboring Arab countries. My answer is no. It is a mistake in our national history, in our retrospective of the period, to understand it separately from the neighboring countries. We have to keep in mind that Palestine's history was an integral part, politically, culturally, socially, economically, and historically, of the Ottoman period in general, and certainly of Greater Syria. Otherwise, we impose our national ideological perspective on that period when nationalism was not the basic identity or ideology behind the processes and events of that region.

On the question of foreigners, I do see a big difference between those who came from Egypt, Jordan, Syria or Lebanon, and those who came from Europe, whether Christians or Jews.

It is very common in Zionist historiography to speak about Arab immigration into Palestine. But once again, these are not immigrants. Palestinians were also moving to those countries, as it was common and natural for a Palestinian to go study in Al Azhar for instance, and remain there; or for a Hebronite merchant to go to Cairo and live there; or go to Damascus or other places, whether to study or to live or whatever. That's why, if you go to Damascus or many of the neighboring cities, you will find many names that originated from Palestinian cities. This was a natural phenomenon.

But in Zionist historiography, generally the focus was on people from Iran or Egypt or other places who immigrated into Palestine in the 19th century. This is in order to demonstrate that it was not only the Templars, the Germans, the Jews or the Zionists who came into Palestine. Actually, they claim, the people of

34

Palestine are a collection of peoples who came from different parts of the world, and that's why the people of Palestine have no more rights to this country than others who also came more or less at the same time. So this is not an innocent question when raised here.

It is important to remember that there is a lot of continuity in the history of Palestine in the 19th century, up to 1908 basically. Until 1908, we cannot speak about Palestinian nationalism, or even Palestinian patriotism. Here and there, there are names and concepts and phenomena which the national movement would pick up later on and say: here we have the roots of Palestinian nationalism or popularism in the 19th century. But if we delve deeper into these issues, I would say that, until at least 1908, we cannot speak about Palestinian nationalism. We cannot speak about a separate history of Palestine, or an ideology or nationalism separate from the neighboring Arab countries.

This is my basic point. The 19th century is an integral part of the 400 years of the Ottoman period. There is a lot of continuity, even though we generally focus on the transformations in Palestine during this period. Trivializing the continuity obscures the subject and makes us less able to understand the processes during this period.

From a Palestinian national perspective, the Palestinians also make the mistake of becoming defensive, because they are the last to write their history and that of the country. They try to disprove the Zionist point of view. They make the same assumptions about periodization, concepts and processes, but try to insert their input. I think the correct way to read and write the history of Palestine in that period is to see the continuity as well as the changes; to see the history of Palestine as part of the history of the region as a whole, and not separate from the region.

I would like to stress a few points. First, Ottoman rule represents the last century of Islamic control in the region, including Palestine. From the 7th century until the 19th century, interrupted by the Crusades, which I will not address here, there were two basic social and cultural processes taking place in the history of this region. One is the Islamization, and the other is the Arabization of the population. These were gradual processes.

Remember that, until the 10th century, even the early 11th century, before the Crusades, the majority of the population in Palestine, Syria, Egypt and other areas was still predominantly Christian. Islam did not forcefully impose itself on the indigenous population, and the process of Islamization was gradual, as was the process of Arabization. That is why in the 19th century - even in the 20th century - we have ethnic and religious minorities throughout the region, in Palestine, Lebanon, Syria, Iraq, etc. For instance, the Kurds in Iraq or Syria preserved their ethnic cultural and social identity, their customs, and their language. As far as the Jews are concerned, we can talk about them either as a different ethnic national group, as they came to perceive themselves in the 20th century, or as a religious minority.

So we have Christians and Jews under the rule of Islam during the whole period, until the 19th century. The Islamization and Arabization was largely completed by the 18th century. So when we speak about the people of Palestine -

not in national terms, but in cultural ethnic terms - in the early 19th century, we can speak about the majority of the people of Palestine being Arabs and Muslims.

The population of Palestine in the early 19th century was about 300,000. I don't accept Yehoshua Ben Arieh's and Ruth's numbers for some of the cities, but the discrepancies are not large. I think Jerusalem had at least 10,000 people, for instance. Acre had 14,000 to 15,000 in the late 18th century, dropping a little in the early 19th century. So why choose 1800 rather than 1780, when Acre was 15,000?

Local leaders did make changes before Europeans penetrated into the country, and the focus on this or that period is very important in understanding the processes during the entire Ottoman period, and not just during the 19th century, separating it from what happened in the 18th and earlier centuries. Europe does play an important role in the modernization of Palestine in the 19th century, whether Templars, Europeans in general, directly, or indirectly. Jews who came to Palestine also played an important role in the transformation and modernization of Palestine.

But I claim that, in the historiography, the role of the local Palestinian population is absent. They are generally portrayed as victims of the changes, of modernization, as people who are opposed to the reforms and who are trying to preserve the old history, the old society, the old culture. The others are agents of modernization and change, whether Europeans, Christians or Jews, while the local people, even the local elites, are portrayed as generally rebelling against modernization and modernity. They want to keep the country in decline under the old regime. But this is not the case. I don't have time now to give examples, but we can return to this issue later on.

We also have to remember that modernization is portrayed as a totally positive phenomenon. Modernization, Europeanization, and westernization, all are always portrayed as something positive. Whenever Europeans go to Africa or Asia or South America, they are portrayed as modernizing and westernizing the ignorant peoples they find there, while they are actually taking care of their own interests in those countries.

It is the same in Palestine, in the Holy Land. The rediscovery of Palestine is an important concept for this period. This is actually the second discovery of Palestine. The Crusaders first discovered Palestine, and came by sword and by military means to take it from the Muslims, and from the Arabs. The second time the Europeans discovered Palestine - or rediscovered the Holy Land - they made a peaceful crusade, not a militant one, through the states and the missionaries. Don't forget that this was also a crusade. The main interests of the Europeans were to gain access to Palestine and to reduce Ottoman control to a mere formality in economics, society, culture, etc. They put pressure on the Ottomans to modernize their empire, and the Ottomans did so in order to maintain their control. Nonetheless, we should remember the negative implications of those reforms and policies on local Palestinians.

Concerning periodization, I agree that there are different perspectives with regard to the beginning of modernization. Some would say it begins in the 18th century. For instance, why are Omar* and his policies in the 18th century different from Muhammad Ali's in Egypt in the 19th century? The main difference is that Muhammad Ali succeeded, and he was in Egypt and was able, more or less, to separate Egypt from the Ottoman Empire. On the other hand, Omar also succeeded, but only briefly. The Ottomans put an end to his control in Acre in 1775. And Jazzar,* an agent of the Ottomans, had a negative effect on the people and the economy and other things.

If you do not look from the perspective of this century, I would say that the 18th century is no less important to understanding the historical processes of the region as a whole, and of Palestine, than is the 19th century. If we limit ourselves to the history of the 19th century, I do believe, for instance, that the 1830s is an important period in the history of this region, and not only because of Muhammad Ali's reform policies. Those modernization policies in Palestine, Syria and the entire region - because once again, Muhammad Ali's control at that time was not only in Palestine, but in the whole region - were weak processes of modernization which served the government, and not the people. That is why they were superficial and did not survive for long after he was called back to Egypt.

I do think that the rebellion of 1834 is an important event. But unlike Kimmerling and Migdal in their book, I do not think of it as the beginning of a national identity. It was not a nationalistic rebellion. But it is important nonetheless, because when you compare it to other rebellions in Palestine during the 17th or 18th centuries, you see that this was the most effective and the most wide-reaching rebellion. The entire population of Palestine took part, geographically speaking. I have documents from notables in Safed - muftis and so on - calling for people to join the rebellion.

Just as the participation of the sheikhs of the countryside and in the villages was important, so too was that of the elites in the cities - Safed, Nablus, Jerusalem and others - but this was not a peasant or fellahin rebellion. It is a prototype of a national rebellion. Politically speaking, it was not entirely a national rebellion. But socially and economically speaking, and with respect to the interests of the people vis-à-vis the interests of the rulers, it was kind of a prototype of a patriotic or national rebellion.

Socially, economically and culturally - not politically - the fundamental transformation of Palestine took place during the second Tanzimat period, after Egyptian control and until 'Abd ul Hamid's ascent to power in 1876. We can extend this period to 1878 because of the constitution and the parliamentary regime which 'Abd ul-Hamid instituted during the first two years of his reign. He held absolute control from 1878 until 1908, which is the important period. It is important to note that the start of this period precedes the First Aliyah and the beginning of Jewish colonization of Palestine in the early 1880s.

I will conclude by saying that, when we speak about the 19th century, even without taking into account processes before and after, in the early 20th century, it is an important period of which the Palestinians have just begun writing their own history. First the Europeans, and then the Jews and the Israelis wrote the history of the Holy Land, of Palestine. The Palestinians are just now beginning to write, or rewrite, the history of the Ottoman period in general, and the 19th century in particular.

Unfortunately, it was only people like Doumani, Rashid Khalidi, myself and others who began looking differently at the Ottoman period, departing from the Orientalist concept of constant decline, until the region was saved by the Europeans and the foreigners who came and modernized it. Instead, they wrote the history of the whole period in national terms, rather than reconstructing it as it was. This is why the first nationally-motivated Palestinian historians were anti-Ottoman, and anti-pre-nationalism period. And that's why also these historians portrayed this period as a dark period of decline and corruption, for which only Arab nationalism brought about an awakening and a change. This was a mistake that Palestinian historians had made, by which they strengthened the perception of the Europeans and Zionist Jews concerning the real history of 19th century Palestine..

ATA QAYMARI: I can see that the conflict is already leaping to the surface, the conflict between the two narratives, even though we are dealing with a period where the Zionist movement had not yet been established. Still, we hear the main notion that this land of Palestine was almost empty, there were not many people living in this country.

ADEL MANNA: 300,000.

RUTH KARK: No. Between 250,000 and 300,000. These are estimates.

ADEL MANNA: Remember that Egypt was three million, ten times Palestine. Today it's more or less the same proportion. Egypt is 70 million and the Palestinians are seven million.

ATA QAYMARI: Although these numbers are relatively low, many people were actually living here. Instead of mentioning only a few cities – Haifa, Acre, Nablus, Jerusalem, Jaffa – one can mention tens of hundreds of villages where people led their lives, culturally and socially. Many villages have an ancient history, with buildings dating back hundreds of years. It is not correct to say that this country was empty. Others, from Syria and Lebanon, were not foreigners. We have to use words in a very sensitive manner.

BURCKHARD BLANKE: Who says this land was empty?

ADEL MANNA: All Zionist historiography, and for a long time.

ATA QAYMARI: This is a Zionist myth.

ADEL MANNA: "A people without a land for a land without a people."

PAUL SCHAM: We should differentiate between myth and slogan and history. You didn't hear from Ruth's position that the land was empty. There were a lot of questions, but no implications. We are talking about 250,000 to 300,000, not 5,000. The differences are not so huge. We should focus here, as much as possible, on the history. The myths are clear. If you want to attack the myths, we can also attack the Palestinian myths. But the history is more sophisticated on both sides, as I think we have heard.

ADEL MANNA: Are you sure of that?

PAUL SCHAM: I hope so.

ATA QAYMARI: Sometimes things are not said, but implied. The wrong impression is given. When you say there were not many people and the largest city had no more than 10,000 inhabitants, this gives the impression that the country was nearly empty.

RUTH KARK: But what can you do? This is what we found in the studies. Can we just fabricate numbers?

ADEL MANNA: Compare Palestine to the region rather than to Europe. Europeans came here and said, "Wow, Jerusalem has only 10,000 people." If you compare that to neighboring countries, it's very different.

RUTH KARK: I did compare it.

ATA QAYMARI: Then there is the problem of land. I've heard that there was a fluid situation.

RUTH KARK: A fluid inventory of land.

ATA QAYMARI: Yes. That allows land to pass from one hand to another, and land is open for others to take over and become legitimate landowners. But I question this. We are not talking about the 20th century. We are still talking about the 19th century.

How much land was in the hands of the Jews in 1948, and what percentage was that of all of Palestine, even according to Mandatory Palestine? Professor Kark talked about half a million dunams being granted or given to the Jews at that time. But if we mention how much land there was for the Jews, even in 1948, we won't reach that amount.

RUTH KARK: I can tell you exactly: 1.8 million dunams were bought by Jews in 1947-1948, including the Jewish National Fund. That's about eight percent of 27 million square kilometers.

ADEL MANNA: Let's limit the discussion to the 19th century and not 1948.

ATA QAYMARI: I didn't want to talk about 1948. I just want to mention this impression that the land was wide open, that others could take it, and that it was being offered by others. What about the people who were living there, who plowed the land and cultivated it, and built their culture on it? That is the main question.

DALIA OFER: I want to go to the more historical issues that Adel mentioned. These are important and are really the center of the historical debate. Of course, there are ideological implications, but the issue of continuity and change is a basic historical one with regard to any subject that we are discussing.

The question is how to evaluate the importance of the changes during the 19th century vis-a-vis the centrality of the continuation. When we talk about transitions of periods, this is really the question. Certainly there are continuities. That goes without saying. And certainly there are changes. But at what point can we say that there is something so substantial that we begin to talk about a trend towards change, rather than a trend towards continuity?

I'm not a specialist in this period. I don't know the answer. But this is what I would like to ask of those who are dealing with it. When reading Adel's paper, I had the feeling that he put, in the center of the paradigm of modernity in the region, the changes within the Ottoman Empire in general in the 19th century. This really goes back to many changes in the concept of modernity.

If we would have discussed this 50 or 60 years ago, we would have looked at the Ottoman Empire as a society that hadn't changed at all, that didn't go through modernization at all. But the new notion of understanding modernity gives the administrative issue a central role, not necessarily only in technology and so on, but in the way the empire or the state was organized. When you take this trend of modernity, a lot of research about Jewish communities in the Ottoman Empire points to a process of modernization that had occurred among these Jewish communities in the 19th century, even before the First Aliyah came to the region.

So again, we are dealing with an important issue here. How did these processes, if we try to look at them from within, contribute to the notion of nationalism, and more particularly, nationalism in the region? We are talking about Palestinian nationalism or other nationalisms in the region. Then, vis-a-vis the notion of nationalism that came from the West and that affected the Ottoman Empire in the western territory it lost throughout the 19th century, what did that do to this tension between modernization and continuation and change?

My last question relates to how we look at the Ottoman Empire as a multi-ethnic empire vis-a-vis the other empires, all of which collapsed after World War I - the Russian, the Austro-Hungarian – including the Ottoman Empire. And some of the territories were bordering territories. It is the Western perspective to say that national movements were a major cause in the dismembering of these empires, which finally did happen because of World War I and its aftermath. Should we then put the Ottoman Empire into the same kind of basket? Or should we see the Ottoman Empire as a unique case and the other empires as European empires, although they were not necessarily European? Here, the distinction.

MERON BENVENISTI: I would like to understand the object of this exercise, the reason we are here listening to these different perspectives. Then the question is: what are we going to do with them? Reconcile them, or just start arguing about who is right and who is wrong? I have already heard three or four different ways of looking at it, so I need guidance. It's interesting to see how you can have an open and objective assessment of history, as done by Ruth Kark, and then Adel comes and bursts the balloon, not by going into the details, but by questioning the balloon itself.

FATMEH QASSEM: Why do you say she was objective and he was not?

MERON BENVENISTI: That's a good example of just the opposite of what I meant. Maybe Ruth should be offended, not Adel. I am just trying to explain why this thing is so complicated. I thought Adel's point was perhaps the foundation of the discussion. What is meant by Palestine? There was no Palestine, and then the whole question follows about the foreigners and so forth. Should I relate to that or not? I have an opinion about it, but my opinion is totally irrelevant because we are not trying to reconstruct objective history. We are just trying to listen to two narratives. If that is the case, then we have to develop some kind of technique or strategy to be able to do something constructive after the discussion. For that I need guidance. I can become a partisan or just remain an observer. The question is what role you want us to play in that game.

BURCKHARD BLANKE: We do not want to impose any role.

ADEL MANNA: He is raising an important point. When I agreed to participate in this conference and was asked to write about the 19th century, I thought it would be important to discuss this history as an introduction to the discussion on the conflict in the relations between Arabs and Jews.

As Ata said, we are speaking here about different national narratives. There are additional narratives, but we are speaking here, as Jews and Arabs, mainly about these two narratives. And there are also different sections within the national narratives. Nonetheless, there are the basics of the Jewish national narrative, and those of the Arab Palestinian national narrative. Many people who discuss the conflict either don't know enough about the other narrative, or they don't acknowledge it. It's an important exercise, in the beginning of this conference, to become informed, and then to acknowledge the narrative of the other as a jumping-off point for the discussion on the 20th century.

AVRAHAM SELA: It is really a question of acknowledgment. Those who want to comment should simply try to understand the points and the main arguments, even though they are not clearly stated by each side. In other words, what have we understood so far? I can summarize in two sentences what I understood from Adel's presentation vis-a-vis Ruth's, and by trying to identify the specific argument, we would accomplish a great deal of the work that we are here for.

PAUL SCHAM: Again, on methodology, I would also like to emphasize the point that people know more perhaps than they're willing to acknowledge about the other narrative. A perfect example is the old slogan of "A land without a people for a people without a land." I think few people actually believe that anymore. This is part of history now, not part of current beliefs.

What I am hoping for - and which I think is happening - is that the discussion is focusing on trying to bring in the knowledge and insights we have gained, historically and experientially, over the last number of years when Israelis discovered Palestinian nationalism and Palestinians perhaps gained a better understanding of Israeli nationalism. Perhaps there is a sharpening, and also points of agreement, that may have developed in historiography over the last number of years.

BURCKHARD BLANKE: Ran, back to the discussion of the 19th century.

RAN AARONSOHN: I think we should try to find a general common ground that is not concentrated on this or other specific fact, but on some kind of mutual agreement about assumptions and terms. Speaking about assumptions, I completely agree with Adel's basic assumption that one should not observe everything through nationalist spectacles, but also through social, economic and cultural terms. This may be one common ground for us when discussing the pre-World War I period, until 1908 for sure, but maybe also afterwards. The other assumption has to do with the term continuation. I also accept this idea of cultural, spatial and periodical continuums, and that one should look at the specific phenomena. But I have a question about other terms that were used.

Modernization seems to be a focal term used in many of the papers. Most of the academic discussion is focused on this term as if it were the north star. Why? Why only? And where does it lead? I wonder.

I also wonder about another focal term, majority-minority – these

41

quantitative balances as opposed to qualitative. How can we find a common ground for using those data about which we seem to roughly agree? A quarter of a million; 300,000; cities of about 10,000; 20 years earlier or later. For me, it doesn't make much difference, looking at the bigger picture. So the explanation, the implications, and the meaning of those minority-majority quantitative facts are of utmost importance, and I think we should discuss that.

MOSHE MA'OZ: Adel, you seem to complain about the Zionist or Israeli historiography that doesn't deal with or acknowledge the local population. Again, one has to define what is meant. Research by Israelis or Zionists? Studies or official historiography? One can show many exceptions to these generalizations. For example, you say this research shows that the population objected to reforms in Palestine, and you see that as something negative. But I think it is part and parcel of the pattern all over the Ottoman Empire to reject the reforms, which were secular and which changed the character of Islamic life and limited their interests. I think this is legitimate. One shouldn't see it in a negative way, but rather in a positive way. One who writes about resistance to reforms is not blaming somebody. On the contrary.

Also, you complain that modernization is always shown as a positive value or notion, and again, this is not true. I know of some studies that show modernization as a negative phenomenon, promoting inter-communal conflict, damaging local trade and commerce by introducing European imports, and creating a huge schism between classes.

Last is the issue of the empty land. We remember this new bible of Joan Peters, "From Time Immemorial". But we also remember how viciously it was attacked. Here again, generalizations are not convincing texts.

FATMEH QASSEM: When talking about the 19th century, we can't ignore that, behind our terminology, hides our ideological attitudes. I would like to demonstrate this by using the term "modernity". If we agree that modernity means imposing Western values on the East, then that implies that Western modernity is something positive. By inference, we already construct a view about the East in this regard. But there's another way to look at modernity, and that is that local people, local communities, develop their own cultural and economic resources. And maybe they can learn something from the outside.

I want to refer to the victor's discourse-narrative. Adel and Ruth both used this term. I don't know who the victim is exactly, but I think it's related to the years after, when history was written. Who wrote it and why? Who is included and who is excluded? Who is visible and who is invisible? It is common knowledge that women have been excluded from the victims' narratives. This is common to all the participants in this regard.

I have one question for Ruth. You mentioned the "indigenous population," and you ask if this should refer only to Arabs? What do you mean by this? With regard to the 20th century, why do you say "indigenous population?" And what is the research and methodology behind this term?

WALID SALEM: When we talk about the modernization of Palestine, we might also take into consideration the following issues. First, how was the modernization process, introduced by the Ottoman Empire into Palestine at the end of the 19th century, implemented? Most important is not the modernization itself, but how it was implemented. The fellahin, at that time, did not register the land in their names because they were afraid of taxes. So, at the end of the 19th century, they were registering the land in the name of the landlords. The world calls this registration process "modernization," but this practice, in essence, reproduced the feudal system through the process of modernization. Later on, with the advent of Zionism, the people who sold land to the Zionist movement were these feudal lords, and the fellahin were victims of that process. And I agree with what Professor Ma'oz said about modernization not being necessarily a good or a bad process. Sometimes it could be applied negatively against the indigenous people, to use Ruth Kark's words. So this is Ottoman modernization. And Adel, please clarify this more.

Secondly, also about modernization, we talk about Western capitulation in our country. They didn't come to establish some kind of modernization. Modernization instead came as capitulation. This is modernization of the second part of the relation. Thirdly, about the first Jewish immigrants to Palestine, I wonder if there is historical evidence that, during that period when Jews were immigrating into Palestine, they introduced any kind of modernization for the benefit or the welfare of the people already residing there.

About Zionism, we have questions whether it was colonialism or colonization. But we might agree that there was a certain process of Western colonialism. My question to both writers is: What is the role of colonialism in that period in Palestine as part of the area in general? Specifically - and this is sensitive - in what way can we put Jewish immigration in that period within this process of colonialism and within the conflict between the Ottoman Empire and the Western capitulations?

Concerning the emergence of nationalism in Palestine, there is some difference between talking about the Russian Empire and the Ottoman Empire. On the fall of the Ottoman Empire, Arab national orientations were developed in Egypt, Syria and Lebanon. But for Palestine, up until 1923, if I am not mistaken, until the Fourth Palestinian Conference in Nablus, they were still talking about it as part of Syria.

ADEL MANNA: You are mistaken.

WALID SALEM: Then please correct me. But only then did we begin to talk about Palestine as a unit. This happened only after the Ottoman Empire collapsed. Most importantly, one of the reasons for the collapse of the Ottoman Empire was the Western invasion into the area, more so than internal factors. There were also internal factors, but the essential damage to the empire was caused by Westerners.

PAUL SCHAM: World War I.

AVRAHAM SELA: This discussion will lead us nowhere. We are going to hit all kinds of points without going to the main issue. The main issue is that, when I heard first Ruth speak, and then Adel, I heard action-reaction between two narratives. There is much responsiveness in what Adel said to the historiography and the research done by Israelis about that period of time. And what I would like to do now is to say what I heard from Adel.

43

First, the land that you call Palestine - and I still need a good explanation of what the notion was in terms of rules, borders, limitations or restrictions that make a land defined abstractly or practically - was part of the Ottoman Empire and had an Arab or Islamic nature. There was an on-going phenomenon of migration of Arab or Islamic groups from one point to another, from one area to another.

ADEL MANNA: A marginal phenomenon. Ten percent of the population.

AVRAHAM SELA: But there was an on-going process of groups moving between one part and another, which was part of a demographic and social reality. The Jewish immigration - certainly the Zionist one - was very different from those trends because it was representing an extra-imperial phenomenon. It was not even part of the region. It was extra-regional and extra-imperial. The significance is that this kind of immigration was part of the colonial imperialists.

ADEL MANNA: No. I didn't say that.

AVRAHAM SELA: That's what I heard. Especially with the ideological element and the ideological agenda, it was definitely very different and foreign to whatever had happened up to then in that region. The local population and the authorities in the country, as well as in the empire as a whole, had no connection whatsoever to those demographic or social changes. They did not interfere with it and had no role in it.

The same can be said of the change in land ownership. Nobody spoke about the role of local landowners or the authorities in either permitting or preventing these changes, including those of the Zionists or the Jews. The same can be understood from what you said about modernization, as if modernization, whether imposed from above by the Ottoman Empire authorities or brought into the country by missionaries or by foreign European groups or organizations, had nothing to do with the local population. They were only passive. They were not taking any part in it.

If I understood correctly, this is what I got from your presentation, and I would like to know if I understood correctly.

ADEL MANNA: Did you also read the paper? What I presented complemented what I wrote in the paper, and I'm not going to repeat things.

LILY GALILI: I want to make a very personal remark in following up on what Meron said, although he is a historian, and I am not at all. I am getting more and more confused as time goes by about the purpose of this gathering. I don't know who coined the term "shared history". I think we already know we can no longer call it shared history. Maybe "simultaneous history" with a focus on the 19th century is a better term.

RUTH KARK: Part of it is shared space.

LILY GALILI: But not shared history. That's very obvious.

PAUL SCHAM: Shared histories.

BENJAMIN POGRUND: It's a newspaper headline.

ADEL MANNA: Sharing your history with the others.

LILY GALILI: Another thing strikes me. For me, history is so foreign as an academic field, but there is an amazingly striking similarity between history and journalism. What's happening here is exactly what Benjamin told us, about the newspaper with the two columns, each reporting the same events, but coming out with a totally different story. So I would like to suggest that when we talk about history, either this is defined as an academic meeting, and then I would be pleased just to hear information about the region in the 19th century because I know nothing about it.

RAN AARONSOHN: Academic is not equal to information.

LILY GALILI: Don't confuse me with facts. I am confused as it is. Or we can at least try to get to the point where, if we disagree on facts, it does not necessarily follow that it's a denial of the other's rights. If we don't agree on the facts of the 19th century, that doesn't mean that we shouldn't be talking about it.

But the underlying tone of the discussion is that: if we don't agree about certain facts of the 19th century, then we won't agree about the future. I think this is a completely wrong assumption. If we could take this factor out of the discussion, maybe it will help us, and even maybe make it more pleasant. Ata gave a perfect example. Ruth and Adel both cited the same numbers. But Ruth said "only 250,000" and Adel gave the objective number of 300,000. Then they agreed to meet somewhere between. We still agree on the basics, but you heard the undertone.

So let's try to make that effort, unless we say, okay, let's forget history and talk about the present. But if we decide to stick to the original plan, let's try to assume that disagreement does not necessarily imply denial or argument about the future. Maybe it's just an intellectual disagreement. If we can do that, I think we will have done a lot.

BURCKHARD BLANKE: At the start of such enterprises as this conference, of course we are always jumping between the actual historical discussion and the meta-layer of the methodology of the conference. We have to go through this process simply to find a way to speak about historical evidence, and then what lies behind it in our own perceptions, all these ideological - or even emotional - settings which lie behind the historical evidence. But if there is historical evidence, I think it is not just an academic game. It is really the basis of our deliberations here.

MERON BENVENISTI: There is no such thing as historical evidence, I'm sorry to tell you.

PAUL SCHAM: There is a lot of argument about that.

MERON BENVENISTI: Can you define evidence?

AVRAHAM SELA: It is widely-accepted facts that happened sometime, somewhere.

MERON BENVENISTI: Until a new historian comes along, and then all the evidence falls apart.

AVRAHAM SELA: There is no question that Jerusalem was conquered by the Crusaders at a certain time.

MERON BENVENISTI: That's totally irrelevant and immaterial.

FATMEH QASSEM: When and for how long?

AVRAHAM SELA: This is a wonderful way to deconstruct history.

MERON BENVENISTI: The context which I heard now, the object of this exercise, is to set up the evidence.

PAUL SCHAM: No.

BURCKHARD BLANKE: To use common evidence.

MERON BENVENISTI: But for that you have to agree on the evidence. If you think you can agree on evidence, then let's see at the end if you have agreed on one element of any evidence. We are not talking about evidence. We are talking about interpretations of evidence.

PAUL SCHAM: I don't want to get into a terminological debate about the name of the problem. I agree with Avraham's idea about shared history, but one of the paradoxes is that the word "history" refers to different things. It refers to what happened, and also to what people write about what happened.

The idea behind the title of this conference is that we share a history in the fact that there is both a Jewish and a Palestinian presence in the land. This is a fact that perhaps we can agree on. Or maybe I won't even try to find agreement.

There was a presence. There are differences with regard to its size, nature, ideology, role, and effect. But the idea is to look at the fact that we both have an interest in the last 100, 120 or more years that we are talking about.

From the beginning of your paper, Adel, if I can put it in Zionist terms, you were trying to show the Palestinians as the objects of history rather than the subjects of history, which, of course, is one of the traditional goals of Zionism. And, as I understand it, the new Palestinian historiography is also trying to do that. Can you give some specifics of that? We have heard, in the context of modernization, of the things that have come from the Ottomans, from the Europeans, from the Jews. Can you talk about how it came from the Palestinians?

Ruth, you made an intriguing comment about not even being sure that you accept the concept of the First Aliyah because Jewish immigration, as I understood what that referred to, was something continuous. One of the things I have understood - and the reason I picked 1882 as a starting date for this conference - is that that's the traditional date of Zionist immigration and the beginning of the New Yishuv. This is a question.

Several writers, not only in these papers, have talked about the majority of immigrants going into the Old Yishuv rather than being part of the new settlement - the Zionist settlement, perhaps we could say. I wonder if there could be some discussion about how this was new and how the new immigration did or did not differ from the old.

RUTH KARK: I have prepared nine points. The first relates to the purpose of this meeting. I suggest that we concentrate on the topic of the conflict and of shared and non-shared history or histories. This is the main theme.

If we are trying to create a periodization of the main years of the conflict, and then define parameters or reasons for the conflict, for example, let's look at the land issue. Walid mentioned the reforms in land ownership. Was modernization for the benefit of the indigenous people or not? Who initiated this reform? Was it the Jews or the Ottomans? And how did it affect things? This is relevant to the periodization of the conflict because it is one of the main issues that goes back to the 19th century, continues today, and will go on into the future. Another parameter we can choose is population, but I won't elaborate on parameters now. One example from the sphere of land ownership is *musha'* land, which actually was not ownership. It was a system that defined how the land was held, and both the Ottomans and the British Mandate attempted to destroy it. This is important.

My second point relates to the analogy mentioned here between historians and journalists. I must say I don't like it very much. I don't think you should really give up serious historical study. You have to work hard, that's for sure, but it's really necessary. And there are things that I don't think can be interpreted differently. There are some facts. Sometimes we lack data, but, for example, there are facts relating to the size and growth of the cities, or the fact that there were several hundred villages. I studied these villages. I didn't ignore them, Ata. It was just a matter of time. I didn't have time here to relate to everything.

My third point is that I didn't mean to present the Jewish point of view in my paper. I tried to give a general overview of processes and terminology for the 19th century, and general terminology. And I don't think I talked about foreigners. I talked about settlers who came from different places. Not all were foreigners. But we can debate about the Circassians, who were part of the Ottoman Empire, and the Bosnians, who came to settle in Transjordan-Palestine, and whether to include them in this process or not.

My fourth point relates to the boundaries of Palestine. I agree that Palestine was not a separate entity under the Ottoman Empire, and I could have brought a nice overhead to show you the boundaries of the Levant during the 19th century or the Ottoman period. The map changed many times.

But since we are discussing a certain area now, it might be legitimate to go back and relate to this area. I am not sure that, for everything, we have to discuss the 400 years of the Ottoman Empire. I think that's legitimate. We have a lot of separate studies on Syria, Egypt, Lebanon - which was not a separate entity either - Transjordan, etc. It really depends on the topic of the study. If the topic is the conflict, then we have to relate to land issues and settlement, and then maybe it's legitimate to discuss Mandatory Palestine.

You also spoke about the main processes of Arabization and Islamization from the 7th to the 20th centuries. I think you have to add the process of pan-Turkanism during the 19th century, which means the unifying of the people of the area under the Ottoman Empire

ADEL MANNA: How does that relate to the history of Palestine?

RUTH KARK: You spoke about the Ottoman Empire.

ADEL MANNA: I spoke about the region called the Arab states or the Middle East, excluding Turkey.

RUTH KARK: It was not only in Turkey. And it was to develop this entity as superior to the Arab entity in the Ottoman Empire. This is again a matter of periodization and the main topic you wish to discuss. Dalia spoke about the disintegration of empires. This is a big question, and I don't think I can answer it. Maybe we can discuss it later, if you like. It's a very interesting question. The fifth point is women's studies. I second Fatmeh's comment. It's an important topic which has been much neglected and which requires a great deal of study.

DALIA OFER: It's still neglected.

RUTH KARK: Yes. And the absentee women of the history of the region and of Palestine need a lot more attention and study. My sixth point relates to why the question-mark after indigenous populations. Did you mean why the term itself, or why did I put Arabs in question marks?

FATMEH QASSEM: Both.

RUTH KARK: In post-modern, neo-colonial studies, they use this term mainly as an opposite to the agents of colonialism and imperialism, to stress the negative effects of colonialists on the indigenous populations, and to stress that not enough attention - and I totally agree - has been given to the study of indigenous populations and their contributions to developments in the area.

AVRAHAM SELA: But given Palestine's nature, who is indigenous?

RUTH KARK: First let me finish. We can talk about the positive and negative influences between the leaders of the colonialists and the indigenous populations, the contributions of the indigenous population and the interaction between them. The role of the local people, of course, is as much under-estimated as is the role of certain groups within the local population, such as women and others. I put Arabs in question marks because the indigenous populations were not only Arabs, neither in Palestine, nor in the Middle East. Indigenous populations include also the minority populations who were living in the area.

My seventh point relates to modernization. I am not going to define it because I don't think I am qualified to do so. Modernization, continuity, change, good or bad? Who were the agents of modernization? Was it the Ottoman Empire, for example? Maybe under pressure. But we know Moshe Ma'oz's classic book about the Tanzimat in the Ottoman Empire. I want to give an example from a general study I am doing now on missionaries and their contribution. I participated in several workshops on missionaries in the Middle East and it looks like the trend, over the last 15 or 20 years, has been sort of revisionist, totally negating everything the missionaries did in this area. Everything was negative from the point of view of the local populations.

I think the pendulum is now swinging back. We can look at things with a little more balance, and we can separate between the negative and the positive. The missionaries, in fact, did a lot of positive things in different areas. They opened the first schools for girls in the Middle East, and the first hospitals. There was opposition from the indigenous populations, and they themselves then went and opened their own school for girls or their own hospital.

With regard to the first Jews as agents of modernization for the benefit of the general public, I'm not sure that it was directly for the benefit of the general public, but it influenced that in some ways. For example, Jewish or Christian settlers built what was called a model farm in Jaffa. An English missionary came to Jaffa in 1885. He bought land and opened a model farm in which Jews and Arabs and local people could study more rational models of agriculture. This had a great local influence. You can see it in the crops, for example, or special kinds of fruit trees that were brought and then disseminated to the Arab villages, or modern machinery. In the 1860s. McCormack, from the United States, had already brought the first combine machine to Palestine. And then some of these things reached the Arab villages. The oil pumps triggered a revolution in

48

agriculture in Palestine at the end of the 19th century.

My eighth point is the First Aliyah and why I do not agree with this term. First, I don't think the Aliyah of the Lovers of Zion in 1882 was the First Aliyah of Jews to Palestine. The first new Aliyah, if you want, was that of the Hassidim in the 18th century.

ADEL MANNA: The Zionist one or the Jewish one?

RUTH KARK: Jewish.

ADEL MANNA: This is different.

RUTH KARK: But the Lovers of Zion were not Zionists. That was in the pre-Zionist period. We can talk about Zionism only after 1897.

ADEL MANNA: I am not sure about that. You speak about institutional Zionism after the first conference - or Zionism as an ideology - and then you have the ideology of Zionism before that, and then the First Aliyah is Zionist.

RUTH KARK: I claim that, if the Lovers of Zion are Zionists, then the ones who came from North Africa in 1830 were also Zionists. They came and settled in Tiberius, Acre, Jaffa and Jerusalem. They were Lovers of Zion. This is the same.

FATMEH QASSEM: There's a big difference between coming to the Holy Land and coming to the state for the Jewish people. And it wasn't the Hassidim in the late 18th century. It was the Yemenites who came.

RUTH KARK: The first Yemenites came in 1881.

FATMEH QASSEM: Yes. But you can't consider them as having come to the Holy Land. You can't consider them the same as the Hassidim before them.

RUTH KARK: The first settlement society for the settlement of Palestine by Jews was in 1860, so it doesn't really matter. Within this context anyway, usually we talk about the Old Yishuv and the New Yishuv. We came to the conclusion that you really have to refine that definition and talk about the old New Yishuv and the new Old Yishuv. You will find the details in the paper.

The last point, which is important, is about colonialism and colonization, and I turn that over to Ran Aaronsohn because he has been studying the issue and has published about it.

ADEL MANNA: Not everything we are discussing here is a Palestinian-Zionist discussion. Many times it's an internal discussion in the narrative of this or that national side. Whether Hovevei Zion is the First Aliyah or not is an example of that. And I'll be giving examples on the Palestinian side as well. Of course, everything is related because much of what we say about the Jews has some implications for the Palestinians, and vice versa. It's important to keep in mind that we have discussions and debates about the narratives of the past within each camp, within each national movement, even though we are here trying to simplify and speak about this or that national narrative.

I will begin with Paul Scham's comments. You understood me well when you said that the Palestinians are often absent in the history of the 19th century and other centuries. Or that when they are present, they are often objects, rather than subjects of history. There are two main examples. Once again, my criticism of the different historiographies, not only Oriental or Zionist, but Palestinian as well, is also part of the discussion of the history of other parts of the world.

49

For instance, social history is a newly-born history of the last few generations. As with many other fields, it started in the West. Then came the writing of the history of the Third World, and historians of this region just recently began writing social history. Under this criterion of social history, for instance, Doumani and others have tried to write history from the bottom up, rather than from the top down. This is one example of rewriting Palestinian history, putting Palestinians back into history in a way that allows them to claim their rightful role in it, instead of keeping most of them out of the narrative by concentrating on political and military history, for example, as when historians of European history concentrated more on the empire and the queen and the king and the wars.

Another example, also related to the issue of top-down or bottom-up history, is that in books or articles written about the history of Palestine during the Ottoman period - including Amnon Cohen's excellent book on the 18th century - when you read carefully what has been written about Jazzar and Dahar Omar, you see that the Palestinians are almost absent because the focus is on the Ottoman administration and Ottoman reform. Everything is Ottoman. So even if you don't say it explicitly, the reader understands it. There is Ottoman control, the Ottoman Empire, the Ottoman administration. Later on, the nationalists will also start speaking about the Ottoman occupation. But if you read the documents from that period, the people didn't look at the Ottomans as occupiers.

When you look at the elites, Jazzar and Dahar Omar are not the only rulers. The entire local elite is part of that administration. When you rewrite the history of that period and speak of the role of the elite, of the notables and so forth, you put the Palestinians back in history. They are no longer absent from that history, as they had been when many Orientalists and their students wrote the history of Palestine.

MERON BENVENISTI: Assisted by Palestinian nationalists.

ADEL MANNA: Yes. I said that before. I agree. Students of those Orientalists include the Palestinians themselves.

DALIA OFER: In his book, Amnon Cohen did not put the Ottomans as occupiers of the region.

ADEL MANNA: Right. He doesn't say that. But the problem with the historiography is that few people read Amnon Cohen's book separate from the Jewish historiography written by people who know neither Arabic nor Turkish. People who write the history of this country in the Department of The Study of Eretz Yisrael and the Study of the People of Israel in Israeli Universities and so on know almost nothing about Arab society. They don't read the documents in Arabic and Ottoman and so on. That's why you have in your mind this kind of historiography, and the Orientalists and other historians of the Middle East department are few in number.

From my experience teaching Jewish students in Tel Aviv, at the Hebrew University, and Ben Gurion and everywhere, they come to the university - and it doesn't matter to which department, but mainly to the departments which do not concentrate on Middle Eastern history - with all this background, from school, or the street, or the media, where the Palestinians are absent from this history. And even when you introduce a book like Amnon Cohen's, it's taken there as part of the Ottoman occupation, administration or whatever, because in the history of this country, only Jews had rights in this country 2,000 years ago. Then they are absent. Then the Muslims occupied the country. Then you have the Muslim and the Mameluke* occupation.

MERON BENVENISTI: They are all foreign empires occupying Israel.

RUTH KARK: Including the Ottomans.

ADEL MANNA: Including the Ottomans. And the people of the country are absent there, or they are victims of occupiers and others.

MERON BENVENISTI: That's why the Crusades are so important.

DALIA OFER: Look at the textbooks. The Crusaders hardly appear.

ADEL MANNA: Let's get back to the 19th century. It's quite difficult to give one definition of modernization. Generally speaking, in the 19th century and earlier, it meant making reforms in societies outside of Europe on the model of the European societies, cultures and administrations. It's called westernization because it is according to the Western model, the European model, and it is comprised of different layers. It starts from the top down, from the government, the empire, reforms in the army and in the administration and in the government, and so on. Then, in the 19th century, also in the Tanzimat period, you have deeper reforms influencing the day-to-day lives of the people. But that happens later, from the mid-19th century on.

BENJAMIN POGRUND: How do we view it in modern terms? Is it a more enlightened era because of modernization?

ADEL MANNA: There are more critical readings of modernization as a positive process. The classical Oriental reading in the Third World is that you have a state of constant decline - some people say it begins in the Middle Ages - until the beginning of the 19th century. Then the Europeans came to Africa and everywhere else, these discoverers, these enlightened people from Europe, came with their input and reforms. And then you have a so-called linear positive revival or awakening. The society, the culture, and the economy, all are improved.

BURCKHARD BLANKE: What is the Ottoman contribution to the modernization of Tanzimat?

ADEL MANNA: Ruth gave the example of the privatization of land, for example. Until the mid-1850s, most of the land was considered some type of state land or another – part of it was *emiri*, from the word emir or prince, and part was *musha'*. A larger chunk of land was *Waqf* land - Islamic endowment - and Christian and even Jewish endowments. Only a small portion of the land was in private ownership. These are the lands around the houses of the villagers and in the towns and so on.

Maybe I should add something about the privatization of land. The privatization of land had some negative implications on the fellahin. But you also have the investment in land, such as the citrus orchards in the Jaffa area. Ruth wrote a book about Jaffa, where once again the Arabs are absent, I'm sorry to say: But the Palestinians who started the citrus plantation around Jaffa were the ones who exported the Jaffa oranges to Berlin, to Paris, to all the capitals of Europe. Jaffa oranges were already famous in the 1860s.

RAN AARONSOHN: Nobody objects to this. This is common knowledge.

ADEL MANNA: Maybe to you and Ruth, but not to the public.

AVRAHAM SELA: But we're talking about history.

ADEL MANNA: The public perception of Israelis is very different from that of the few specialists who wrote some books here and there, and the impact of their books on the public is really marginal.

RAN AARONSOHN: But are we speaking about public perceptions or about history?

BENJAMIN POGRUND: It's part of our discussion. A lot of people still subscribe to the point Paul made about the empty land.

AVRAHAM SELA: I also have experience with a lot of students. This is endless, because I can talk about how ignorant Israeli students are about various things.

ADEL MANNA: So let me take my words back and say that Palestinians are absent in the books of many Israeli historians writing in Hebrew. I'm not speaking about the public anymore. I'm speaking about historians who wrote books about the history of Palestine until the 19th century. You can point out four, five, six historians who wrote about the Palestinians and Palestinian citrus and so on. I can give you 100 historians, writing mainly in Hebrew, who didn't write about Palestinians. Who influenced the public? But this is not the issue.

Avraham, you more or less summarized my presentation very well, except for one point. You understood me as having said that Jewish immigration in the late 19th century was similar to the Europeans as foreigners, meaning that it was also colonial. I didn't say that and I didn't mean that. However, I would say that the Zionist ideology was born in Europe during the period of colonialism and was influenced by colonialism and its ideology, by its Euro-centrism, and by European perspectives of non-European societies and cultures. The process of immigrating into Palestine was also similar to the colonization of other parts of the world.

RAN AARONSOHN: No.

ADEL MANNA: This is my perspective. Maybe I'm wrong and I'll learn something from you later on. It's obvious that there was no Jewish superpower which sent the Jews into Palestine the way France sent the French or supported the French who went to Algeria. But it's part of the colonial phenomenon, part of the colonial period. And it's a national movement.

RAN AARONSOHN: And modernization, universal modernization, and urbanization.

ADEL MANNA: This is colonialism using modernization in order to further its interests.

RAN AARONSOHN: And industrialization and other processes. This is very general. Let's use specific terms.

AVRAHAM SELA: What was the role of the "indigenous" population from top to bottom in the process of migration, including the migration of Zionists? Migration is a neutral word that can be used by both sides.

ADEL MANNA: You mean the landlords?

AVRAHAM SELA: Everything. There's lots of talk here about the ignorance of the role of Palestinians by these and those historians. There is a lot of projection of historical blame. I just want to know what the role of the local population was. Did they collaborate with any of those trends coming from abroad?

ADEL MANNA: No. First, I wouldn't use the word collaboration.

AVRAHAM SELA: Collaboration in the positive sense.

BURCKHARD BLANKE: Cooperation, not collaboration.

ADEL MANNA: Cooperation with the process. I wouldn't use the same value judgment on that period that you use for the selling of land to Jews, for instance, later on when we have a national conflict. At that time, until the late 19th century, who sold land to the Jews? Ruth knows more about that. She can give you more numbers and examples. Most of them were what she called absentee landlords.

RUTH KARK: Some of them.

ADEL MANNA: Some of them. Absentee landlords in Beirut, in Jaffa and in other places, and some Palestinian landlords here and there.

AVRAHAM SELA: When you call them Palestinian, we come to this name and it's a problem.

ADEL MANNA: Arab locals. It's not Palestinian in the national or political identification. But they lived in Palestine. I'm speaking of the indigenous people of Palestine, the Arabs of Palestine. It was mainly not the indigenous people, but rather Lebanese, for instance, who bought the land from the government and then later sold it to Zionist Jewish communities. At least in the 19th century - and later in the 20th century, but that's a different story, more complicated - the settling communities in Palestine looked for huge expanses of land with less population. That's why there were no fellahin there to begin with to sell their land. Most of the fellahin lived in the mountainous areas. So we have few examples of fellahin. The majority of the people who did sell their land in the 19th century were landowners, whether indigenous people of Palestine or people from outside - Syrian, Lebanese or others.

Once again, the most important point here is that we can't blame them for doing that. There was no national identity. The conflict at that time was not a national one. It was a socio-economic issue. If that landlord thought he could get a good price for that land, he would sell it, whether to Jews or Christians or Muslims or whoever. The Jews had the money. They wanted to buy big plots of land, thousands and tens of thousands of dunams, and that's why they sold to Jews. There was also almost no resistance to that, and this is also important. It's true that you can speak about problems between the indigenous people and the settlers in Metula or in Petah Tikva or in other places, but those were local, not national conflicts. The attempt of Zionist historiography to begin the conflict already in 1882 is wrong, including with respect to this issue. If you take the incidents before 1904 - and I limit myself to 1904 …

MERON BENVENISTI: Rashid Khalidi does the same. He tries to use those clashes and make it something nationalistic. It's not only the Zionists, but also the Palestinian nationalists.

ADEL MANNA: Nationalists look for roots of resistance already in the

18th century. There are classical works on that. Everybody is defensive and trying to respond. Palestinian historians as well.

RAN AARONSOHN: Few Zionist or Israeli researchers try to go back to those roots and say what you said. Very few.

DALIA OFER: One of our criticisms of Jewish historiography of the land is that it ignored the conflict altogether until the 1920s. If you're talking about a land without a people for a people without a land, you completely ignore that there was even the possibility of a conflict. It's only the new trends that are trying to revise this conceptually.

ADEL MANNA: I return to Walid's question. The episode between 1918 and 1920, not 1923, continues the ideology of pan-Arabism before World War 1. During that war, Arab nationalists cooperated with Sharif Hussein and his sons in order to have an Arab kingdom. The Palestinians, who were part of this ideology, thought at the time, tactically, that it would be in their interest to be part of the Faisal kingdom in the Bilad-al-Sham*.

That's why it is the only two years during which they speak about Palestine as the southern part of Syria. You don't find that earlier. Khalidi speaks about southern Syria. So once again, this is a small episode until 1920. After Faisal is kicked out of Damascus, the next conference doesn't speak about being part of Syria or the kingdom of Faisal. In the summer of 1920, this episode is finished and the Palestinians begin to talk about three major points important to them - demographic migration, land economics, and the independence of Palestine and the end of the Mandate. Those are the three basic issues of the Palestine national movement.

MERON BENVENISTI: I think the question of borders is more complicated. The community model is more appropriate. Once the colonists established borders, the subject people accepted them. This is important for us to realize, for both the Jewish national movement and for the Palestinians - and for all occupied people, colonized people. The borders fixed by the colonialists became the borders of nationalism.

ADEL MANNA: I return to the issue of land and fellahin and registration of land in the name of landlords. This is tricky and complicated. So far, we cannot draw conclusions because much work and research still needs to be done. There is the myth or story that many fellahin registered their lands in the names of landlords. I don't know how true it is. I don't know what Ruth thinks about that.

The facts are that the lands of the fellahin in the hilly and mountainous areas were not registered at all in the names of landlords, and the fellahin who cultivated their lands in these areas registered their land in their own names. You don't have landlords in the hilly areas. You have landlords mainly in the valleys and along the coastal region, where there were very few fellahin, if at all, or where there were some Bedouins who didn't register the lands as their own.

This is a different story, but this is a national myth which is not that true. All this Marxist discussion about the fellahin vis-a-vis the landlords and the landlords did this and that to the fellahin and so on, historically speaking, this is more myth than history and fact. So I don't buy this hypothesis. A lot of work should be done on this subject. The facts that we know, in the later period, where we have landlords and where we don't, teach us that this is more fiction than fact. I don't say there were no cases like this. But this is not the basic reason why we have landlords in Palestine from the 1860s on, like the Husseinis and the Nashashibis. But even their lands were not in the Jerusalem area. They were in Gaza and Jaffa and other places where they could buy the land from the government or from others, but not the land of the fellahin in the Jerusalem area, in the villages.

RUTH KARK: Also in Jerusalem.

ADEL MANNA: There are exceptions. We are speaking in general. But if they bought land, this is different than fellahin going to the landlord and telling him to register their land in his name.

RUTH KARK: There was also an interesting stage of auctioning off the land by the Ottoman government.

ADEL MANNA: That is the Ottoman state selling lands, and those who had money to buy were the notables. This is not the fellahin going to the landlords and telling them to register the land in their name. This is a different story.

MOSHE MA'OZ: Do you have evidence that it was not the case?

ADEL MANNA: I said much work needs to be done on this. But we can come to this conclusion. We don't have enough data to support the other conclusion, but, as I said, the facts later on with regard to where we have landlords, in which areas, makes us believe that there were very few cases in which landlords registered the lands of the fellahin in their own names. Rather, there were other, perhaps political, ways in which they became big landlords.

I would like to speak about the 1834 rebellion and Moshe's comment about it being a rebellion of the notables. The notables are the leaders of the rebellion, but it is a rebellion of the whole population - the notables of the cities, the sheikhs of the villages and the Bedouins. That's why this rebellion is important and we need to study it much more. Not enough has been written about it.

I went to Egypt many years ago - when the Hebrew University told me: If you go and study Egypt, maybe you'll get a job at Hebrew University. I spent two years there, not so successfully trying to collect documents about the history of Egypt. It wasn't easy to get permission to go to the archives. But when I did, and started collecting data about the 19th century. I found hundreds of documents about the 1834 rebellion. I made use of some of these documents in my book in Arabic, in the chapter about the rebellion. I could write a whole book about the 1834 rebellion because I have literally hundreds of documents in Arabic which shed more light on it.

PAUL SCHAM: Some of the discussion here is something that only people who have spent their careers studying land tenure in Palestine in the 19th century would know about. I hope we can be a little more general.

DALIA OFER: Perhaps more details have to be given. I disagree. I'm not acquainted with all this, but I think it's important and I am glad it was raised.

RAN AARONSOHN: With regard to Paul's remark, I would also request that, when you go into some less familiar subjects, please think of us as students and give examples or explanations.

ADEL MANNA: Ran, concerning your comments about assumptions and terminology: yes, assumptions and terminology are important for the writing of history. For instance, with regard to "majority" and "minority," it's true that we don't speak about Palestinians as such at this period, but we can speak about the Muslims as a majority and the non-Muslims as minorities - really just minorities. We can speak about the Arabs in Palestine, which could include Jews as well. Many of the Sephardic Jews were Arabic-speakers. Their culture was mainly an Oriental Arabic culture, and some Arabs in Palestine and Iraq and other places called them Arabs, Arab Jews. Like Muslim Arabs and Christian Arabs, there are Jews who are Arabs. That's why I spoke earlier about the social and cultural dimension of the Arabs of the country, the indigenous people vis-a-vis the foreigners who came in. And when we speak about foreigners, it's not only Europeans and Jews who came from Europe.

Many of the documents that I read from the 18th and 19th centuries refer to sons of Arabs or sons of Turks, or this person is ibn Arab or ibn Turk. This means that the indigenous people did consider the Turks, who do not speak Arabic, as foreigners also, and different from the local indigenous people who did speak Arabic and whose culture and traditions were Arabic. So we can speak, socially and culturally, about whether Arab and Islamic peoples were a majority here. Circassians came later, in the 19th century, and they settled in different villages. Many of the Arabs from outside who came into Palestine lived in the villages of the indigenous people. They didn't go and establish villages for themselves.

RAN AARONSOHN: In many cases they did. Not always, but there were some.

ADEL MANNA: In many other cases they were included in the local population. They integrated into the local population.

RUTH KARK: Not exactly. Usually they founded new villages with some segments of the local population.

ADEL MANNA: I know that some Egyptians didn't integrate and didn't live entirely with the villagers. I am jumping to a different period. When refugees came to the West Bank and other places, sometimes they lived with the other Palestinians - and we are already speaking about the national period - and sometimes they lived in camps. And the local indigenous people looked differently at the refugees. So again, it's more a social issue than a national one.

In general, they managed to integrate into the population. In contrast, the settlers, whether the Templars or the Jews, intentionally excluded themselves from the population and lived in different settlements, and had an entirely different project, one that involved not integrating into the population, but rather having their own settlements separate and apart from the local population. The ideology of Zionism - not the First Aliyah and the Hovevei Zion, but the Second and Third Aliyot and later - was an exclusionary one which kept out the local population, rather than wanting to integrate into it.

AVRAHAM SELA: Exclusion is not correct. Segregation.

ADEL MANNA: Segregation and exclusion, because in the later period, even when you have socialist settlements, the kibbutz residents would never agree to have Arabs in their settlements, even if they were Marxist, or communist, or socialist. So it was an exclusion of the Arabs, and it made no difference whether they were leftists or right-wing. It was only for the Jews and the Zionists.

FATMEH QASSEM: Exclusion was discussed in the First Zionist Congress.

MERON BENVENISTI: During the Zionist period, there were at least four or five Jewish villages with Arab neighborhoods.

ADEL MANNA: Which villages are you speaking about?

MERON BENVENISTI: Rosh Pina, Nes Ziona.

ADEL MANNA: This is during the First Aliyah. I said from the Second Aliyah on.

RAN AARONSOHN: Nes Ziona existed until the 1940s.

ADEL MANNA: This was the ideology from the Second Aliyah onward.

MERON BENVENISTI: It continued until 1948.

AVRAHAM SELA: For example, Arabs could come and get medical treatment in Zionist institutions. This is not exclusion.

ADEL MANNA: This is exclusion when we speak about it as a national project.

MERON BENVENISTI: When you speak about that, yes, but there are enough details to make it not so clear-cut.

RUTH KARK: Maybe there was also exclusion of Jews from Arab villages.

ADEL MANNA: Not at all. Jews could come live in Jaffa and anywhere else where Arabs were living. But Zionist settlements after the Second Aliyah excluded the Arabs.

Dalia asked a question about the Ottoman Empire in comparison to other empires. Once again, I'm not a specialist on the Russian or the Austro-Hungarian empires, but from my knowledge, we can make some comparisons and speak about whether or not nationalism was a basic factor in the destruction of the empire. Specifically, my examples are from the Ottoman Empire in which we have to differentiate between, for instance, the eastern European region, the Balkans, and the Middle East. In Europe and the Balkans, the people were mainly Christian, not Muslim. Nationalism there began earlier, and the national movements were supported by the Europeans in an earlier period, whether in Greece or among the Serbs or among other nationals of the Balkans. I think the national movement supported by Europe did play an important role in destroying or weakening the Ottoman Empire.

When we take the same period of the 19th century in the Middle East, there had been no national movement in Palestine until 1908. I don't think there was a national movement anywhere in the Arab world until 1908, not even in Lebanon. There is local patriotism, but not an Arab national movement, neither in Egypt nor in Syria, nor anywhere else in the Middle East. There were a few thinkers – Khawatbi, Assouri and others - but that does not constitute a national movement. It's something different. We have to differentiate between some people who have a national consciousness and a national movement.

That's why I don't think the national movements played an important role in destroying the Ottoman Empire in the 19th century. Later on, in the two decades before World War I, and particularly after 1908, there is something different. There are examples, for instance, of Muhammad Ali and others who did play a role in weakening the Ottoman Empire. The fact that Muhammad Ali was able to gain control in Egypt and make reforms is already a sign of the weakening of the Ottoman Empire, a weakening which had already begun. Had Muhammad Ali become a stronger ruler in Egypt, he could have fought the sultan himself. He helped the sultan in Greece, but wanted the government of Syria, including Palestine, in return. And when the sultan refused, he simply sent his army in 1831 to occupy the region.

During the 18th century, or even earlier, we have local leaders and elites, from Syria to the Galilee, who took advantage of the weakening Ottoman Empire, and actually weakened it further, because the Ottoman Empire should have invested money and soldiers to suppress these local leaders. But this is still not a national movement.

MOSHE MA'OZ: Ultimately, the Muslim rulers were mostly loyal to the Ottoman Empire. You said yourself that the notables were part of the bureaucracy.

ADEL MANNA: I differentiate between the rulers of the districts and the lower local elite. The local elites are part of the administration and loyal to the Ottoman Empire. Nonetheless, when we speak about the weakening of the Ottoman Empire, they played a role here and there.

MERON BENVENISTI: There is also a difference between here and the Balkans. Here, there was no input from the imperialists to weaken the Turkish regime. I am talking about the 19th century. They had no interest in dismembering, except the Balkans.

ADEL MANNA: Just a few remarks to Ruth. With regard to the issue of foreigners or settlers, I take your point that you spoke about settlers, not foreigners. Nonetheless, there are different kinds of settlers - Circassians or Templars or Jewish Zionists versus others who would be ready to integrate into the population. Egyptians and Houranis* integrated into the population and become part of the Palestinian people.

RUTH KARK: There has not been a definitive study on this. But the local population did not marry them. They settled in separate places.

ADEL MANNA: This is a social issue, not a national one.

Concerning an issue you raised earlier, persecution or not of Jews in Palestine in the 19th century, I put that in my paper. In Palestine, like elsewhere in most of the Middle East and North Africa - I'll speak more about Palestine now and not other places - in the Ottoman Empire in general, and under Islam also, Islamic rule and Islamic society were much more tolerant of Christians and Jews - particularly Jews - in the 19th century. We have bloodshed and conflict between Christians and Muslims from the 1840s, and in Palestine, we rarely encounter massacres or persecution of Jews as such. The entire population suffered under the rulers and the governments.

When I speak with Israelis today about our situation as Arabs in Israel, and the inequalities and discrimination, they say, "Well, people in Syria are not living under any better conditions." But this is not a comparison because all the Syrians suffer from the Syrian regime. All dictatorships inflict suffering on their people. We are speaking about a state which declares itself a democracy and which should give equal treatment to all its citizens, whether Arabs, non-Jews, Jews or others.

This is also the case here. Speaking about the Ottoman Empire in the 19th century, the Ottoman administration in Palestine, and the indigenous people of Palestine in the 19th century, I think the attitude was very tolerant. There was not equal treatment, but there was tolerance. Tolerant does not mean equal. Once again, here and there you can find some examples, in 1834 in Jerusalem or in Safed, on this or that date. But if you take the entire 400-year period of Ottoman control, generations of Jews, Christians and Muslims living under Islamic control, you cannot say that the Islamic attitude or the Islamic rulers were not tolerant towards the Jews.

Bernard Lewis, Mark Cohn and others wrote books making this comparison, and they said that the Jews, under the rule of Islam, did not suffer the lot of Jews under Christian Europe. A few examples that they raised are the Jews and Muslims under the Crusaders, the Jews in Europe, the Muslims and Jews in Jerusalem and in Palestine, the experience of the Muslims and Jews in Spain under Islamic rule and then when the Spanish people conquered Spain, and modern anti-Semitism in Europe from the 19th century to the Holocaust. Do you have anything similar to those experiences of the Jews in Europe? This is the comparison between tolerance and intolerance.

I may also add that you don't have segregation of the Jews by Muslim rulers in general. Once again, you can pick out this Fatmid ruler, or that experience. The Jews did live in many Jewish towns and neighborhoods, but this was more a choice of the people, Christians, Jews or others. Jews also lived in the 16th century and in other periods under Islam. There were no vetoes against Jews in the Muslim world, and no limitations on the jobs they could hold.

RAN AARONSOHN: Evidence, facts, data, versus understanding, explanation, meaning, implication. Objective versus subjective.

I found this session very disturbing with regard to the twins in our bellies, research vis-a-vis myth. If we believe we have common ground, Meron, and that reality has not yet been written, we should stick to the historiography and to research, and not go on with general observations about the populations we are involved with. We should exploit our professional advantage and proceed with that, and not look around too much.

Another thing, if we do try to look at things professionally, I would point out that there is a difference between inductive and deductive methods. As I sat here and listened, I personally tried to be as inductive as possible, and not to let my personal set of conclusions and models and generalizations color what was presented here. I believe we should first try to find a common ground of evidence, facts and data.

I would also like to share with you the uneasy feeling I got from the discussion here about methodologies. There was an imbalance between what I heard from Ruth's presentation, that tried to put forward ground rules with question marks, and the other approaches that, for me, didn't lead to much more than conflicts and disagreements. This also impacted our time.

AMNEH BADRAN: "Palestine", the historical word, as opposed to "Palestine" relating to Palestinians and national identity. I feel as if I am now asked to question how to use the word "Palestinian" in referring to a people who were living in Palestine during the 19th century. As someone who is not a historian, I need to think aloud with you. If the Westerners who have been coming to this area have been using the word "Palestine" and I cannot use it, speaking about the 19th century, then how can I relate to the area where my ancestors have been living? And because there were no borders defining Palestine, then is there any real attachment to the area?

ADEL MANNA: Nobody said that. You can have an attachment with different ideologies and identities. You don't have to have a national consciousness and identity in order to have an attachment.

AMNEH BADRAN: In addition, we are trying to impose the form of a national state, a modern state, on a period with no such context in terms of socio-political development. How can we take something Western and modern, and try to impose it on a period that is not yet ready for it? I'm not saying I don't have an attachment. But how can I use the word "Palestinian" only when speaking of building a national identity or a Palestinian national state? This is a very tricky matter.

Let's go back to history and look to the word Palestine and see if this is related to the area and why the word Palestine was chosen then. If anyone can enlighten me about the history of the word, that might help.

DALIA OFER: It's a Roman word.

BURCKHARD BLANKE: It's the narrative of victors. The Romans, as occupiers, invented this word. And it's very funny to note that they used the "ph" of the Greeks - Philistine - which, over hundreds of years, is converted into "p" - Palestine, a word Arabic-speaking people cannot express because they don't pronounce the "p".

ADEL MANNA: They say ph.

BURCKHARD BLANKE: Yes. They say Falastin. Throughout the world it is now adopted as Palestine.

WALID SALEM: Instead of talking about indigenous people, can we say the majority of these indigenous people were Palestinians?

AVRAHAM SELA: Only if you can prove that they were consciously understanding and accepting this identity. I think this is the problem we are really talking about. When we say these people were Palestinians, would they themselves at that time define themselves as such? Or are we only using the term so we can communicate and understand each other?

AMNEH BADRAN: There are Palestinians belonging to areas of Palestine. The question of national identity was developed later.

AVRAHAM SELA: I am talking about an awareness of one's identity, even if we're talking about small groups of people, not the whole country.

RUTH KARK: Have you heard of the *sanjak* of Jerusalem and of Nablus?

AVRAHAM SELA: I think this is what you meant. If not, please correct me. We're using it only as a technical term because we want to understand each other. And when we communicate using this terminology, we understand we are talking about the indigenous inhabitants of this country in that period and nothing beyond that.

AMNEH BADRAN: I am differentiating between belonging to an area and belonging to a national identity. It's not only a technical matter.

DALIA OFER: I really don't agree with what Ran said. I don't think what happened in Ruth's and Adel's presentations was basically different from a methodology point of view. Each of them asked correct historical questions and related to the historiography, and came to different conclusions because of different periodizations, or because of different viewpoints.

RUTH KARK: It's not a matter of viewpoints.

DALIA OFER. We all have viewpoints. So what? The question then is whether, in our work and in our research, with all our limitations as human beings, we can try to be as neutral as possible relating to basic methodologies and disciplines. And I think this happened in both these cases, although they presented things in a different way.

Looking at the whole session, particularly at both their responses, I think we were on sound ground. Let's think about it. We don't have to change our credo. What we have to understand is the other point of view. We want to know the other point of view, and not out of tolerance, but out of respect. I think this is a major thing that happened here, and I want to thank both of you.

THE BEGINNINGS OF JEWISH SETTLEMENT AND ZIONISM TO WORLD WAR I

Ran Aaronsohn

WE address four specific questions and issues. The questions: How did early settlers and Zionist leaders see the land and its people (to the extent they did)? What form of organization and what borders did they envision? The issues: The emergence of Arab and Palestinians nationalism and identity (including movements and ideas), and the Palestinian reaction to Zionist settlement.

In thematic and chronological terms, this summary is divided into two secondary periods according to the *Aliyot* (the sequential periods of Jewish immigration to Eretz Yisrael/Palestine prior to 1948). The reason for this is not only that this kind of division is the accepted approach in Israeli historiography, but also because of the turning point that came with the transitional period between the First Aliyah and the Second Aliyah in terms of the Arab question. It should be taken into account lastly, that this summary is naturally subject to limitations − both objective (i.e. the short space available) and subjective (mainly the fact that the author is a Zionist).

THE FIRST ALIYAH PERIOD (1882-1903)

Jewish settlement

This wave of immigration comprised some 50,000-60,000 Jews, almost all from Eastern Europe. Approximately half left Eretz Yisrael before the end of this period. Most of those who remained settled in towns, where they generally integrated with the members of the veteran Old Yishuv* Jewish communities in Jerusalem and the other holy cities. The remainder − no more than a few thousand − founded new urban communities. A minority of the immigrants established agricultural settlements around the country, the *moshavot* (colonies), primarily on land bought from the Arabs. By the end of the period, the 28 moshavot of the First Aliyah included approximately 5,000-6,000 people living on some 250,000 dunams (62,500 acres). The total Jewish community in Eretz Yisrael was doubled during the First Aliyah period, reaching an estimated figure of 50,000 by its conclusion.

The New Yishuv in the moshavot and towns began to develop in all spheres of modern life − from agriculture and economics to the social and cultural aspects. They faced many difficulties: natural (an undeveloped country) and human, internal (lack of capital, know-how and organization) as well as external (opposition from the Ottoman authorities and from the Arab neighbors). They were assisted on the one hand by the *Hovevei Zion* (Lovers of Zion) organization of Eastern Europe, from which most of the immigrant settlers came, and on the other by Baron Edmond de Rothschild of Paris, who became a key figure in the moshavot through his officials ("The Administration").

Zionism, organization and political ideas

Throughout this period, the leading ideological grouping was Hovevei Zion. The Zionist Organization was established in 1897, and its institutions only began to operate in Eretz Yisrael during the Second Aliyah period, as discussed below. The general goal of Hovevei Zion and of the New Yishuv immigrants was to renew Jewish identity in the Holy Land through economic and cultural means, focusing mainly on the development of a network of productive settlements and the revival of the Hebrew language. The organizational character was primarily individualistic, both in terms of the personal activities of immigrants and settlers, and in terms of the autonomy of each community or colony. National frameworks were of marginal importance. In political terms, the new Jewish identity in Eretz Yisrael was thought of as an integral part of the dominant Ottoman Empire. Thus, there could be no public discussion or practical action relating to the question of borders. Accordingly, it is anachronistic to see the adjective "national" in the context of political ideas or organizations of this period.

The Arab Question

Contacts with and attitudes toward the Arabs were conducted on two levels and two planes. First, on the general national level, and in terms of principle, it became an "invisible" question. There was only a limited and obscure discussion of the Arab issue, consonant with the poorly-developed and proto-national atmosphere of the time. None of the important elements of the developing society, including the New Yishuv establishment (the Baron's administration) and public opinion figures (the leaders of Hovevei Zion) formulated any coherent political philosophy; nor did they develop any practical tools in this respect. Discussion of the Arab question was marginal, inconsistent and highly individualistic.

On the local and practical level, it could be considered a "banal" question. It was here that the main significance of the contacts with the Arabs should be observed. These contacts appeared as part of the fabric of everyday life, and as a practical and purpose-oriented matter. The relations were double-edged; on the one hand, contacts and cooperation, characterized by the purchase of Arab land (mainly from the urban *effendis*) and neighborly relations with peasants and Bedouin on the part of the moshavot established on the land. These relations ranged from hired labor (including work as guards) by numerous Arabs, through mutual trading relationships with buying and selling on both sides, and culminating in the provision of public services for Arabs in some of the colonies. On the other hand, tensions and struggles were also evident, in both directions. Trivial disputes were not unusual, according to a format that was also common among the Arabs themselves at the time, and often related to rights of pasture and water, the use of roads and, in particular, thefts. There were also graver incidents relating to the ownership of purchased land, borders, and farming rights. While these incidents created hostility, the overall picture was one of neighborly coexistence.

THE SECOND ALIYAH PERIOD (1904-1914)

Jewish settlement

A second wave of Jewish immigration from Eastern Europe comprised some 40,000 people, of whom fewer than half were more or less permanently absorbed in Eretz Yisrael. This immigration had a mixed character; on the one hand, a continuation of the pattern of the First Aliyah, whereby immigrants joined the urban Jewish communities, settled in the existing moshavot and established additional ones. On the other, we find a new class of immigrants, most of whom worked as laborers in the towns and moshavot, and a minority of whom settled in the newly-erected "national farms" or established the first collective settlements (*Kibbutzim* and *Kvutzot*). Some 26 Jewish settlements were founded during the Second Aliyah period, as well as the city of Tel Aviv. On the eve of World War I, the total Jewish population in Eretz Yisrael was approximately 85,000. The immigrant laborers established professional organizations and created two labor parties, which formed the basis for the labor movement. The collective settlements of the laborers were established with the funds and assistance of the Zionist movement institutions, which began to be active in the country during this period. The continuing "private settlements" activities took place mainly under the auspices of the ICA (Jewish Colonization Association), the organization that inherited Baron Rothschild's activities in Eretz Yisrael. Both bodies continued to purchase land, so that by 1914 the Jews owned over 500,000 dunams (125,000 acres), the majority held by ICA, and a minority held by the Zionist movement institutions, individuals and private companies.

Zionism, organization and political ideas

The leading ideological body during this period was the Zionist movement (although Hovevei Zion continued to exert influence). The institutions of the World Zionist Organization also began to operate in Eretz Yisrael: the Jewish National Fund, Anglo-Palestine Bank, Hakhsharat Hayishuv and the Palestinian Office. In terms of practical settlement activities, however, ICA was the leading body. Zionism formulated political goals, which related essentially to the creation of an autonomy (with Ottoman and/or international approval) in selected parts of Eretz Yisrael in which a Jewish majority would be created. There was no accepted territorial definition, and certainly no precise borders; but the general orientation was to the areas of the new Jewish colonization along the coastal plain, in the valleys, and in parts of the Galilee. The representatives of the Zionist movement expressed a vision of a national Jewish society in the country, and of self-sufficiency and Hebrew labor as the basis for an autarchic national Jewish economy – in opposition to the local Arab society and economy. This vision was shared also by the laborers of the Second Aliyah, who advocated the "conquest of labor." That trend led to the emergence of "Hebrew guards" effort, and organizations were established to replace Arabs in this role.

The Arab Question

A transition took place during the period, due to dramatic changes in circumstances − both external (the revolution of the Young Turks and the rise of Palestinian-Arab nationalism) and internal (the institutions of the Zionist Organization and organized labor). These changing circumstances had a direct impact on the Arab issue. The important changes in this sphere may be summarized by two key trends:

(A) Sharpening and extremism. The "Arab question" became the "Arab problem." The tension and disputes of the earlier period continued, particularly on the subject of land. New manifestations also developed, primarily relating to the replacement of cheap Arab labor by Hebrew labor, and the "conquest" of the profession of guarding as a national Zionist statement. As a generalization, there was now a conscious attempt to develop an autarchic society and economy, distinct from the non-Jewish (i.e. Arab) local surroundings.

(B) Awareness and fears: the "invisible" issue now became "visible." Public debate began with an article published in 1907, clearly revealing the problematic dimensions of the relationships between the Jewish settlers and the Arab population. "Top-down" actions were taken to reduce tension. The policy adopted by leading bodies, both under the Palestinian Office and under the ICA, was one of reconciliation and restitution. Compensation was provided for tenants and other land tillers, while in the political arena the Zionists attempted to reach an understanding with the young Arab national movement. In the labor movement, uncertainties developed on the moral and ideological level with regard to the Arabs, particularly in the context of the usurpation of the role of Arab laborers.

SUMMARY AND CONCLUSIONS

During the First and Second Aliyot, the number of Jews in Eretz Yisrael more than trebled; over 50,000 immigrants arrived in the country. The majority of the immigrants joined the Old Yishuv, while the minority founded the New Yishuv, which was roughly divided into a private sector and a laborer sector. During this era, more than 50 new Jewish settlements appeared on the map of the country, many private (moshavot) but some collective (kibbutzim) or of some other kind. These settlements − of whichever kind -- formed the heart of the New Yishuv, which developed an economic and cultural life separate from that of the local population. The New Yishuv was supported by global Jewish organizations, particularly Hovevei Zion and later the World Zionist Organization; these public bodies played a leading role in shaping the ideological and political character of the endeavor. From a practical viewpoint, private bodies such as Rothschild's administration and ICA were of greatest help. While throughout this formative period the quantitative scale of Jewish colonization was limited, as were Zionist

65

aspirations, the basic characteristics of the whole Jewish resettlement in Israel/Palestine may already be discerned.

During the course of this period, the "Arab question" underwent a process of exposure and exacerbation. A parallel process was the development of "Arab discourse" from the local and practical level to that of national principle. The spontaneous and mutual neighborly relations that typified the early period became less frequent due to the Zionist policy of separation regarding the "Arab problem" by the end of the period. This process was manifested not only in ideological and political forms, but also in increasing tension and struggles on the grassroots level. Until World War I, the conflict with the Palestinians was limited in scope, and possessed only an extremely marginal international character. Nevertheless, the essential elements of the Arab-Jewish conflict could already be seen during this early stage.

The approach of most Jewish settlers and Zionist leaders during this period, as well as of the historiographical mainstream approach to this day, is that the Arab question was merely one problem out of many. It confronted the Jewish settlement movement in Eretz Yisrael, alongside issues of equal importance (the attitude of the authorities, the shortage of means of subsistence, internal struggles, etc.). Accordingly, the prevailing approach to the Arab question was local and internal in nature. Only on the margins (narrow at the time, though broader and widening today) could a critical perspective be found, viewing the Arab question as THE primary issue facing Jewish settlement in Eretz Yisrael – sometimes as part of a broader view arguing that the settlement ignored the realities of the land, sometimes combining this tendency with the phenomena of colonialism and capitalism. According to this alternative approach, "Arab discourse" should thus be examined from a comparative and generalized viewpoint, in a much wider context.

Selected Bibliography

Aaronsohn, Ran, *Rothschild and Early Jewish Colonization in Palestine*, Magnes Press and Rowman & Littlefield, Jerusalem and New York, 2000

Bartal, Israel (ed.), *The Second Aliyah: Studies,* Yad Izhak Ben-Zvi, Jerusalem 1997 (esp. Gorny Yossef, "Between historical activism and contemporary activism", pp. 419-434) [Heb.]

Ben-Porat, Amir, "Opportunity, desire and the break into Palestine", Iyunim Bitkumat *Israel, Studies in Zionism...* 4 (1994), pp. 278-298 [Heb.]

Eliav, Mordechai (ed.), *The First Aliyah, vol. 1*, Yad Izhak Ben-Zvi, Jerusalem 1981 (esp. Ro'i Yaacov, "Jewish-Arab relations in the First Aliya settlements", pp. 245-268) [Heb.]

Gorny, Yosef, *The Arab Question and the Jewish Problem,* Am Oved Publishers, Tel Aviv 1985 [Heb.; English translation: *Zionism and the Arabs, 1882-1948: a Study in Ideology,* 1987]

Kolatt, Israel (ed.), *The History of the Jewish Community in Eretz Yisrael since 1882: The Ottoman Period, I,* The Israel Academy and Bialik Institute, Jerusalem 1989 (Esp. Lamdan, Yosef, "The Arabs and Zionism, 1882-1914", pp. 215-256) [Heb]

Ram, Uri, "The Colonization Perspective in Israeli Society", Journal of Historical Sociology 6/3 (1993), pp. 327-350

Shafir, Gershon, *Land, Labor and the Origins of the Israeli-Palestinian Conflict, 1882-1914,* University of California Press, Berkeley and Los Angeles, 1996

Shapira, Anita, *Land and Power: The Zionist Resort to Force,* Tel Aviv 1992 [Heb].; English translation: Stanford University Press, 1999

Stern, Menachem. et al. (eds.) *Zionism and the Arab Question*, Zalman Shazar Center, Jerusalem 1979 (esp. Kolatt Israel, "The Zionist movement and the Arabs", pp. 9-36) [Heb.; English translation: *Zionism and the Arabs: Essays,* 1983

THE PRE-HISTORY OF PALESTINIAN NATIONALISM

Issam Nassar

THE premise from which this essay starts is that nations and nationalism are modern products with histories that date back to a few centuries at the most. Although the emergence of nations and nationhood appear to be a hallmark of the last two centuries, the birth of a single nation was not necessarily a matter of "historical determinism." Rather, each nation emerged as a result of certain particular events, circumstances and incidents combined with certain activities and rhetoric produced mostly by what we can call the nation's elite. In other words, the production of the *imagined community;* i.e. the nation, to use Anderson's phrase, combines economic and political process with cultural-rhetorical one. [1] Therefore, writing its history must not be limited to the political events that produce the nation-people, but must also include the discourse through which the nation is produced and constructed, and the history employed in this production process.[2] Accordingly, the study of the emergence of the Palestinians as a nationed people, in my opinion, ought to go beyond the narrow angle of the development of their political institutions. But it should primarily include the study of the Palestinian imagination of the self, the kind of discourse it produced, and the historical factors influencing it.

Palestine, as we have known it since 1923, was a part of *Bilad al-Sham* (commonly equated with the name Greater Syria), a distinct region that fell under Ottoman control in the second decade of the 16th century. Under the Ottomans, this region was divided into several administrative units that fell under the direct rule of different administrators. The region known as Palestine did not constitute one administrative unit but different parts belonged to larger units that crossed between Palestine and other Syrian territories. However, despite the absence of administrative unity of the region in question, evidence suggests that Palestine was the name used by various people to refer to the territory that stretched from Acre in the north to Gaza in the south. In what follows, I am attempting to highlight some of the elements that led to Palestinian self-identification with Palestine.

Recent studies on Palestine suggest that the emergence of a self-identification with Palestine on the side of its population predates the inception of Palestinian nationalism itself. While the latter can be linked with various outside elements beyond the direct control of what would become the Palestinians, the first reflects the internal socio-economic processes that were gradually taking place since the middle of the Ottoman period in Palestine. In other words, the emergence of an Arab Palestinian national movement was no doubt connected with, among other things, the rise of Turkish nationalism within the ranks of the Ottoman establishment, the start of the Jewish Zionist colonization of the country, and direct British colonial control of Palestine after World War I. However, historical evidence suggests that the idea of Palestine as an administrative, social and economic unit was already in existence in the second half of the 19th century. In his study of Jabal Nablus, Beshara Doumani argues that the "economic, social, and cultural relations between the inhabitants of the various regions of Palestine during the Ottoman period . . . [illustrate] why Palestine became a nation in the minds of the people who call themselves Palestinians today."[3] Doumani supports his point by showing that Palestine "produced large agricultural surplus and was integrated into the world capitalist economy as an exporter of wheat, barely, sesame, olive oil, soap and cotton during 1856-1882 period."[4] Nablus, as Doumani argues, constituted the main commercial center in the 19th century for the villages in a region that spread from Hebron in the south to the Galilee in the north. Its trade relations with the Greater Syrian hinterland, particularly with Damascus, made Jabal Nablus, in effect, the actual center of the web of relations that constituted Palestine.

Still, despite the existence of an actual commercial center for the region in question, as pointed out by Doumani, one cannot argue that the loyalties and identifications of the residents of Palestine at that time were national in nature. Rather, a combination of local, regional and religious affiliations existed within Palestine that often were more potent than any sense of belonging to the country. As Rashid Khalidi showed, a multiplicity of identities existed among the people of Palestine in the late Ottoman period. Ottoman, Arab, tribal, and religious identities coexisted among the urban elite and the residents of the villages, who often assumed local, rather than national or regional, identities.[5] However, such multiplicity of identities did not necessarily reflect conflicting loyalties, for loyalty to the Ottomans did not negate being proud of Arab heritage nor defending Palestine against foreign greed. The coexistence of multiple loyalties remains to this day one of the characteristics of Palestinian identity.

The mere emergence of the idea of the land of Palestine, with defined borders similar to the ones relied on later by the British Mandate, reveals that the idea of a Palestine distinct from its neighbors existed in some circles. The Palestinian imagining of the boundaries of their national group is a product of conditions that largely existed in the 19th century. Among such conditions is the centrality of Jerusalem in the popular imagination of the Muslim, Christian, and Jewish residents of land that made it [Jerusalem] a symbol for all other places in Palestine and turned visiting it into an important part of the religious identity of the residents of Palestine.[6] This centrality of Jerusalem was enhanced even more from the middle of the 19th century by its growing importance as an administrative center which affected the lives of the people of the region. The city became the de facto administrative and political capital for all nearby areas, particularly in the period after 1887, when it became the capital of an independent *sanjak* (district in the Ottoman Empire) carrying its name and sending delegates to *Majlis al-*

Mab'outhan (the Ottoman parliament). As Kimmerling and Migdal point out, such a special administrative status for Jerusalem was important for the eventual birth of an independent Palestinian identity in the aftermath of Ottoman rule.[7] Kimmerling and Migdal base their argument on an essay by Butrus Abu-Manneh in which he argued that the autonomy of Jerusalem "was of tremendous importance for the emergence of Palestine."[8]

Equally important was the image of Palestine in the 19th century European imagination. Depictions of the country as the Holy Land, as expressed in writings by European travelers, missionaries and archeologists in the 19th century, played an important role in shaping a local recognition of the distinctiveness of Palestine and its geographic unity, even though its frontiers were not clearly and accurately drawn.[9] Alexander Schölch stated this case when he wrote:

> One can easily assume that in the second half of the 19th century the image of Palestine as a unit (as in the "Holy Land" or the "Land of Israel") was more precise and more strongly formed among the Europeans than it was among the local population and the Ottoman administration. But beneath the fluctuating surface of administrative boundaries, an image of the region's coherency was recognizable, at least after 1830. During the 1870s it took on contours that were clearer. To this extent, the Mandate zone of Palestine was no artificial, colonial creation.[10]

Schölch goes on to show that in the second half of the 19th century the port of Jaffa—because of its connection with Jerusalem—was Palestine's window onto the world. Using Ottoman and European statistics, Schölch argued that from this port Palestine exported to Europe and imported its different products, and consequently Jaffa played a central role in shaping an independent meaning for Palestine.[11]

Therefore, in light of the above, it should not come as a surprise that a portion of the urban intellectuals in Palestine and of the *mashreq* (the eastern part of the Arab world), began to imagine—and speak of—Palestine as a distinct political unit well before colonial divisions and intensive Jewish immigration, even though this imagining was yet not accompanied by a distinct Palestinian national consciousness. An early articulation of Palestine as an entity came from the writer (and former Ottoman official in Jerusalem) Najib 'Azuri who proposed in 1908 the idea of expanding the *sanjak* of Jerusalem to include northern Palestine, explaining that this was necessary to develop the land of Palestine.[12] Not only did 'Azuri's vision of Palestine correspond with the borders as they were drawn a decade later by the British—who drew the map based on biblical imagination—but also corresponded with the borders for Palestine as stated in the statement issued by the First Palestinian Arab Congress that was held in Jerusalem on 3 February 1919. In the protest statement sent by the participants to the Paris Peace Conference then in session, they stated that they represent "all Muslim and Christian residents of Palestine, which is made of the regions of Jerusalem, Nablus, Arab Acre."[13] In this regard, it might be worth mentioning that the protest letter sent a few months before by the Muslim-Christian committee in Jaffa to General Allenby in 1918 spoke in the name of "the Arab Palestinian".[14]

Still, it is important to keep in mind that that conference held in Jerusalem in 1919 which was called "the Arab Palestinian Congress" and issued the statement mentioned above emphasizing the importance of the independence of Palestine and of preserving its unity, asserted that Palestine was part of Greater Arab Syria.[15] Such dualities that seem to be expressed in the statement, however, do not diminish the importance of the fact that to the attendees of the Congress, Palestine presented a unit in itself. Such dual national allegiance was also in existence in the 1950s and early '60s. Examine the political program of any of the Palestinian political movements at the time—say the Arab Nationalist Movement and you will notice that the Palestinian concern with the liberation of Palestine from the Zionist movement was always expressed in the language of Arab nationalism.[16]

The point that I am trying to suggest is that an imagining of Palestine as an entity was evolving even before Zionism presented a threat to the Arab nature of Palestine. Still, the conflict with Zionism played a central role in shaping the nature and the articulation of the emerging Palestinian nationalism. If the colonial division of the region based on the Sykes-Picot agreement (1916) was what finalized the borders of the imagined Palestinian entity, Jewish immigration to Palestine played the largest role in the evolution of a distinct Palestinian nation, which began to assume new directions and develop new characteristics. Because of the nature of Jewish settlement, which generally sought to build agricultural colonies, the Palestinian clash with the Zionist project began in the villages, not in the cities. This produced one of the most important characteristics of Palestinian identity and one of its problems at the same time. The peasant character became an essential part of the way Palestinians view and represent themselves. Later on they would adopt peasant forms of dress, such as the *kufeyeh* headscarf, and the village dance, the *dabkeh*, as symbols of Palestinian national identity. At the same time, the fact that the city did not play the larger role in shaping local consciousness is responsible for not generalizing this consciousness, which continued to compete with a number of other national perspectives. However, this would change later on. During the British Mandate period, the peasant feeling of distinctiveness found its political expression not in rural areas but in the city, through articles in local newspapers, political discourse, and emerging parties. The various Palestinian newspapers, *Al-Karmel, Filasteen,* and *Al-Munadi,* all without exception conducted one campaign after another against the Zionist movement and its project in Palestine, demanding that Palestine remain for its people and become politically independent. Najeeb Nassar, the most prominent of Palestinian journalists and owner of the Haifa-based *Al-Karmel* newspaper, asked in 1914—a few years before British rule began—that the Arabs of *Bilad al Sham* (Greater Syria) support the people of Palestine, whom he called "the Palestinians." In 1914 Nassar wrote:

> We, your Palestinian brothers, share with you all your difficulties. So why don't you, at least, feel with us a little the disasters raining on us…and on our country. [17]

Nassar's text reveals recognition of the borders of the Palestinian group at that time. It also reveals the awareness of the difference of this group from another neighboring group—the people in the rest of Greater Syria. This awareness becomes deeper after the Balfour Declaration in 1917 and during the British Mandate period generally, when it starts to take a political bent. In 1923, for instance, The National Arab party announced in its founding statement that its goal is "preserving Palestine for its people [...] and establishing a constitutional government in it."[18] Although the Arab identity of Palestine will continue to be an important part of Palestinian discourse during the Mandate period, this discourse will focus more and more on the particularity of Palestine. In other words, despite the fact that Palestinian particularity was rooted in historical conditions preceding intensive Jewish settlement activity, it crystallized as a consciousness only after the Palestinian encounter with Jewish settlements.

The peasant rejection of settlements and the political expression of this rejection through urban institutions constitute, then, the practical starting point at which the Palestinians saw themselves as an independent people. The emergence of the Zionist project into the light, and the British support of it through the Balfour Declaration, accelerated the development of a distinct political Palestinian identity. This identity began to express itself through societies and organizations that characterized themselves as Arab, Syrian, Islamic, or Christian but whose aim was defending Palestine against the Zionist threat. Imagining the Palestinian collectivity begins to take a practical bend with the convening of several Palestinian conferences as a reaction to Zionist threats and with the unambiguous demands for the right of self-determination for Palestine. This imagining will take a more formal vein in the period after 1922, following the official establishment of the mandate and with it the political borders of Palestine. It will develop later to become a collective imagining in which the majority of the population in mandate Palestine participates, until 1948 that is.

Nevertheless, since the development of a Palestinian national consciousness did not produce its own nation state, as was the case with the Arab neighbors of Palestine, but instead went through a period of disruption and discontinuity as a result of the events of 1948, i.e. the *Nakba*, it is not possible to speak with certainty about what that imagining would have produced. For Palestinian identity as we know it today owes its nature and characteristics to the experience of expulsion and exile of a significant portion of the Palestinians since 1947. No doubt a tragic event on different levels — familial, personal, and national — the catastrophe resulted in, first, the dismantling of the social structure for a significant part of the population in Palestine, who became refugees; and, second, the disappearance of urban centers from the lives of those Palestinians remaining in Palestine, who were transformed from city dwellers into groups living on the margins of cities. These two consequences mark a turning point in the nature of Palestinian discourse and in its continuity. The first one significantly aided the emergence of the Palestinians as a distinct group united by their shared experience of displacement. The second put an end to the development of a Palestinian collective imagination, which used to be formulated in the cities.

The two issues are closely related, but the first is especially important because it encouraged the emergence of a new kind of Palestinian identity. The disappearance of local identifications as a result of uprooting accelerated the confirmation of a Palestinian particularity that can be called national. After all as Homi K. Bhabha correctly noted the "nation fills the void left in the uprooting of communities and kin."[19] The exodus and the forced expulsion of the Palestinians in 1948 and the eventual erection of refugee camps all over the Middle East presented the perfect context for the transformation of the old Palestinian local and communal belongings into a nationalist one. The construction of such a new form of a living *locality* that is far more complex than the *old community* and far more symbolic than *society* to a large extent transfigured "the meaning of home and belonging."[20]

In other words, the point can be made that at the refugee experience played a central role in defining the nature and the meanings of the Palestinian identity, as we know it today. Still, narrating the history of Palestinian nationalism can not be done without taking into account that even before the encounter with Zionism, there were certain developments that were paving the way towards the emergence of a kind of identity particular to Palestine and its people. After all, nations, to borrow the words of Homi Bhabha, "lose their origins in the myths of time."[21] The Palestinian nation is no different. It lost its origins in myths connected, in this case, with the struggles against colonization that the Palestinians had to wage in their history. And in doing so, it constructed new myths about its origins that connected it, not with the socio-economic and political developments of the last 150 years, but instead with an imagined past that predates nations and nationalism by centuries.

---

[1] For further elaboration on this issue, see Benedict Anderson's *Imagined Communities: Reflections on the Origin and Spread of Nationalism* (London: Verso, 1991).
[2] The dominant tendency in the study of the evolution of Palestinian identity is the history of the evolution of the Palestinian political institution. An example of this is the Palestinian historian Maher al-Shareef's book *Al Bahth 'an Kiyan: Dirasat fi al-fikr al-siyasi al-filastini 1908-1993* (The Search for Being: Studies in Palestinian Political Thought (Nicosia: Markez al-abhath wal-dirasat al-ishtirakeyeh fil-calam al-carabi, 1995).
[3] Beshara Doumani, *Rediscovering Palestine: Merchants and Peasants in Jabal Nablus, 1700-1900* (Berkeley: University of California Press, 1995), 245.
[4] Ibid., 4.
[5] See, Rashid Khalidi, "Competing and Overlapping Loyalties in Ottoman Jerusalem" in *Palestinian Identity: The Construction of Modern National Consciousness.* (New York: Columbia, 1997), 63-88.
[6] Ibid.
[7] Baruch Kimmerling and Joel S. Migdal, *Palestinians: The Making of a People* (New York: The Free Press, 1993), 68-69.

8 Butrus Abu-Manneh, "The Rise of the Sanjak of Jerusalem in the Late 19th Century," in Ben-Dor, Ed., *The Palestinians and the Middle East Conflict: Studies in Their History, Sociology and Politics* (Ramat Gan: Turtledove, 1978), 25.

9 I briefly refer to this possibility in my doctoral dissertation. See Issam Nassar, *Imagining Jerusalem in the 19th Century: A Study in Religious and Colonial Imagination.* (Doctoral Dissertation, Illinois State University, 1997).

10 Alexander Schölch, *Palestine in Transformation 1856-1882: Studies in Social, Economic and Political Development* translated by William Young and Michael C. Gerrity (Washington, D. C.: Institute for Palestine Studies), 16.

11 *Ibid.*, 134-148.

12 Azuri suggested this to the Ottoman Parliament that was restored in 1908 in a newspaper article that appeared on September 23, 1908. See Rashid Khalidi. *Palestinian Identity: The Construction of Modern National Consciousness.* (New York: Columbia, 1997), 28-29.

13 Documents of the Palestinian Arab resistance to the British occupation and to Zionism 1918-1939. (Beirut: Mu'ssast al-Dirasat al-filasteneyeh): 3.

14 Documents of the Palestinian National Movement 1918-1939 (Beirut: Mu'ssast al-Dirasat al-Filasteneyeh).

15 See the text of the statement in Nweihed al-Hout's *Al-kiyadat al-seyasiyeh* (Political Leadership) (Beirut: Mu'assast al-dirasat al-filasteeneyeh), 96.

16 Established in the early fifties by a number of Palestinian activists such as George Habash and Hani al-Hindi, this movement declared that the liberation of Palestine is not possible without Arab unity. See the interview of George Habash with Mahmoud Sweid published in a book in the series *Marjé'iyyat filasteeneyeh*, # 3 (Beirut: Mu'assast al-dirasat al-filasteeneyeh, 1998): 11.

17 Al-Karmel, Haifa 6/12/1914. Quoted in Ali Mahaftha's Ali Mahaftha, *Al-fikr al-siyasi fi Filasteen: min nihayet al-hukm al-ʿUthmani wa hata nihayet al-intidab al-biritani 1918-1948* (Political Thought in Palestine: From the End of Othoman Rule Until the End of the British Mandate) (ʿAmman: Markez al-kutub al-ʿurduni, 1989), 23-24.

18 Ali Mahaftha, *Al-fikr al-siyasi fi Filasteen*, 225

19 Homi K. Bhabha. "Dissemination" in *The Location of Culture* (London: Routledge, 1994), 139.

20 Ibid., 140.

21 Homi Bhabha. *Nations and Narrations* (London and New York: Routledge, 1995), 1.

DISCUSSION 2

Ran Aaronsohn and Ata Qaymari/Issam Nassar

Note: Because of Israeli travel restrictions, Issam Nassar, who lives in the Palestinian Authority, was unable to travel through Israel's Ben Gurion Airport, and would have had to make the difficult journey to Amman, and then fly to Cyprus. He was unable to do so, and his paper was therefore presented by Ata Qaymari. Since he could not respond to the comments at the time of the seminar, he was given a transcript, and his response appears at the end of this discussion.

RAN AARONSOHN: I would like to stress my Israeli viewpoint. I am not only fifth generation, of the first year of the First *Aliyah* - sorry for the term - origin, but I'm also a Zionist. So I'm not neutral at all, but I'll try to stick to facts and be as objective as possible. Considering some of the underlying issues raised by most of the Palestinians and sometimes the Israeli participants, I'd like to concentrate on one basic term - actually a couple of un-identical twins - colonization vis-a-vis colonialism.

In Issam's paper, you see a reference to the "Zionist colonial project", for instance. I think this is of great importance, and I'd like to shed some light on it from my viewpoint. Colonialism has to do with political and economic operational projects in which a political entity conquers a new extra-territorial territory, country, place, whatever, and exploits its resources by different means. Colonization, on the other hand, involves other disciplines, mainly geography, because it has to do with the immigration of people overseas - meaning extra-territory - and their structural resettlement apart from the network of settlements of the local indigenous population.

The characteristics of colonialism have to do with metropolization and, with occupation, which are features of super-imposed power, while colonization is characterized by a mechanism of creating a new geography, a new reality next to the old one. Colonialism may exist without any colonization, illustrated by the British in India and Kenya and the Belgians in the Congo. There may be colonization without colonialism. The Templars, the Germans, the Americans in the Holy Land - in Palestine at the time - are a close example. But we may also point to the Japanese in Argentina, in Brazil, in South America; the Italians in Tunisia, who were of much more importance than the French till the beginning of the 20th century; and many other examples.

Colonization may be used as a tool of colonialism, within colonialism, as a vehicle to promote it. An example is the French colonization in Algeria - almost not at all in Morocco - and which, in some ways, expanded in Tunisia.

Colonization there was one of the vehicles of the conqueror, of the colonialist power, to promote colonialism; and there it had to do with a super-imposed power and with infrastructure that worked in favor of the French. All the railways and markets and enforced laws and regulations resulted in privileges for the settlers in contrast to the local native population.

We see a completely opposite phenomenon regarding Jewish colonization in the Ottoman Empire. The Jewish settlers - sorry about the term, I am trying to use it neutrally - were under-privileged under Turkish rule. Even those inhabitants who maintained European citizenship did not benefit from it. In general, but also with regard to many details, they were under-privileged. They were restricted in many ways with regard to buying land, obtaining building permits, drilling wells, and so on. Of course, it wasn't always the same. I am speaking in generalizations. It was not a linear process. But overall, I think this is a correct observation.

One may say that we are now speaking about a specific form of colonialism. This is not a new argument. It has been used for decades by many scholars, Arabs, Palestinians, Communists at the time, and New Zionists as well. They claim that specific people or institutions inside the Jewish endeavor should be seen as colonial agents. And because of their great importance, they do shed light on the general Zionist project as a whole. The person that I looked at very carefully was Baron Edmond de Rothschild who represented, in my perception, the most important factor explaining many of the phenomena of Jewish resettlement in Ottoman Palestine until World War I. He was much more prominent till about 1900, but he influenced that entire period. You may know about the administration he established, especially his agents - because he himself was in Paris, an absent landlord. One may easily draw some general inferences from a very few of his characteristics - the fact that he was a capitalist from a very well-known, wealthy French family, absent from the area and so on. Even so, I cannot find many reasons to identify him and his administrative activities - which should actually be referred to as something like national institutions of the time - as colonial. I looked at equating this with the Jewish national institutions in general during the Mandate period, and I found significant parallels.

All the money flowed one way, from France to Israel. Not a single franc, to my best knowledge - and I looked into the archives on both sides of the sea, and others - went the other way. This is completely contrary to one of the most important features of colonialism. Even if we say there was real political power, a real metropolitan entity, Baron de Rothschild gained nothing at all from it. Not a single franc that he earned - such as from the two wineries which are still in operation today in Rishon Lezion and Zichron Ya'akov - went the other way. It all stayed within the Jewish sector of Palestine. There are many other examples, which show that Rothschild had nearly no features of a colonialist agent. He was not working in connection with the French government. I did not find any realistic basis to the claim that he was a colonialist agent, and not even that he was a peripheral agent of the French colonial power.

A question was raised here about exclusion or separation. Adel is correct in saying that those who came with the First Aliyah did not behave this way, and no wonder. They were individual enterprises. Once the Zionist political entity and bodies, on the one hand, and the Palestinian embodiment of a political self-identity, on the other, began to act on the ground around 1908, we begin to see exclusion and separation between the two markets, the two communities, the two societies, the two nations. That began in 1908, and was only embodied after World War I.

Even today, there are societies which call its settlements colonies. So the colonial project was not colonial, and the colonial claims we have spoken about is something we should approach with a question mark.

Let's discuss this after we know what were the real features and characteristics of Jewish resettlement in Palestine in the late Ottoman period. It did not overlap structurally with colonialism. Essentially, it was a different kind of phenomenon. Colonization was universal at the time, and one should take this in the context of what was happening all over the world.

ATA QAYMARI: [*presenting the paper of Issam Nassar, who was unable to attend – see his comment at the end of this discussion*]: Issam's assumption is that Palestinian identity, contrary to the prevailing idea, is not a by-product of the Zionist colonial project in Palestine. He refutes this latter assumption and posits that the roots of Palestinian identity were products of events, circumstances and discourse that predated the Zionist project by decades, although the Zionist struggle and colonial project affected it. It was shaped by the struggle against Zionism.

When any nation emerges, Issam stresses, it combines economic and political processes with cultural and rhetorical ones. Therefore, the history of any nation must also include the discourse through which the nation is produced and constructed. Accordingly, the study of the emergence of the Palestinians as a nationed people should primarily include the study of the Palestinian imagination of the self, the kind of discourse it produced, and the historical factors influencing it.

With regard to the historical factors that influenced the imagination of Palestinian identity, Issam begins with the fact that there was a commercial economic center in Jabal Nablus. He refers to Doumani who argues that the economic, social and cultural relations between the inhabitants of the various regions of Palestine during the Ottoman period contributed to the vision of geographic Palestine from Acre to Gaza. Second is the centrality of Jerusalem. In the 19th century, Jerusalem became a symbol for all of Palestine, and visiting Jerusalem became an important part of the religious identity of the residents of Palestine. Eventually, we have the image of Palestine in 19th century European imagination. The image in the minds of missionaries, archeologists, travelers who came to Palestine in the 19th century played an important role in shaping a local recognition of the distinctiveness of Palestine and its geographic unit.

Politically, the discourse of the Palestinian people is reflected in the statement issued by the first Palestinian Arab Congress held in Jerusalem in February 1919. The participants stated that they represented all Muslim and Christian residents of Palestine, which was comprised of the regions of Jerusalem, Nablus and Arab Acre. In this statement we see a kind of unity of Nablus, Acre and Jerusalem as the three parts of Palestine. A protest letter, sent a few months earlier, in 1918, by a Muslim Christian community in Jaffa to General Allenby, spoke in the name of the Arab Palestinian. Still, at that time, the Palestinians had dual identities. In spite of the fact that they call themselves Arab Palestinians, they also speak of integrating into greater Arab Syria.

What Issam argues here is that such dual identity does not diminish the importance of the fact that, at this Congress, Palestine is presented as a unity in itself. Congress participants call for a unification of Palestine with Greater Syria, so there is a sense of belonging to Syria, but there is also a stress on the unity of Palestine and its uniqueness. Issam's point here is that imagining Palestine as an entity was evolving before Zionism presented a threat to the Arab nation of Palestine. The conflict with Zionism played a central role, he insists, in shaping the nature and articulation of emerging Palestinian nationalism. It plays a central role in shaping the nature of this identity, but it is not its origin.

The rural and agricultural characteristics of Zionism also affected Palestinian identity, and the Palestinians found a parallel identity connecting themselves to the land and to its symbols - such as the kufeyeh and the dabkeh - which became symbols of their identity later on.

After the Nakba, Palestinian identity owes its nature and characteristics to the experience of expulsion, and the refugee question becomes central to this identity. This Palestinian experience plays a central role in defining the nature and meaning of its identity.

LILY GALILI: I would like some elaboration referring to Ran's original paper, not to the presentation. You go from the concept of what is defined as the Arab question to what is later defined as the Arab problem, and some of the characteristics remain basically the same. So what accounts for the difference? How did the Arab question turn into the Arab problem, and what triggered it?

RAN AARONSOHN: That was in the transitional period between 1908 and 1917 or 1918, about a decade.

LILY GALILI: So it correlates to Issam's presentation.

RAN AARONSOHN: I accept nearly everything in his paper.

DALIA OFER: Why don't you connect it to the ideology of the Second Aliyah and the fact that the national visions were defined in a more clear and operative way? On the social level, the transformation, the Second Aliyah people were looking to change the image of the Jew to that of a producer, a self-supporter not dependent upon others. Gordon's* notion was that you have to really work the land in order to own it. You cannot just buy it.

ADEL MANNA: *Kibbush avodah** and *kibbush adamah.**

DALIA OFER: The articulation of these two kinds of concepts were of the Second Aliyah, not necessarily of the Zionist movement at that time, because the Second Aliyah and its ideology were not generally accepted by Zionists at the time.

We see that side by side, Gordon's articulations and the embodiment of the awareness of the national movement among the Palestinians. So here you have the reason why it's not a question but becomes a problem for each of the movements, for the Jews and for the Palestinians. "I am far from the *wattan* and I can't wait to come back to it, meaning Jerusalem, not Palestine." There are many examples. But unfortunately - or fortunately - we don't have Palestinian nationalism or a Palestine in the 17th or 18th century.

I agree with your comment concerning the British. Although the Zionists were not the agents of British colonialism, nonetheless, the British - the Anglican Church and so on - played an important role in promoting the notion of the Jews going back to Palestine. This is in all the biblical research, all the travelers' books. This did help promote the idea and the ideology that this land belongs to the Jews and that they have the right to go back to it. And it probably helped some Jews to pick up on this idea.

I would add to Avraham's comment concerning the period between 1917-1923, during which I do believe the Palestinian movement crystallized, the fact that in the neighboring Arab countries - Syria, Lebanon, Iraq, Egypt and elsewhere - local national movements crystallized during this period. The Palestinians were left alone. Should they become the only pan-Arabists while all the others are taking care of themselves? So they said, okay, everybody has their local national movement. Why don't we do the same thing? This is another reason why the Palestinian movement crystallized during this period.

AMNEH BADRAN: Going back to the relationship between the Zionist movement and Britain, from what I have read, I understand that Britain had no constituency in Jerusalem and no followers for the Anglican Church, and therefore they took on the holy role of the Jews. They did that furiously during the late 19th century, and they were even involved in pushing for Jewish representation in the the municipality of Jerusalem. They arranged through the British and other consuls that not only Muslims would be running the city, but also representatives from the Christian and Jewish communities. From then on, things accelerated, and the representation of Jews and Christians became similar to that of the Muslims. In fact, there was a great deal of support between Britain and the Zionist movement, not only in terms of services, but also politically.

ATA QAYMARI: I don't feel comfortable defending this article. I wanted to present it in a critical manner, but I thought it wouldn't be fair to Issam, so I presented it as it is. I agree that it is problematic. The title is problematic with relationship to the data within the article itself because it tackles more than one period that shouldn't be discussed when the emphasis is on the 19th century.

But if we just rephrase the argument in his article, we can trace Palestinian identities - not roots. It's less than roots. Maybe it's the seeds of this nationhood as a community as even before the Mandate, if not as an actual nationhood. These seeds would not have grown into a nation without the Mandate. This should be stressed. Playing with words by saying "by-product"' or "shaped by" or "were the products of" is not academically, politically or theoretically correct.

We can say there were many elements. Along with those were the economic and social development of Palestine as a community, with the development of the cities of Nablus, Jaffa and Jerusalem, making the whole area into a kind of nation within other elements that interfered in this identity.

BURCKHARD BLANKE: I would like to ask somebody neutral, what do we gain by knowing that the emergence of Palestinian identity is not related to the Zionist movement or the British Mandate or the other events we are talking about?

AVRAHAM SELA: The argument is not that it doesn't relate to the Zionist project. It says that, in the period until World War I, this is what we have. And then there is a different process. The Zionist movement, when you look at it historically, looks like a linear process, but it could end at any time in history. It depends on powers, on various international developments.

RUTH KARK: It depended on the British.

PAUL SCHAM: From 1882 to the beginning of World War I, what was the attitude of Zionist leaders and the Zionist movement about what would happen to the Palestinian inhabitants with the realization of the Zionist dream? Obviously, those attitudes underwent transformations during that period. My impression is that it was not something that was thought about very much. Perhaps the ultimate Jewish Commonwealth or other entity would encompass the Arabs? Of course, Herzl thought the Palestinians would be happy about Jewish immigration. They would benefit and there shouldn't be a problem. But I would imagine some people were a bit more sophisticated than that.

Was there thinking about this, how did it change over time, and how did this affect the attitude towards the indigenous Palestinian inhabitants, to use a polemical phrase?

AZIZ HAIDER: Many Palestinian researchers are trying to prove that the national identity of the Palestinians crystallized and developed before the Zionist movement came to Palestine, or before the immigration to Palestine. I think that it is because there are political implications if we prove that we are a nation, and if we prove that we developed and crystallized according to European nationalism or idea of nationhood. So there are implications with regard to rights, who has the right to take this stand or to be here or to develop and to establish a state here.

I think this is the wrong idea. I also think the population and number of inhabitants is not the point. So what if the population was lesser or greater in Palestine among the Palestinians themselves? The right to be in Palestine and to establish a nation state is not related to the size of the population or to the crystallization of this identity.

Most researchers don't distinguish between political identity, national identity, religious identity, and social and cultural identity, and this is a problem. If we talk about cultural and social identity, it could be okay. If we talk about religious identity, it could be okay. But to say that the Palestinian identity crystallized, or that among the Palestinians there was a national identity that crystallized, I think it's the wrong thing, and we don't need it. But they say the Westerners or the Americans developed this way, and they think that being a nation according to the Western definition affords you more rights. This is a problem. I don't feel that I have to make any attempt to prove something like this. At the same time, I want to historically place the seeds of this political identity. Some Palestinian researchers claim that Palestinian identity is still not completely crystallized. I think this is true. We have some problems with the social basis of this identity.

WALID SALEM: One point in Issam's defense. I think that what he was trying to do was to elaborate on the seeds of the development of Palestinian identity, which was a combination of Islam, Palestinianism and Arabism. These are the three components. As Dr. Haider said, the conflict between these three components continues. We don't know what the future holds for the Palestinian state, whether it will be more Islamic, more Palestinian, more Arabist. The local community is a component as well, of course. The identity of the Palestinian state will be the outcome of the conflict between these four components.

My second point relates to Ran's terminology. If it was a process of colonization and not colonialism, then where did these lands come from where Zionists and Jews established their settlements? From the moon? Was it without owners? Was it a gift from God? If these lands didn't come from the moon and are not a gift from God, then they are based in a certain geographic area and there were landowners, even if they were *musha'*, that is, community.

So are we really talking about peaceful colonization? People who came in a peaceful way to reside beside other people and to live with them in peace? Or are we talking about people who came and seized land in various ways - ways which we need to talk about. So I challenge your idea of colonization.

AVRAHAM SELA: Be a little more specific. What means are you referring to?

WALID SALEM: Some parts of the land of Palestine were marshland which were expropriated by the Zionist movement with the help of the British.

RUTH KARK: That is absolute nonsense. You are mistaken.

WALID SALEM: If I am mistaken, then please inform me.

LILY GALILI: Dr. Blanke asked earlier if it really matters how many Palestinians and how many Jews there were in the 19th century, and on the political level, it really doesn't matter. In terms of all the suffering, a political solution must be found regardless. But all of us here know that the conflict also operates at a very different level, in the sphere of ethos and myth, and we cannot completely disregard that because it is very present in the minds of both sides. One example to illustrate how much it matters is that the settlers used history and myths and Jewish ethos as powerful arguments in favor of settlement.

On the other hand, I watched a shocking segment on Palestinian television, a debate among Palestinian historians on the subject of mutual shared history, but ancient history. And they said the Jews don't belong here. There was never a Jewish presence here. They were just passing through, coming from other parts of the world. Then there was a comment about the common patriarchs, at least Abraham in Hebron, and the response was that this is a very common mistake. There was Ibrahim, one of the fathers of the Muslims, and someone named Abraham also passed by, but they were absolutely not the same person. I think this question of relevance or importance is unfair to the Palestinians because Israeli has already had 54 years of statehood, and has already established myths and an ethos, although some are still in process and some are already being revised. But the Palestinians are still constructing and creating their national ethos.

So we cannot say it's unimportant and irrelevant. If it's important for us, then it's important for both of us. Therefore, the question should be separated from the political question. The political question is to resolve the conflict as quickly as possible.

AVRAHAM SELA: I want to get back to the question of the British-

Zionist relationship because I think we'll see it in even stronger ways in the coming sessions. We should be very clear about what we mean when we speak about the foreign power - local power relationship. That the British consul in Jerusalem had close contacts with Jews in Jerusalem doesn't mean anything about British policy towards the Zionist movement. When we speak about this issue, we have to be very clear in showing the reasons and motivations of the British government in supporting or not supporting the Zionists.

During the Mandate, and definitely by the end of the Mandate, these issues of whether the British were pro-Arab or pro-Jewish become entirely legendary. We should be specific and accurate on this point, and very careful about the historical "facts". For example, when the British High Commissioner said, sometime in early 1948, "I don't understand why the Jewish community here hates us so much", this is some kind of historical fact. But things that are not facts should be classified as myth or perception or narrative, but not necessarily part of history.

ATA QAYMARI: Why don't you elaborate a little?

AVRAHAM SELA: This is following what Meron said earlier about the connection between the Consul and the Jews. During World War I, the reasons why the British supported the Zionists were divorced from that reality. It had to do with British interests.

MERON BENVENISTI: But this doesn't matter. The motivations of the British have nothing to do with what the Zionists did.

DALIA OFER: It's important to remember that, particularly after the Balfour Declaration, during the Mandate period, anything the British did in Palestine - whether it complemented Zionist activities or whether the Zionists thought it did not complement them - was important in promoting the Zionist project. Without them, as Meron said, it would not have succeeded. However, to say this is colonialism is a mistake. You cannot understand Zionism without looking at its origins as part of a national movement of the Jewish people, and it was not the only national movement of the Jewish people. There were others. This was the one that succeeded. Most of the others were simply murdered by the Nazis. I mention, for example, the non-Zionist Bund in Europe, which was also a kind of socialist national movement, although of a special character.

So nationalism is extremely important. It is true that it emerged during the time of colonialism or imperialism in the late 19th century. Without understanding that atmosphere or milieu, we cannot understand it, which does not mean one equates it with colonialism. We will still have to deal with it, and it's important to put it on the table.

PAUL SCHAM: The general point being made is that, even if, in Palestinian eyes, the actions of the British aided Zionists and Zionism, and therefore were pro-Zionist in the Palestinian perspective, it is essential, for a true historical understanding, to look at it from the British point of view as well and ask, Was this being done for British reasons. Was there a sympathy with Zionism? This depends, obviously. In 1918, there was more British sympathy with Zionism than in 1947-1948. But this brings up the larger issue of what we are trying to do here, which is to look at this from two different sides. We are talking about two different narratives, and here we are bringing in the British narrative as well.

It's relevant here as well to bring in the point Walid was making about Ran's distinction of colonization as something that did not distinguish among the inhabitants. But from the point of view of the people living there, when a landlord sold the land and the tenants had to leave, the distinction may have been lost on the people who had to leave. In other words, you were looking at colonization from the point of view of the colonizers; and understandably, Walid and other Palestinians are looking at it from a different point of view. Certainly both are valid in this forum.

RAN AARONSOHN: I tried to categorize the questions and comments into three main topics. First, Paul and Walid. Concerning the plans of Zionist leaders with regard to the Arabs, I don't know much about it, I should admit. I didn't look at it specifically.

MERON BENVENISTI: There's not much to look at.

RAN AARONSOHN: That's it. I would dare say there were nearly none. But then we should cut the limited answer into two, following the two-part periodization in my paper. In the first sub-period, meaning the First Aliyah till about 1904-1908, none to my knowledge. I guess this is because, through their eyes, there was no need to think about it. From their point of view, their nonpolitical thinking and aims - and from the point of view of present-day researchers - there were no activities on the political or national level that would lead to the need to develop future plans for the Arab population

PAUL SCHAM: What I meant is how were they thinking. There wasn't national planning.

RAN AARONSOHN: I thought the question was with regard to plans. If we want to consider views afterwards, I would really need to rethink it. Views, of course, are another matter, but I'm not sure that they are very different. Ahad Ha'Am may be an example of someone with some overall views and that's it. And even he looked at it on a very limited, micro scale.

WALID SALEM: What do you think about A.D. Gordon? He talked about the value of the land coming from its use.

DALIA OFER: From cultivating it. Not from its use.

WALID SALEM: The Jews have the right to own land if they cultivate it.

RAN AARONSOHN: During the second sub-period, I think Herzl's idea of Arab cultural assimilation as an ethnic minority with full civil rights is quite representative, even for the big thinkers representing the workers at the time. Even Gordon may be included in this broad classification - Arab cultural assimilation as an ethnic minority with full civil rights in whatever political future framework of the Jews in Palestine. That's the best I can say, considering my orientation.

And yes, Walid, it was, until World War I, a completely peaceful process of land acquisition. The Jews bought land only in the free market, and as I said, they were underprivileged as compared to the local Arab effendis, not to mention the owners or the sultan - who was of great importance at the time - and even the fellahin here and there, and so on.

AVRAHAM SELA: Can you relate to the question of dispossessed people?

RAN AARONSOHN: It's of great importance. In my period of interest, dispossession was very limited. In the beginning, during the British Mandate, there was a governmental inquiry into it, and they found that most of the land that was to be bought by the Jews was in the relatively empty lands of the plains, and it had already been through other processes of buying and selling in the free market of the effendis in the 1870s and 1880s. The permanent tenants of those lands numbered - I don't know if it's a few hundreds or many hundreds, but that's it. I tried to make a list of the first ten colonies bought in the 1880s, and I found around 150 tenants who had to leave their places. And those ten include more than one-third of the First Aliyah colonists. It was very limited, I think, even considering the then Arab population.

ADEL MANNA: Every tenant has a family.

RUTH KARK: Most of the tenants were brought in by these landowners when they bought the land. It was not settled before. The Valley of Israel was empty when they bought the land. They brought in tenants who sat there for ten years, maybe fifteen years, sometimes even less than two years. Then they sold the land and evacuated these tenants.

ADEL MANNA: They also evacuated Bedouins who had been living there for hundreds of years.

RAN AARONSOHN: Some of them. I was referring to the permanent tenants, those who lived there even tens of years, not only hundreds. Those numbered between 100 and 200 altogether - not families. The others were not settled there on a permanent basis.

Considering segregation, Dalia and Adel, during the Second Aliyah, I may agree on principle that it was mainly because of internal and not external aspects - Palestinian nationality and crystallization, as we just mentioned.

I agree that one should consider notions and perceptions of the Second Aliyah elite, the leaders of the workers.

The next point is in response to Meron and Amneh regarding British interests, including missions, colonialism and so on. Yes, of course. British agents tried to use the Jews and their potential bodies and sections as a vehicle to promote their own interests. But it's no wonder that the few examples you mentioned were all very early and had nothing to do with our title. To my best knowledge, almost none of them can be mentioned after the beginnings of Jewish settlement and Zionism up to World War I. That's why it ends in 1917. Right you are.

Of course, the Balfour Declaration is very prominent in the background. Nevertheless, we have no hard evidence, no primary documents of any kind, showing any kind of Jewish settlement or colonization in Palestine as being part of British colonialism.

MERON BENVENISTI: That's a very limited perception of the relationship.

RAN AARONSOHN: I am open to other evidence.

MERON BENVENISTI: We are not talking about the fact that there was a British Commissioner who gave money or soldiers or aid, like in Kenya. We are talking about a situation where a general atmosphere was created in which

Zionism could use the British influence - as the British used Zionism - in order to promote their own interests. I'll give you an example. The 19th century Kitchener drawing of the map of Palestine creates the imaginary perception of Palestine based on the Bible. Then Lloyd George uses George Adam Smith's book on Palestine in order to obtain the British Mandate for Palestine from the French so he can implement his own millennium. This is what we mean by British influence in making Zionism viable. Not the money or armaments they invested.

RAN AARONSOHN: Taking your example, each time anybody from the Christian world, from Europe to the States, uses the Bible for his own benefit or for his country's benefit to promote colonial interests, does that prove that the Jewish enterprise is a colonial project? And we should have evidence about the facts, not the general atmosphere. It was a time of colonialism which means it was colonialism.

MERON BENVENISTI: Why are you so defensive? I think it's very good that the Zionists expropriated the British Empire; and moreover, that the Jews could have exploited the British administration in Palestine in the 20th century. They had more access to it, and that is why, even if the British built a road, the Jews, as Europeans, benefited from it more than the Arabs did. That is a very important relationship that could be understood by the Palestinians, no matter what the High Commissioner said, as demonstrating that Zionism is an offspring of British colonialism. I understand their perception.

AVRAHAM SELA: According to your approach about the coalition of interests between the two sides, it's as if we're talking about a linear process of British and Zionists collaborating or cooperating and understanding each other.

MERON BENVENISTI: I said exploiting each other, and both were clever enough to exploit the other.

AVRAHAM SELA: They could be adversaries. They could be coalescing their interests. They could be on different parts of the spectrum. We are trying to avoid essentialism, and the danger in your point is that you actually suggest to us to think in an essentialist way. In other words, between British colonialism and Zionism there were some close points; hence, we can take it for granted. What we are suggesting is to take everything for its merits and not to talk in general about alliances.

MERON BENVENISTI: There is no hindsight? I think it is relevant.

RUTH KARK: I agree with Meron about the atmosphere regarding Palestine and Jews and Britain at that period, based on religious aspirations, and maybe even some politicians as well who had religious aspirations.

RAN AARONSOHN: Even through the eyes of those who say never mind the facts because there was a general atmosphere, I would expect them then to explain what was wrong with the British - who had interests - in the context of this so-called colonialism, trying to use Jewish identity or whatever at the time as a vehicle to promote their own colonial interests. So what? Does that automatically change the reality? This general perception that the Zionist project was part of a universal plot or colonialism leads nowhere.

ATA QAYMARI: This is a dangerous approach politically and academically, this denial process. You are saying, "We came here, we built settlements, we didn't dispossess anybody, we acquired the land in the free market, everything went according to the book".

RAN AARONSOHN: Until World War I. Don't forget that we are in a specific session.

ATA QAYMARI: Even so, we have to judge things also according to results.

RUTH KARK: In 1860, in order to develop the lands, the Ottomans invited settlers from Europe, gave them land in the Ottoman Empire, and freed them from paying tax on those lands. They invited people to settle.

ATA QAYMARI: Dalia also mentioned that the Jewish national movement was developing at the same time. We have several simultaneous processes, one of which is the development of the national Jewish movement - the successful Zionist movement. At the same time we have the British interest in cooperating with the Jews and then the Zionists. All these processes are part of a process of colonization - and colonialism at the same time - with the cooperation of the British, and resulting in the dispossession of the Palestinians.

You can't come to a land and say, "It's empty. We built colonies in neutral terms and bought the land in the free market and there were no tenants there. Only 200 without their families."

RAN AARONSOHN: All together, with their families. 200 persons.

ATA QAYMARI: Which accumulated into millions of dispossessed Palestinians.

ADEL MANNA: This is something different from history.

ATA QAYMARI: It is different. I'm now looking at the results.

ADEL MANNA: You can't mix this subject with that of the refugees. There's a limit to how much we can mix things together.

ATA QAYMARI: I accept your protest. I just wanted to stress that we don't have to rely on general atmosphere to see the results. When Balfour declared the right of the Jews to a homeland in Palestine, the Palestinian people were surprised. He was promising things that weren't his to promise.

AVRAHAM SELA: Can you say that what happened until 1914 inevitably, no matter what happened later, led to the dispossession of hundreds of thousands? This is the problem.

ATA QAYMARI: The results and the accumulation of this process would, in any case, lead to the dispossession of the Palestinians.

AVRAHAM SELA: So you do argue this, and this is quite basic. But historically speaking, you can't do it .

RUTH KARK: You must blame the Ottomans and the Arab landowners.

DALIA OFER: We don't have to blame.

AVRAHAM SELA: It's not a question of blame. It's a problem of causality. You can't explain the later process of the Mandate - and definitely not of 1947-1948 - by what happened in or until 1914. There is no connection. You can say the phenomenon is similar.

ATA QAYMARI: These are the beginnings.

MERON BENVENISTI: It's a problem for us because we are always deciding to start a new page.

AVRAHAM SELA: Historically, every moment is a new page.

MERON BENVENISTI: They try to say 1948 is 1936. We say no, we started in 1947.

RAN AARONSOHN: You can't rewrite the first page according to the last page. That's what you're doing.

MERON BENVENISTI: That's precisely what they are doing. That's why we're here. You can't attack his causality. Why is your causality right and his not? You also have a causality. Your causality is break and bond. You decide where it breaks and where it bonds. He has something different.

AVRAHAM SELA: There are ground rules we have to follow, and they are that we are dealing here with some kind of cause and historical process. You can't say that every statement is possible.

MERON BENVENISTI: That's not what I am saying. I am saying that the problem is that there is no single perspective. What for us is cause is for them effect, and vice versa. You cannot say that his perception of causality and where things started and ended is logically and basically wrong, and that's what you're saying.

He's not wrong. That is his perception. He understands causality differently than you do.

RUTH KARK: If you use this line of thinking, we're going to go back to Abraham.

BURCKHARD BLANKE: This is a fundamental problem of historians. In every discussion we have this matter of layers where people speak not only about the narrative, but also about the task of historians.

ATA QAYMARI: What I am trying to say is that the denial of any dispossession, of any negative effects of that process at that time on the Palestinians, is not a good approach academically or politically, because denial works in both directions. The other narrative could also deny processes that happened on the other side. This does not contribute to mutual understanding. It does not help the relationship between the sides.

RUTH KARK: As long as we stick to the facts.

ADEL YAHYA: I am devastated by this notion among Israeli historians and scholars denying the important role of the British and its integral relations with the Zionist movement, the colonial power and the fact that Zionism emerged from this colonialism. To me, this seems politically and ideologically motivated. Indulging in this detailed discussion of whether the British were pro-Zionist or pro-Palestinian doesn't really make sense to me as somebody who is involved with the oral history of 1948, especially the perception of Palestinians that the British were as much at fault as the Jews and the Zionists in the dispossession and expulsion of hundreds of thousands of Palestinians.

ADEL MANNA: Is that the British Mandate period?

ADEL YAHYA: The Israeli historiography leads us into a lengthy debate about whether Zionism is a colonial phenomenon by which Palestinians were expelled from their country. This discussion tries to evade the historical responsibility of the Zionist movement, together with the process of colonialism, of the first sin of expelling hundreds of thousands of Palestinians. It's depressing because it doesn't seem that we are coming to terms with the facts whereby the Israelis would admit the historical wrong that was done.

RAN AARONSOHN: When?

ADEL YAHYA: It culminated later in 1947-1948, but it started right there. Zionism helped colonize the country through British interference, and this is something that Israeli historians are trying to deny. The result was the expulsion of three-quarters of a million Palestinians from their country. Israel doesn't want to admit that. They say they were not a colonial power. This thing happened for some magical reason that nobody can define, and Israelis are not willing to confess to this sin.

MOSHE MA'OZ: Was there a war or something in 1948?

RUTH KARK: And 1914?

ADEL YAHYA: That resulted in the expulsion of the people. What is disturbing in all this is that we started with this motivation of trying to evade responsibility. That is not promising. We will not reach any conclusion this way. Unless we admit that the Palestinians were subjected to an injustice in the first place, there is no way out of this cycle of violence we witness today and which will be with us for another hundred years.

AZIZ HAIDER: What I hear from Ran and Ata and others goes to the core of our discussion. We are not going to agree about historical events, about myths. We have two narratives. We have come here to listen to each other. We will never agree about these narratives. Ata has the right to say what he says and Ran has the right to say what he says, and we listen to each other.

PAUL SCHAM: This question of narrative is absolutely essential. It goes to the heart of what history is. Ata and Adel expressed it, and I don't see this as a point of fixing blame. We didn't come here for that.

ATA QAYMARI: I didn't mention blame.

PAUL SCHAM: I know. I am responding to the statement that Israelis are trying to evade responsibility. If this were a non-academic forum trying to fix blame for the refugee problem, the discussion would be different. This is not the point here. We are not trying to come to a single conclusion.

It's important, in understanding the role of the British and that of the Zionists, to look at what either side thought they were doing at the time. The British records show that they were following their own interests. It's not as though the British records say, "We think it's important to have a Zionist state in Palestine". In addition, the British record of support of Zionism is very mixed. Palestinian mythology is that the British were on the side of the Zionists. Jewish/Israeli mythology is that the British were helping the Arabs from 1945 or even earlier, and the Zionists were fighting against the British.

MERON BENVENISTI: I am very happy that we were able to exploit the British Empire. You want to blame us for that. I am very proud of it.

ADEL YAHYA: But your colleagues are not proud of it.

ADEL MANNA: I would like to make a sharp methodological comment about what's going on here. I am troubled by Ran's ultra-positivism as a historian. He stresses looking only at hard evidence. What is hard evidence? Do you think that the general atmosphere is not a good enough factor to influence things, even without documentation or hard evidence?

RAN AARONSOHN: Yes. By itself, it's nothing. It's not history.

ADEL MANNA: I don't think it's nothing. It's important. Too much positivism is a problem in many cases. For instance, this is one of the problems of Benny Morris's book. He speaks about the refugees and the expulsion of the Palestinians only when he has hard evidence, a report in a *Tzahal** or other Israeli archive. This is hard evidence for him. But if the whole village of Majdal Krum tells him that, in our village, the soldiers killed six or four or nine people and kicked us out, this is not hard evidence.

RAN AARONSOHN: That's not general atmosphere. And you are now speaking about a different time period.

ADEL MANNA: I know exactly what I am speaking about. The general atmosphere of that time. Try to listen to me. The general atmosphere at that time is that soldiers were allowed to kick the Palestinians out.

The other side of the coin is, while over-positivism is a problem, the post-modernist relativist attitude is not less problematic. I think we should differentiate between political discourse and academic arguments. We are mixing things together. I don't agree with Meron, for instance, when he tries to support the Palestinian side by saying that every narrative is his narrative. When we study a subject academically, or try to understand what happened in a specific period and in a specific place, we have to stick to the facts and try to study the issues as historians.

Concerning the issues of blame and denial, once again, there is a big difference between the denial of kicking the Palestinians out in 1948, for instance, and the denial of taking the land of the Palestinians before 1917. We don't have enough data to establish a case here different from Ran Aaronsohn's. I want to be as fair as possible. Ran has a case when he says that the Zionist movement before World War I was not colonial. It was a colonization movement, but it wasn't colonial, although you can raise the points that they had this and that support, ideological or whatever. But he has a case.

We also have a denial by the Palestinians of the Zionist movement as a national movement. We stick to the idea that it was colonial because we don't acknowledge the Zionist narrative that the Zionist movement was also a national one, one that had negative implications for us.

My point is that, while we ask the Israelis to acknowledge our narrative when we have a case, we also, from time to time, have to acknowledge the Jewish Zionist narrative when the facts support their case.

AVRAHAM SELA: We came here as historians who try to stick to some basic professional ground rules. A basic approach is to understand the difference between perceiving history as something that proceeds according to a specific principle or according to some perceived path, and one that is subjective to various changes, decisions and so on. It can be drawn very simplistically. If A is a certain year and B is five, ten or twenty years away, the best thing is to say that the shortest line is the correct line. But history doesn't work like that. There are endless points, regressions, progressions. Each point in history presents different options, possibilities, decision-making, decision-makers. You cannot start a process before 1914 and say anything about the connection between that, in terms of causality, and what happened in the 1930s or the 1940s. That will bring us to nothing but a dead end.

If we accept that history is full of junctions in which there are many possibilities, and the basic perception of the freedom of human beings in decision-making, then we have to accept the need to explain processes through causality. As historians, we cannot accept that everything is possible. It's contrary to the basic rules of the profession.

DALIA OFER: I agree very much with Adel Manna's comment. I would like to give an example that perhaps might be helpful to us. About a year or two ago, Goldhagen's book about "Hitler's Willing Executioners" came out on the market, was translated into many languages, and received a lot of press. The main thesis was that the Germans were anti-Semitic in their culture, their folklore, in all their thinking, starting from the time of Luther. This eventually resulted in the killing of the Jews by the police units. He examined this very thoroughly in World War II. So he went from Luther to 1941, after the invasion of the Soviet Union.

This deterministic approach to history is completely wrong. The fact that Luther said - and many historians quote it - that Jews must be expelled and killed does not mean, from that point until the execution of the Jews, things progressed in a linear manner. Along the way there was Jewish emancipation. There were relationships between Jews and non-Jews in Germany. Jews felt there was a full friendship between Jews and Germans. We have to deal with the killing of the Jews in the context of Nazism and World War II, in the context of development at that time. That doesn't mean that anti-Semitism does not play a role, but we cannot take this as a deterministic process. Similarly, we can't say that what happened in 1948 started with the idea of the Zionists who came to settle in Palestine because, at any point between 1882 or 1840 or whatever. Until 1948, the whole project could have been destroyed for a variety of reasons.

WALID SALEM: We have heard that there was colonization, not colonialism. We have heard something about the relationship between Jewish colonization and British colonialism. There are different ideas about that. We also heard information about 100 to 200 tenants, a small number, who were evacuated from their land. Different studies show that Jewish-Palestinian relations during that period were tolerant ones. Salim Tamari wrote about the good relationship between Jews and Palestinians in Jerusalem. This is something we know. We know Palestinians were working in the Zichron Ya'akov wineries. And there are other examples.

So these things co-existed. Tenants were evacuated, regardless of the number. There were tolerant relations among Jews and Palestinians at the same time that there were disputed relations with British colonialism, which we have different opinions about. All of these were present during this period. If Jewish existence in Palestine before 1914, whether colonization or colonialism, developed into some kind of colonialism after 1917, this is tomorrow's discussion.

RAN AARONSOHN: First, yes, the Jewish enterprise in the Palestinian territories after the 1967 war may be considered as a colonial phenomenon. Second, yes, the Jewish enterprise during the Mandate period was colonization under a colonial umbrella and, here and there, as a colonial vehicle. Third, no, this doesn't say anything about any other period. That shouldn't be done within any academic paradigm. That would be a deterministic and anachronistic and an ahistorical way of looking at things.

ADEL MANNA: Agreed.

RESPONSE BY ISSAM NASSAR:

I WOULD like to take this opportunity to answer some of the points that were raised in the discussion in my absence.

I found the hostility towards my use of the term "colonization" to describe the early Zionist Jewish settlement in Palestine quite puzzling. It seemed to me to represent more an exercise in historical teleology than anything else. I do agree that Zionism (not Israel and its occupation of the West Bank and Gaza, though) does not fulfill the exact meaning of colonialism as it relates to 19th and early 20th century European history. Yet we should not forget that Zionism was a settler movement—and an ideologically informed and motivated one, for that matter— whose goal was to settle European Jews in Palestine in new, exclusively Jewish communities apart from the communities that already existed there. The final aim of the movement was the establishment of an exclusively Jewish national entity through a gradual acquisition of the land regardless of the feelings, desires, interests or will of the indigenous population.

In this sense, at least in the eyes of those excluded by it, the Zionist movement was a settler colonial movement in the same sense as other similar movements in places like South Africa or North America in previous periods. Colonization of the land and ridding it of its native population, which was deemed less "civilized" and hence incapable of determining its own interests and destiny, certainly fits a central element of the colonialist imagination of the 20th century.

If my colleagues review some of the contemporaneous literature they will find that—unlike them—the Zionist movement did not shy away from using the term. Early Zionists had no problem whatsoever in referring to the "colonizing" of the land in their plans for, and settlement activity in, Palestine, without feeling the need to qualify the use of the term. Indeed, examples of the use of the term "colonization" in early Zionist literature and documents are abundant. It is enough to browse through the papers or the autobiography of Chaim Weizmann to find the concept used quite regularly. In his discussion of the Zionist Commission in the period after World War I, for instance, Weizmann described Arthur Ruppin as "our able colonization expert" ("Chaim Weizmann," 1949, 122 and 221). As is public knowledge, he also discussed the establishment of a Colonizing Department in Palestine headed by Ruppin himself.

But, again, my original presentation was hardly a discussion on Zionism itself. It dealt, rather, with the historical development of the way Palestinians articulated their own sense of identity. It is my hope that my contribution to the subject can enhance the debate in a way that undermines the need to control even the discourse of the other.

DEVELOPMENT OF THE PALESTINIAN NATIONAL MOVEMENT, 1919-1939

Manuel Hassassian

THE awakening of Arab consciousness in modern times and the consequent rise of Arab nationalism can be attributed, *inter alia*, to the activities of the Zionists and to the impact of the First World War. The Palestinians were part of the Arab World, sharing with it many internal developments as well as some of its external influences. Zionism was particularly influential in shaping their politics and in determining their political destiny.

Along its historic continuum, Palestine became the object of conflicting political claims and intense religious attachments. Over the centuries, Arabs and Jews have developed deep roots and emotional attachments to it. In time, the roots and the attachments became important in the development of two separate, but conflicting nationalisms. Arab nationalism and Zionism. Both nationalisms strove to ultimately gain control of Palestine.

Historically, the Palestinian question can be related to the problem of Western intervention-cultural penetration in the form of ideas of nationalism and political penetration in the form of colonial rule. However, while Jewish nationalism originated in the intellectual and emotional response to the pogroms of eastern Europe, the nationalism of the Arabs was a direct reaction to Ottoman (Turkish) oppression and European colonialism.

One should keep in mind that the two nationalisms appeared around the same time, towards the end of the 19th century, and reached the peak of their political strength later in the 20th century. In the meantime, they were tied to the outcome of political decisions made in Europe. Although their aspirations were to be realized in Palestine, far away from Europe, their fortunes and misfortunes depended heavily on the politics of Europe, particularly those of the big powers.

After World War I, political fragmentation became a very serious problem in the Arab World. In addition to the traditional socio-political divisions, which had characterized Arab society (i.e. varieties of localism, parochialism and clan loyalty), there were now new political entities created by the European powers. In time, these entities began to demand from the populace absolute loyalty as well as total obedience to their institutions and symbols of authority. The new colonial creations prompted the development of national liberation movements whose

92

object was the assertion of independence through the expulsion of the colonial powers and the establishment of Arab sovereignty over Arab Land.

In Palestine, the quest for independence and political freedom took a slightly different turn than it did in the neighboring Arab states. Palestinian Arabs had to deal with a second threat to their future independence and territorial sovereignty and this threat was embodied in the goals and aspirations of Jewish Zionism. Of course, the Zionist movement had obtained, in 1917, the Balfour Declaration from the British Government promising them the creation of "a Jewish national home in Palestine". It is impossible to understand the Palestinian national movement without the constant reminder that the movement was profoundly influenced, and, to a certain degree, shaped by its long and difficult struggle with the Zionists.

One would expect that the ferocity of the struggle between the Palestinian Arabs on the one hand and the Zionists and their British ally on the other would unite the Palestinian Arab movement and would consolidate its forces to make it a more formidable force. Unfortunately, the Palestinian Arabs could not escape their traditional rivalries. The Palestinian national movement fell victim to internal divisions and political fragmentations. At times, Arabs fought Arabs while their Zionist enemy confronted them with unusual stubbornness and determination to succeed in their ultimate goal of creating a Jewish state in Palestine.

The Palestinian Movement in its early stages of development
Initially, the British governed Palestine through a military administration known as Occupied Enemy Territory Administration. Beginning in 1917, this administration was headed by General (later Viscount) Allenby, assisted by his personal appointee General Clayton (later Sir Gilbert) as chief political officer, and Sir Ronald Storrs as Governor of Jerusalem.

During this period of military rule, 1917-1920, a number of political groups and associations appeared on the scene. They were the rudiments of the nascent movement which later became the official leadership of Arab Palestine. These clubs were offshoots of their Syrian prototype *Nadi Filastine* (The Palestine Club) which was organized in 1919 in Damascus to press upon the government of King Faisal the Palestine cause. The club was led by Shaykh Abd el-Qader Muzaffar and it included a number of young Palestinian activists like Hajj Amin Al Husseini, Izzat Darwazeh, Rushdi al Shawwa and Salim Abdul Rahman al-Haj Ibrahim, whose names later become well known among the leaders of Palestine.

Similar political groups were organized in the towns of Palestine but only three of them had any appreciable impact upon political events in Palestine: the Muslim-Christian Association, the Arab Club *(Al-Nadi al-Arabi)*, and the Literary Society *(Al-Muntada al-Arabi)*. The Muslim-Christian Association promoted the principle of political cooperation between the Muslims and Christians of Palestine for the purpose of forging unity and organizing a political front to deal with the Zionist enemy. Its membership came mainly from the ranks of the political elites of urban Palestine, who aspired to retain the political influence they had secured under the Ottoman Empire, which preceded the new British military administration. They also hoped the Arabs would obtain an appreciable measure

93

of justice under British commitments made to the Arabs in the well-known Hussein-McMahon correspondence of 1915. The two other political groups, the Arab Club and the Literary Society, were similar to the first in that their recruits were mainly from the ranks of urban elites. But they were different in many other respects. For one, they rejected the creation of a British mandate in Palestine and desired instead to become part of Faisal's Syrian Kingdom.

However, the more interesting aspect of the two organizations was that they represented the first political manifestation of the Husseini-Nashashibi rivalry which, later, would divide the Palestinian national movement. Until this time, the two great Jerusalem families competed by means of the traditional methods which owed very little to modern political organization. The Husseinis led the Arab Club and the Nashashibis led the Literary Society. According to Zionist sources, the two groups were in contact with the more radical secret organizations known as *al-Fidai* (Self-Sacrificer) and *al-Ikha'Wal'Afaf* (Brotherhood and Purity). These latter groups were involved in political agitation, mainly in the cities of Jaffa and Nablus, and they condoned the use of terrorism as a political weapon of the last resort, though no evidence has proved that they actually resorted to terrorism.

The initial period in the development of the Palestine Arab movement, from about 1919 until 1934, was marked by the convening of a number of congresses. These congresses, like the political clubs of Palestine, drew their inspiration from the General Syrian Congress of which they were initially a part. The Syrian Congress was organized in 1919 and became widely recognized as the nationalist leadership of geographic Syria, including what later became Palestine, Lebanon, Jordan and the present-day Syrian Republic. This was the congress that elected Emir Faisal, the actual leader of the 1916 Arab Revolt, as King of a united Syrian state.

An all-Palestine Congress was held in Jerusalem between 27 January and 10 February 1919 to formulate a common policy, called a "program", on Palestine to advise Faisal while attending the Paris Peace Conference. The Congress was presided over by 'Aref Pasha al-Dajani who was then the president of the Jerusalem branch of the Muslim-Christian Association mentioned earlier. Representatives of the Association also attended the General Syrian Congress in Damascus. The Jerusalem Congress resolved to reject political Zionism and to accept British assistance on the condition that such assistance would not impinge upon sovereignty in Palestine. Basically, the Congress wanted Palestine to be part of an independent Syrian state to be governed by Emir Faisal of the Hashemite family. It also preferred US political tutelage, should this be necessary, or British tutelage as a second choice, but under no circumstances would the Congress accept French political guardianship.

Late in 1919, the 'Higher Committee', *al-Lajneh al-Ulya*, was formed at a special congress in Haifa, following a similar meeting in Damascus. Soon, branches of this committee were organized in Jerusalem, Nablus and Haifa, and they were granted jurisdiction over other political groups such as the Arab Club, the Literary Society, the Muslim-Christian Association, the Self-Sacrificers and the Greek Orthodox Club. The President of the Higher Committee was Rashid al Haj Ibrahim of the Haifa Muslim-Christian Association.

Another Congress was held in Haifa on 14 December 1920, consisting mainly of the then existing political clubs and associations as well as the Palestinian members of the General Syrian Congress. It was at this Third Congress that the Arab Executive Committee was selected, with Mousa Kazim al Husseini as its head and 'Aref Pasha al-Dajani as his deputy. The membership of the Third Congress was exclusively Palestinian, an indication that Palestine had become a separate political entity with its specific political needs and requirements.

Collectively, the Executive Committee was to become the official leadership of Arab Palestine. It consisted of nine members, who were to carry on the work between the plenary meetings of the Congress, while a permanent Secretariat was organized in Jerusalem to take charge of day-to-day aspects of Palestinian politics. Basically, members of the Executive came from the landowning families of Palestine. The Third Congress passed resolutions demanding self-determination for the Arabs of Palestine and the establishment of an Arab government. Obviously, it was preoccupied solely with the problem of Palestine. Its connection with Syria was becoming more symbolic than real.

The same was true with the Fourth Arab Congress, which was held in May 1921 in Jerusalem. This Congress resolved to send a Palestinian delegation to London to make a plea for the Arab Palestinian cause. The delegation did go to London where it did no more than correspond with the Colonial Secretary, Winston Churchill. The gist of the delegation's position was not to cooperate with the British government in drafting a constitutional document for Palestine unless the policy of creating a Jewish national home in Palestine was altered. This was probably why a meeting with Churchill never took place. Now, the Palestinian nationalist movement was becoming more radicalized.

To understand Palestinian Arab politics one must be familiar with the social structure of Palestinian society, and the position of influence of the great families of Palestine during the British Mandate. One must keep in mind that the politics of Palestine was largely the politics of these families, who derived their influence mostly from their ownership of vast tracks of agricultural land.

The social division

The Arab Muslims of Palestine, who constituted the vast majority of the country's population, were divided into three distinct social groups: the Bedouin, the rural population (usually referred to as the *fellahin*), and the urban populace.

The Bedouin were concentrated mostly in the southern part of the country but were also present in appreciable numbers in the Jordan Valley. In 1922, according to the official census, there were about 60,000 Bedouin in Palestine, or about 10 percent of the total population. In general, the Bedouin stood outside the society as a whole, not fully integrated into the mainstream of political life. They usually resisted interference in their internal affairs, disliked centralized political authority, and strongly opposed any restrictions upon their freedom of movement. According to one source, the traditional leadership of Arab Palestine used the Bedouin to obstruct Jewish efforts to colonize the southern part of the country.

The fellahin were mostly poverty-stricken people, illiterate and village-oriented even when they lived in urban centers. At the end of 1946, less than two years before the establishment of the state of Israel, they numbered 747,970, or 65.44 percent of the total Arab population. They lived in about 865 villages scattered throughout the country. According to the 1922 official census of Palestine, they had numbered 430,000. Probably, one percent of them were wealthy landlords, half of them were middle and small land owners and the rest, about 200,000 people, were wage earners. In the rural areas, the traditional rivalries involved the extended families, known as *hamulas*, and the clans. One aspect of the rivalry was historical, involving the Qaysis and the Yamanis. According to Raphael Patai, the rivalry originated in the tribal feuds of North and South Arabia which spread into the whole of Arabia as well as the Fertile Crescent. In the 1920s and 1930s, the rivalry affected the Palestinians but Western sources exaggerated its strength and political implications. The urban population numbered much less than the rural, but it was politically much the more active, playing a significant role in the national movement of Palestine.

At the bottom of the social ladder of the urban society of Palestine, there was the proletariat class, which usually contained two substrata. The first included the multitude of the unemployed and servants doing menial work at the homes of the well-to-do and in the streets as venders, porters and helpers. The second included the impoverished unskilled workers, boatmen and artisans. They usually lived in the old part of the cities and were mostly illiterate. Politically, they provided the human element needed for agitation, demonstrations, protesting crowds, and mobs, as well as spontaneous riots and violent action.

Moving up the social ladder there was the middle-class which consisted of minor government officials, teachers, shopkeepers, wholesale merchants and the more affluent artisans. Most of this small middle-class came into being during the Mandate period when the British began to introduce European economic activities and new modes of production. A large proportion of this class consisted of Christian Arabs and other minorities, many of whom were educated in missionary schools.

The urban upper-class was the center of political power and both the national and local leadership came from its ranks. Although members of this class lived in the city, many of them owned land in the villages as absentee landlords. Some members of this class were high officials in the religious hierarchy who derived a great deal of influence from their role as patrons of the major religious festivals, of which the *Nebi Musa* (the prophet Moses) was the most important. Members of the urban upper-class, usually known to Westerners as the *effendi* class, were usually literate and well-educated in the "outward forms of European culture". The social cohesion which characterized this class was somewhat impaired by the political rivalries which involved the major families of Palestine, whose power and influence during the 1920s and 1930s should not be underestimated. In Jerusalem, the capital of Palestine, the rivalry between the Husseinis and the Nashashibis was typical. The power and influence of these two families predated the British Mandate, back to the period when the Ottoman state helped them extend their influence over the peasant class and the rural areas.

The divisions and rivalries which characterized relations among the great families of Palestine were in part a by-product of a rigid social structure. According to J. C. Hurewitz, "the Muslim community was atomized by clannish separatism". The clan was the basic unit of social class. Headed by a *shaykh*, the clan in the small village aligned itself with a particular clan in the larger village and also with a clan in the town or city where the powerful landowning families always resided as absentee landlords.

As noted above, rivalries among the big families went back to the Qaysi and Yamani rivalries of pre-Islamic time. The latter divisions had a geographic dimension involving north Arabia, where the Qaysi's power rested, and south Arabia where the Yamani's influence extended. Yet Palestinian factionalism carried with it no ideological connotations, for the simple reason that big families competed for the control of existing resources and did not aim at changing the social structure. In Jerusalem, as elsewhere in Palestine, ideology and politics rarely went together. In fact, the Palestinian national movement never manifested genuine ideological inclination. At any rate, prior to 1948, family feuds and factional politics were responsible for the failure of Palestinians to successfully challenge the Zionist movement in its attempt to create a Jewish state.

Factionalism in the PNM (Palestinian National Movement)

From the first year of the British Mandate in Palestine, the traditional leadership of the Arabs was spilt between the Husseinis and the Nashashibis. The divisive nature of Arab leadership had its effect on the whole of the Arab national movement. In essence, that movement was never united or strong enough to confront its British and Zionist adversaries. As mentioned earlier, part of this problem was the outcome of the existing social structure which was unproductive as well as rigid.

Nevertheless, Western influence in the form of secularism and modern development did have some effect on the demography of Palestine many years before the British created it as a separate political entity. A new urban elite had come into being towards the end of the 19th century. During the Mandate, this elite became politically influential, causing the traditional elites in the villages to feel resentful and insecure. Not until the 1930s was the urban elite able to dominate the politics of both the rural and urban populations and become in effect the national leadership of Arab Palestine.

The British, who naturally wanted to control the country, exploited almost every aspect of the demographic and social cleavages existing in Palestine. They encouraged the establishment of "peasant" type of political parties, hoping such political organizations would prevent the union of the rural and urban elites into what might become a viable and genuine national movement.

However, the rivalries between the Husseinis and the Nashashibis remained the British best hope for a weak and ineffective national movement. Herbert Samuel distinguished three basic movements in Palestine, namely, Arab nationalism, Islamic unity, and anti-Zionism. He understood that these three movements were interrelated and that the Husseinis were trying to combine them into one single movement which would become powerful and thus difficult for the British to control. Consequently, he resorted to a policy of "divide and rule." This was the policy of balancing family interests which attempted to distribute offices between the Husseinis and the Nashashibis. As we have seen earlier, Hajj Amin was chosen as Mufti after Ragheb al-Nashashibi was appointed Mayor of Jerusalem.

The British policy succeeded, and the rivalry between the two families became more adversarial during the first decade of the British Mandate. These families manipulated all ties of kin, class and patronage to win over new supporters. As mentioned earlier, family feuds were behind the formation of some of the early political parties. It was the Nashashibis who, in 1923, encouraged the creation of the National Party, headed by Shaykh Suleiman Taji al-Farouqi of the city of Ramleh and the owner of the newspaper *al-Jami'a al-Islamiyyah*_(Pan-Islam). Even earlier, in 1921, the opposition led by the Nashashibis established the National Muslim Association with branch offices in a number of Palestinian towns. According to one source, Samuel was encouraged by the Zionists to support opposition of the Husseinis in an effort to divide the Arab national movement.

During the British Mandate, Arab opposition to Zionist aspirations was never a transient phenomenon. In fact, it grew in strength with the development of Arab nationalism. Naturally, the desire for self-determination and independence also increased among the Arabs of Palestine. Ironically, after ten years of Mandate rule, the national aspirations of Arabs and Jews became so crystallized as opposite forces that the success of one meant the inevitable failure of the other.

The Palestine national movement, in all of its critical stages, failed to achieve diplomatic success in redressing its grievances. Consequently, extreme alienation made it resort to violence as the only means by which it could express its frustration and anger. Undoubtedly, violence also related to the social and economic dilemma within the Palestinian Arab Society. These social imbalances contributed to the ultimate failure of the national movement.

The outbreaks of violence in 1920, 1929, 1933 and 1936 illustrate Arab frustrations in achieving their goal of independence. Although each outbreak differed in intensity and duration, the constant factor remained the Arab sense of political deprivation, which resulted from the growing fear of Zionist domination and the awareness that Zionist ambitions and activities were the only obstacles to the achievement of Arab independence. It was natural then that Arab nationalism in Palestine would become fiercely anti-Zionist and anti-British in forms as well as in substance.

The desire to dominate the political scene as manifested in the struggle between the Husseinis and the Nashashibis was marked by the former's manipulation of the religious sentiments of the people. At the end of the 1920s, Hajj Amin's position became precarious due to the successful challenge put up by the opposition in both the municipal election of 1927 and in the Arab Executive elections of 1928. However, the conflict between Muslims and Jews over the Wailing (Western) Wall in 1928-29 presented a golden opportunity for Hajj Amin to regain political influence for himself and the SMC which he headed and directed. At the time, Muslims and Christians were bound together in the struggle against Zionism.   Indeed the issue of the Wailing Wall had mobilized all Palestinians including the *Mu'arada*, who were the Nashashibi-supported opponents of Hajj Amin.

The Wailing Wall, which had religious significance to Jews, was adjacent to a Muslim holy place and the dispute involved the extent of rights and practices of the two religious groups.   It is important to note that the Mu'arada in the beginning did not actively participate in the protest and demonstration preceding the riots and the violence associated with the 1929 Wailing Wall controversy. But when the violence became widespread the Mu'arada's attitude changed significantly. The Wailing Wall incident became a national issue around which Muslims of all walks of life rallied. The Mu'arada feared the issue was enhancing the Mufti's prestige and influence and did not want the trend to continue. Its attitude was best reflected in its newspapers *Mirat al-sharq, Sirat al-Mustaqim* and *Filastine*, whose editorials supported the struggle for the defense of Muslim rights in the Buraq al-Sharif, the Muslim religious shrine adjacent to the Wailing Wall.

The failure of the partition concept induced the British to take severe measures against Arab intransigence. The assassination in October 1937 of Lewis Andrews, the Acting District Commissioner of Galilee, convinced them that the Arab Revolt was becoming more daring in its violent attacks and more determined in its political demands. Consequently, it outlawed the AHC as well as all existing national committees throughout Palestine. As for Hajj Amin, who by now had become the sole and most popular leader of Palestine, the British decided to oust him as SMC president and head of the Waqf committee. The oppression extended to every level of the political leadership. Hundreds of political activists were arrested, and the five most important members of the AHC were deported to the Seychelles in the Indian Ocean. Realizing what was happening, Hajj Amin took refuge in the Haram al Sharif. A few days later, during October 1937, he escaped and left the country on a small boat to Lebanon where he stayed for some time while his revolution was being mercilessly quelled by the British.

The revolution failed. According to W.F. Abboushh, "With the national leadership imprisoned or out of the country, the revolution became politically uncoordinated. It was clear that the British desired an end to it without making concessions to Arab demands. There was no alternative for the guerrillas but to aimlessly continue the fight. The failure of the political leadership and the reluctance of the British to make concessions made the national aims unattainable. From then on, the rebellion gradually turned inward. Arabs began shooting Arabs."

When the revolution "turned inward", the pro-Husseinis went after the pro-Nashashibis and killed a number of them. Perhaps in self-defense, the latter became active in opposing the rebels. They organized a strong force to retaliate openly. Beginning with in autumn 1938, the pro-Nashashibis were able to tip the scale in their own favor.

The British had, since autumn 1938, been quite successful in dealing with the rebels. There was no doubt that the rebellion was losing team and coming to an end. Because of the numerous incidents of assassination people desired an end to violence. By 1939, the rebellion was no longer active, except for few sporadic incidents. However, there were a number of incidents of retaliation by Palestinians against those who had been less than completely supportive of the rebellion.

Ironically, in 1939 the British government changed its pro-Zionist policy and became clearly pro-Arab. Thus, it seemed as if the Arab rebellion, which the British had successfully crushed, did win. However, the reason for the change in British policy had nothing to do with the rebellion but, rather with the international situation and the coming of World War II. The British government, facing the likelihood of a wider war with Hitler's Germany, decided it could not afford to alienate the Arabs. Consequently, it issued the White Paper of 1939 to conciliate them. This paper severely limited Jewish immigration, restricted Jewish purchase of land and held out hope for an independent Palestine in which the Arabs would have a majority. The most striking feature of the White Paper policy was its clear pronouncement that the British government never promised the Jews a state in Palestine.

Ironically, the AHC rejected the paper because it did not meet Arab demands for immediate and full independence. Obviously, they had lost confidence in the British, believing that they had made too many promises in the past and did not live up them. For obvious reasons of their own, the Zionists also rejected the White Paper and vowed to get it reversed as soon as the war was over.

After 1939 the world was busy with the war. Most of the Zionist leadership kept quiet, believing correctly that Hitler was more threatening than the White Paper. They would later stage their own rebellion and succeed in getting the British out of Palestine, something the Arabs could not do when they had their rebellion.

As for the Arab national movement, 1939 was its last year. Its leadership was no longer in the country. The people were tired of fighting, and were now quiet and resigned to accepting their fate. As for the Mu'arada, it was optimistic that the future would give it a bigger role, a more dominant one. Unfortunately, it did not realize that the future did not belong to it, for the Arabs would in less than ten years lose Palestine. A Jewish state would in 1948 be established in most of the country and the rest would go under Jordanian and Egyptian rule. Worse yet, down the line the future was even gloomier. The whole of Palestine would go under Jewish rule in 1967 and there would be no assurances that stability in the region or peace might one day prevail.

ZIONIST DIPLOMACY, 1914-1939

Norman Rose

FROM a Zionist perspective, perhaps from any perspective, the Zionism experiment - for such it was in its early period - must be regarded as a huge success story. Fifty years after the first Zionist Congress convened, the United Nations granted international legitimacy to Israel, with an independent Jewish state to be established in a partitioned Palestine. From little more than a hyper-active pressure group that had constituted a tiny minority in the Jewish world, the Zionist movement became a factor of international consequence. Its most cherished aim had been fulfilled, some would say against all the odds. How did this come about?

Allow me to suggest three main motifs to this story: an ability to exploit changing international circumstances to its advantage; securing a responsible, moderate balance of forces within the Zionist movement; and the quality (or otherwise) of the Zionist leadership. And all this against the background of the first half of the 20th century. Among the most dramatic periods in contemporary history, it saw two world wars and startling changes in the international system, namely, a shift from a multi- to a bi-polar system that also witnessed a new balance of power.

Another factor intruded, independent of Zionist influence but which worked to its benefit. National self-determination, enshrined in President's Wilson "Fourteen Points", became a guiding principle to be honored by the international community.

World War I was the turning point. Until then, Herzl and his immediate successors had placed the Zionist case before the Great Powers, but with few concrete results. It was not for nothing that the immediate pre-war period was categorized as the "Zionist Doldrums." With the outbreak of war a great dilemma confronted the Zionist movement. Should it support the Allied or the Central Powers, or should it adopt a policy of neutrality? All options were risky, threatening to deprive Zionism of the fruits of victory by whatever side. By moving its headquarters to Copenhagen, the movement plumped for what seemed to be the safest course, neutrality.

World War I was a turning point for Zionism for another reason. It saw the emergence of a new leader, Chaim Weizmann. From the outset, Weizmann placed his faith in a British-Allied victory. There was no rational justification for this, for Allied victory was not assured until the late spring of 1918. How then to explain Weizmann's stand? Weizmann himself would put it down to *Fingerspitzengefühl* (literally: finger-tip feeling, or instinct; intuition, or flair). It amounted to a finely honed sense of timing, to know when to bang on the table and when to compromise, to grasp the right moment to advance or to retreat. This faculty - a prerequisite for a successful leader - would characterize Weizmann's (and Zionist) diplomacy throughout this period.

The period under consideration coincided with Weizmann's dominance of the Zionist movement. Indeed, such was his pervading influence that he has been justly nicknamed the "Benevolent Despot". This was particularly true in the field of diplomacy, where Weizmann's touch, and connections, were judged as being the key element in Zionist diplomacy. This was decisive, for it was axiomatic, at least for Weizmann and his followers, that ultimately Zionism could attain its aims only through cooperation with the Great Powers.

It is true that by the mid-late 1930s Weizmann's position was being challenged by Ben Gurion. But despite differences in temperament, and occasional clashes over policy, more of emphasis than of substance, they managed on the whole to work harmoniously together, ultimately to the benefit of Zionist policy.

In these circumstances it is worth asking what moved Weizmann? What principles, if any, did he adhere to? Did he cling to a guiding political philosophy?

Perhaps the following might serve as some general guidelines to Weizmann's approach. First, his concept of "Synthetic Zionism." Weizmann had criticized Herzl for his strictly "political" approach. By contrast, Weizmann maintained that "political" and "practical" Zionism must go hand in hand. He said: "I consider practical activity to be the means of attaining the political aim - the Charter!" In effect, this was to recognize the external constraints imposed upon the movement; of adapting its limitations to international reality. For Zionism was still a minority movement of little consequence to the international community. It could not face the Great Powers with *faits accomplis*: it could not, for example, demand or declare a Jewish state. It had to prove, by mass immigration, by building and strengthening the Yishuv, by constructing the infrastructure of a national existence in Palestine, that Zionism was worthy of international support. This could not be achieved overnight. It would be a long, drawn-out process. Above all, everything would depend on how the Jewish people would respond to the challenge. The first signs were not auspicious. And this basic situation would not materially change until the advent of Hitler turned the Jewish world topsy-turvy.

Secondly, there was Weizmann's well-publicized pragmatism. Was this a natural trait? Or was it imbibed from the British (Weizmann emigrated to England in 1904 and later assumed British citizenship)? We'll never know. But it was there! He made the apophthegm, "politics is the art of the possible" his own. When facing internal opposition, he often said: "The Jewish people, for all its genius, is apolitical: far too intolerant, far too uncompromising, too given to ideological nit-picking". Like the British Foreign Office, Weizmann held that you could not conduct diplomacy by a series of "No's!" or categorical demands. He would certainly have adhered to Lloyd George's quip: "I am a man of principle and expediency is one of them".

102

Then we must consider his charisma, his much-commented upon charm. He possessed in abundant measure what the French call *présence*. But more than anything, he commanded a unique ability to kindle the imagination of those with whom he came into contact, to impart to them his faith in the destiny of the Jewish people and the significance of its survival. Opponents no less than supporters bore witness to these aspects of his personality: Balfour, Lloyd George, Winston Churchill, Georges Clemenceau, Ronald Storrs, Jan Smuts, T. E. Lawrence, Franklin D. Roosevelt, Harry Truman. Anthony Eden, no friend of the Zionists, tended to avoid meeting Weizmann, remarking "that he would see ministers and turn them inside out".

It is generally acknowledged that the Balfour Declaration of November 1917 was the first step on the road to Jewish statehood. Although Weizmann was the key figure on the Zionist side in procuring the Declaration, he did not act in a vacuum. Gradually, there evolved a merging of British and Zionist interests, best personified by Lloyd George's resolve to "grab" Palestine for imperial, and other, reasons. The Declaration was not entirely to the Zionists' liking. It had gone through five drafts. It spoke not of Palestine "reconstituted as the National Home", but of "the establishment in Palestine of..." (Was this the first hint of partition?) Nor was there a definite British pledge to administer Palestine, a condition Weizmann considered a *sine qua non* for the fruitful development of the National Home. Moreover, this opened the door for an international regime to administer Palestine - a prospect anathema to the Zionists. Of course, the Balfour Declaration does not state this explicitly; but neither does it contradict it. (Note that most British wartime documents, from the de Bunsen Committee Report to the Sykes-Picot agreement, speak of an international regime for Palestine.) And what precisely was a National Home? - a novel, untested concept in international relations. Clearly, the Zionists had wanted a more clear-cut commitment. As Weizmann put it, "I did not like the boy [the Declaration] at first. He was not the one I had expected."

Despite these caveats, the Zionists acknowledged the Declaration as a document of extraordinary historical moment. For the first time, a Great Power had recognized the legitimacy of the Jewish people's right to a National Home. It didn't reward the Zionists with all they wanted, but as Weizmann was wont to say time and again, "It is better to take 50 percent of something than 100 percent of nothing."

What did the British mean by the National Home? Later, a frustrated Weizmann asked British leaders whether they thought the Declaration meant "an ultimate Jewish majority". Yes, chorused Lloyd George and Balfour, we always understood it to mean "an eventual Jewish State". These thoughts were not for publication, but they slotted neatly into Weizmann's overall strategy. When pressed why he didn't demand a Jewish state, Weizmann patiently explained: "We didn't demand one because they wouldn't have given us one. We asked only for the conditions which would allow us to create a Jewish state in the future. It is simply a matter of tactics."

Meanwhile, the British had to square the Declaration with other promises and agreements they had made during the war, in particular, but not only, the

Hussein-MacMahon correspondence of 1915-16. Encouraged by the British, Weizmann came to an arrangement with Emir Feisal, widely considered to be the effective leader of the Arab nationalist movement. They met first near Aqaba in June 1918, confirming their compact later in London and Paris. It called for the "closest possible collaboration" between Arabs and Jews in the development of "the Arab State and Palestine"; it agreed that there would be "definite boundaries between the Arab State and Palestine"; it envisaged the implementation of the Balfour Declaration and "large-scale" Jewish immigration while protecting the rights of the Arab peasants and tenant farmers; it also provided for Jewish economic assistance to the Arabs, and a united Arab-Jewish front at the forthcoming Paris peace conference. It made no mention of a Jewish state. Feisal added one proviso: "If the Arabs are established as I have asked ... I will carry out this agreement. If changes are made, I cannot be answerable for failing to carry out this agreement." These sentiments were confirmed in a letter, dated 1 March, from Feisal to Felix Frankfurter. Weizmann waxed enthusiastic about Feisal's qualities. "He is the first real Arab nationalist I have met. He is a leader," he confided to his wife.

Although Weizmann's estimation was highly colored, it is clear that a basis, however shaky, existed for a Jewish-Arab accord. But whether Feisal was powerful enough to deliver the goods, or whether the French and British would allow him to do so, was an entirely different matter. These were matters over which the Zionists had no control. In the event, the Feisal-Weizmann crumbled before the greater interests of Britain and France: the need to preserve their alliance, for European as well as imperial reasons. In March 1920, at San Remo, the mandates for the Lebanon and Syria were awarded to France, those for Palestine and Iraq to Britain. France was given the green light. By June, Feisal had been ousted from Damascus and his newly-born Kingdom of Syria destroyed. France had imposed its own rule on Syria. The cohesiveness of Arab nationalism, never robust, had been shattered.

These events also cast their shadow on Palestine. Anti-Zionist riots (by definition also directed against the British) had broken out in March-April 1920. They were but the prelude to decades of mounting inter-communal violence. Palestinian Arab nationalism, hostile to Zionism from the outset, took a more belligerent course, its batteries recharged from Feisal's tragedy. In this manner, both nationalist movements fell victim to the global interests of the two imperial powers who now ruled the Middle East.

In the summer of 1922 the League of Nations ratified the British mandate for Palestine - and a year later the United States followed suit. In some ways, this was no less an achievement for the Zionists than the Balfour Declaration. The document that incorporates the text of the ratification reads as a Zionist paper. It was preceded by a period of intense lobbying, both by the Palestinian Arabs, who were attempting to abrogate the Declaration and nullify the mandate, and the Zionists, who were striving to fine-tune it. Both parties drew heavily on their friends in British political life. But the net result can only be viewed as another step forward for the Zionists. Official government publications, notably the so-called "Churchill White Paper", confirmed that the Balfour Declaration "is not susceptible to change", although it redefined the Declaration in less enthusiastic terms than the original. There was one significant setback: it effectively limited the Jewish National Home to the area west of the Jordan.

These shifts in British policy were a far cry from the Zionists' original hopes. Grudgingly, out of a sense of *force majeure*, the Zionist Executive acquiesced in them. But they also clung to the flexible phrasing of Churchill's paper, confident that it did not contradict Weizmann's formula of securing "the conditions which would allow us to create a Jewish state in the future". There was another substantial bonus for the Zionists, particularly for Weizmann. Britain, tolerant and democratic, noted for its (relatively) liberal imperial philosophy, and endowed with a rich tradition of Gentile Zionism, was now recognized as the mandatory power. This had always been Weizmann's aim.

Thus was inaugurated the official Anglo-Zionist period in Zionist diplomacy. It began with high hopes, but ended in deep crisis. Despite appearances to the contrary, it was a stormy relationship from the outset. One cynic noted that the process of whittling down the Balfour Declaration began on 3 November 1917, the day after it was approved. Weizmann, in his darker moments, would have heartily concurred.

In some ways the 1920s were, as the saying goes, both "the best of times and the worst of times". The best of times because those years witnessed the arrival of a further 61,000 Jewish immigrants, in particular the so-called Third *Aliyah* of immigration, a group of dedicated, ideologically committed (mainly Labour) Zionists. The foundations of a genuine National Home were laid: in agriculture, in light industry, in urban growth, in the founding of health and educational systems. The *Histadrut* (the General Confederation of Jewish Labor) was formed, a mammoth organization that was a key instrument in the economic, social and political development of the *Yishuv*, and that by the end of the decade encompassed about three-fourths of the Jewish working population of Palestine. Here was the embryo of a pioneering Jewish working-class. Then there was the Jewish Agency, with its myriad departments that mirrored faithfully the departments of any legitimate government. Small wonder that the British would wryly refer to it as "a state within a state."

With hindsight - when viewed from a historical perspective - it is possible to assess these achievements as significant breakthroughs. Yet, for the contemporary observer, it was also the worst of times. The rate of Jewish immigration had not lived up to expectations. In one year alone, 1927, more Jews left Palestine than came in. These were shocking figures that heralded a bleak future. To compound matters, the Zionist movement verged on bankruptcy. Zionist leaders spent much of their time on fundraising excursions. It was not for nothing that Weizmann dubbed himself "the greatest tax collector in the history of the Jewish people." The ramifications of these trends, unless checked, threatened the very existence of the National Home.

One factor that gave the Zionists some room for hope was the relatively tranquil state of Jewish-Arab relations. Since the flare-ups of 1920-21, things had considerably quieted down. Both sides had maintained contact, although there was still no meeting of the minds. In August 1929 all this changed - for the worse.

Ugly communal riots broke out. In all, 472 Jews and 268 Arabs were either killed or wounded. Not only Zionist settlements were attacked, but also the ultra-Orthodox, non-Zionist communities in Hebron and Safed. For many Zionists this confirmed their view of the Palestinian national movement as militant, intransigent and violent. There was some truth in this, for it had fallen under the sway of Hajj Amin Al Husseini, the Mufti of Jerusalem, who would brook no compromise, neither with the Zionists nor with those Palestinians who opposed him. The concept of a bi-national state (or even of some form of cooperation as envisaged in the Feisal-Weizmann agreement), not explicitly ruled out by either the Balfour Declaration or the terms of the mandate, had effectively been shunted aside, and was now promoted only by fringe groups.

In the wake of this unprecedented cycle of bloodshed, the government set in motion a series of inquiries, none of which were favorable to the Zionists, culminating in the Passfield White Paper of 1931. This document undermined the Zionists' interpretation of the National Home. It was considered so damaging that they cut off all official contact with the government. Anglo-Zionist relations had plummeted to their nadir. But by an inspired bout of lobbying, the Zionists, led by Weizmann, launched a successful counter-attack. Eventually, the MacDonald Letter emerged. Whatever its faults - for it was bitterly criticized in some Zionist circles - it allowed the Zionists, once again, to realize Weizmann's formula of creating the conditions necessary for a eventual Jewish state. The Letter proved to be the legal basis for the administration of Palestine until the White Paper of May 1939.

One result of Hitler's rise to power in January 1933 was to see the spread of anti-Semitism, not only in Germany, but throughout central and eastern Europe. As a consequence, Jewish immigration to Palestine rose to unprecedented heights. In the course of three years, 1933-35, almost 150,000 Jews officially entered the country. If this trend continued unchecked it would have substantially altered the demographic character of Palestine, to the Jews' advantage. In November 1935, the Arab Higher Committee, headed by Hajj Amin, responded with a series of radical demands: the prohibition of Jewish immigration, the cessation of land transfers to Jews, and the establishment of a national government responsible to a representative council. The British turned down this appeal. The following April the Committee called for an Arab general strike that imperceptibly evolved into an armed struggle against the British administration and the Yishuv. The ensuing Arab revolt lasted intermittently until the outbreak of World War Il.

These were the immediate circumstances that led to the appointment of the Peel Commission in 1936. It was authorized "to investigate the underlying causes of the disturbances" and "to inquire into the manner in which the mandate for Palestine is being implemented". In July 1937 it reported that the mandate was "unworkable" and recommended the partition of Palestine into Jewish and Arab states, leaving some areas of strategic importance under British control. In this way began the great debate on partition - one that has yet to be settled.

Initially, the Zionist attitude was unclear. When Weizmann was asked what he thought about the Peel boundaries for the Jewish state, he replied: "standing room only." Yet his political sixth sense told him that here was a genuine turning point, a unique historical moment that had to be seized less it be lost forever. As he was wont to say, *"C'est le premier pas qui compte!"* (It is the first step that counts). His frame of mind was compounded by the rapidly deteriorating condition of European Jewry. Weizmann, together with Ben Gurion, fought strongly for partition. This was an uphill battle, for opposition to the idea was widespread in the Movement. Nevertheless, at the Zionist Congress in August 1937 they succeeded in passing a resolution that endorsed the principle of partition, while at the same time empowering the Zionist Executive to continue to negotiate its details. This was a triumph for *realpolitik* over ideology.

It was short-lived, however. Opposition to the scheme was rife. The Arab world fiercely resisted it, as did the Palestinian Arabs. Weizmann's friends in Britain, his Gentile Zionists, also challenged the idea, on imperial grounds. But more significantly the Foreign Office and the Chiefs of Staff damned the concept, arguing that partition could only be implemented by the use of force. Given the current international climate, with the European powers moving towards outright confrontation, this was not a viable option.

So partition was put into cold storage. What remained? There were always Peel's so-called "palliatives". In the event of partition proving impractical, Peel had suggested a number of proposals that it was hoped would calm down the situation. These included drastic restrictions in immigration and land purchases, the two most sensitive issues for the Zionists. At a series of meetings with the Zionists in September 1938, as the Czech crisis was unfolding, the government made crystal-clear its intention. The link between these events is obvious. "Baffy" Dugdale, one of Weizmann's closest advisers, remarked: "They are going to sell the Jews also - give up partition, for fear of Arabs, the Germans, the Italians."

Lord Halifax, the British Foreign Secretary, bluntly defined the government's policy as ensuring that "the Arab states would be friendly towards us". The deteriorating international situation demanded it. He told the Zionists they must "reconcile administrative necessity and fundamental and eternal spiritual claims and rights."

Lord Halifax's "administrative necessity", together with Peel's "palliatives", eventually metamorphosed into the May White Paper of 1939. Despite intense Zionist canvassing, both in Britain and the United States, the paper was published and became official British policy. It called for a level of immigration of 75,000 over the coming five years - further immigration being dependent on Arab consent. There were also to be draconian limitations on land sales, and the promise of a Palestinian state in ten years' time was held out. The paper was rejected vehemently by both the Palestinians and the Zionists - which did not deter the government from implementing it. The Zionists, however, achieved one minor success: the May White Paper was savaged in parliament - partly as a result of Zionist lobbying. In the Commons, the government – which normally commanded a majority of 290 - squeezed through by just 89 votes. This was generally interpreted as a vote of no-confidence. (It is worth recalling that just a year later, in May 1940, in the debate over the Norwegian campaign, the government scraped through with a majority of 81, a "victory" that forced Neville Chamberlain's resignation and elevated Churchill to the Premiership.)

With war only weeks away there was little room for maneuver for the Zionists. They had no trump cards to play. In official circles, the feeling was prevalent that in the coming struggle against Nazi Germany the Jews had no option but to support Britain. And they were right. Of course, there was no way the Zionists could become reconciled to the White Paper. The provisions that rankled most deeply were those concerning immigration. This was not just a question of crippling the National Home, however iniquitous and unacceptable this was in Zionist eyes. Of far greater import was the fate of European Jewry, the doomed six million, in Weizmann's words. As Ben Gurion said, "the Jews of Palestine were well able to look after themselves ... it was not the fate of the Yishuv but that of the Jews who were not yet in Palestine" that was at stake.

Was the May White Paper **the** "turning point" in Anglo-Zionist relations, as it has so often been described? Surely not. The Zionists were acutely conscious that, in the event of war, immigration would in any case be restricted; they were confident, rightly as it turned out, that they could evade the restrictions on land sales; while the prospect of a Palestinian state ten years in the future, and dependent for its establishment on Arab-Jewish cooperation, seemed a sufficiently remote possibility as to remove it from the realms of political reality. If it is necessary to talk in terms of "turning points", it would be far more profitable to see one in the Labor government's refusal to rescind the White Paper at the end of the war rather than in the actual formulation of that policy by Chamberlain's government on the eve of war.

For all that, could something be salvaged from this callous blow to Zionist aspirations? Weizmann's mind went back to World War I. Once again, he believed implicitly in an eventual British victory. Would he again be able to pull off a stunning coup, another Balfour-type declaration? Was this a desperate case of the wish being father to the thought? Perhaps - but that is another story.

DISCUSSION 3

Manuel Hassassian and Norman Rose

MANUEL HASSASSIAN: The Palestinian National Movement has been in existence for almost the last hundred years, and has acquired certain characteristics to the point that they have became a phenomenon. When we talk about the Palestinian National Movement in the early 1920s and 1930s, we talk about factional politics of the Palestinians. My thesis has always been that the internal struggle within the Palestinian National Movement was based on clan loyalty and on factional bickering. The turning point, the catalyst, was the rapid Zionist colonization of Palestine.

Before talking about the Palestinian National Movement in its earliest stages, I must shed some light on the genesis of Arab nationalism. We can't talk about Palestinian nationalism in isolation from the creation of a pan-Arab movement in the latter part of the 19th century, during the Ottoman domination.

Several factors led to the creation of consciousness among the Arabs. One was the cultural penetration of the West in terms of its ideology; second, the dissatisfaction of the Arab Muslims in the Ottoman Empire with being treated as second- or third-class citizens. We have an expert here on Ottoman history – Moshe Maoz - who can tell us that all Tanzimat and land reforms failed, which exacerbated the sense of alienation of these national minorities within the extended Ottoman Empire.

As a result, with the rise of awareness of modern nationalism in Europe, they could not sit idly by, but had to be affected by the basic geo-strategic interests of the Western colonial powers in the Middle East. That, in itself, played a dramatic role in raising consciousness in opposition to Ottomanism *per se*, although Ottomanism, at that time, supposedly epitomized what we call the Islamic empire. So the challenge came from the Arabs in terms of an ideology called Arab nationalism. Ironically, the avant-garde among the Arab nationalists were the Arab Christian intellectuals who lived in the Levantine area, the Fertile Crescent, who were greatly affected by Western ideas of nation and nation-states, which they rapidly transformed into a mobilizing force in raising consciousness among the Arabs.

The Arab Christian intellectuals played this role for many reasons. First, it was important for Arab Christians to cling to something called Arab nationalism because, by doing so, they removed the discrepancy between Muslim and Christian Arabs. The concept of nation and nation-state being removed from the concept of an Islamic state put them on an equal footing. Second, the Christian intellectuals, and the Arab Christian minority per se were, one way or another, tied to the West because of early emigration from Lebanon, basically from the Fertile Crescent, to the Americas. This played a significant role in keeping contact between the population living in the Fertile Crescent as well as in the Americas. Third, the Christian intellectuals were exposed to the Western value system, and also were more versed in European languages than were the Muslims. Therefore, with regard to the penetration of the Western cultural value system into the East, they played a key role as go-between, basically translating values from English or French or whatever into Arabic. In addition, the Christian communities in the Fertile Crescent were a thriving community. They were considered upper middle-class. They were entrepreneurs. They were involved in trades and what have you. This gave them an upper hand within the social strata of Arab society.

For all these reasons, the Christian Arab intellectuals were the spearhead of Arab nationalism, which put the Muslim Arabs at that time in a position in which they needed to identify with the changes that had been imposed upon them because of colonial rule. And because of their frustration with the Ottoman Empire for its lack of reforms and not giving the Arabs a certain independence, they started to reconsider Islam from a more modern perspective. In other words, they started looking at Islam through Western lenses, trying to justify democracy through *Shura**, trying to justify the concept of *'Umma** and connect it with that of the nation. That led to Muslim intellectuals identifying with Arab nationalism, but from an Islamic perspective, modifying and reinterpreting Islam within this new cultural penetration. This is called Islamic reformism. However, they never admit that corruption ever touched Islam per se. Corruption was found in those rulers who misused or abused Islam. Corruption never touched Islam. However, Islam is a way of life. It could be adjusted at any time. Time and space are immaterial because Islam has a complete value and material system which can accommodate, at all times, Arab Umma or Islamic Umma.

So Islamic reformism was put in a situation where it had to reconcile its difference with Arab nationalism, which epitomized secularism, and secularism - separation of church from state – which was a driving force in Europe. That put the Muslims, especially the Islamic reformists, in a critical position. Since Islam is a way of life, how can you separate church from state?

A reinterpretation of nationalism within the parameters of Islam gave it a new twist and a new dimension. However, the battle was lost by the Islamic reformists to the pan-Arabists at a later stage, after World War I. These two ideologies, that were the driving force for change in the Ottoman Empire, played a crucial role in changing political as well as ideological discourse in the Arab Middle East.

The Palestinian National Movement has always been an offshoot of Arab nationalism. So why did this specific Palestinian nationalist movement arise? The Palestinian Arabs were fighting British colonial rule in Mandatory Palestine, but they also faced an additional problem, and that was the colonial Zionist settler movement. Ironically, both ideologies, Arab nationalism and political Zionism, emerged as a result of and a culmination to objective factors in the West as well as in the Middle East. The emergence of Jewish nationalism concretized in a

110

program called political Zionism coincided with the emergence of Arab nationalism, and each one had a certain kind of impact.

The Palestinian National Movement, to a certain degree, had a different twist from Arabic nationalism because of its nemesis, political Zionism. Therefore, political Zionism played a crucial role in crystallizing Palestinian nationalism. From this perspective, it is important to note that the Palestinian National Movement started to emerge and to crystallize in its shape and struggle for independence immediately after World War I. The greatest catastrophe for the Arabs was the double pledge made by Britain to the leaders of the World Zionist Organization and to the Arabs, to Hussein, who decided to fight with the Allies against the Turks.

Those ten letters between High Commissioner MacMahon in Egypt and Sharif Hussein proved to be very controversial, especially letter No. 8 in which the British were very specific and very cunning, saying, "We are willing to give independence to all Arab provinces except the western part of Hama". This was for two reasons. One, they wanted to confirm their pledges to the Zionists; and second, they didn't want to disturb their relationship with the French. The French at that time were inclined towards colonizing Palestine since it was considered the southern part of Lebanon. This letter was misinterpreted by Hadi, a law graduate from the Sorbonne, to imply the independence of Palestine. But MacMahon and the British High Commissioner were very clear in what they said. However, the greatest surprise to the British was when George Antonius published his book, "The Arab Awakening," in 1938, in which he exposed the controversial position of the British during the war, the contradictory pledges they made to the Arabs and then to the Zionists, creating a national home for the Jews.

In 1917, with the Balfour Declaration, we start witnessing the alienation of the Arab population in Palestine from Britain and from the Allied powers. In 1918, we had the Syrian conference; in 1919, the Weizmann-Feisal communique. The Palestinian National Movement started showing its teeth in the early 1920s, and the 1920s and 1930s witnessed three stages of its development. The first stage of British civil administration runs all the way from 1920 to the Wailing Wall incident of 1929, and could be considered a stage of peaceful resistance. The Palestinians opted to use obstructionist methods to express their dissatisfaction with the Brits and with British colonial rule in Palestine, believing themselves entitled to sovereignty and political independence. At the same time, the British were facilitating Jewish immigration into Palestine in total contradiction to their pledges to the Arabs.

We cannot avoid talking about factionalism within the Palestinian National Movement, particularly epitomized in the 1920s and 1930s. The Palestinian National Movement was a culmination of a rigid social structure based on an atomized clan system which played a significant role in creating impediments to consensus-building and unity within the movement. I would say it was not the Brits and the ingenuity of the Zionist colonists at that time with regard to land confiscation and taking over Palestine, but it was this inner weakness within the national movement that exacerbated the situation to the point that I accuse the leaders of that period of the loss of Palestine and of the consequent Nakba of

111

1948. The major contradictions of Jewish immigration and British colonialism were always there, but our internal weakness and this factionalism played into the hands of the Brits and, at a later stage, of the Zionist movement, when they were creating their modus vivendi at a time when we were very weak internally and couldn't defend ourselves or win any war against the Brits or against the Zionists.

This rigidity in the social structure in Palestine, based on the politics of notables, reached a turning point in the history of the national movement. We ask today what went wrong with Camp David and Taba, and we always used to ask what went wrong with the nationalist movement. We had total control of the land and 98 or 99 percent of the population. But eventually, demographically and geographically, we ended up the minority. We lost Palestine, and in 1967, we lost whatever remained of Palestine. And we draw parallels between this and what went wrong in the 1960s, 1970s, 1980s, 1990s and the year 2000.

My main focus will be on factionalism. Hajj Amin Al Husseini turned out to be the undisputed leader of Palestine. His appointment was extremely controversial. We wonder how the British policy of divide and rule succeeded in creating the balance between the two notable families, the Husseinis and the Nashashibis. How did they create this leader out of a 26-year-old artillery commander like Hajj Amin Al Husseini, who wrote vociferous articles about the Brits and incited the Jaffa riots of 1920, and who sought refuge in the tribes of Jordan? It's amazing that Herbert Samuel, the first Commissioner of Civil Administration in Palestine, acted on the recommendation of his advisor and lawyer to give Hajj Amin Al Husseini clemency simply because they needed a Husseini, as his half-brother was Mufti of Palestine.

The center of power in Palestine was in Jerusalem, and that power rested in two positions that carried important political weight. One was the Muftiship of Palestine, which was situated in Jerusalem; and the second was the Mayoralty of Jerusalem. When the British came in, they realized there was a certain imbalance there because both the Mufti and the Mayor were Husseinis. They wanted to appease the opposition, the Nashashibis and so on, so they basically decided to oust the Husseini mayor in 1920 because he led the Jaffa riots with Hajj Amin Al Husseini, and immediately appointed a Nashashibi as mayor of Jerusalem.

There was to be an election for the Muftiship within the 'Ulema. But when the election resulted in someone from the opposition becoming the Mufti, the Brits said no. They needed a Husseini. So they looked around and found this young redhead, and they brought him over and gave him clemency. He was sent to Cairo to university in order to became a sheikh because, as Mufti, he had to understand *Shari'a** laws. He started studying with Rashid Rida, a modernist, and of course he failed. After six months he came back, and the Brits were really confused about what to do, and they decided to send him on pilgrimage. So he went and became a *hajji**. However, he was never elected into the Shari'a court system. He was appointed by the Brits, but it was never officially gazetted. So Hajj Amin created that kind of a balance.

Of course, once in power, he started dealing with factionalism by going back to the old traditional classical ways of nepotism and corruption and what have you. He started appointing Husseinis to all the key positions and institutions in Palestine, to the point where the British realized that Hajj Amin Al Husseini was becoming less and less popular because he was appeasing the British by being more royal than the king.

The Husseinis, who were known as the Majlesiyoun, were related to the Supreme Council created by the British in 1923, presided over by Hajj Amin Al Husseini. Those in opposition were called the Mu'arada. It was not Mu'arada against Zionism. It was Mu'arada against the Majlesiyoun, that is, Hajj Amin's rule in Palestine.

From there, the factional bickering over political power in Palestine increased. In 1927, when municipal elections took place, the Mu'arada basically swept all the towns and villages except for two places, Gaza and Majdal Shams. So Hajj Amin felt his position was precarious at best. Then, the Wailing Wall incident takes place in 1929. The Mu'arada could not stand against Hajj Amin because, if they did, they would have been considered traitors. In this way, he eventually managed to gain control and popularity and to challenge the British. From the Wailing Wall incident onwards, he became the arch-enemy of the British system.

This peaceful resistance that I talked about from 1920-1929, epitomized best Hajj Amin's cooperation with the British Mandatory rule. However, from 1929 to almost 1935, with the advent of political parties in Palestine, there was radicalization of the national movement. In 1931, for the first time, we see an uprising against the British and not against the Zionists. We see, in 1933, 1934, 1935, the development of the political parties representing family interests and notables - not political parties in the sense that we understand it- but of course factions, that basically radicalized the situation.

And from 1936 to 1939, we see the third phase, what I consider to be outright rebellion, the culmination of economic and political frustration of the Arabs with British policies in handling their affairs. This eventually led to the downfall of the traditional leadership in Palestine. Hajj Amin was ousted and managed to escape to Cairo.

After 1939, we never had a national consensus leadership. Eventually, the Shaw Commission which came as a result of the 1929 Wailing Wall incident, the Peel Commission which came as a result of 1936, and then the Anglo-American Commission in 1946, all recommended partition. The 1947 UN partition plan did not arise out of a vacuum. It was based upon earlier recommendations made by the commissions of inquiry that concluded that there was no way to resolve or reconcile the basic differences between the Jewish communities and the Arabs except by means of two separate entities.

Unfortunately, now, but maybe fortunately at that time, the Arabs refused the partition plan, and the war that led to the creation of Israel was the blow which caused the early Palestinian nationalist movement to take a different course, not only in the 1950s, but in the mid-1960s, with the PLO.

NORMAN ROSE: One looks back at the beginnings of the Zionist movement in the late 19th century and the first Zionist Congress and it's impossible to define the Zionist movement except in terms of an international pressure group, a minority movement within the Jewish people that did not command widespread support. On the contrary, it was violently opposed by many important groups within the Jewish world, and in fact did not achieve a majority standing within the Jewish world until sometime during World War II. Nevertheless, 50 years on - a comparatively short time in historical terms - the United Nations, in November 1947, internationally legitimized the idea of a Jewish state, Israel, which was the aim of Zionism from the first Zionist Congress or from Herzl's famous pamphlet, "A Jewish State," first published in 1896.

Therefore, the question I think everybody has to ask themselves is, How did this come about? What happened? How did a minority pressure group manage to achieve, within such a short space of time, its declared aim?

Of course, there are many reasons for this but I want to suggest three main points. Firstly, the movement had to work within the framework of the international community. It had no power. It had no money. It had no influence, at least in the beginning. What it had was the hope of manipulating - and I use manipulating in its broader sense - the international community, the great powers that existed at the end of the 19th century, which in a sense continued until 1939, or even to the end of the World War II.

This was no easy task. One could not command a majority opinion within what we define as the European system since all these Great Powers - England, France, Russia (later the Soviet Union), Germany, the United States later on - all had conflicting interests. One had to balance one set of interests against the other, by no means an easy task.

The second point is that, within the Zionist movement itself - and here I was very impressed with the previous presentation, perhaps in a negative sense, but nevertheless it's reflected in my own paper - that the Zionist movement itself had to produce something organically, a balanced realistic leadership that knew how to work within the international system. Again, no easy task because the Jews were thought of by many people as too apolitical, too ideological, too uncompromising. Weizmann, of course, had to work within this framework. Nevertheless, on the whole, the Zionist movement produced this balanced leadership, although we know there were conflicts within the Zionist movement. There was a great deal of opposition to Weizmann later on, and to Ben Gurion.

The third point, which is connected to the second, is that, in the long run, the Zionists had to produce a leader or a leadership that was capable of combining all these factors, working with foreign governments and persuading them somehow - because this seemed such an illogical thing to do - that the Jewish people had a historical and legitimate right to a claim in Palestine. Again, one turns back to the late 19th century and the rise of nationalism in Europe from which Zionism sprang ultimately. And one thing that worked in the Zionists' favor, over which they had absolutely no control whatsoever, this was the elevation of the principle of national self-determination that evolved after World War I, as one of President Wilson's Fourteen Points, which became a kind of icon in international politics. Everyone, every nation, every tribe, every community, could claim national self-determination. One only has to look at the map of Europe in 1919 and 1920, and compare it with the map of Europe before World War I, to see how this principle of national self-determination expressed itself in the world community. And why shouldn't the Jews be part of this? So this was an added factor that worked to the Zionists' advantage.

Another factor which worked to their advantage was Theodor Herzl's pre-World War I diplomacy. Herzl didn't achieve anything in concrete terms: he failed to persuade the Germans, the Turks or the British. However, his achievement in a larger sense was that he presented the Zionist case before the great powers, and they realized what he was talking about. They didn't accept his argument for various reasons. Nevertheless, when later leaders, such as Weizmann or Ben Gurion, came to talk to the leaders of the governments of Britain or America or whatever, those leaders understood what was being spoken about. They had an idea at least of what the aims of Zionism were.

The question presented by the outbreak of World War I was: What do we do? Do we support the Allied powers or the Central powers or do we take a moderate neutral stance? Whichever way the Zionist leaders looked at it at the time, they were bound to fail. They were going to fall between, not two stools, but three stools. If they supported the Allied powers and the Central powers won, they would lose out, and vice versa. And if they were neutral, both sides would say, why didn't you support us. This, again, would not be to their advantage.

Ultimately, the official Zionist leadership opted for neutrality. They moved the Zionist headquarters to Copenhagen, which was neutral, and they began to work, in a sense, in a vacuum. Here we have the beginnings of a political sense, of realizing, of hoping - because there was no more than a hope at the time - that one side would prove decisive in World War I, and therefore, if the Zionist movement supported that side, it would reap the rewards at the end of the war. Of course there was absolutely no guarantee as to who was going to win World War I. It was a stalemate until the late spring of 1918. There were four or five years of prolonged warfare between the Allied powers and the Central powers.

Chaim Weizmann was elected head of the World Zionist Organization in 1920, and headed the Zionist movement from then until sometime in the World War II, almost a generation, a career I think unprecedented in modern political history. I've named him elsewhere as the benevolent despot because he ruled, not with an iron hand, but by persuasion. Nevertheless, his policies were more or less adopted by the Zionist movement.

In 1914, Weizmann was nothing. Now he is seen as the second greatest leader in the history of the Zionist movement. Of course, he was a very charismatic figure. He lived in England and read at Manchester University in organic chemistry. But going by his natural political instinct, he said that Britain's allies would win World War I. This was in the late summer or early autumn of 1914. Why? No one knew. It's really impossible to pinpoint how he reached that conclusion. But he never deviated from it until the Allies actually won the war in late-1918. And he focused all his energies in trying to foster contacts between the Zionist movement in England - again, a kind of minority group within the Zionist movement as a whole - with members of the British government.

He was successful and unsuccessful. I don't want to go into the question of his scientific work, but as a result of that, he was brought into contact with leaders of the British government - the Prime Minister, the Foreign Minister, Churchill and so forth. Nothing came of these initial contacts, but again, Weizmann presented himself as a Zionist who was firmly committed to the British cause, and they were impressed by his loyalty to Britain. This was something because he was Russian, and the British did not like the Russians. Russian Jews were not favorable to Russia fighting Germany. There was a kind of dual loyalty there.

The first substantial contacts between the Zionist movement - Weizmann - and the British government took place at the beginning of 1917, and here it's very important to understand the overall political context.

In Britain, a new government had emerged. Lloyd George, a Welshman, in the framework of the United Kingdom, and from a minority race, was a very dynamic Prime Minister. In my opinion, he was the most talented British politician of the 20th century. He formed what we now call a kitchen cabinet of five people - Lloyd George, Miller, Smuts, and two others. Three out of the five were committed Zionists - Lloyd George, Miller and Smuts. We call them the Gentile Zionists. He had a cabinet secretariat consisting of two people who were also very pro-Zionist - Sykes and Leopold Hayman - and, of course, Balfour was the Foreign Secretary, although he wasn't a member of the kitchen cabinet. So there was a constellation that had not been planned at all, at least by the Zionists, that was inclined to take a pro-Zionist stand if a British pro-Zionist policy could be integrated into British imperial policy. These two things had to slot one to the other.

The culmination of these contacts was positive, although there were ups and downs. The Balfour Declaration of November 1917 went through five drafts. First the British government turned to the Zionists and said, "Present us with a draft." That initial draft proposed establishing a Jewish national home, or making from Palestine a Jewish national home. The last draft severely curtailed that very widespread commitment to establish in Palestine a Jewish national home. This is the first hint of partition.

There are two things to take note of from the Balfour Declaration. First, there is no British commitment to administer Palestine. It's an overall commitment. Weizmann did not want this. He wanted a firm British commitment to administer Palestine. He didn't trust the French. He didn't want the Americans. He didn't want the Dutch, who were also proposed at the time. He wanted Britain. He believed implicitly in British democracy. He thought, of all the imperial powers, that Britain would be most suited.

Second - and this again points to his political sixth sense - Weizmann did not believe the Zionists could go to Britain or to the international community and say, We want a Jewish state. We demand a Jewish state. You have to give us a Jewish state. We supported you during the war. This is what we deserve. He knew very well that the imperial powers, Britain and France, would not give him one. Therefore, there was no point in demanding it.

The first thing you have to do, of course, is build up the Jewish national infrastructure in Palestine. This depends on Jewish immigration. How would the Jewish people respond? We know they didn't respond very well in the initial period. All we could get was some kind of Great Power commitment to establish a Jewish national home in Palestine. But what is a national home? No one knew at the time. It was a novel concept in international terminology.

Nevertheless, Weizmann seized upon the Balfour Declaration as the great historical turning point. Why? Because the greatest power in the world at the time - Great Britain - had recognized the national legitimacy of the Jewish people. For him, this was the achievement. He felt, from Britain he could go on and persuade other powers, as indeed they did, not only Weizmann, of course, but other Zionist leaders as well, until the League of Nations eventually enshrined the Balfour Declaration in the terms of the Mandate published in 1922. In 1923, the United States, which was not a member of the League of Nations, also ratified this idea. So by 1922-1923, the international community as a whole recognized the national legitimacy of the Jewish people that had to be expressed in Palestine. For the Zionist movement, there was no other place.

In the 1920s, Weizmann was the undisputed leader of the Zionist movement, on first-name terms with the leaders of the Western world. Quite a few years ago, I wrote a book about Weizmann. One of the things that really staggered me about him was the way in which world political leaders, from whatever country, were so impressed with his personality. He had charisma, a word which is impossible to define in concrete terms. Either you have it or you don't. When you walk into a room and you have charisma, everybody knows. President Wilson, Lloyd George, Churchill, Balfour, Georges Clemenceau (the French Prime Minister), Lawrence of Arabia, all these people were so impressed with Weizmann. When Weizmann put his case before them, they were convinced. Somehow, in his inner self, his spirit, he expressed the national aspirations of the Jewish people, and it was through him that they became convinced of the - I wouldn't say righteousness - but rightness of Zionist claims.

This is an important factor. Either you gain people's trust or you don't. If you gain it, then you take it. This was one thing that Weizmann managed to achieve for the Zionist movement during this period.

The other thing was how the Jewish people responded to the challenge. Of course, in the 1920s, they did not respond. There was a wave of immigration, the Third Aliyah, which was ideologically committed, mainly Labour Zionists strengthening the kibbutz movement and Labour institutions, the Histadrut and so forth. But it didn't represent the Jewish people, only a tiny minority within them. More Jews left Palestine than came in 1927. The Zionist movement was on the verge of bankruptcy, not only in terms of support they were receiving from Jewish people, but also in terms of money. You can't work unless you have money. You can't finance activities in the United States and Britain and France and so on. It's not for nothing that Weizmann spent a great deal of his time in the United States fund-raising.

All this changed with the 1929 riots. The Zionists were worried by the British reaction to the riots, which expressed itself in a series of White Papers that were all severely damaging to the Zionist cause, limiting immigration and land purchases and so on. Weizmann's commitment to the British here was a conflict of interest. The British were a great imperial power, particularly in India with its great Muslim population, and it was an uphill struggle between the Zionists and the British government.

I want to jump to the partition plan, which again came as a result of the Arab revolt in 1936-1939. The Peel partition plan was a three-way partition - a Jewish state and an Arab state, with the British retaining a certain strategic area. This is 1937, two years away from World War II.

How did the Zionists respond to this? Again, characteristically of the Zionist leadership at the time, Weizmann's first response when he heard the terms of the Peel report - which were leaked to him by a friend in the cabinet before it was actually published - was, "Standing room only." It was a kind of handkerchief in size. I mean there was nothing there. But this is the first time that a Great Power had proposed a Jewish state. Therefore, you take what's on offer and you negotiate the details.

This was not the majority opinion within the Zionist movement. He had to struggle hard. There was opposition from the extreme left, the Marxists, working-class cooperation, so forth and so on; and from the extreme right - Greater Israel, as we would call it today. Nevertheless, he managed to get through. He managed to persuade the Zionist Congress of 1937 to accept the idea in principle, and let's go on to negotiate the details. Weizmann's slogan was, "It's better to take 50 percent of something than 100 percent of nothing." You take what's on offer. Then you go forward. Of course, the Peel partition plan fell through for many reasons, and it evolved naturally into the White Paper of 1939, considered to be catastrophic for the Zionists.

I ask the question, Was it? Again, I look to Weizmann as a leader and I say yes and no. Yes, because it was really catastrophic in terms of immigration and land purchases and whatever. But this was World War II, and Weizmann knew - they all knew by May 1939 - that the war was about to break out. It was inevitable. In the event of war, immigration would be restricted. But the Zionists felt confident that they could evade land restrictions, as they did, during the war. Weizmann looked back in history - a dangerous thing to do because historians, or politicians, who think they can learn from history usually learn the wrong lessons, not the right lessons.

Weizmann thought World War II would repeat World War I, and he would get another Balfour Declaration. So he again supported Britain. But what he got was the Labour Government of 1945, a complete disaster for the Zionists.

MANUEL HASSASSIAN: I would like to confirm what he said. History is past politics and politics is present history.

LILY GALILI: A question to Manuel Hassassian. First of all, it was a very important presentation because I think most Israelis still believe that the Palestinian national movement was established by Shimon Peres in Oslo. So it's good to hear that it started some time ago and to put it in context. There is a missing link for me. I am certainly not an expert in political science nor in the Palestinian national movement. You started your presentation with a description of the general background of European and Western influence on the birth of national movements in general, and how it influenced the Arab, Palestinian and Zionist national movements. You mentioned in passing, and I would like you to elaborate, on the interdependence or mutual interest between the Palestinian national movement and the Zionist movement and how each defined the other, if

118

at all. What was the interaction between the two, if there was any?

In your paper, you attach great importance to the tensions between the two families, the Husseinis and the Nashashibis, as to some extent failing the national movement. You also mentioned it in your oral presentation. What is the importance or value of this personal aspect as opposed to tendencies and processes and so on?

You also insinuated that these problems within the Palestinian national movement persist until today. You implied that whatever went wrong in the past somehow affects the current situation as well. Could you please elaborate a little more on that?

DALIA OFER: These are the first two papers that we can look at as part of a shared history, the first two papers that look at a period in a way that tells us how the understanding of each enriches the situation. Perhaps if we had a paper on the Nakba, which we really did not, that could have been the same thing, looking at it from different perspectives, but somehow complementing each other on the issue of the Holocaust and Nakba.

Amneh and I had a conversation, before leaving for the airport in Cyprus, about the origins of Zionism and Palestine, looking at it as a colonization movement and as a national movement. I said I think the difference in our approach is that I agree that part of it is colonization, of course. But it's a national movement in its essence.

Manuel's paper was impressive in its ability to combine the critical issue of colonizing Palestine from the Palestinian point of view, but viewing the movement as a national movement. This point of view doesn't portray one as better or worse. It's not a matter of values, but of analysis.

It surprised me that Norman's paper did not at all relate to the opposition, the difficulties, the feuds, the conflicts within the Zionist movement, but only to the political issue - which was really the issue of the paper. The social history of Zionism - we can't say of the Jews because that goes beyond this - was not in your paper, looking at it from an understanding of world politics and diplomacy and how to use that for the benefit of the goal of Zionism.

In Manuel's paper, the social issues were so important - the structure of the village, the structure of the town, the differences between the townspeople, different groups of townspeople, etc. In this respect, it's important to put this kind of social history of the Zionist movement into the story of Zionism in Palestine. There were a lot of conflicts between towns and settlements, between kibbutz people and townspeople, between the left and what we call the right. It wasn't only a political right, but also a different social issue.

My last comment is about the facts. You say, Norman - and I agree with you completely - that a lot of Zionism's success was not so much because of what they did, but because of world politics as a result of World War I, self-determination and the dismemberment of all the empires into national states, with the difficulties and the benefits for the national movements. When we look at the successes of the Zionist movement, the obvious success of the partition resolution of 1947 and what followed, we should note that, in a way, all its political programs and decisions at various stages - what to do after the Holocaust and World War II, etc. - none of what they thought would happen actually happened. You can say that, in a way, all its programs failed because the end of World War II was a completely different story from the end of World War I. The notion of working with the British in the war and against Hitler, etc., thinking that the result would be another Balfour Declaration, was completely wrong. Fighting the British, the terrorist acts against the British, all that was a complete failure. By the summer of 1946, they realized it would not work and they retreated from it. Yet in the end, they did succeed. In this respect, we have to introduce into the story some consideration of the impact of the Holocaust and of the political structure after World War II.

But it's true also in the 1930s and the late 1920s, because you didn't mention the Fourth Aliyah. You talked about the Third Aliyah. When we think of the social history of the Jews in Poland, the Fourth Aliyah is extremely important, a result of the national economic policy of the Polish government at that time that pushed the small Jewish middle-class - not the major one - outside the economic field that they were previously part of. The same is true for the early 1930s - Nazism and the persecution, etc.

This period is really so dramatic, the asymmetry between what happens to the Jews in Palestine and what happens to the Jews in the Diaspora on the one hand, and the asymmetry between what happened to the Jewish national movement - Zionism - in Palestine, and the Palestinian national movement really crystallizing and becoming a modern movement. If you read the two volumes of Shuka Porath, he describes not only families and clans, etc., but also, from 1935, 1936 onward, the formation of a modern national movement. And the asymmetry between these two movements is really what we are experiencing today.

MOSHE MAOZ: Norman, did you coin this phrase, Gentile Zionism?

NORMAN ROSE: I'm afraid so.

MOSHE MAOZ: Congratulations. There is also another phrase, Arab Zionism, which is a different notion. I suppose you'll agree with me that this Gentile Zionism preceded the Balfour Declaration.

NORMAN ROSE: Of course.

MOSHE MAOZ: To that extent there was public opinion that encouraged this idea of the Balfour Declaration. It was already published in 1840. There was Zionism before Herzl. But again, in a short paper you cannot elaborate on everything.

You convinced us as to the charisma of Weizmann, but you didn't mention his charisma was vis-a-vis the Gentiles but not vis-a-vis the Jews, his fight with Ben Gurion. In fact, Ben Gurion was more powerful to the extent that Weizmann said he cannot stick his nose except into the handkerchief. What was the balance there? This is a fascinating story during the British Mandate, the balance between Ben Gurion and Weizmann. Ben Gurion had the upper hand. But we never heard you mention the name Ben Gurion.

Manuel, you said something daring about the impact of Zionism on the Palestinian national movement. Was there also any impact regarding the system? I think about this word democracy, democratization, and you described very well that there was none. But was there any tendency among Palestinians to also

120

imitate - as in the case now since 1967, without admitting it - the democratic institutions of the Jews, of Israel? Was there also an attempt to look at it, especially since the British also had a model of democracy?

My question is why you didn't have this tendency of democratization among the Palestinians although, as you mentioned, you had parties that were more family parties, notable parties. If there were a democracy - this is a theoretical question - and the municipal elections were won by Nashashibis, or let's assume that crucial questions of the White Paper in the 1947 partition were determined by democratic vote among the Palestinians, would it have been different? There was discussion among the Palestinians about it, I'm sure, about 1939 and 1947. These are two missed opportunities. So I'm asking whether there was a kind of debate among the Palestinians regarding these issues, or if there is now some soul-searching about it. How can you explain that, especially the White Paper which in fact answered the demands of the Palestinians, was rejected? Was it a majority? Was it the position of the leadership that you mentioned?

AVRAHAM SELA: Listening to the two presentations, I could hardly tell I was in a forum discussing shared histories. There was hardly any connection between the two other than a mention of the word Zionism here and there and the question of Arab nationalism here and there. The missing part in both papers is more discussion about the positions and efforts by the two movements vis-a-vis each other. There was huge Zionist diplomacy towards the Palestinian Arabs. It was futile, and not only ineffective, but maybe not even intended to bring about any substantive results, but rather to ease the conflict and to buy time. Still, it's an important chapter in Zionist history during the Mandate and should be included in both papers, whether as a negative position or as a positive one. We have to discuss it because there was some consideration, some contact, some effort, at least during some part of the conflict, to mend things or ease things, and to respond to opportunities as well as certain threats to each side. There's been quite a lot of writing on this issue, including my own contribution.

Second, a historiographical point, namely, the fact that both of these papers end in 1939 has no basis. We have to talk about the period of the Mandate, and that goes up to 1948. Yes, 1939 is a milestone in the process, but it is definitely not the end of the development of the Palestinian national movement. It is not the end of the struggle between the two movements. And most importantly, to understand what happened in the 1940s, one has to base his analysis on the previous part of the Mandate, especially the later 1930s.

I make this point because there's a prevalent tendency in Palestinian writings, if you look at the biographies of the Mufti, almost not to mention the history of the Mufti after 1939. 1939 or 1938 was the apex of his achievements or his activities, even after he was expelled - or actually fled - out of Palestine. Still, his leadership continues to be very decisive about whatever concerns the Palestinian national movement, and his decisions and the factional politics continue to overshadow the fate of the Palestinian-Zionist struggle, so I think it must be included. And it must be widened to also include the 1940s, because it never ends until 1948, and the Mufti's experience during the war and afterwards, in his later attempts to build the Palestinian national movement on a new basis and to prepare for the inevitable - or what seemed to be inevitable - confrontation with the Zionist movement. All this is part of the story and cannot be disconnected from it.

In this context, it's interesting to see that, during this period that you're talking about, there's a very important shift in terms of the center of gravity of the two movements. While the Zionist movement moves from outside in, the center of gravity of the Palestinian national movement moves from inside out.

MANUEL HASSASSIAN: In Oslo, it switches.

MOSHE MAOZ: In the Intifada, it switches.

AVRAHAM SELA: It switches after 1982. The question is, what is the turning point? In 1983 and 1985, in two articles by Sabri Jiryis, then director of the PLO Center for Palestinian Studies and one of the most profound thinkers of the PLO at that time, he made it quite clear that, after 1982, and after the expulsion of the PLO from Lebanon, the center of gravity shifted back to the territories. This was the only asset left in PLO hands. In 1985, he actually prophesied the Intifada when he said, "It's the only way we can do something." The Palestinian population will initiate some kind of protest and mass action. It's an important point because eventually the struggle was decided in Palestine, and because of the changes in the centers of gravity, the Palestinian movement was in a state of weakness. This can be seen when comparing the two movements.

With regard to Manuel's paper, one or two points are important to mention. Many times we forget that the Palestinian Arab population was no different from the Lebanese or the Syrian - maybe the Lebanese a little - but Syrian or Iraqi or other Third World post-colonial states. In other words, yes, there was factionalism. Yes, it was a traditional society. Yes, the fellahin comprised more than two-thirds of the population. All this is true. But there was one thing that differentiated this movement from other national movements that emerged on the basis of colonial division of territories, and that was the struggle with Zionism. And the struggle with Zionism was a main obstacle to the process of institution-building. In all other Arab countries in the region, by the early 1920s, the colonial powers started establishing national governance, governments composed of indigenous personalities, people from the same population.

In Palestine, the attempt was made exactly along the same pattern. In 1922, the British government came up with the idea of elections for the legislative council. The reason the "Palestinian national movement" - and I'll explain immediately why I put that in quotes - boycotted it, not on the basis of boycotting any kind of national representation, but on the basis of rejecting the Mandate, which included the Balfour Declaration.

You talked about notable politics and about the major proportion of the rural population and the villages and so on, about the democratization of Palestinian society and elections. Don't forget that, in the elections for local government councils, only those who had landed property could participate. So we're still talking about a very small proportion of people who could actually take part in these processes.

This is less important here, thinking in current terms about the 1920s and 1930s. The question why this couldn't happen and why modern institutions were not built, I think has to be very tightly connected to the type of population, the kind of traditions, the norms of the society. You can't demand that such a society would produce something which was entirely foreign to its basic understandings and notions about the process of using and implementing power.

MANUEL HASSASSIAN: Thanks, Avraham. You answered Moshe's question.

ATA QAYMARI: Can the struggle really be portrayed as resulting from the failed national Palestinian leadership and the victorious ingenious Jewish leadership who achieved, at the end, the State of Israel and the entire land of Palestine for the Jews? I see here two opposite images, upside down from each other, and I think there are deeper currents that affected this process, not only the failure of the Palestinian leadership and the great actions of the Jewish leadership.

Suppose we had had, at that time, the best possible leadership in Palestine. Could the Palestinians objectively, on the basis of their cultural, historical, economic structures, have faced the Zionist national movement and the will of the British to make Palestine into a home for the Jews? Or the other way around. If the British had not been interested in adopting and furthering the Zionist goals, could the ingenuity of Weizmann and the pro-Zionist government in Britain have achieved such a thing? These questions are deeper than this kind of critical view towards our history.

It's very important to look at our history in a critical manner, but there are other things that formed the national movement in addition to just feuds and notables and conflicts among families in Palestine. We can't blame the whole Palestinian national movement on its leadership. How could the Zionists affect the national movement in the conflict, in their goals, in their approach towards Jewish immigration, towards the question of land purchase and the whole question of the British Mandate? Who was the enemy at that time?

It's a matter of both sides. The Palestinian national movement at that time couldn't read the map. They didn't understand that the British were the main enemy of Palestinian independence and achievement of nationality. They concentrated on Jewish immigration as their main enemy, and maybe that's why they refused the quota thing.

The British wanted to establish a civil government in Palestine in which Jews could be represented. Palestinian leadership refused this, maybe because they didn't want to sit with the Jews. On the other hand, the only difference with the Jews was that they could read the map correctly. Could the Palestinians face this great international legitimacy afforded the Zionist movement, and struggle against it and stop it, or did they have to accommodate themselves and try for the half recognition that they got, and maybe more? We had the majority at that time. We could have formed a majority government in Palestine of Arabs, Palestinians, even under the Mandate. So I want you to explain the deeper currents that affected both movements and that led to the end results, not only the guilt on one side and the marvelous deeds on the other.

RAN AARONSOHN: I also found great common ground between the presentations and the papers, and I would also like to draw your attention to some common land that both parties shared. The common grounds were not only through the external framework, but also from internal terminology that was used mainly by Manuel. Secularism, and even fragmentation, also characterized the Jewish Zionist side at the time. I am speaking about practical Zionism. As I said, common land, not only common ground. Practical Zionism also featured fragmentation among the left - the Labour Movement, organizations, settlements, the kibbutz people and the moshavim, which actually became the most important basis for the Zionist presence in the Holy Land at the time - vis-a-vis the right, the so-called civilian movements and organizations and settlements, the moshavim which were the majority and the main core of the Zionist presence till the 1920s.

There were also important internal divisions within the Jewish national infrastructure, and not only in the political external framework which worked in parallel. Look, for instance, at the new Zionist organizations, the Revisionists, who were not mentioned in this discussion. So also looking through this focal process that you, Manuel, talked about in Palestinian society, I think we may discuss some parallel processes and phenomena in the counterpart.

BENJAMIN POGRUND: Ata developed a point which Manuel spoke about - the Brits facilitating Jewish immigration - and there was also reference to the Jews driving the Brits out. Yet, in many Jewish eyes, it's not seen like that, and you mentioned it. You spoke about the catastrophic White Paper of 1939. In Jewish eyes, Britain was the enemy. They did not help immigration. They imposed very strict limitations. And to the Brits, it was not just the Jews who drove them out of Palestine. It was the Jews and Arabs together. They had had enough. Both the Jews and the Arabs gave the Brits such a hard time that they just wanted to get out of there.

Now a sentimental question. Avraham spoke about Zionist diplomacy. One reads sentimental stuff, even today, and people talk about friendships with Arab neighbors. They tried to organize football among the children and the Arabs wouldn't cooperate. There has been this thread over the years of Jews wanting peace with the Arabs. I am wondering if, at any time over the period of history we're talking about, any kind of accommodation was vaguely possible that could have been accomplished either in a joint state or separate states. Or were the competing interests so great and the competition for the land so devastating, that it was always an unavoidable conflict?

One other point addressed to Norman. You talked about the growth of Zionism in the 20th century in the international framework and all the other factors and the leaders. You talked about Weizmann. And there were also all the other people. You drive around Israel and see all the street names. An extraordinary range of talented people in the 20th century arose and took part in this process. If it's relevant to this discussion, why did this happen in the 20th century? You had the international events. You had to have World War I and all the other events. But you also had the individuals. I wonder if that perhaps has to do with people coming out of the European ghettoes, coming out of the schools where they had studied Talmud, and there was then an outburst of energy which led to the Jewish pianists and violinists and painters of the 20th century. Did this contribute to producing these extraordinary people who did so much in the 20th century and were one of the factors you talked about?

PAUL SCHAM: I saw it a little differently. What struck me was the inevitability of the conflict. Certainly, as Avraham pointed out, there were efforts of various sorts on both sides to try to engage each other. But primarily, both sides were not interested in talking to each other. They were talking to the rest of the world. The Palestinians saw the Zionists as interlopers, invaders, who basically they didn't have anything to say to. On the national level, they recognized, I think correctly, that the thrust of the Zionist movement was inherently destructive to Palestinians. In a sense, it's a cliche and completely obvious. On the other hand, it points towards the fact that the efforts of Brit Shalom and other well-meaning organizations, whose ideologies I think were very fair, were not really possible. I suppose you can never say something was not possible, that an alternative could not have been followed, but the two goals were so very different.

Though this is not at all the focus of this seminar, I think there was that inability to engage the core of the other side and to find some common ground. So to some degree, we have to proceed with great caution as far as using history, and I think you're right. When people fasten on history to understand current events, they often fasten on the wrong things and make mistakes. But this inability to deal with the core of the other side and to find some core connection, to some degree was paralleled in the 1990s. And it would be interesting to expand on that, because you were talking about some of the similarities between the mistakes of the 1930s and those of Oslo.

I really feel there was this inevitability. There were two national movements headed towards a confrontation. However, the confrontation did not have to end up the way it did. That was partly a matter of military developments and other things. But the confrontation itself was basically almost unavoidable.

AMNEH BADRAN: Professor Hassassian, I agree that the Palestinian leadership at that time was not up to its responsibility, but there are other factors as well: the colonial powers and their interests; the project of the Zionist movement; Abdallah and the Hashemite goals, and their understandings with the British and the Zionists; the inner rivalry within the leadership; no history of self-rule and no sophistication in addressing the Palestinian belief that there was no legitimacy for a Jewish homeland in Palestine; the repression of the grassroots leadership during the late 1930s. And I would like you to elaborate more about the establishment of this grassroots leadership. I agree that we can blame them, but not accuse them alone of the whole thing. They weren't up to their responsibility because of many reasons.

I would also like your help with the use of the term riots instead of revolts or uprisings when speaking about the Palestinian uprisings in Jaffa or at the Western Wall or the Wailing Wall. Why did you use the term riots instead of revolts?

MANUEL HASSASSIAN: I said the great revolt and I said the 1929 disturbances and I said the 1920 riots, because they were riots against the British. I know exactly which term I am using.

AMNEH BADRAN: And why did you use the term Wailing Wall?

MANUEL HASSASSIAN: That's the accepted British concept. We refer to it either as the Wailing Wall or the Western Wall. In their writings, the Arabs refer to it as the Wailing Wall, and they use it interchangeably with the Arabic term.

RAN AARONSOHN: I also noticed your use of different and parallel terms when referring to the 1936-1939 revolts, rebellions, disturbances. It was quite prominent. Why did you use them interchangeably?

FATMEH QASSEM: I think we hide our ideology behind our use of language. I mentioned this in Cyprus, and I have many questions about it. When we refer to 1936, most Israeli historians will use the word riots, and all the Palestinians use revolt or uprising.

DALIA OFER: Israeli high school textbooks, since Shuka Porath's book was published, use *mered* - revolt - even the Shimoni books before 1948 or 1947.

FATMEH QASSEM: Concerning the Balfour Declaration, the Arabs understood it as a promise, while the British and the Jewish Zionists conceived of it as a declaration, and there is a big difference between the two. What can we learn from this usage of language?

The same declaration, on 2 November 1917, recognized Palestine as the national home of the Jewish people and refers to the Palestinian people as non-Jewish. So the term non-Jewish was known not only within the Zionist movement. What do we understand from this, that the British referred to us as non-something? Maybe the destiny of Palestine was determined right then by their seeing us as non-something.

I have so many questions about the Balfour Declaration, and again, not as a historian, but from a narrative point of view. The Balfour Declaration was given to the Zionist movement at a time when the Jews were not a huge community in Palestine. And Britain, as a Great Power, had not occupied Palestine, or hadn't completed the occupation of Palestine. What should I learn from that? Who gave them the right to allocate the land? They allocated land around the world in 1916, but it raises so many questions.

ATA QAMARI: That's imperialism.

FATMEH QASSEM: I have so many questions about the historians' discussions of the legitimacy of the UN or of the League of Nations or if the Palestinians were a nation or not. The Palestinians had communities. They lived here peacefully. So why did Britain have the right to give these communities, together with their land, to other people? Regardless if they were a nation or not, or if they were part of pan-Arabism or not. There were towns. There were cities. There were institutions. They were integrated into the Mediterranean, the Levant. Less developed, more developed, what's the big deal? I don't understand.

My last point is about something that the Palestinian national movement and the Zionist national movement share, a common ground, and I think this is the main point that Palestinians and Zionists in Greater Palestine or Greater Israel have to deal with. Neither movement succeeded in separating religion from state. This is a core problem. It relates to Judaism as a religion, and it relates to the Palestinians because they find it hugely difficult to separate Islam from the state, as do Arab countries around the world. It's very problematic because Western democracy - and I'm not suggesting that we have to adopt this form of democracy

- but democracy and civil society will be very hard to develop in this country without dealing with this fundamental problem of separation of church and state.

WALID SALEM: There is a lot of discussion about the mistakes of the Palestinian leadership and how that relates to the socio-economic situation at that time, and with the status of the people in that period. Were the people absent? Did they have no influence on the Palestinian leadership in that period? Did they reject the Zionist invasion into Palestine only because the Palestinian leadership asked them to?

My other comment relates to the international strategies. What was the role of international strategies and policies in this situation at that time? There was imperialism, and we were its victims. So where does the responsibility lie? Is it really mainly the Palestinian leadership, or does it have something to do with the social situation, with the people, and also with the imperial powers around the world?

The question of democracy needs deep discussion. We have the example of the Palestinians democratically electing municipalities, the High Islamic Council and the British standing in the way. So were the obstacles to Palestinian democracy internal or external factors? Finally, some new Palestinian historians are also questioning the idea that the Palestinians were atomized. I don't think that Palestinian society can simply be described that way, full stop. This is an injustice to Palestinian society.

MANUEL HASSASSIAN: I won't go into detail for each question. I got the gist of the general trends that have been discussed here.

In response to Avraham, we were restricted to eight or ten pages about a specific period of time, about which I published a book called "Factionalism in the Palestinian National Movement from 1919 to 1939." The whole book is on all those dimensions you mentioned. I thought it important, since this is a thematic approach, to eyeball a certain aspect of Palestinian history exclusive of the Zionist movement on the other side. Just to talk about how internal Palestinian politics developed and how they were influenced by Zionism and the international balance of power. Factions were a phenomenon. And by the way, I was the first Palestinian - and the last - to talk critically about this era of our history, looking at the internal political rivalries that exacerbated the divisions among Palestinians and inhibited the consolidation of their power in their fight for independence and against Zionism and the British Mandate. I felt that I needed to add that twist to the literature of Palestinian history.

An answer, Ata, for what you asked - the position of the Palestinian national movement vis-a-vis the international imperial system mandating the Levant, the French, the British, the Palestinian national movement vis-a-vis Zionist Jewish immigration - all Arab history books have addressed exactly that same political discourse, but they never dealt with the inner dynamics, how the identity of the Palestinians was shaped by the contradictions within the Zionist movement as well as within the British Mandate. In a sense, I twisted the perception of history because I thought there was a missing link that had to be addressed.

Talking about nationalism within the context of factionalism, I needed to allude to social divisions - and I want to come back later to the question of democracy. I support what was said, that a traditional society like Palestine couldn't have been influenced by these modern trends because of Islam and other features of the culture. But going back to the political discourse, this is my answer to Fatmeh in a nutshell: Since the invasion of Napoleon until today, we are still debating the same political discourse - how can we modernize without changing the traditional pristine character of Palestine? How can we reconcile the Western value system with the traditional concept of Islam? So far, we haven't come up with an answer. It's a haunting obsession of Arab intellectuals, trying to find a solution, because there is no compromise between Islam and Western value systems. There is acceptance of physical aspects of Western civilization, but an adamant rejection of the value system of the West because democracy doesn't coincide with Islam's value of consensus. How can you reconcile those two? In Islam, there is consensus. In democracy, there is majority rule and minority right.

Since Islam is a state of religion and a way of life, you cannot really get into the question of secularism - separation of church and state. It's impossible. That's why I said that the Christian Arab intellectuals were the *avant-garde* of Palestinian nationalism, a concept borrowed from the West. In Islam, there are no nations. There is one Umma. It can't accept the concept of nation-states. From this perspective, Arab Christians had no problem with the separation of church and state. They adopted this Western value system and emulated it in the context of nation-state building.

In a sense, the classical historic Arab narrative, when dealing with the Palestinian question, has always been very banal because they exactly follow the same traditional pattern of blaming the other side, of saying that the Zionists were helped by international allies - Britain and what have you. It's true to a certain degree, but it could not be the only reason why we failed. There must be other reasons we have to allude to. That's why we need to be very daring and critical about our history.

The question of factionalism was based on "notables" in the cities, and large families who owned large tracts of land in Palestine. It happened that most of these notables lived in Jerusalem, and they created a certain patron-client relationship. They were the ideologues, but those who took up arms were the fellahin, and sometimes they did not wait for the traditional leaders. Look at all the uprisings in Palestine, even in modern times. Neither the first Intifada nor the second Intifada were initiated by leadership. Thank God for a lame-duck leadership. It was always a popular mass movement. From this perspective, the traditional leadership in Palestine gained control because of its various influences and also because of the relationship with the West.

The problem here is that the Husseinis, who were considered the nationalists, were also considered idealists who historically missed opportunities. The pragmatists were the Nashashibis, who were always dubbed traitors and compromisers. However, if you really look into their platforms and political positions, they were the pragmatists of the time. They did not want to miss those opportunities. Politics were in the context of a basically traditional society that was not politically conscious enough to understand ideology beyond rejecting colonialism and Zionism as two colonial settler states coming to Palestine to dismember Palestinians, uproot them and take their land.

That was the simple concept the fellahin had. The sophisticated concept was a state with political freedom, independence and sovereignty. Those were the key issues reiterated time and again when our delegations from the Arab Executive Committee went to London. That's why I say that, in the first period, 1920 to 1929, we used obstructionist methods, demonstrations, civil disobedience, continuing all the time to send delegations to London to address our grievances and to demand an independent, sovereign Palestinian entity.

To tie the question of factionalism to the present, look at the structure of the PLO. Look at its structure in the Oslo agreement. And from 1982, with Hamas coming to power, with Islamic Jihad, factionalism - even apart from the opposition outside the PLO structure - has always been a phenomenon within the PLO structure, but it was as interpreted as pluralism rather than factionalism. However, in terms of practice, it has not been pluralism because of the simple fact that one dominant political faction - Fatah - always maintained the majority in the decision-making process. That's why there are all these splinter groups who are part of that structure, and yet have never achieved the passing of any resolution because they are a minority. In theory, it looked beautiful, but in practice, it is factionalism. And we have all kinds of splintering outside the PLO by those who did not accept the *status quo*.

The question of learning democratization from Zionism came at a later stage, after 1967, with the occupation. I alluded to that in the chapter about relating democracy to peace when I said that democracy affected the cultural sub-culture of Palestinian society as an impact of the occupying power, which is, ironically, the rule of law on one side of Jaffa Gate and the rule of an occupying power on the other side.

It's true that we failed to begin an institution-building process in the early 1920s, and the Zionists succeeded. We learned this under the occupation of 1967, and that's why we were very successful, in the 1970s and 1980s, in building a nascent civil society. Unfortunately, in the 1990s, the total advent of the National Authority and the establishment of all the ministries overshadowed the NGOs which had really created the fledgling democracy of nascent civil society.

Concerning 1939, I have to admit that all commissions of inquiry and all British papers favored the Palestinians and the Arabs, but it was all lip service. They never concretized those recommendations on the ground because they didn't want to upset the entire Arab world and they didn't want to upset the Muslim communities in India and the subcontinent. However, they clung to their promise in the Balfour Declaration by facilitating Jewish immigration. The Brits wanted to create a balanced view by issuing White Papers, but at the same time, they were allowing Jewish immigration on the other side.

The year 1939 did not come from a vacuum. Even if they had asked me to go up to 1948, I would have stopped at 1939, because the 1940s are a different story. The traditional leadership of the Palestinian national movement was finished in 1939. We lived with the resonance of the charisma of Hajj Amin Al Husseini in the 1940s, with the establishment of an Arab Palestinian party led by Jamal Al Husseini.

In opposition, we had the Communist Party which really asserted its presence in the 1940s, and was much stronger than the Arab political party. They really pulled the rug out from under what we call family politics, and for the first time there was an ideological political perspective with a structured way of going about liberating Palestine. Unfortunately, World War II and what happened then really disrupted our national aspirations.

There is a long debate about the question of periphery and center of gravity. I agree. What I meant by the Oslo process was basically the advent of the PLO leadership from exile. But the actual question of influence started with the dismemberment of the PLO in Lebanon in 1982, and the creation of a political vacuum between 1982-1985, when the Muslim Brotherhood became more and more daring in trying to fill that political vacuum, and the thrust of support that these people got from Israeli occupying forces.

AVRAHAM SELA: Another myth.

MANUEL HASSASSIAN: Let's not forget that the occupation has always tried to concoct an alternative leadership to the PLO. It started with the Village League, with the Muslim Brotherhood, with Hamas and what have you. It's debatable. You can look at it the way you want to see it.

Paul, I cannot but agree with you that these two nationalisms - political Zionism and Arab nationalism - which were created for common and different reasons, have always been at loggerheads because of their conflicting claims over Palestine. So the conflict was inevitable.

To the question of terminology, it's not I who called it the Balfour Declaration. The British called it that. But I will deal with the content. There were 52 different interpretations of the Balfour Declaration in the League of Nations, 52 different readings of its contents in 1922, which became part and parcel of the League of Nations Article 22 giving international legitimacy to the Zionist movement's having a national home for the Jews in Palestine.

We say our catastrophe starts with the Balfour Declaration. I published an article on the Balfour Declaration discussing why the Brits issued this declaration. Norman talked about Weizmann being a distinguished chemist and who played an instrumental role in World War I by discovering a new method of manufacturing acetone which, was used in guncotton. Because of that - and many other reasons - the Brits wanted to give lip service to the Zionist movement.

We are not trying to say the Husseinis or the Nashashibis were traitors. We are simply saying that, if we scrutinize what happened in the past, given the political realities and the objective conditions, maybe I would have done the same had I been a leader at that time. But this does not prohibit me from drawing inferences from history in order to look at the present and seek the future.

With regard to terminology, we refer to the 1936 revolt because it was a major uprising all over Palestine. All the villages took up arms. We started having brigades shooting at the Brits and the Jews. It was a big revolt, not only in the sense of an armed struggle. It was more than that. We call it a revolt because, for the first time, we had the challenge coming from the fellahin and not from the notables. It was a popular uprising to change not only the struggle against the Brits and the Jews, but also a message against the traditional leadership of

Palestine. A revolt means a drastic change in perception.

In 1920, there were riots and demonstrations. It was a demonstration against the British in 1920 which ended up in a riot. We started throwing rocks and beating on the British army. They retaliated and killed six or so at that time, and they ousted Hajj Amin Al Husseini and they fled. These are riots. You cannot call it a revolt. There should be a sense of ideological change when you talk about a revolt, a drastic change in perceptions accompanied by the use of arms and what have you.

The Western Wall incident was an incident. It started with a kid playing football. He kicked his football into some dried tomatoes, and the Arab woman was so mad she took up a knife. That's how it started. And then it was like an avalanche. It was not prepared. It was not systematic. It was not structured. It was an avalanche of riots which eventually ended up with what it had to be.

AVRAHAM SELA: You minimize the whole year from the summer of 1928. You make it a matter of a football game.

MANUEL HASSASSIAN: The objective conditions were always there - that the Palestinians would never accept Jewish immigration in Palestine. They needed a spark, and that spark ended up in these riots. That's what I'm saying. There was objective historic background for this.

NORMAN ROSE: I'll try to answer some of the questions together because there were so many questions asked.

I always think it's dangerous to judge past events in terms of contemporary values. Anybody saying the word colonization today is deemed to be on the wrong side of the fence. But in the pre-World War I period, or in the immediate World War I period, colonization was an accepted value of international politics.

I can tell you with absolute certainty that no one expected that the Great Powers would relinquish their hold on the Middle East after World War I. They were looking for some kind of compromise between Great Power imperial interests and the local national aspirations of the indigenous peoples, including, at the time, the Zionist presence in Palestine. In that kind of conflict, you are not going to expect the indigenous population of the Middle East to triumph over the great imperialist powers, and that is precisely what happened.

Social history is not my field, but let me add one point. During the 1920s, 1930s, 1940s, 1950s, 1960s, up until 1977, I think it's true to say in the general sense that the Palestinian Movement, and then the Israeli Labour movement, dominated Israeli politics and the politics of the Yishuv up until the proclamation of the state. I don't negate the influence of Jabotinsky* and the new Zionist organizations and other political groups and factions that made their presence felt in Palestine, but if you look at the elected leadership of the Yishuv up to 1948, it all stemmed from the same source. That's the most important point, from my point of view.

Differences between Weizmann and Ben Gurion. These were the two great leaders of the Yishuv and of the Zionist movement In my opinion, the differences ultimately between them were tactical and not strategic. Look at the Biltmore Program. Although it was adopted by Ben Gurion, and he came back immediately afterwards and started canvassing the Yishuv, this was actually

Weizmann's program in an article written in *Foreign Affairs* in the beginning of 1943. It was signed by Weizmann, but in fact written by two of Weizmann's closest advisors, Dugdale and someone else. The difference, in my opinion, was more personality than policy. Weizmann was the old established leader. Ben Gurion was a comparatively young man looking for his chance to take over the leadership of the Zionist movement. He had come to the conclusion during the war that the emphasis for Zionists was to face America, not Great Britain. He wanted to lead the Zionist movement, and Weizmann stood in his way. Weizmann was, by then, an elderly gentleman, and the questions of health and leadership in politics are very important. Was Weizmann strong enough to be able to carry the struggle through? It didn't work out. After the Biltmore struggle, Ben Gurion came back to Palestine and Weizmann had to recuperate in the Catskills for about three months to get over the shock of this conflict.

Again, you can dispute this, but, in my opinion, Weizmannism triumphed, and it became an integral part of the Zionist movement's diplomatic and political policy right up until the summer of 1946. This is the struggle after the united resistance movement collapsed and the Zionist movement officially adopted partition and rejected cooperation with terror groups - Lehi and Irgun - and this is Weizmann's policy.

It was impossible to forecast, in 1939, what was going to happen in 1945, and that Labour would come to power in 1945 as a majority government. You have to remember that Labour leaders and the Labour Party in Britain were pro-Zionist up to 1945. Weizmann and other Zionist leaders had very close relations with Labour leaders, and they were strongly disappointed when the Labour government refused to rescind the May White Paper, which was the be-all and end-all of Zionist policy at that period.

It's also important to remember - and Manuel knows this much better than I do - that there were very strong pro-Palestinian groups within the British political establishment. It wasn't only pro-Zionist. I'll just give you two examples. One is that, in the summer of 1922, the House of Lords adopted an anti-Zionist decision which in effect abrogated the Balfour Declaration. Of course, the House of Lords has no power. Nevertheless, it was symbolic of the kind of opinion that was floating around British political circles at the time. The other thing, which might sound paradoxical, is that the Gentile Zionists opposed the Peel partition for British imperial reasons. To have adopted the partition within the context of, as I use the word, the Arab revolt, within the context of an Arab rebellion, would have been a very dangerous precedent for the British government in imperial terms, with regard to India in particular. This is an important key.

Gentile Zionism is kind of rooted in the British Protestant tradition and can be traced back to the revolutions of the 17th century. A colleague of mine wrote a wonderful article on the return to Zion in Protestant thought. You see it in pamphlets. So it comes as no surprise that people like Balfour, Lloyd George, Churchill and Leopold Avery kept on with this tradition. Of course, it's not a question of whether Gentile Zionism exists or not. It's a question of how you exploit it or manipulate it, and this is what Zionists did to very good effect in the period under question.

Of course there were Zionist-Palestinian contacts - well, not Palestinian - but again, you've got to look at the events as they developed during World War I and immediately afterwards. As far as the British were concerned, there as only Feisal and Sheikh Hussein, and they met and came to this kind of compact. What did Feisal have in mind at the time? We don't know exactly, but I am prepared to make an educated guess. Weizmann was prepared to accept the concept of a bi-national state, and this wasn't ruled out by the compact. They were talking about an autonomous Jewish area within a greater Arab state - or Palestinian. This wasn't ruled out. I don't think Weizmann or the Zionist movement ruled it out of hand. We preferred a Jewish state, and then one thing can lead to another. It could lead to a confederation or a federation. These things are not incompatible.

The turning point came in 1929, and the complete domination of the Palestinian national movement by Hajj Amin Al Husseini. Weizmann felt very strongly in 1929-1930 that the Palestinian national movement had turned into an ultra-national, chauvinistic and violent movement. Therefore, it was very difficult, if not impossible, to find a common language.

The decision to abandon Palestine and to bring the Palestinian issue to the United Nations was taken in February 1947, at exactly the same time that the British decided to partition India, and the two things are intimately connected. The British adopted a different imperial strategy: We have India. We have no need for Palestine. We will protect our imperial interests - what is left of them - in West Africa, across Africa to Egypt and the Canal. No one thought differently in 1948. This is the reason in my opinion, and it is backed up by the latest research.

There were many reasons for the Balfour Declaration. Weizmann didn't invent acetone. He invented a cheap method of producing it, which is slightly different. It wasn't because of that. The importance of acetone and Weizmann's scientific work was that he presented himself to the British government as a person they could trust. He participated in the British war efforts at a very difficult time. He built an international conglomerate to produce acetone factories in Canada and the United States and South Africa and so forth. This was important in terms of trust. He didn't know, in February of 1915, what was going to happen in 1917. When it happened, he could then rely on the early contacts that he had made.

It's true that the Balfour Declaration does not refer specifically to Arabs or Palestinians or whatever, but rather to the non-Jewish community. You can say this was an oversight. Perhaps it's true that the British didn't know what was going on in Palestine in 1917, before they had actually conquered and explored and established a civil military administration there. There was a continuity in British policy between the Balfour Declaration and what went on beforehand. Look at all the British documents concerning Palestine from the Inter-Departmental Committee set up to examine British interests in the Middle East after the collapse of the Ottoman Empire through the Sykes-Picot agreement up to the Balfour Declaration. The British speak of an international regime for Palestine, and the Balfour Declaration doesn't specifically exclude this possibility.

Again, this might come as a surprise. The British themselves were not anxious to take over the Mandate of Palestine. We have on record Balfour turning to the Americans to take it on. We don't need it. What do we need it for? To take on the Mandate means money and administration and army and police force. We have an empire. We don't need this. The British wanted to involve the United States in all post-war settlements in the Middle East and also in Europe. They thought this was an excellent way to get the Americans involved in the Middle East. They also wanted them to take the Mandate for Constantinople and the Bosphorus. Of course, that didn't work out.

We can say that when the British took the Mandate, they sensed something was wrong. They had been receiving reports from the military administration about the basic conflict. But the great imperial reason then about Egypt, the Canal, Sinai, Palestine, was keeping the French away. If the Americans didn't take it, the French were only too anxious to step in. It was part of British policy to keep the French as far away as possible from the Suez Canal. The Balfour Declaration was for strictly imperialist reasons.

One silly point about bi-nationalism. Again, I don't look in contemporary terms because, in contemporary terms it turned out to be a complete catastrophe. But in terms of 1918, 1919, 1920, the League of Nations and the Great Powers were thinking in terms of bi-national states - for example, Yugoslavia and Czechoslovakia. The Middle East was not setting a precedent. It was very much in the context of international politics at the time. Of course, the peoples concerned had to agree, which is what happened in the other places. But the idea of a bi-national state in Palestine wasn't such a far-fetched idea, provided that the Zionists and the Palestinians would agree to it.

PAUL SCHAM: On behalf of the culprits who set up arbitrary divisions in time, just as imperial powers set up arbitrary divisions in space, we thank everybody who participated. We hope everybody shares our feeling that this was really, at a difficult time, a very productive interaction.

134

THE HOLOCAUST, THE CREATION OF ISRAEL, AND THE SHAPING OF ISRAELI SOCIETY

Dalia Ofer

THERE are two different aspects to the issue of the Holocaust and the State of Israel. The first deals with the relationship between the Holocaust and the establishment of Israel, focusing on the pre-1948 period and what led to the decision to create the Jewish state. The second relates to the influence of the Holocaust on the shaping of Israeli society during the state's formative years.

Scholars are divided on whether the Holocaust had any tangible influence upon the creation of Israel. There is no controversy, however, concerning the Holocaust's effect on shaping Israeli society. All agree that it was a powerful force, both socially, due to the integration of Holocaust survivors into that society, and in the cultural sphere, resulting from the influence of the memory of the Holocaust on Israeli culture.

The primary historical players are: Great Britain, the USSR and the US; the Zionist leadership in Palestine and abroad; Jewish organizations, primarily in the US; and the survivors of the Holocaust. The Arabs will not be presented as major players, nor will the 1948 War of Independence be discussed. However, comparisons will be made between the Jewish Holocaust survivors and the new Palestinian refugees.

Diverging opinions: the Holocaust and the creation of Israel

Evyatar Friesel argues that there is no historical connection whatsoever between the Holocaust and the creation of Israel, and that claims to the contrary appeared at a later period, the outcome of a certain climate of opinion that emerged within the Jewish public at large and in the academic community.[1] According to Friesel, the *Yishuv* (the Jewish community in pre-state Palestine) and the Zionist movement had set their political objectives prior to the Holocaust. The Zionist movement had opted for the establishment of a Jewish state as early as 1939, in the wake of the White Paper published that year that reflected Britain's changed policy towards the creation of a Jewish National Home. The 1942 Biltmore Conference gave formal expression to that decision.

Moreover, the UN resolution to partition Palestine and create two states therein was adopted in 1947 by the General Assembly after unexpected agreement by the US and the USSR. This agreement stemmed from diametrically opposed political considerations of the two powers, which were then in the midst of the Cold War, considerations that had nothing to do with the Holocaust. Both believed that the creation of a Jewish state would serve their own interests: the Soviets hoped that the UN decision would hasten the withdrawal of the British from the Middle East, while the Americans believed that it would lead to stability in the region and thus prevent Soviet penetration.

Yehuda Bauer differentiates between the direct effect of the Holocaust and the influence exerted by the Holocaust survivors.[2] He accepts the claim that the Holocaust per se was not a factor in the creation of the State of Israel, and that neither the efforts by the Yishuv, nor the Cold War considerations of the Great Powers, were the outcome of the Holocaust. He thus agrees with Friesel that one cannot view the Holocaust and the establishment of Israel as being a case of cause and effect, for the chronological connection does not necessarily create a causal link.

Bauer does, however, assign importance to efforts of Holocaust survivors who helped mobilize public opinion throughout the world in favor of Zionist objectives. He believes that it was this public opinion which enabled the Yishuv to place the question of a Jewish state on the international agenda. Bauer believes that Holocaust survivors in Poland—members of the Zionist youth movements together with repatriates from the Soviet Union, who began to organize the *Briha*[3]— became the moving force behind the mobilization of widespread international support to establish a Jewish state. Through the activities of the survivors and their vigorous efforts and participation in illegal immigration and the political efforts of the Zionist movement, they supported the claim that only Palestine could provide the solution to the homelessness of the Jewish people. The terrible catastrophe that was liable to wipe out every prospect of establishing a state was now transformed into a factor that helped strengthen the Yishuv.

Efforts to establish the state: the role of Jewish organizations

Various studies deal with the role played by diverse Jewish groups in convincing world Jewry and the international political community of the necessity to establish a Jewish state in the Middle East. Those dealing with American policy on the Palestine issue stress the efforts of the Zionist movement within the Jewish community as a factor that influenced the judgment of President Harry S. Truman and his advisors (including his Jewish advisors).[4] Some historians attribute the ability of the Zionist Organization of America (ZOA) to mobilize American Jews for mass public demonstrations, as well as the cooperation between the ZOA and other Jewish organizations, such as the American Jewish Committee, to the influence of the Holocaust and the great concern felt by American Jewry for the fate of the survivors.[5] Help for the Holocaust survivors was forthcoming from several Jewish organizations, above all the Joint Distribution Committee (JDC). The aid efforts of American Jewry influenced the viewpoints of these organizations on possible political solutions for the resettlement of the Displaced Persons (DPs). Moreover, the establishment of Communist regimes in post-war Eastern Europe also made emigration to Palestine a desired solution for many Jews in these countries. The joint efforts of the JDC and the Yishuv's emissaries and leaders, already begun with the Nazi rise to power in Germany, created a basis for greater acceptance of Zionist objectives by local Jewish leaders, including American non-Zionists, and strengthened Zionist inclinations among the survivors themselves.[6] Thus did the Holocaust survivors become a unifying force for the Jewish communities of various countries.

Further studies are needed to determine whether the Holocaust and its outcome had any real effect on the thinking, mentality, political assessments, and modes of operation of elements—Jewish, as well as non-Jewish ones in the international community—that were involved in the efforts to create a Jewish state. These influences must be considered within the totality of all the other factors that motivated action in favor of or in opposition to the creation of a Jewish state. It is also necessary to determine to what extent the "Jewish Question"—the problem raised by the survivors and the DP camps on German soil, as well as the issue of whether Jews should return to their countries of origin—was part of the agenda of the international community in the immediate post-war era.

It is especially important to study the Jewish Question in the context of the new East European Communist regimes that gradually emerged after the war. What was the role of Jews as a social and political factor in these societies? On the one hand, individual Jews were actively involved in efforts to firmly establish the Communist regimes. On the other hand, the Jews, as a social group, belonged to the middle class, the social group that posed a problem for these regimes. This condition was most obvious in Romania, but also existed in other countries.

The Yishuv and Zionism

What was the impact of the destruction of European Jewry on the consciousness of the Yishuv? Did the Yishuv conclude that it now had the responsibility to plan, formulate, and execute a Zionist strategy that would consider the mutual dependence between the Yishuv and the Holocaust survivors? Most studies answer that question in the affirmative. They trace the slow process of change in the Yishuv's self-understanding by which it gradually realized that it was no longer the "darling child" of the Jewish Diaspora and must now accept responsibility for the fate of Diaspora Jewry by extending what help it could.[7]

One manifestation of this attitude was the gradual abandonment by some Zionist statesmen, including David Ben Gurion and Moshe Shertok (Sharett), of the concept of "selective immigration", which called for cutting the conceptual connection between the economic absorptive capacity of the country and the extent of immigration. As a result the selection of immigrants according to their ability to be pioneers in the land of Israel lost its centrality in Jewish immigration policy. These changes were a prerequisite to the new policy of mass immigration after the establishment of the State of Israel. Another is the preliminary planning conducted in anticipation of the dispatch of emissaries to the survivors, and the sending of such immigration emissaries to Romania and Bulgaria as early as September 1944, immediately after these countries were freed from Nazi rule.

A year later, Ben Gurion visited the DP camps in Germany and spoke with high-ranking US officers there. His encounter with the survivors in the American zone of occupied Germany moved him to believe that their difficult human condition could become a moral force to pressure public opinion in Europe and the USA. Early in 1946, when the flight of survivors from East European countries into Germany greatly increased, Ben Gurion realized the great opportunity that lay in turning these camps into a huge human reservoir of survivors. Through the Americans, he thought, it would be possible to create a focal point of pressure on the Allies to permit immigration to Palestine and to create a Jewish state. This shows that Ben Gurion's pre-war attitude and strategy remained unchanged in the aftermath of World War II: to utilize the weakness and distress of the Jewish people as a political lever. The major means of achieving this was to demand that all survivors be allowed to immigrate to Palestine.[8] Historians who accept this line of argument claim that the Yishuv leaders believed that enlisting the Holocaust survivors for the Zionist cause would provide a double solution—for the survivors and for Zionism—and would be a key instrument for mobilization of Jewish and international political support. However, at that time it was unclear whether it would be possible to enlist the survivors on behalf of Zionist objectives after all they had suffered.[9]

The literature devoted to the activities of the Yishuv emissaries in Europe also deals with the relationship between the Yishuv and the survivors and how it developed. There are two opposing viewpoints on this matter. In her book, Irit Kenan touches upon the ambivalence engendered by this meeting of the two sides as a result of the different expectations held by each of them. She claims that despite the fact that negative images of the survivors were prevalent, the emissaries made every effort to bring them to Palestine.[10] A different view emerges from the study by Idith Zertal, which focuses on Aliyah Bet (illegal immigration) and the Mossad Aliyah Bet (the organization responsible for it). Zertal presents the attitude of the Yishuv and its leadership towards the survivors as one of political manipulation, an instrumentalist approach that had the objective of advancing the idea of a Jewish state. According to Zertal, these leaders were not motivated nor at all influenced by the outcome of the Holocaust or by the great suffering of its survivors. All they bore in mind was the political interest of establishing a state.[11]

The survivors

The relevant question concerning the survivors is whether they turned into a political pressure group which joined and influenced the struggle to establish a Jewish state If so, what was the process that transformed an unorganized public into not only a central but also an active and creative element in the political struggle? Did they become "instinctive" Zionists in the wake of the Holocaust? In what ways did the survivors express their support of the efforts to establish a state, and how did they participate in them? Can we discern similar—or different—patterns of organization that developed among different groups of survivors and in various countries, and can we point to their experiences in the Holocaust and its outcome as central factors influencing these patterns of organization?

The studies that deal with the Holocaust survivors in the DP camps for the most part concentrate on the camps in Germany, generally dwelling on social developments and the processes of rehabilitation and self-determination in the camps. Most scholars do not believe that the survivors became "instinctive" Zionists due to what they underwent in the Holocaust. They do, however, agree that diverse Zionist approaches did develop among them, some of them in line with accepted Zionist concepts while others were reactions of sorts to the destruction of their homes, families, and communities. The social group created by the survivors in the camps became an important unit for the individual members, one that created ties and identification. Many of the survivors claimed that they must continue their lives together, and this in a Jewish environment. It would seem that a new Zionism was created among the Holocaust survivors, a Zionism at whose core lay their ability to live as Jews, and its significance. Immigration to Eretz Israel and their life in that country were central manifestations of this feeling.[12]

Research points to the creation and crystallization of a Jewish community in the DP camps that engaged in the rehabilitation of individuals, but also began the work of preserving the memory of the Holocaust by collecting historical testimonies, thus bridging the gap between personal and general experiences.[13] The message of Zionism and mobilization for Zionist activity were highly important factors in shaping the survivors' process of rehabilitation, a fact that explains their willingness to join in the struggle to achieve Zionist aims, most clearly expressed in Briha, on the one hand, and Aliya Bet, on the other.

Even the leaders of Agudat Yisrael and the non-Zionist rabbis in the DP camps in Germany came to the conclusion that after the destruction wreaked by the Holocaust there had been a true change in the role of Eretz Israel, which they now saw as a focus for the renewal of religious life.[14] Thus was the idea fostered even among non-Zionist circles that immigration to Eretz Israel was a necessity, and that a demand should be made of the international community to enable immigration.

There is a consensus among scholars dealing with this issue that the survivors, despite the horrors they had undergone during the Holocaust, possessed the great strength and high motivation necessary to rehabilitate themselves. They also agree that despite the obstacles and hardships along the Zionist track, this was the most positive and significant one for the survivors. In terms of a return to normal life (such as economic activity, creating and raising families, acquiring a trade or a profession, and more), the survivors were tremendously successful. This holds true for those who found new homes in Israel, or in the United States, Australia, and elsewhere.

The Holocaust survivors and Israeli society

The impact of the Holocaust on Israel should be divided between the role of Holocaust survivors in shaping the country's social, economic, political, and cultural life, and the meaning of the destruction of European Jewry for the self-understanding of the Israeli public.

Research on both aspects is still in its early stages and is developing rapidly. Among the relevant topics are: absorption of the survivors into Israeli society and their contribution to its development; Israeli identity and the Holocaust; shaping remembrance of the Holocaust and its commemoration; and how the Holocaust influences attitudes towards the conflicts in which Israel and Israeli society are involved. This includes both Israeli Palestinians who are citizens of the country and Palestinians in the occupied territories, and relates to the attitudes towards the Arab states, and other countries. One aspect of this last topic is the abuse of the Holocaust for domestic and foreign political purposes.

Contending with the Holocaust is not a phenomenon unique to Israeli or Jewish society. Various European nations are also directly or indirectly facing up to the Holocaust and in recent years the issues concerning the treatment of the Jews by populations and governments, both in occupied Europe and in the neutral states, looms heavily over these countries. Similar patterns can be discerned in the development of reactions to the Holocaust in different countries throughout the world.

Absorption of the survivors in Israeli society

The primary conclusion that emerges from research literature is that, despite the difficulties, what meets the eye is the great extent to which the survivors have been absorbed into Israeli society and participate in the economic, social, and cultural life. All this notwithstanding, how their past affected their activity in various aspects of life in Israel still awaits to be studied.

Hanna Yablonka presents a complex picture of the difficulties and successes that accompanied the absorption of the survivors in different frameworks, and also records the negative images assigned to them by many Israelis.[15] Jacob Markovitzky, who documented how Holocaust survivors were treated in the armed forces, found that the greatest effort to absorb them militarily was made by the *Palmach*, the unit glorified and identified as comprised of soldiers born or educated from an early age in the Land of Israel,[16] and indeed it was in its units that they served most successfully.[17]

A study devoted to the survivors who were detained by the British on Cyprus surveys their relatively successful later absorption in Israel, as a test case of the entire corpus of Holocaust survivors, in comparison with the great difficulties faced by immigrants from Islamic countries who reached Israel during those same years.[18] The survivors accounted for about 40 percent of the immigrants to Israel during the great wave of immigration, doubling the Jewish population.

Shlomo Bar-Gil's book on survivors of the Holocaust and Youth Aliyah[19] documents how successful Youth Aliyah was in providing tens of thousands of young boys and girls, many of whom had lost both of their parents in the Holocaust, with the necessary means for integration into Israeli society.[20] A leading official in this organization once commented that Youth Aliyah was instrumental in moving immigrant youth from the margins of society to its center. This was achieved, claims Bar-Gil, despite the fact that those involved in receiving and absorbing the youngsters did not understand the traumatic experiences through which these girls and boys had gone in the Holocaust; moreover, they gave no thought to this aspect and did not provide their charges with the tools and means with which to contend with their past experiences. The young immigrants were unequivocally called upon to forget the past and integrate into their new social milieu, to become exactly like native-born Israelis. One of the bluntest means of achieving erasure of the past was forced replacement of their "foreign" names by Hebrew ones, an act that met with opposition.

Studies devoted to the second generation of Holocaust survivors were conducted from the perspective of psychology. The research stresses the special problems of those who grew up in such families, and the significance of these problems in efforts by the children of survivors to understand themselves.21 Very little research was done from the economic or sociological perspective. Noteworthy is the work by Gila Menahem and Ephraim Ya`ar who demonstrate that despite the success of these groups in the economy and in achieving social status they still lagged behind the second generation of native-born Israelis.22

Remembrance and commemoration

During the past two decades, the shaping of a nation's memory and identifying the concepts and role of collective memory, individual memory, and historical narratives have became central issues of social and historical discourse. Research on nationality and national identity has reflected on the manipulation practiced by the elite and ruling classes in the shaping of a national memory. It provoked many questions relating to the representation and authenticity of concepts and conventional knowledge, which became milestones and even symbols of a national culture.

In relation to the remembrance of the Holocaust, these questions were first raised in Tom Segev's book, "The Seventh Million."23 He argues that the Zionist movement, and later, the State of Israel, appropriated the memory of the Holocaust to further their political objectives. He claims that already during the first months after news was received concerning the harsh fate of the Jewish communities in Nazi-occupied Europe, Zionist leaders were quick to suggest how this could be utilized to strengthen the Yishuv and to raise donations for Zionist enterprise in Palestine from Jews the world over.

Segev detects apathy, a lack of compassion, and abuse by the Yishuv relating to the possibility of rescuing European Jews during and after the Holocaust, this at the initiative of its political leaders, especially Ben Gurion. He believes that the roots of this policy lay in some of the basic concepts of Zionism: negation of the Diaspora and the desire to create a new type of Jew.

I disagree with Segev. I believe that those who were instrumental in deciding how to commemorate the Holocaust and nurture its memory did not follow a pre-conceived plan. Like almost every other matter in the Yishuv and in the early years of the state, in this case too, diverse Zionist and Jewish approaches were brought to bear. The manner in which the Holocaust should be commemorated was the subject of controversy between secular and religious Jews, between various sectors within the Labour Movement, and between other groups.

To a great degree, what was finally adopted was the result of how people began to realize the extent of the Holocaust, as well as of its influence on the political efforts of the Zionist movement and the leaders of the pre-state Yishuv and of the State of Israel. Another influential factor was the challenges that Israeli society had to face, such as the War of Independence, the great wave of immigration in the first years of the state and the search for the means to absorb these immigrants, the reparations agreement with West Germany, and more. Patterns of commemoration in Israel were also influenced by those developed among the survivors in Europe and by those adopted by other Jewish communities throughout the world. It may be claimed, therefore, that it was not only this or that ideological concept which shaped the patterns of commemoration. The form they took was also influenced by developments on the various levels of Israeli society, the degree to which the political framework exercised control over extensive areas of public life, political rivalries, literary works, and to a large extent by the reactions of the survivors themselves.

I believe that the patterns of commemoration and remembrance were shaped in a process in which a dialogue was taking place between "the Israelis" and the Holocaust. It was conceived within the realization of the meaning of the Holocaust for the Jews and its implication as to the responsibility of the Jewish State to ensure the future of the Jewish people.[24] It also reflects interaction between the memory of individuals—survivors and Jews who immigrated from Europe prior to the war and their family and friends who remained behind and were murdered—and the images and concepts of the collective shaped by institutions, commemoration ceremonies, and historical and contemporary narratives. In this process Holocaust and Heroism Commemoration Day and the establishment in 1953 of Yad Vashem—the national institution responsible for the commemoration of the Holocaust—played a role as active and intentional social and cultural agencies of remembrance.[25]

Don Handelman's studies of days of commemoration and the form they take place the memory of the Holocaust and its significance within the context of the national memory and commemoration of the fallen of the Israel Defense Forces. Handelman stresses the chronological time span—the seven days that separate Holocaust Commemoration Day from Memorial Day for the IDF soldiers—and its symbolic significance in the Jewish tradition of the shiv`ah the seven days of morning. He also places emphasis on the space of commemoration—the geographic proximity of the sites at which the major commemoration ceremonies are conducted: the military cemetery, the tomb of Theodor Herzl, founder of political Zionism, and Israeli prime ministers on Mt. Herzl, and the site of Yad Vashem. Furthermore, he points to the chronological continuum from Passover, the historical festival of freedom (the exodus from bondage in Egypt), through Holocaust and Heroism Commemoration Day, Memorial Day, and finally Israel's Independence Day, all falling within a few weeks.[26] James Young's volume is a comparative study of "the texture of memory."

He describes the sites dedicated to commemorating the Holocaust in Israel, Poland, Germany, and the United States, placing special emphasis on their architectonic aspects, and connecting them with the social and cultural meaning of the Holocaust in each country and society. In relation to Israel he accepted the commonly-held notion that heroism was the major message that Israeli leadership encouraged.[27] My studies, as well as those of Roni Stauber and Hannah Yablonka, present a more complex message. The use of the word heroism (gvurah in Hebrew) related to both spiritual and armed resistance, while the exhortation to understand the situation of the Jews from within, in all of its complexity, encouraged the legitimization of different responses to the Nazi assault. Yet, armed resistance was still glorified and the story of the ghetto fighters and partisans was an important source of Jewish pride in this dark period.[28]

The Holocaust and Israeli identity

Research on the Holocaust's influence on Israeli identity has until now focused on the realms of education and culture.[29] Israeli identity and its connection to the Holocaust have been studied by Simon Herman, Charles Liebman, and Eliezer Don-Yehiya.[30] According to Herman, the Holocaust has become one of the important factors contributing to a sense of a common destiny shared by Jews and Israelis. Liebman and Don-Yehiya believe that the crisis engendered by the transition to statehood during Israel's early years, which demonstrated that non-religious Israelis were not satisfied simply with the centrality of the state, encouraged its secular population to seek new roots in Jewish culture. As a result, "Jewish consciousness" became part of the curriculum in Israeli schools, one aspect being conceiving of the Holocaust as an episode that strengthens the bonds of a common Jewish destiny, serving as a connecting link between various segments in Israeli society.

The authors claim that this process began in the late 1950s and was given impetus by the Eichmann trial conducted in 1961. (In 1960, Adolph Eichmann who had been responsible in the Nazi bureaucracy for the deportation of the Jews to the death camps, was abducted from his hiding place in Argentina and brought to trial in Jerusalem a year later.)

The testimony presented by several Holocaust survivors from the witness box during this trial transferred individual memories of the Holocaust from the margins to the very heart of public consciousness. It made the voice of the survivors legitimate for all sectors of Israeli society and helped it identify with the suffering through which Jews went during the Holocaust.[31] This is a process that continues to develop in Israeli society to this very day; Liebman and Don-Yehiya claim that the Holocaust has become the "civil religion" of Israel. It is my opinion that the increasing consciousness of the Holocaust cannot be put down solely to the decline of the ethos of etatism, to the increasing role of individualism in Israeli society, and to the search for Jewish roots. One should also take into account the change in the attitude towards the Diaspora among Israelis: A more positive approach towards Jewish life outside the State of Israel has developed through the relationship between Israel and the Jewish communities in the West. Thus, the life of Jews in Europe prior to the establishment of the state is viewed with more empathy by younger generations of Israelis who never experienced living as a minority.[32]

Suggested avenues of research

The Holocaust plays an important role in the process by which Israeli society is slowly becoming conscious of the implications of the great loss sustained by the Jewish people during the Holocaust. This is happening several decades after the arrival and absorption of Holocaust survivors in Israel. In this process, private experiences have become part of the public domain. Survivors began relating what befell them only to their grandchildren, when they could present themselves as successful people, many years after they had rehabilitated themselves and created families. The increasing consciousness of the destruction of the Jewish people is a possible explanation for the patterns of remembrance and commemoration that are developing in small communities such as kibbutzim, moshavim, and communal settlements: the establishment of a commemoration room in the school or community center or a commemorative site in the local cemetery, and the shaping of a permanent pattern for Holocaust and Heroism Commemoration Day ceremonies. Visits of high-school and university students to death camps in Poland have become routine. In schools and kibbutzim, commemoration ceremonies are organized and executed by these youngsters.[33]

Research of such developments should be integrated into a wider, more extensive study that will encompass social history (issues connected to immigration and absorption), cultural history, and political contexts (such as the use of the Holocaust made by various political parties, relationships with Jews in the Diaspora and with the international community). Such a study should also analyze developing relationships with and images of "the other"—the Palestinians living within Israel and in the West Bank and Gaza. A recent study dealing with how Israeli society relates to anti-Semitism examined the sources from which youngsters and youth gained their information on this topic. It transpires that what they learn about the Holocaust in the schools and the media are the primary source of the concepts and the images they form of the Palestinians. What emerges from the study is that how these young people relate to discriminatory behavior towards Palestinians in Israel is completely different from how they relate to similar behavior towards Jews in the past or the present.[34]

One should abstain from polemics while studying the role played by the Holocaust in shaping the attitude of Israelis towards the conflict with the Palestinians. Every effort should be made to understand the emotional undertones that are hidden in certain terms and memories. There is, of course, also a manipulative political stratum, and steps should be taken to isolate it from the study.

Another issue worthy of research is the degree to which Arab leaders of diverse hues and shades are aware of how the Holocaust influences the self-understanding of Israelis and thus the political conflicts. We are aware of the Arab claim that the problem of Jewish refugees was solved by creating another problem of Palestinian refugees. Many are acquainted with the image of the "house on fire" used by leading Jewish historian Isaac Deutscher after the Six Day War in 1967: people trapped in a burning house have no alternative but to jump out of the windows. During their fall to the ground they crash into and wound persons standing at the foot of the house, people who want to see what is happening and perhaps want to help, but are unable to do so.[35]

Research of the influence of the Holocaust should be executed in a comparative framework, one that compares different countries, but also various groups within Israeli society. Interdisciplinary cooperation is the order of the day. Historians must internalize concepts used in anthropology and other social sciences, and employ them in their own studies.

[1] Evyatar Friesel, "The Holocaust: factors in the birth of Israel? in *Major Changes within the Jewish People in the Wake of the Holocaust*, ed. Yisrael Gutman pp. 519-544, (Jerusalem 1996; henceforth: *Major Changes within the Jewish People*).

[2] Yehuda Bauer, "The Impact of the Holocaust on the Establishment of the State of Israel", in *Major Changes within the Jewish People*, pp. 545-552.

[3] The clandestine mass movement towards southern European ports from where the refugees embarked on illegal immigrant ships bound for Palestine, or to Displaced Persons camps, primarily in Germany.

[4] See, e.g., Amitzur Ilan, *America, Britain and Palestine: The Origin and Development of America's Intervention in Britain's Palestine Policy, 1938–1947* (Hebrew) (Jerusalem 1979); Zvi Ganin, *Truman, American Jewry and Israel, 1945–1948* (New York 1979); John Goodall Snetsinger, *Truman, the Jewish Vote and the Creation of Israel* (Stanford 1974).

[5] Menahem Kaufman, *An Ambiguous Partnership: Non-Zionists and Zionists in America 1939–1948* (Jerusalem 1991).

[6] Dalia Ofer, " 'Oldtimers' and New Immigrants as Perceived by Jewish Organizations in Europe and America, 1946–1951" (Hebrew). Pp. 20–51 in: *Israel in the Great Wave of Immigration, 1948–1953*, ed. Dalia Ofer (Jerusalem 1996; henceforth: *Israel in the Great Wave of Immigration*); Yehuda Bauer, *Out of the Ashes: The Impact of the American Jews on Post-Holocaust European Jewry* (Oxford 1989).

[7] Hava Eshkoli (Wagman), *Silence: Mapai and the Holocaust, 1939–1942* (Hebrew) (Jerusalem 1994); Dalia Ofer, *Aliyah, Golah*, and the *Yishuv*: Ben Gurion's Policy during the Holocaust" (Hebrew), *Cathedra* 43 (March 1987): 69–90; Yechiam Weitz, *Aware But Helpless: Mapai and the Holocaust, 1943–1945* (Hebrew) (Jerusalem 1994; henceforth: Weitz, *Aware But Helpless*); Shabtai Teveth, *Ben Gurion: The Burning Ground, 1886–1948* (Boston 1987); Tuvia Friling, "Ben Gurion and the Holocaust of European Jewry, 1939–1945: A Stereotype Reexamined," *Yad Vashem Studies* 18 (1988): 199–232; idem, "Changing Roles: The Relationship between Ben Gurion, the Yishuv, and She'erith Hapletah 1942–1945." Pp. 480-456 in: *She'erith Hapletah 1944–1948: Rehabilitation and Political Struggle*, ed. Yisrael Gutman and Avital Saf (Jerusalem 1990; henceforth: *She'erith Hapletah*).

[8] Dalia Ofer, "From Survivors to New Immigrants—She'erith Hapletah and Aliyah." Pp. 304-336 in *She'erith Hapletah*; Hagit Lavsky, "The Survivors of the Holocaust and the Establishment of the State of Israel" (Hebrew), *Cathedra* 55 (March 1990): 175–81; idem, "A Community of Survivors: Bergen-Belsen As a Jewish Centre after 1945," *Journal of Holocaust Education*, 5:2–3 (1996): 162–177, (henceforth, Lavsky A community of Survivors)

[9] Weitz, *Aware But Helpless*; Dina Porat, *The Blue and Yellow Stars of David: The Zionist Leadership in Palestine and the Holocaust, 1939–1945* (Cambridge, MA 1990).

[10] Irit Kenan, *Holocaust Survivors and the Emissaries from Eretz-Israel: Germany 1945–1948* (Hebrew) (Tel Aviv 1996; henceforth, Kenan, *Holocaust Survivors and the Emissaries*).

[11] Idith Zertal, *From Catastrophe to Power: Holocaust Survivors and the Emergence of Israel* (Berkeley 1998).

[12] Hagit Lavsky, "Liberated, But Not Free: The Nature of the Jewish Organization of Bergen-Belsen" (Hebrew), *Hatzionut* 18 (1994): 9–37; idem, "A Community of Survivors. Ze'ev

Mankowitz, "Zionism and She'erith Hapletah." Pp. 211–30 in: *She'erith Hapletah* (henceforth: Mankowitz, "Zionism and She'erith Hapletah"); Kenan, *Holocaust Survivors and the Emissaries.*

[13] Shmuel Krakowski "Memorial Pprojects and Memorial Institutions Initiated by She'erit Hapletah." Pp. 388–398 in: *She'erith Hapletah.*

[14] Gershon Greenberg, ">From Hurban to Redemption: Orthodox Jewish Thought in the Munich Area, 1945–1948," *Simon Wiesenthal Center Annual* 6 (1989): 81–112.

[15] Hanna Yablonka, *Survivors of the Holocaust: Israel after the War* (Basingstoke 1999).

[16] The Palmah was a selective unit for special operations established in 1942 by the underground Jewish defense forces. Its members combined life in kibbutzim with military training and activities. In the Israeli ethos it became the exalted symbol of the new Jewish defense force. See Alon Kadish, *To Arms and Farms: The Hachsharot in the Palmah* (Hebrew) (Efal 1995).

[17] Jacob Markovitzky, *Fighting Ember: Gahal Forces in the War of Independence* (Hebrew) (Tel Aviv 1995).

[18] Dalia Ofer, "Holocaust Survivors as Immigrants: The Case of Israel and the Cyprus Detainees," *Modern Judaism* 16 (1996): 1–23.

[19] An organization, established in 1934, to assist in the immigration of youth from Nazi Germany. Some 6000 youth from Germany and countries it annexed reached Palestine through the organization. After the establishment of the state it was also involved in the immigration and absorption of youth from Islamic countries.

[20] Shlomo Bar-Gil, *They Sought a Home and Found a Homeland: Youth Aliyah and the Education and Rehabilitation of Holocaust Survivors, 1945–1955* (Hebrew) (Jerusalem 1999).

[21] Dan Bar-On, *Between Fear and Hope: The Story of Five Families of Holocaust Survivors to the Third Generation* (Hebrew) (Tel Aviv 1994); Dina Wardi, *Memorial Candles: Children of the Holocaust,* (London 1992).

[22] Gila Menahem and Ephraim Ya'ar, "Emigrants, Refugees, and Survivors in Israel: The First Two Generations" (Hebrew). Pp. 191–209 in: *Israel in the Great Wave of Immigration* (above, n. 6).

[23] Tom Segev, *The Seventh Million* (New York 1993).

[24] Dalia Ofer, "Israel". Pp. 836–923 in: *The World Reacts to the Holocaust;* idem, "Linguistic Conceptualization of the Holocaust in Palestine and Israel, 1942–53," *Journal of Contemporary History* 31 (1996): 567–95.

[25] Dalia Ofer, "The Strength of Remembrance: Commemorating the Holocaust during the First Decade of Israel," *Jewish Social Studies: History Culture and Society,* 6:2 (winter 2000): 24–55; *Memory and Awareness of the Holocaust in Israel,* ed. Yoel Rappel (Hebrew) (Tel Aviv 1988); Roni Stauber, *Lesson for This Generation: Holocaust and Heroism in Israeli Public Discourse in the 1950s* (Hebrew) (Jerusalem 2000).

[26] Don Handelman, *Models and Mirrors: Towards an Anthropology of Public Events* (Cambridge 1990).

[27] James Edward Young, *The Texture of Memory: Holocaust Memorials and Meaning* (New Haven 1993).

[28] See above, nn. 24, 34, and 35.

[29] E.g.: Nili Keren, "The Impact of Public Opinion Shapers and of Historical Research on the Development of Educational Thought and Educational Programs Concerning the Holocaust in High Schools and in Informal Education in Israel (1948–1981)" (Hebrew), Ph.D. thesis, The Hebrew University of Jerusalem, 1985; Ruth Firer, *The Agents of Zionist Education* (Hebrew). Haifa and Tel Aviv 1985; Nurit Govrin, "The Holocaust in the Hebrew Literature of the Younger Generation" (Hebrew), *Zafon* 3 (1994): 151–60; Hanna Yaoz, *Three Generations of Israeli Poets on the Holocaust* (Hebrew) (Tel Aviv 1990); Sidra Ezrahi, "Revisioning the Past: The Changing Legacy of the Holocaust in Hebrew Literature," *Salmagundi: The Literary Imagination and the Sense of the Past* 68–69 (fall 1985–winter 1986): 245–70.

146

[30] Simon Herman, *Jewish Identity: A Social Psychological Perspective* (Beverly Hills 1977); Charles S. Liebman and Eliezer Don-Yehiya, *Civil Religion in Israel: Traditional Judaism and Political Culture in the Jewish State* (Berkeley 1983). A study by Uri Farago on Israeli high school students has supported Herman's findings. See Uri Farago, "Jewish Identity of Israeli Youth, 1965–1985" (Hebrew), *Yahadut Zemanenu* 5 (1989): 259–85.

[31] Hannah Yablonka, *The State of Israel vs. Adolf Eichmann*, (Hebrew), (Tel Aviv 2001).

[32] Dalia Ofer, "History Memory and Identity: Perception of the Holocaust in Israel." In: Uzi Rabhon and Chaim Waxman (eds.), *Jews in Israel: Contemporary Social and Cultural Patterns,* (University Press of New England, in print)

[33] Micha Balf, "Between Mt. Carmel and the Mediterranean: The Development of Public Commemoration of the Holocaust in Kibbutz Ma'agan Michael and Ma'ayan Tzvi" (Hebrew), M/A. thesis, Hebrew University of Jerusalem, 1998; Baumel Judy, " 'In Everlasting Memory': Individual and Communal Holocaust Commemoration in Israel," *Israel Affairs* 1:3 (1995): 146–70; Jackie Feldman, "It is my Brother Whom I am Seeking: Israeli Youth Voyages to Holocaust Poland" (Hebrew), Ph.D. thesis, Hebrew University of Jerusalem, 2000.

[34] See, e.g., Nili Keren, Gila Zakovitch, and Yair Auron, *Antisemitism and Racism: A Study of the Attitudes of High School Students in Israel* (Hebrew) (Tel Aviv 1997).

[35] Isaac Deutscher, *The Non-Jewish Jew and Other Essays* (London, New York, and Toronto 1968), 136–37.

THE HOLOCAUST IN THE PALESTINIAN PERSPECTIVE

Ata Qaymari

THE Holocaust, as an extreme event in history that happened to a very special, and what could be described as a controversial group of people, aroused a wide range of reactions throughout much of the world. These cover the whole spectrum of human response to historical events from end to end, from complete denial and denunciation to total identification, affection and solidarity.

This description largely fits the Palestinian people's stand on the Holocaust, but with some significant difference. It differs from the European stand, especially that prevailing in Germany where there is a great sense of guilt and responsibility for spawning a racist movement that, when it came to power, led the country to such extreme deeds. There is, too, the other extreme in Germany, which comprises total denial and rejection of any responsibility. It also differs both in kind and degree from the attitudes among other European countries and peoples, many of whom also feel guilt for having allowed the Holocaust to happen and for leaving the Jews to their horrible fate, though with less of a sense of accountability.[1]

The Palestinian situation also differs greatly from that of other countries and peoples who are far away from responsibility, and thus guilt, such as other Third World countries. It must be recognized that the Palestinians are in a special situation because, although they were not directly affected by the Holocaust, either as victims or perpetrators, their indirect connection is unique.

'Nothing to do with us'

From this particularity, of being totally innocent of any responsibility for the Holocaust, that terrible catastrophe of the Jewish people, which ended with a metaphorically identical Catastrophe of their own, stems the whole reaction, response and stand of the Palestinian people. The particularity leads almost all Palestinians to the conviction that whatever happened in Europe has nothing do with us. We are not Germans, not to say Nazis, and do not bear any responsibility; we are not an imperialist power who could have helped or rescued the Jews from their fate; and we are not anti-Semitic nor do we hate the Jews nor sympathize with anti-Semitism, for we ourselves are Semites.

Thus, why on earth should we bear the results of the other's deeds?

Despite some difference in nature, cause and form from denial of the Holocaust elsewhere, denial does exist among Palestinians. The strongest denial relates to the numbers. The man in the Palestinian street finds it difficult and incredible to accept the extreme number of six million Jews being deliberately driven to their death in gas furnaces.[2] He would relate this to what he is deeply convinced is the global widespread propaganda of the Jews, or the "Almighty" Zionist movement which, he believes, tends to exaggerate events and numbers in order to extract affection, support and financial compensation for the claimed descendants of those killed in Europe during World War II.

And although it does not help to promote any of the Palestinian goals, the denial or diminution of the numbers killed in the Holocaust is widespread, partly because it is really unbelievable in its extremism, and partly because the events of World War II are far away and intangible for most Palestinians, while Palestinian suffering is close and visible.

Another major form of Palestinian denial relates to the way in which the Jews were killed. Some would say that even if there was deliberate killing in gas furnaces, it could only refer to Nazi pilot projects and not to a program of total destruction of the Jews. This is so in spite of awareness of the racist and murderous nature of the Nazis, and of the fact that many people, including Jews, were killed during the war in places subject to occupation by troops or bombardment or other suffering due to military action.

Related to the same line of thought, another method of reducing the magnitude of the numbers involved is to make a comparison with other World War II statistics. Some contend that even the number of six million should be seen in the perspective of the 50 million people killed during the war.

On the other hand, there is a widespread feeling among many Palestinians of solidarity with the Holocaust's survivors. This is common in leftist circles and among ex-Communists, who tend to be acutely aware of the political and historical background of World War II, in which the racist Nazis were the devil confronting almost the whole world, including the Communist Soviet Union. It also stems from political, cultural, ideological and sometimes religious affiliations. Those who adopt liberal, democratic and especially communist values strongly condemn the Holocaust and express affection for and solidarity with its survivors. Among others, Islam, as a culture or a religion, can also be the basis for a special reaction towards the Holocaust whereby the cruelty and racism of Western civilization is denounced in contrast with Islam's *Tasamoh* (tolerance) under which Jews were legally protected, socially accepted and religiously justified.

Thus, alongside those Arabs and Palestinians who dismiss the Holocaust as a Zionist exaggeration, are other voices that call for sharing the grief over a universal human tragedy.

Many Palestinians perceive the Holocaust directly through the prism of their *Nakba*, the counterpart of the Holocaust in Palestinian history, in which their whole social, economic and cultural fabric was destroyed and uprooted. This perception is usually a reaction to the national ethos which the Jews have constructed out of their Holocaust, accompanied by very strong criticism and rage by Palestinians who maintain, "We are not the cause, but still we are obliged to bear the effects."

This rage is frequently expressed through astonished questioning by many Palestinians: "How can a state that claims to be the refuge of the descendants of the people who had such a horrible experience in human history advocate or support the oppression of any other people?" Equally provocative to Palestinians is the ambivalent Israeli popular stand towards the atrocities by Israeli soldiers and officials in the occupation of Palestinian lands. While Palestinians see a strong reaction to any practice or event which has the slightest connection with or connotation of the Holocaust, such as soldiers drawing signs or numbers on the arms of Palestinian detainees, hardly any response can be discerned with regard to other actions of exploitation, torture or harassment.

The greatest cause for rage is that Israel attracts considerable support and solidarity because, or against the background, of the Holocaust while continuing to deny Palestinians their basic and legitimate rights to self-determination and a return to their homeland. Israel exploits world understanding of the Zionist claim that, without a strong Jewish entity, it will never be possible to guarantee that the Holocaust will not recur.

Who is the victim?

A widespread view among Palestinians is that the Jews are using, indeed abusing or misusing, the Holocaust not only to rally support for Israel's aggression against Palestinians, but also to diminish or underestimate Palestinian sufferings. This Jewish claim as the "ultimate victim" is provocative to Palestinians. They see its expression in the absolute rejection by many Jews of any comparison of any kind of other tragedies and catastrophes with the Holocaust. "How dare you compare anything with the Holocaust!" is the usual Jewish reaction." "In the Holocaust an entire people was persecuted and doomed to total annihilation!" they (rightly) say.

The impression among Palestinians is that the Jews tend to claim a monopoly over suffering and assume the image of the ultimate victim, thus negating the sensitivity which the descendants of the Holocaust should show towards the suffering of others. For many Palestinians, the Holocaust seems an excuse and a camouflage for the atrocities and injustices which Israel thrusts upon them.

The envy

In the eyes of many Palestinians and Arabs, the Zionist movement has converted the Holocaust into a means to gain political and economic benefits, besides exploiting it for the advancement of the occupation and settlement. This seems a response of envy of the part of Palestinians, more than anything else. For although it implies an objective criticism of the occupation and settlement of their lands, this response insists on connecting the Holocaust with further Zionist activities without being able, psychologically at least, to denounce the latter while missing the opportunity to identify with the former. The indifferent and negligent stand of many Palestinians towards the Holocaust thus plays into the hands of Zionism.

This "envy" - and I stress that I use the term metaphorically, as with rage - again expresses itself in competition over the question of "who is the victim?" While the Jews claim the status of "ultimate victim", the Palestinians compete with them by assuming the status of the "present victim". "We are the only people left in the world who still live under occupation," Palestinians frequently say. Or even, "We are the Jews of the Middle East", in half-recognition of Jewish suffering throughout history, accompanied by a half-claim for the status of principal underdog of current times.

The Palestinians further argue that, even if our catastrophe does not include such comprehensive annihilation as in the Holocaust, it is no less catastrophic to destroy a whole society with its material, social and cultural presence on a certain land and to drive its people out their homeland into exile, thus depriving them of their natural right to return for generations, and all within the continuation of injustices, occupation, suppression, oppression, ethnic cleansing and apartheid policies. "While your tragedy is in the past, our tragedy is still going on," we rightly say.[3]

The Nakba versus the Holocaust

It is obvious that each of these two events has its own particularity, and it is impossible to match or compare them. However, because of the context that fate has forged in bringing both peoples together; it is instructive to realize how common human tragedy is. Although it is not possible to trace it back to the effects of the Holocaust or of Zionist practices, there are significant similarities in the ways in which both communities address their catastrophe, the Holocaust on the one hand and the Nakba on the other.

In dealing with their Nakba, Palestinians adopt a similar approach, in commemoration and historiography, to that adopted by the Jews towards their Holocaust. The Palestinians are trying, just as the Jews did and are still doing, to gather a kind of collective memory that preserves their own social, cultural and historical fabric. Oral history collection is a popular historiographical approach among Palestinian historians and researchers. Attempts are being made to build up the national museum as a culmination of attempts to restore the heritage and formulate the national ethos of the Palestinians, both as a political tool for preserving the national entity and as an effective way to mobilize the people into a process of national struggle to gain their legitimate rights.[4]

Palestinians stress folklore, costumes and wedding traditions in addition to preserving symbols of the Nakba - keys of the refugees' original houses, memories and refugees referring to themselves by the original names of their villages and towns and not the refugee camps they live in - "I am from Zakariya", a Palestinian refugee who lives in Deheshe camp near Bethlehem will most likely say when asked where is he from, or the general name Returnees (*'Aidun*) instead of Refugees (*Laji'un*). All this and other forms of identification recall the Israeli attempts to create a part of their national ethos out of the Holocaust - such as the Yad Vashem institution - along with historical and religious myths.[5]

To a great extent, the Palestinian ethos is built around the refugee question and peasant culture, as a symbol of the right of return of the refugees to their land

- the object and subject of fellaheen activity and as the source of life, dignity and existence.

In my opinion, further research should be undertaken to examine the similarities in the human response to catastrophes such as the Holocaust and the Nakba. Both events left large numbers of people with destroyed lives. They found themselves obliged to face the demands of survival that could sometimes be even more horrible and heroic than facing death itself. To any possible extent that the Holocaust and the Nakba are compatible, it would be illuminating to see what similar and perhaps even almost identical means and human forces the survivors of both catastrophes used to face the challenge of survival. Go and listen to a Holocaust survivor and a Nakba survivor and ask them what they did to overcome the trauma and to continue living and you might find almost the same adjectives and superlatives. Just as human nature is similar, so too are human reactions to the trauma of catastrophe and tragedies.

These similarities, were they to be traced and compared in the two cases, could bring more mutual understanding and solidarity.

The future

As much as it was, is and may still be necessary for the Jews to remember the Holocaust as part of their national ethos, it is no less necessary for them to overcome it and, in one sense, even to "forget" it. As long as the Jews cannot overcome the trauma of their Holocaust and continue to fear future integration with others, it will be impossible for them to reach forgiveness and reconciliation. In this regard, it is not the Germans who need this change of attitude by Jews, but the Palestinians, who were affected by the results of the Holocaust and who continue to carry the consequences of the refusal by Jews to overcome their trauma and thus accept the implication of a reconciliatory attitude towards the Palestinian cause as part of a solution of the conflict.

If the Holocaust continues to shape our present and our future, it will not enable the Jews to overcome their fears and thus establish normal relations that are not based on historical psychological precipitants, but instead on future prospects and potentials.

The responsibility

It is obvious that there was no responsibility whatsoever, direct or indirect, by Palestinians for the Holocaust. But this innocence did not exempt them from the effects of the Holocaust that culminated in the establishment of the State of Israel, the widespread international recognition of it, and all the accompanying Palestinian tragedy.

However, Palestinians must understand that innocence is not the rule of the game, but rather the different political, economic and cultural circumstances that constitute fate.

Palestinians have to work on their reaction towards the Holocaust in the direction of being able to recognize and to acknowledge the other's agony and suffering on a human basis, and to stand alongside the Jews in honoring the memory of Holocaust victims. They should learn not to mix their anger against occupation with a human reaction to the suffering of the other. They should learn the need to identify with the wretched of the earth, even if these happen to be their enemies at the moment, for these same people will surely be their friends when the time comes and a solution to the conflict is found. Such an attitude will help the Jews not only to overcome their trauma, but also to identify with the three forms of the Palestinian agony, namely, racial discrimination, occupation and exile.

The Palestinians should recognize the Holocaust and its victims, not only in their numbers, but also explicitly, using the names of the victims. When names substitute for numbers and the conflict is thus humanized, the solution will be round the corner.

---

[1] In her book, *Denying the Holocaust* (Penguin, 1994,) Deborah Lipstadt passionately evaluates Holocaust denial as a set of cranky ideas that sometimes takes the form of respectable academic accounts.

[2] See *The Destruction of the European Jews* by Raul Hilberg, (Holmes & Meier, 1985). It is the internationally acclaimed first major account, originally published in 1961, of the Nazis' Final Solution. Based on reliable historical sources, it estimates the number of Jews killed as 5.1 million. Subsequent studies have amended this figure to 6 million.

[3] *The Holocaust and Collective Memory* by Peter Novick (Bloomsbury, 2000), argues that portraying the Holocaust as a uniquely Jewish catastrophe has the effect of downgrading other genocides.

[4] Oral History and Testimonies is a widespread approach among Palestinian historians and researchers. A wide range of internet sites provide the oral testimonies of survivors and photo galleries of people and destroyed villages in Palestine . See for example www.alNakba.org.

[5] For a more detailed account of the experience of the Jews in Europe during World War II, see *The Holocaust* by Martin Gilbert (HarperCollins, 1987), which draws on archival documents and the words of ordinary people.

DISCUSSION 4

Dalia Ofer and Ata Qaymari

DALIA OFER: I would like to make a few major points to place my paper in the context of our discussion, in particular, the importance of the role of the Holocaust, not only its historiography, but also its perception in the awareness of Jews in general, not only Israeli Jews. Although I cannot say that research on the role of the Holocaust is comprehensive, we have learned so far that this is a formative event in the memory of the Jewish people and of Israeli Jews. As time goes by, it becomes even more important in Western civilization.

Perhaps 20 years ago I began to confront how difficult it is - and was already so in 1948 - for Palestinians to understand Israelis as victims because of their experience. But this does not diminish the fact. By Israelis, I mean those Jews who lived in Palestine. We must remember that a large proportion of the people who immigrated to Palestine from the end of World War II until the establishment of the state, and during the first years of what we call the mass immigration, were Holocaust survivors.

The definition of Holocaust survivors is broad. They felt they were living the construction of memory, that they were the real survivors of the Holocaust, and that the Jewish community, as a community, continued to exist as a community of survivors, although not all of them were survivors in the precise sense of the word. And with the passage of time, in the Israeli mentality, the feeling was that they continued to be potential victims of the Palestinian-Arab, Jewish-Palestinian conflict. This is, again, a concept that is important to grasp about Israeli self-understanding.

Despite the fact that the attitude of Israelis to the Holocaust is diverse, and despite the fact that it changed over time and was formulated differently in different periods of the development of the state, it did become a formative event in Israeli awareness. For example, during the war itself, the information about mass killings came to Palestine - and not only to Palestine, but also to the democracies - and was confirmed. There was a lot of information in the papers all the time, but it was difficult to comprehend it. Something that is so unprecedented is hard to grasp. But, at least formally, from December 1942, the government acknowledged it and the Jewish Agency announced it. So we can look at this date, although I think it took years for the people really to internalize it. When we read the documentation, what was written in the papers, the discussions among the Jewish Agency and other committees, we see that there was a lot of questioning about how this could be.

Why did the Jews go like sheep to the slaughter? This is the famous expression that arose out of Vilna, Krakow, in the Diaspora, but that was also repeated in Palestine. The context is important when it was said in Palestine. This is almost a blaming of the Jews. How could it happen that Jews were killed in such large numbers? This is one example of how difficult the process was.

With time, things changed, not linearly, but with different players and different voices coming up to the public stage, expressing either personal memories or memories of communities. Books were published. Historiography was developed. There were debates such as the Hannah Arendt debate. All these things contributed to the formulation of the understanding of the process and of the events that had taken place, and along with that, the awareness and the role of the Holocaust within Israeli society.

We have talked about the Palestinian catastrophe, the Nakba. But we don't lack sources about the fate of the Jews. Right away, when the war ended, they were available. We didn't have to wait 30 years or 50 years according to the rules of archives. First, archival papers were taken by the Allies, some by the Russians which are only becoming available now, but a large proportion was in the hands of the Western Allies, and the Nuremberg trials already made use of that documentation. In fact, the Jewish issue was completely marginal in the Nuremberg trials. This testifies to the fact that, just after the war, and despite the shock of the discovery of the concentration camps - Auschwitz was the only death camp that was not destroyed and that was captured. It was taken by the Russians who did not release all the photographs until much later. There was a great deal of suspicion between the Allies - the Cold War actually started during the war - and what the Russians released was limited and not necessarily trusted.

But the pictures were in people's minds. All the documentaries that came out in the beginning were about Bergen Belsen, Mauthausen, not death camps but forced labor and concentration camps. In the last stage of the war, when the Germans were in retreat, they didn't want to leave the prisoners in Eastern Europe, so they took them in death marches to these places, and there was great shock at their discovery.

But the Jewish Holocaust, the genocide of the Jews, was not a major theme at that time. Academic historical writing began in 1961 when Raul Hilberg's book, "The Destruction of European Jewry," came out.

The problem was Jewish sources. Most of the Jews were murdered. This was perhaps the only war goal that was nearly achieved by the Nazis. But already, during the war, there was a great historical sense among the victims that they had to leave documentation for history. They didn't want that period to be remembered through the eyes of the murderers, through the documentation of the Nazis. They were thinking that it was not feasible that the world would be conquered and transformed by the Nazis, and therefore, they must leave documentation so future generations would know what had happened.

We see two pulls in their writings, one the future of the Jewish people - and they did believe there would be a future. They couldn't imagine a world without European Jewry, Eastern European Jewry mostly. The other was the universal pull, man to man. We see these two main motivations which led them to feeling

155

compelled to leave documentation. Another element of the importance of the Holocaust was the role of the survivors in the struggle for the creation of the Jewish state. This also changed in the historiography. It began with emphasis on the Jewish emissaries who came from the Yishuv to Germany. The first were soldiers in the Jewish Brigade in the British army who, already in 1945, made contact with survivors.

But more research has been done on the survivors themselves, from Poland, Germany, Italy, Austria. The activism and the will to return to life of the survivors played an extremely important role in the process of activating the Jewish community in general. This was one of the great moments of the Zionist leadership, particularly of Ben Gurion. These people had suffered so much, had been under such duress and yet survived, and he felt that what should be done was to create rehabilitation centers because they would be completely broken. In the fall of 1944, Ben Gurion went to Bulgaria. He wanted to go to Romania, but the Soviets would not allow him in. There were about 400,000 Jews there. In Bulgaria, about 40,000 Jews. Ben Gurion realized their potential, and how he, as a politician, a leader, a statesman, could mobilize this power.

Ben Gurion's concept, which was formulated and crystallized during this time, was that, in order to push forward their political goals, the Jews should use their weakness as a source of strength. They would not be able to fight the British. They would not be able to fight the world of Nazism. The only power they had was perceived as justice.

In the 1930s, when Nazism came to power, the issue of Jewish refugees had already come up. Throughout the war, but particular afterwards, this crystallized in his mind. That's why illegal immigration became so important. That is also why he thought, after the summer of 1946, when the terrorist acts against the British came to a dead end, that we have to retreat to the basic idea of using the weakness as a mobilizing force. This is important in the crucial period between 1944 to November 1947. And again, it is amazing when we look at these Holocaust survivors. Not all of them had been in Nazi death camps or forced labor camps. In fact, there were fewer of those because most people who entered Nazi camps simply did not survive. Some had been in hiding, and many people in countries occupied by the Nazis had not yet been deported because the governments of Rumania and Bulgaria resisted deportation for different reasons.

In the summer of 1946, the British decided to deport illegal immigrants to Cyprus. Over 55,000 people went through Cyprus. One boat carrying 15,000 people arrived at the shores of Israel, and then was turned back. The people on the *Exodus* ship were deported to Germany. But these people were willing. Had they not been willing, nothing could have happened. And not only were they willing, but there was always tension about who would go and who would remain. There were rules. They didn't want to take pregnant or older women. Demographically speaking, it was a young community of survivors, for obvious reasons. In many other respects as well, the will of the survivors to return to life is amply demonstrated. There were many marriages and many babies born in the DP camps from 1945 on. Waves of people arrived in the DP camps between 1945 and 1948, and the camps were finally dissolved in the 1950s. One camp remained for people who were sick until arrangements were made to bring them to Israel.

The role of the survivors in constructing and formulating and impacting the Jewish community in Israel, Israeli Jews, is extremely important and far beyond their numbers. The number of survivors in Israel after the establishment of the state, after May 1948, was 360,000 to 400,000. The overall immigration to the end of the 1950s, together with the immigration of North African Jews of over one million, amounted to only about a third of the population. But their impact on the society, culture, economics, politics, and certainly the construction of memory, is extremely significant. It was that first generation who established how Yad Vashem worked.

Members of the first and second Knesset already included Holocaust survivors. This is amazing when you think about first-generation immigrants to a country. There was the Berman coalition which later became *MAPAM*. I think he became part of the Communist party, although I'm not sure. Barhoff, Grossman, many Holocaust survivors, were not only members of Knesset, but also of the committees before the Law of Yad Vashem was passed in 1953, and their impact was important.

All this contributed to the ethos of "From Holocaust to Revival" that became fixed in Israeli society and the Jewish community in general. This ethos is based on a traditional Jewish ethos of *galut* and *geulah*, exile and redemption. Galut and geulah were not imposed, but grew up in a way with the dialogue and with confronting the present situation, while also taking a lot from other traditional Jewish sources. Even the expression, "Holocaust survivors", in Hebrew is not actually Holocaust survivors. In Zionist and Jewish rhetoric it is *shearit haplita*, the remnants.

In one of my articles I tried to go through the history of this expression, beginning with the Bible, in Isaiah, when he talks about the destruction. Then he says the redemption will be of the remnants, and these remnants will rebuild the Jewish people. The expression, "remnants," first arose within the community of survivors. One American sociologist who worked with the survivors called this community of survivors in Germany and in DP camps "a community without an elite." I think this is incorrect. Every community has an elite. It just depends on how you define it. There were people, despite their youth and the fact that the war had interrupted their education, who did have a great deal of cultural heritage.

The last point I want to make is something that disturbs me very much. Many years ago, we held a small conference at the Van Leer Institute of various people working on the Holocaust. We called it "The Use and Abuse of the Holocaust." Without going into all the phases after 1967, there was - and still is, although I think it is a little less now - a lot of manipulation of the Holocaust among the political leadership, both right and left. This is a disturbing phenomenon, entirely contrary to the magnitude and meaning of the events, and to the fact that we have still not absorbed all the impact. It should be treated with more respect than what we have seen, not only before 1967, not only before that war, but even much earlier. We see it mostly after the 1970s, but even Ben Gurion compared Nasser to Hitler.

157

The Holocaust became a tool of combat between the Labour party and Herut in the 1950s and 1960s. German reparations, the Kastner affair*, the selling of armaments to Germans, and the Holocaust entered into each of these discussions. But we begin to see it on a much larger scale after 1967, and a great number of historians and educators resented it. Dealing with this is still an important part of my educational role when teaching this subject in the university.

ATA QAYMARI: Dalia's presentation was quite illuminating and very helpful in understanding the relationship and the contributions of the Holocaust and its survivors to the establishment of the State of Israel and its aftermath. In a way, I can't understand how someone could think - and I am quoting - that the terrible catastrophe that was liable to wipe out every prospect of establishing a state was now transformed into a factor that helped the Yishuv. This is a contradiction.

The claim was that the survivors of the Holocaust did not contribute to the establishment of the State of Israel. The State of Israel was the development of the interior Yishuv itself, without the Holocaust. Maybe the Holocaust accelerated the process, but it could not have been stopped or its direction changed. Also no less illuminating is the heroism of the survivors in rehabilitating themselves and returning to life with prospects and with prosperity.

But this is not what I want to stress in my reflections on Dalia's paper. I want to describe the Palestinian perception of the Holocaust. It starts with, "What do we have to do with it? We are not the Nazis." This first reaction might lead to strong identification and solidarity with the survivor.

The other reaction is based on an awareness of the political and international circumstances. Those with a liberal democratic - or even communist - background, understand the global circumstances during World War II and its results and the position against the Nazis of the Soviet Union and the other Allies, and their stand results from that point of view. But whatever position they hold, Palestinians have nothing to do with the Holocaust. We are innocent. We haven't done anything to you. Why do we have to bear the responsibility or the consequences of this Holocaust? Furthermore, why should this affect our demand for the right of return to our homeland? Even if you suffered in Europe and through the Holocaust, what does that have to do with our right to come back to our homeland? A widespread claim among Palestinians is that the Jews use the Holocaust to diminish our cause. Israeli Jews say, "We had the Holocaust. How can you compare that with what happened to you? We were killed. We were annihilated. Nothing to that extent happened to you." But anybody who is suffering will revolt against someone who tries to diminish his suffering and tell him it's all right. This stance stems from the perception that the Jews try to give the impression that they have a monopoly over suffering and victimhood. There can be no comparison. The Jews say they are the ultimate victims

ADEL MANNA: Ultimate and eternal.

DALIA OFER: Not eternal, but ultimate.

ATA QAYMARI: No comparison is accepted. The argument is that people were physically annihilated. Six million Jews were killed, and that is the ultimate victimization.

Another question relates to the number of six million. Sometimes Palestinians claim that the Jews are exaggerating. It did not reach such huge numbers. But in fact, what does it matter? If the Jews say six million, we should accept the number to the last person, to the last name, not only the number. Each one of them matters. We are talking about human lives, and maybe that's why some Jews reject any kind of comparison between Israeli behavior now and Palestinian claims that their behavior is like that of the Nazis.

"Why are you doing to us what the Nazis did to you?" This is the Palestinian reaction. And along with diminishing the number, some also mention the great numbers of other victims in World War II, just to imply a lessening of the impact on the Jews. In other words, not only millions of Jews were killed, but 50 million others were also killed in that war. This is an attempt to diminish the Jewish catastrophe as we feel the Israelis diminish our catastrophe.

Palestinians question why Israeli society did not revolt against its soldiers who put signs or numbers on the arms of Palestinian detainees. Of course they must revolt against such a thing because of the Holocaust connotations. But to the contrary, most also do not react to even worse civil actions and forms of torture against these detainees.

Moreover, it is the Palestinian perception that Israel is widely exploiting and manipulating the Holocaust for political purposes in order to continue to deprive Palestinians of their legitimate rights of self-determination and return to their homeland. Palestinians believe this is deliberate on the part of Israelis. It is not something authentic. It is a political manipulation rather than an existential expression.

Palestinians do not understand how Israelis could do these things to us if they are victims. If they are really victims, why are they victimizing us?

Another reaction is that of envy, or a kind of competition over who is more of a victim. We say we are no less victimized. The Holocaust survivors revived themselves and rehabilitated themselves and now are doing well. They live comfortably. They have a strong state. They can raise their children in good and comfortable conditions, while our tragedy is still going on. The problem is not the victim who was a victim, but the one who continues a victim.

Palestinians are now trying to create similar kinds of historiography, oral history, a commemoration of their Nakba. They are working on rebuilding the national museum and the collective Palestinian memory of the Nakba. There is envy when they see what the Israelis have done with their Nakba, while we are not doing what we should to revive and to exploit our Nakba in order to achieve our own goals.

There is an emphasis on culture, on traditional costumes and wedding rituals, in addition to the preservation of symbols of the Nakba - keys, memories, names of villages. Above all, there is the continuing identification with the original homeland: "I am not from such and such refugee camp, I am from this or that village." In Jordan, I asked many refugees where they were from, and I never met one who didn't name a place in the homeland. They say, "I am from Jaffa." I asked one of them, "Would you really want to go back to Jaffa? Jaffa now is totally Jewish. I doubt you would feel comfortable where there is no education for

159

Arabs and where there is a high percentage of drug dealers. And what would you do there without any work?" The response was, "Even so, I want to come back to my place. This is my only identification." I asked, "What about Ramallah?" He said "No, Ramallah would be another form of exile for me. This is not the way."

That's why the Palestinians even try to change the terminology used to refer to the survivors of the Nakba. Instead of saying refugees, they call themselves returnees. This has to do with the potential. We are potential returnees, not only refugees. The stress is on the future, not only on the past.

I say that in spite of the fact that there really is no comparison between the two cases, quantitatively and qualitatively. But maybe the similarities that can be traced can bring more mutual understanding or more mutual identification and expressions of solidarity.

What is the responsibility of the Palestinians? Are we really responsible for what happened? I once wrote an article saying that the Palestinians are as innocent as a village that sinks on one side of the ocean when there is some geographical disturbance on the other side. Something may happen as a result on the other side of the ocean and a village could sink. How is it responsible? But it has a shared fate.

Finally, as much as it was - and maybe still is - necessary for the Jews to remember the Holocaust, it is also necessary to overcome it, even to forget it in the context of the Israeli-Palestinian conflict. It is not the present. There are other things that should be improved or corrected. One day the Israelis should say, "You know, we have to stop this process of self-victimization, try to be normal and to address real and future questions, try to address the other's tragedy in a somewhat human way, react to it and understand it, and maybe even resolve it."

RUTH KARK: I found Dalia's paper comprehensive and interesting. But I think it's a good illustration of what we discussed earlier, that history is not an exact science, because she presented many historical studies with many different conclusions and ideas. So this is a more general thing we must take with us. Sometimes there are contradictory ideas. More specifically, I relate to the Yishuv's attitude towards what happened in Europe, but also to a more general concept that Dalia mentioned as inter-disciplinary - or I think multi-disciplinary - research .

I did a study on Jewish settlement in the Negev and found that, already in 1933, Ben Gurion and many others were changing their land policy towards the Negev. Earlier, on many occasions when they had to decide which areas they more urgently needed to purchase with the limited amount of money they had, they said the Negev could wait. The change happened early in 1933 - and I have some proof in the documents - and that had a direct relationship to what happened in Germany at that time. This is maybe another event to support what you said about the attitude of the Yishuv.

Going back to another discussion, this change of land policy in the Negev led to what happened when the United Nations Committee came to Palestine. At that time, there were already about 20 Jewish settlements in the Negev. The United Nations Committee was taken there and shown how the Jews were making the desert bloom, as we spoke of earlier. After analyzing political documents, we think this was one of the main reasons why, in the division of Palestine into a Jewish state and an Arab state, the Negev was included in the Jewish state. Many claimed that, in any case, the Negev was deserted and the population was limited, and see what the Jews are accomplishing there. And when they came to President Harry Truman, they brought him this description of the Negev to show why it should become part of the Jewish state. So there was the 1933 change in policy, then the establishment of Negba in 1939, the three observation points in 1943, then the 11 settlements and so on. So this was very instrumental in that process. This is just one example of how we can gain from multi-disciplinary cooperation.

My last point relates to something that I would like to hear you elaborate about more: Arab Israelis or Palestinian Israelis and West Bank Palestinians and Gaza Palestinians and the Holocaust. I would like to hear more about it with reference to two places in your paper. First, you speak about the effect of Holocaust survivors on Israeli society, and you bring up the question of how the Holocaust influences attitudes towards the conflicts in which Israeli society is involved. Then you say that this includes both Israeli Palestinians who are citizens of the country, and Palestinians in the occupied territories, and relates to the attitude towards the Arab states and other countries. One aspect of this last topic is the abuse of the Holocaust for domestic and foreign political purposes.

Second, about Palestinians, you say, in the context of the social history research that you suggest, that it should also analyze developing relationships with and images of the other, the Palestinians living in Israel and in the West Bank and Gaza. I would like to hear more about what you think. Then you quote a study by Zakovitch and Auron, and say that what emerges regarding the images of young people is how they relate to similar behavior towards Jews in the past or the present. And then it also relates to the Palestinians, but I didn't understand that paragraph at all. So please explain the conclusions of this study.

LILY GALILI: There is an ongoing change, not only in the perception - actually, I don't think the perception is changing - but in the rituals, maybe of the ethos, of the Holocaust, with the coming to Israel of a million Russian immigrants. They bring a totally different view. Many of them lost members of their families in the Holocaust, but the Holocaust was never commemorated in the Soviet Union because it was against the law. Instead, they commemorated their victory over the Nazis on 9 May. I think what can be marked as their first real contribution or infiltration into the very closed Israeli ethos is that the Knesset just passed a law that doesn't replace Holocaust Memorial Day, but adds this other day. Now we officially commemorate the day of victory over the Nazis on 9 May

MERON BENVENISTI: We commemorate the 8th. We should understand that what we did to make the Israeli Soviet Russian Jews happy was to add 9 May. But for those of us who remember it, it's 8 May, not 9.

LILY GALILI: It was not done only to make them happy. We are not very good at making our citizens happy.

MERON BENVENISTI: It was a political gesture.

LILY GALILI: It's more meaningful than that. When I speak with them, they tell me that they're always hearing that the State of Israel is the immediate outcome of the Holocaust. But then they say that's the wrong way to look at it. The State of Israel is the outcome of the victory. Without the victory, with just the Holocaust, there would not have been a state. The state is here thanks to the victory. Slowly this is infiltrating into the Israeli ethos. People listen to them, and it's an interesting shift.

PAUL SCHAM: I have three points, one of which was brought up by Ruth about the understanding of enemies. It seems to be a truism that nations are always preparing for their last war, not their next war. This is one of the elements that is almost impossible to escape, given the close connection between the Holocaust and the fight against the Palestinians. The rhetoric, the mindset, was essentially transferred from the Nazis, to some degree, to the Palestinians. The most obvious one who did that was Menahem Begin but, as Dalia mentioned, also Ben Gurion. The imagery is so present that it's almost impossible to escape. I'm not defending it, certainly, but I am saying it's inescapable, after the last experience, that you are trying to prevent that. The sense of awesomeness of the terror of the Holocaust is something you are trying to prevent, and perhaps excessively trying to prevent vis-a-vis Palestinians and the Arab world.

Second, in response to some of the points that Ata raised, is why Israelis can't forget it. I think this is part of the secular religion of Israel. For Jews who cannot relate to traditional Judaism as a religion, this is something that has acquired a status of its own with its own symbols and its own understanding. It has become one of the kinds of glue that hold Israeli society together. This is even more true of the society in which I grew up, the United States. Among American Jews, there are even fewer things holding them together. This is why sometimes Israel and the Holocaust are considered the two main Jewish symbols in the United States, but there's also a lot of truth to that in Israel. Therefore, I believe it is transferred over to the Israeli-Palestinian conflict.

A fundamental question was implied by both of you on which I don't think research has been done. It's an incredibly sensitive topic. Just raising it as a question brings up lots of feelings. And that is, why is it that, ultimately, the survivors of the Holocaust were able to rebuild their lives and the survivors of the Nakba were not? There are many answers and we don't have to rehash them here. But looking at this in a fundamental sense, a neutral sense, it seems that there was a decision by the survivors, aided by the outside, to move on and to rebuild their lives in other countries. On the other hand, the decision by the Palestinians was clearly to wait and to try to return. And we see the results 50 years later.

The context in which I bring this up is that, as someone who works primarily on Israeli-Palestinian projects, many people have raised this issue with me. It is the perception of Israelis and American Jews that Palestinians have stayed in the camps and not done something for themselves, whereas Jewish survivors moved on. The context is to understand that this is the mindset of many Jews, contrasting themselves and saying, "See, we did something for ourselves and the Palestinians didn't." .

ADEL MANNA: Dalia's paper and presentation were very good. I learned a lot. And thank you, Ata, for your reflections.

As a child, I starting thinking about this issue. In the late 1950s, when I was in primary school in Israel, we had to celebrate Israel's independence. The teachers and the headmaster would tell us that Israel liberated us. It was a war of liberation and they liberated us. I started asking questions. Liberated us from whom? At home, I heard my family's personal stories about having been kicked out from our village in January 1949, when I was a year old, six months after the occupation of the village. And my parents called it occupation.

So at home it was occupation. In school it was liberation. And I was puzzled. What was the truth? I told my parents what they taught us in school, and my parents said, "They're collaborators. That's why they tell you what the Minister of Education wants them to tell you." But the main point is that, on the day of celebration, the school was full of Israeli flags. And the next day, the police would come and interrogate some of the students - this happened more than once - because someone drew swastikas on the walls of the school, and there were rumors about who did it.

I began to ask questions: What's the connection between the day of independence and the Nazis? The Jews were the victims of the Nazis. We are the victims of the Jews who kicked us out of our village in 1949. All this began to puzzle me, and I didn't receive adequate answers from my teachers nor from my father. My father is not well-educated. He told me whatever he knew, but I continued to be puzzled. And I think many Palestinians are not only puzzled, but also have been troubled about this issue ever since 1948. According to the Palestinian narrative, they are the victims of the State of Israel, and when they have to study about the Holocaust and to acknowledge that the Jews are the victims - the ultimate victims as was mentioned here - that troubles their narrative. It is difficult to face this issue and to try to study it academically, neutrally, like any other subject.

That's why I think that for many years - maybe still today - most Palestinians, if not all, try to do what Ata more or less told us - either denial, just not to speak about it, or to try to diminish it by claiming it's an exaggeration, it's Israeli Zionist propaganda. Or even, okay, it's all true. So what? What do we have to do with it? We are the victims of the victims, and we are the present-day victims. This is also important. Six million were killed. It was a Holocaust, a great catastrophe for the Jews. But a state was established. The survivors and many other Jews now have a state and they can go on and build themselves up, while we Palestinians continue to suffer from the establishment of this State of Israel.

Most of the time, the two narratives are portrayed as if one side is bad and the other side is good. One side is the victimizer and the other side is the victim. And for the Palestinians, it's clear that they are the victims and the other side is the victimizer. That's why it is so fundamentally difficult for the Palestinians to tackle this issue without emotions, without the background of their suffering. And the abuse of the Holocaust by Israeli or Jewish propaganda makes it even more difficult.

In the late 1950s, when I was a child, Egypt's President Gamal Nasser was, to me and to many others, the hero of pan-Arabism. Those were the years of Syrian-Egyptian unity. And Ben Gurion compared him to Hitler. I couldn't

163

understand the connection. We knew that Hitler had died. He lost the war. But Nasser was trying to do something else. So what's the connection between Nasser and Hitler? Once again, I was puzzled.

So this is the memory I have from my childhood concerning the Holocaust and the connection between the Holocaust and the Nakba of 1948, and how I and many Palestinians tried to deal with it, and are still trying to this day.

As I said, we still don't have good Palestinian research into the Nakba. Not surprisingly, we also don't have any good study of the Holocaust. There is some literature, but this subject awaits historians and others to produce good books and studies. There is also a lot of ignorance among the Palestinians about what happened, in addition to the psychological dimension. The younger generation of Palestinians, at least inside Israel, are ignorant even about the 1948 war. When I give lectures at the university sometimes, they know very little about the history of Palestine in general, or about the details and the facts of the war of 1948. They speak more with slogans than with facts or with an analytical approach to this subject, and they deal with the Holocaust the same way - with slogans and with emotions, rather than academically or realistically.

Earlier we spoke about the fears of the Jewish side, their paranoia and their feeling that they're a minority. These are connected to the Holocaust. And when there are suicide bombs - particularly, for instance, in Netanya, where one or more of those killed were Holocaust survivors - and I see the reactions in the media, I understand how the memory of the Holocaust is revived and the image of the Palestinians becomes even more connected to the victimizer of the Holocaust.

So now the Palestinians are the devil who is coming to kill us and those survivors who fled the Holocaust. This is a tremendous accusation, to portray the Palestinians as if they are continuing what Hitler didn't finish. If I were on the other side, I could see how that can influence and affect public opinion of the generation who doesn't know much. They are spoken to with slogans and with emotions, and the reactions of the people towards the Palestinians are a result of portraying them as if they are continuing the Nazis' mission.

But the Palestinians often don't understand Israelis' reactions when they say, "We are frightened. You are waging an existential war against us." The Palestinians say, "You are frightened? But you are killing us. You have the planes and the helicopters. You are invading our cities. You are not letting us leave our homes. You are demolishing our houses. How are you frightened?"

So without taking the narratives into account, the emotions and the images these days are difficult to understand. And this is now a question for Dalia: Do you feel, particularly in the last year or two, that there is a fusing of the issue of the Holocaust - intentionally or not - with the conflict and the relations between Palestinians and Israelis?

Concerning the question that Paul raised, this is a good example of fast and sometimes provocative comparisons, without intention in this case. As somebody who teaches in Israeli universities and lectures to various audiences, I am also often asked these kinds of questions: "Why do you do this and you don't do that, why do we have Peace Now and you don't have something equivalent, why did we accept this or that and you didn't?" The conclusion underlying those provocative questions is, once again, "We are the good guys and you are the bad guys. We are productive. You are lazy. We are modernized. You are backward." The images behind those questions are clear.

Take the subject of the survivors. First, it's not a good comparison. The Palestinians don't have a state to help the refugees build a life from scratch. You can say, okay, the survivors started to rebuild their lives even before the State of Israel was established. Once again, if you take into account the two societies, what kind of survivors are we speaking about? Most of the refugees are fellahin, peasants who lost their land and homes. The only profession they know is cultivating the land. And when they find themselves living on the margins of the cities of the Arab states, they have no land to cultivate. They are jobless, and they find themselves in those camps, or sometimes in places like Lebanon that don't want them.

There are many other factors why the comparison is not a good one. Nonetheless, if we have to deal with this issue, the assumption that the Palestinians didn't rebuild their lives is not even true. They did. They did it differently than did the Holocaust survivors, but they did it. They didn't just sit in their houses or cafes and do nothing. It is true that, in the first year or two or three, there wasn't much they could do, and most of them thought it would take a month, two months, a year, and then they would be going back. There was no point in dramatically changing the way of life because they would be going back to their villages, to their homes, to cultivate their land. You don't want to invest much in a temporary place because you'll just lose it when you go home. If you build a house, you can't take it with you. That's why they didn't do much in the first few years. But later on, they did begin to revive their lives, or at least the lives of the next generation, within their new context.

One of the conclusions of the Palestinian refugees after the catastrophe was that, in war, in a catastrophe such as that of 1948, you may lose your house, your land, everything you ever built, and the only thing you can take with you is either money or jewelry, if you have it - but most of the fellahin didn't have those things - or education. Education is in your head

This is why there has been so much investment in educating the younger generations. The refugees saw that those who were educated, townspeople or others, made it. They immediately found jobs and started working, whether in Jordan or Lebanon or Syria, or later they went to the Gulf states and made fortunes out of their education. So it might have been too late for them, but they revived their lives by investing in educating the next generation. That's why, from 19 or more percent literacy among the peasants in 1948, within 10 or 20 years you find 90 percent literacy among the Palestinians in the refugee camps. This is a tremendous way of rebuilding your life. The fact that they continued to live in refugee camps doesn't mean that they didn't revive their lives or that they didn't do anything with an eye to the future. Once again, we are dealing with assumptions and images, and we formulate judgments without questioning those assumptions.

MOSHE MA'OZ: Going back briefly to the pre-1948 period, the period of 1947 and the partition resolution, Dalia, you mentioned the debate between historians about the contribution of the Holocaust to the 1947 decision, and I'd like to hear more about that, especially your view. You also mentioned non-Zionist survivors. Of course, many Zionists arrived before the Holocaust, but I want to know about this, the Bundists, for example. Most of them preferred to go to America. But those who came to Israel and were integrated into the Zionist ideology, to what extent did they play a role? Again, I cannot escape going back to what Ruth Kark and others addressed. You called it disturbing. I think it's more than disturbing. I am referring to the impact of the traumatic experience of the Holocaust on Israeli attitudes towards the Palestinians.

In another discussion I mentioned Arab rhetoric and its impact. Here you have Jewish rhetoric and its impact. We mention time and again the equating of Arafat and Hitler, Ben Gurion's statement about Nasser. Of course, the comparison was false. Nasser had an army and a state. Arafat, poor fellow, is no danger to the State of Israel. There have been meetings recently, involving one Israeli scholar in particular, who deals with anti-Semitism and compares Islam to Nazism. Good God! We cannot even imagine how dangerous an impact this has on the mindset of the public.

WALID SALEM: What I have to say falls more in the area of human rights than in history. What we are talking about is something that we cannot address in historical or academic terms alone. This is something that has to do with human values and respect for those human values in our daily lives and relationships. No matter what the rhetoric is about the Nakba or the Holocaust - which is greater and which is less, which is the ultimate - from the point of view of human rights, what happened in the Holocaust and what happened in the Nakba both illustrate a process of dehumanization of the other. The idea that these are sheep and not people, that we the Germans are the superiors, that Arafat is like Hitler, all this results from the dehumanization of the other, feeling that the other is not a human being like me.

ADEL MANNA: And the demonization. Both.

WALID SALEM: When this mentality persists, it leads to danger. This is one of the main questions we need to tackle - the mentality, the beliefs, the values. When people's values contradict human values, what can we do to protect and promote those human values? Because Palestinians see themselves as victims, their minds have been narrow on this subject. They feel what happened to them. They didn't refer to the world outside. They didn't have the money or the opportunity to see other people's problems. They are isolated from the Israeli public, so they cannot be sensitive to the needs of the Israeli people.

ATA QAYMARI: This works in both directions.

WALID SALEM: Okay. And speaking about this only from our side, I feel that, because we have our problems, we have become narrow-minded in a way. As a Palestinian who is committed to human rights, I feel ashamed because my people have not recognized and empathized with the problems of the other. The Israelis also have not empathized with our problems. This, however, might be an idea for a healing process.

Since both our peoples are victims, it seems that healing must be a process that accompanies the political solution, or maybe even precedes it. In this regard, I have a suggestion for both academic research and for human rights. Why don't we use these two catastrophes as a tool for healing? Dalia talked about it being used as a political tool. Why don't we, who believe in human rights, use it differently, in a positive way, as a healing process for both peoples? In order to do that, we need to not only talk about our sufferings - and Ata, I disagree with you that we must forget the Holocaust. We must not forget it. It is forbidden to forget such a huge crime against humanity. We will not forget such a crime at all. But maybe we can use it for healing our relations, in two ways.

First, if possible, I suggest that Israeli researchers and research teams studying the Holocaust stop excluding Palestinians. Include the Palestinians in the process of research. You mentioned a Van Leer seminar about the Holocaust. Next time, include Palestinians so they can integrate this other view into their research on the topic. Second, we talk about our historical relations. I haven't studied Jewish-Arab relations throughout history. There might be bad experiences. There might also be good experiences. Let's talk about them both. Let's try to develop research about when our relations were good, when there was tolerance between us, that could be taught to people on both sides.

This is my suggestion about using the Holocaust and the Nakba in a positive way, to lead to a tolerant future and to a political process combined with a healing process.

ATA QAYMARI: I used "forget" between quotation marks. I don't mean to forget it, but to overcome it.

RAN AARONSOHN: Concerning Ata's comments, you spoke about Palestinian denial of the Holocaust after the Israeli denial of the Palestinian Nakba, and also of mutual suffering. My first question was about research, and I ask again: Has there been any kind of research, even in the context of other studies, in which Palestinians tried to refer to the Holocaust? Has there been any systematic written research? Do Palestinian researchers and academics try to rebut the mainstream Israeli claim that the Holocaust was a unique event by, for instance, comparative studies on the Armenian disaster and so on? Or by relating to Uganda, Kenya, Rwanda and so on? One may go on, unfortunately.

BENJAMIN POGRUND: One theme that seems to come up all the time is a cry for acknowledgment and understanding from each side of the other side. Among Israelis, there is a huge amount of arrogance and obtuseness about Palestinians. If you ask someone if he ever speaks to Palestinians, the guy will say, of course, when I have my car repaired I talk to the mechanic. It's generally at that crude level, and there tends to be a huge amount of misunderstanding and ignorance, and really not wanting to know.

This is relevant to our present reality. At breakfast yesterday, we talked about Camp David when Barak refused to meet Arafat. This was viewed, on the Palestinian side, as an act of dishonor towards Arafat, and was taken really badly by the Palestinians. And I've heard repeatedly, with regard to the Nakba, that the lack of acknowledgment of the hurt that was done is deeply felt. Among Israelis, there is very little understanding of the need to acknowledge what was done. Regardless of what might be done to resolve it, just the need to acknowledge it.

On the Palestinian side, when I talk to friends such as Walid and Adel, I make the point all the time that there's a lack of appreciation on the Palestinian side of Jewish history. We have been talking about the Holocaust, but that's only one aspect. There is a history of centuries of anti-Semitism and of Jewish suffering. In 1948, when there were some who proclaimed aims of driving the Jews into the sea, that reinforced the Jewish experience of anxiety, fear and paranoia. Then there was 1973, and other problems over the years. Today you hear statements by Hamas insisting that they are after all of Israel, not just the West Bank and Gaza. Every Jew is a settler and every Jew must either be killed or driven out. This is a constant reinforcement of age-old Jewish fears.

You can say, "That has nothing to do with us." In many ways, you are right. Why should Palestinians pay the price for the European sins and guilt that helped bring about the State of Israel? The question I put to the Palestinians here: Don't you have to take all this on board? If you want to live in the real world, as Adel and Walid were saying, don't you have to pay heed to this if we are going to move forward?

Israelis have to become more heedful, more caring, more understanding about Palestinian feelings, and Palestinians have to do likewise, or we go nowhere. That's what Walid was getting at, and that's why we work together, particularly in this area.

Adel Manna spoke about how the Israelis view Palestinians as the devil. You're right. But how do we overcome that? What can a group like this do to overcome this?

Ervin Staub, a psychologist at the University of Massachusetts at Amherst, wrote an interesting book called "The Roots of Evil," published by Cambridge University Press. His specialty is why people do terrible things to other people and why people do good things to other people with no hope of reward. I expect Jews, because of our history, to be more caring and more concerned about persecution. I've asked Staub, "Surely you expect Jews, more than anyone else, to be conscious of the effects of persecution, and so to be more careful about it?" His response was, "That's right. On the other hand, people who have survived a terrible trauma can go the other way. They can become like rats in a corner and fight more viciously if they think they are under threat."

So if we are going to try to resolve things here, that is also a factor we have to take into consideration. But I'd like to hear reactions from Palestinians and Israelis about how we can apply all this wonderful knowledge we are gaining here.

FATMEH QASSEM: As a Palestinian raised and educated in Israel, I know much more about the Jewish people and their suffering than I do about Palestinian history or their suffering. I learned about Palestinian suffering only at home, not in any institution or educational system. When I went to the university and said I was Palestinian, my Jewish Israeli colleagues told me I was anti-Semitic. When I was working towards my history teaching certificate, I was required to take 16 or 18 credits in Jewish history and nothing about Palestinian history. There is no such thing as Palestinian or Islamic history at Ben Gurion University.

I think the comparison between the Holocaust and Palestinian-Jewish relations is unfair. Germany, as a state, politically and morally, takes responsibility for what they did. The Israelis not only do not take political responsibility, but they systematically exclude us.

I wonder whether sometimes we might use the Holocaust for some human insights, whether we might look deeply into this historical event and learn from it on the local and the universal levels, and see where it has begun to be used emotionally and manipulatively against the Palestinians. I once went to Yad Vashem with a group of Palestinians and Jews. The first reaction of the Palestinians was, "Oh, this is built on the land of Deir Yassin." I don't even know if that's true or not.

RUTH KARK: No. It's actually Ein Kerem land.

FATMEH QASSEM: But the fact is not even important. The assumption is what shapes our attitudes. Then, on the way out of Yad Vashem, I saw a big picture of the Mufti. Give me a break. What is he doing here, and why? What are you trying to say with this?

My mother and her family were forced to evacuate their village in 1948. I wonder what would be the response if I talked about what happened to this woman, to this family. Do we have the courage to admit the legitimacy of her loss?

I was in Germany five or six years ago with a group of Palestinians, and was very impressed by how the Germans talk about their guilt and their shame and their willingness to take responsibility for what happened to the Jewish people under the Nazi regime. But when I talked about my suffering as a Palestinian - and I was not ranking the suffering, I don't want to say one is more or less than the other - I was surprised by the hostile responses I received.

Again, I'm not talking in general. This was a very personal experience. But what makes people take responsibility for what has happened to others? What motivates us to see the devil in the actions of others? What makes us exclude the other? This is a huge and confusing question.

LILY GALILI: I think this is relevant to our discussion. Walid, Ata and Fatmeh talked about the abuse of the Holocaust, comparing Arafat to Hitler, and I want to remind us that this equation has not been restricted to Palestinians only. We also had Yitzhak Rabin depicted in Nazi uniform. There is also internal abuse of the Holocaust, inside Israeli society. It's not divorced from the other abuse, but it's a more holistic kind of phenomenon than we have been admitting, and we have to deal with it on both levels. We saw depictions of Rabin in Nazi uniform and then in a Palestinian kafiyah, and that sets up the equation between the swastika and the kafiyah. It goes on and on in its impact on society.

ADEL YAHYA: I agree with Ata that the Palestinians feel it is not their problem. The Holocaust is not their fault. It's a European phenomenon and they had nothing to do with it. They actually resent any kind of education about the Holocaust because they feel it is being forced upon them. They are being forced to learn something about a mistake that was committed by others, and they resent that. They say, "What do I have to do with this? It's not my business. And even worse, I've been victimized by it."

They hate the fact that Israelis and Jews have used this massacre against them in order to victimize the Palestinian people. It's impossible to teach Palestinians anything about the Holocaust under these circumstances.

BENJAMIN POGRUND: You told me at one time that that was the

reaction of some people. Others said it was important to know Jewish history and to understand it.

ADEL YAHYA: That was in a special context. We were in Acre, and went to visit the museum at Kibbutz Lochamei HaGeta'ot. Most of the people resented it. They said, "What the hell do we have to do with this? This museum is built on our land. What the hell is a museum about the Holocaust doing on Palestinian-occupied land?" That was the initial response. Those who thought it a was good experience said, "We have to learn from these people how to express our own disaster, our own memory." That was the only rationale they found for themselves to see anything about the Holocaust. They were not willing, at any cost, to learn something about Jewish suffering. They said, "Look at these people. They started from the illegal position of building a museum on our occupied land, and now they're trying to convince us that their Holocaust justifies the suffering we have been subjected to from 1948 to the present."

So it's almost impossible to bring this topic to Palestinians, and even more so to other Arabs outside of Palestine. Somehow, Palestinian intellectuals can understand listening to something about the Holocaust because they feel victimized, and that's a strong feeling. We are victims. This is the biggest issue. And therefore, they understand the language of victims. In other Arab countries, you can't even mention the word Holocaust. You will be attacked immediately, even if you're a Palestinian and talking about it in any context. You are not permitted to bring up the issue of the Holocaust.

MOSHE MA'OZ: In Lebanon, there was a conference about Holocaust denial among intellectuals.

ADEL MANNA: It didn't take place. And the discussion in the press was about not letting them come .

ADEL YAHYA: About a year ago, I was in a conference in Egypt where the Holocaust came up. I was immediately attacked by my Egyptian colleagues.

ADEL MANNA: I have had a different experience in Egypt. I've been there at least eight times in the last 15 years, and have spoken to intellectuals and others. It wasn't difficult. On the contrary .

ADEL YAHYA: Because the Palestinians feel that the issue of the Holocaust is forced upon them, they usually misuse it. Like the Israelis. If the Israelis are misusing it, so can we. There is always the equation. In demonstrations, you will always see the Star of David equaling the Nazi swastika. I have never been in any Palestinian demonstration where there wasn't this equation of Zionism with Nazism.

AMNEH BADRAN: This is a generalization.

ADEL YAHYA:: There is always this tendency to equate Israeli actions in the Palestinian areas with Nazi behavior towards the Jews. The Nazi analogy was also used when Israeli soldiers stamped Palestinian youth in the territories with the Star of David. It happens even more in this current Intifada. Palestinians also trying to use it because they feel it is forced upon them. This European phenomenon was forced upon them, and now they want to use it in their favor.

AMNEH BADRAN: Dalia spoke about victims of the Holocaust feeling themselves victims of the Jewish-Palestinian conflict.

DALIA OFER: Not only the victims of the Holocaust. Israelis in general.

AMNEH BADRAN: The general Jewish public, but you related also to the question of Holocaust victims. Haven't they seen the Palestinians also as a people, whether they accept them as a nation or not, who also have rights, individually or collectively, to defend themselves? It's a question of the right to defend your home, your land, yourself and your attachment to a place. I think this is a fair question because we also have the experience of suffering and of persecution in our past.

Walid spoke about feeling shame because the Palestinians do not empathize about the Holocaust. I agree when he says we should both empathize with each other's suffering, and acknowledge the suffering. But what was missing there was recognition of responsibility.

In the case of the Holocaust, I acknowledge the suffering and I feel empathy. But it's not my responsibility. But on the Israeli side, if they acknowledge the suffering, then they also have to address the question of responsibility. Who did what to whom? When we speak about healing and reconciliation, it is an important element in any future process. And when we speak about responsibility, it's not only a matter of numbers and political responsibility, but also a matter of moral responsibility.

Benjamin spoke about Hamas' political declarations and how they are perceived by the Israeli public. One of the problems of the latest Intifada is that the media has been driven by the political establishment. Instead of focusing on the 80 percent of Palestinians who are ready to accept a compromise, they focus on the 20 percent who are not. The media is used as a means to support the political government that is in place.

Again, with regard to the media and the question of image, it was mentioned that Palestinians are portrayed as devils, so I think it's fair to say how Israelis are portrayed in the Palestinian media.

BENJAMIN POGRUND: Israelis always say the Palestinians are liars. They haven't kept their word about the numbers of arms. Palestinians always point to Israeli lies about settlements. There are lies on both sides.

PAUL SCHAM: Walid suggested looking at positive relations between Israelis and Palestinians. The Truman Institute has begun a program like this under the impetus of Moshe which, unfortunately, was stopped due to the Intifada. But it's something we hope to be able to revive.

My perception is that suffering rarely ennobles. Only in extraordinary cases. Mostly it makes people want to make sure it doesn't happen to them again. An excellent example is our own Minister Natan Sharansky, who was a human rights hero in the Soviet Union, and is now somewhat less solicitous about Palestinian rights than he was about Jewish rights.

AZIZ HAIDER: I would like to share with you some experiences I have regarding mutual acknowledgment or the asymmetry of acknowledgment regarding our narratives about the Holocaust and the Nakba. Three years ago, the Israeli Ministry of Education invited me to be part of a group of about 15 people to work on a common curriculum for Arabs and Jews, using the same texts for both Arabs and Jews, and among the Jews, religious and secular. We started with everybody's narratives, first with the Jewish one which everybody already knew. There was no discussion of it. It is not my role to debate with you about what you say is your history. I have to accept it. We started with the Holocaust, the Aliyah, the Yishuv, independence liberation. I accepted everything.

The second year we started with my narrative. The first time I mentioned the names of our heroes whom we want to teach about to our children, such as Deir Kassam, we stopped working for six months. I said, "I accepted every element of your narrative. Now you also have to accept mine. For you, this is the enemy. But for me, Menachem Begin was an enemy, and I accepted him in your narrative."

When I mentioned the 1936 revolt, there was a problem with the word, the term. Was it a revolt? Then we got to the Nakba. I said, "It's your independence and it's my Nakba. I have to teach about that, and about Hajj Amin and all these other elements." And the same thing happened. We stopped working for seven months. This term Nakba could not be included. I said, "But you invited me here with my narrative, the entire narrative. I accepted everything. You can't accept the term Nakba?" Out of the three years of that group's existence, we didn't work for at least a year and a half because of these things. Still, we did finally come up with a curriculum which is now on [Minister of Education] Limor Livnat's table.

One side was ready to acknowledge the narrative, and the other side was not, because of arrogance and patronizing. We are the enemy, and because of the political situation and the confrontation, they are still not ready to acknowledge the other side. This was my experience.

BURCKHARD BLANKE: What do you mean when you say, "They are not ready"? A certain group of intellectuals in Israel?

AZIZ HAIDER: It is difficult for the Israeli side because we are still in confrontation. They still feel they are the powerful side and can impose their narrative on us, but not vice versa.

ADEL YAHYA: That's what's happening here in this discussion.

RAN AARONSOHN: One of the weaknesses of our discussions is the high level of generalization, and it goes in both directions. Maybe it's structural and cannot be avoided. Even when we try to specify specific groups, it's still a generalization. We should be aware of this. This goes directly to a personal experience I want to share with you. Don't forget we are speaking about the Holocaust .

DALIA OFER: And Nakba.

BURCKHARD BLANKE: We are now aware it has to be included. When we speak about the Holocaust, we must also open the discussion about the Nakba.

RAN AARONSOHN: When I was a boy, a young adult, I made a personal boycott of Germany. But once, on my way to Europe, we had to land on German land, and I didn't want to get out of the plane. I had no personal reference to the Holocaust, but it was part of my national identity. I now see that I felt such a strong emotional reaction based on a very high level of generalization. Eventually I was able to understood and to separate between the then German government, institutions and people, and the present generation. It took time till I was slowly able more and more to connect with them, then even to visit Germany. The first time I was there, I still tried to avoid sleeping there. Even later, when I did spend some time there, I couldn't help thinking, when I looked at the older people, what were they doing during the World War II. Now I would never consciously blame the people present in Germany at this time, especially the new generations. And I think I was able to overcome those feelings by trying to avoid generalizations and to look more individually, consciously and rationally.

RUTH KARK: Then you went and bought a German car.

RAN AARONSOHN: Exactly.

BURCKHARD BLANKE: Mr. Abraham Burg, Speaker of the Knesset, recently declared that one cannot buy German cars because of this relation with the Holocaust. On the one hand, it's ridiculous. On the other hand, it has symbolic impact.

One short anecdote. When the leader of Germany's Liberal party came here recently, [Meretz leader] Mr. Yossi Sarid didn't want to meet him because of the ongoing discussion in Germany about a Syrian-born ex-member of the Green party who wanted to move into the Liberal party. He had made some political statements comparing the Israeli military incursion into Jenin during the Defensive Shield operation to the Nazis. He broke a taboo in Germany because one cannot speak openly about these things. And this is why Yossi Sarid didn't want to meet the president of the Liberal party. You see how symbolically it converted into a political scandal. You cannot blame the leader of one party for the statements of somebody else who wants to join that party.

WALID SALEM: I want to say something to my Palestinian colleagues. It will not be helpful for us to put the question of the Holocaust under the carpet.

BURCKHARD BLANKE: Is there anybody who wants to hide it?

WALID SALEM: We can say it's a European problem and so it should be solved there, but this will not be helpful. Europe bears a lot of responsibility, but the problem exists now in our country. The Holocaust survivors are now in Israel, and so we are the ones who need to deal with this problem. If we put it into the framework of human rights and values, we will be able to address this question, and we must address it.

If we want to confront the process of dehumanization, even in this project then why don't we raise questions about the human beings who were living in Palestine at that period, talk about citizenship in Palestine, the question of democratization, institution-building during the Mandatory period, the modes of life, how people in the cities and villages were living, fashion, cultural values, the question of land use. If we talk about the people, we will begin to humanize each other again.

MERON BENVENISTI: I find one difficulty in the comparison. There is a problem equating the situation that occurred in the land of Israel-Palestine and outside, not from the point of view of responsibility, but from the point of view of a person who believes he is indigenous. For me, everything starts from the land. This is a very important element in understanding the Nakba, and it's not very easy for me to understand the Holocaust. I admit that I'm a neo-Canaanite. I was born and raised on the negation of the Diaspora. At the same time, my uncles perished in the Holocaust, so it's not that I am outside this. But as an ideology, there is a vast difference. The fact that the Holocaust is important in understanding Israeli identity is clear.

But my affinity with the Palestinians is based on the fact that we belong to the same land. That, for me, is the formative connection which makes me not only sympathize with the Nakba, but also with the origins of everything that has to do with the lost civilization. We are not talking just about the victimization of 1948. We are talking about an entire civilization being lost, one that was also part of my upbringing.

Some Palestinians say that when I say things like that, I am taking their history from them. But it's part of my history too because I was born in a place where Jews and Palestinians lived together. I don't pretend that it was like the Golden Age in Spain, but it is my shared history. That's why I am so fascinated with everything that has to do with the history of my land, although it's a history I have destroyed. But from that point of view, in the possibility of understanding and of being sympathetic with the Nakba, we have a very important common ground, unlike the artificial attempt to force you to understand the Holocaust.

This is artificial, no matter what people say. Lip service will be paid. All Palestinians who are politically correct will say we must, and so on. But there is something else that can be a real common experience, if we concentrate on the land, on the fact that we must live in the same land. Therefore, the features of that land and how it influenced us are very important and can be developed. For example, we have not talked about Israel's monopoly over nature. Anything having to do with nature is Israeli, and Palestinians have no place in that beyond their villages. I have no time now to go into this, but this is also the case with regard to the perception of history, the perception of archeology. Israelis accept the fact that archeology ends in 1700. Everything else since 1700, including the civilization of the Palestinians, is outside the realm of archeology.

RAN AARONSOHN: But then it's modern history.

MERON BENVENISTI: There's a difference between saying that this place is protected by the Law of Antiquities and therefore cannot be touched, and the destruction of hundreds of Arab villages because they were after 1700.

RUTH KARK: Again we have to blame the British. That's a British law.

RAN AARONSOHN: But now we have a new law.

MERON BENVENISTI: The new law says the same thing. Palestinian civilization is totally erased. What I am saying is, let's turn the victimization and responsibility around and see how we can create history. If history is too painful, there are other ways. I am familiar with a taxonomy project that is identifying local plants by their Hebrew and Palestinian names. To me, this is a symbolic way to make both sides part of the same land. And of course, if you teach about the civilization that has perished, then people might understand the loss represented by the Nakba. No matter what we say about the Holocaust and how important it is, the civilization that has been lost here is no less important - no matter that I am a destroyer of this civilization - and the comparison between the two is artificial.

FATMEH QASSEM: By generalizing and using the word Jews as equivalent to Zionism and the Holocaust, and by focusing on the Eurocentric conception and importance of the Holocaust in shaping the mainstream

Eurocentric Jewish state, we are avoiding a huge discourse within Israeli society, that being the narrative of the Mizrachim. They have a different point of view, and I would like to know more about it. They haven't been represented here, and I draw that to the attention of the organizers of this project.

RUTH KARK: This is an important point. This year, I started teaching a course called "Sephardim and People from the Middle East in Palestine-Israel." There is always the question, if the Ashkenazim had not become the majority and had not become leaders in politics and other spheres of life in Palestine and Israel, maybe the scenario of our conflict would have been very different.

DALIA OFER: Before the Holocaust, Jews within the Islamic community were only a demographic fraction. The change occurred because of the destruction of European Jewry. Zionism was a national movement that emerged in the context of European communities in that particular context.

I thank you all for your comments. The way Adel and Fatmeh expressed their personal experiences is important. It's not always only about knowledge. It's also about something that happens between people when we relate to each other. It should not be forgotten.

Of course, the Holocaust is not the responsibility of the Palestinians or the Arabs. The Holocaust is, first and foremost, the responsibility of the Germans. I say the Germans because I don't think the Nazis are a special creature. It was a phenomenon of German history at that point, and the participation of the German people with the Nazi project was very wide. Again, it was not all Germans, of course. There was opposition, and a lot has been written about it. And in this respect, other nations under occupation - Poland, Ukraine, Latvia, Lithuania - also collaborated with the Nazis, and many of them were directly involved in the killing. Still, their responsibility is different from that of the Germans.

The Arabs are certainly outside this realm. I agree completely that, despite the fact that the Mufti collaborated with the Nazis - and I have a lot of documentation of his direct acts in relation to hindering Jewish illegal immigration - he does not belong in Yad Vashem. The fact that he appears there is a political statement of those who created the museum. I hope this will not be the case in the new museum. I see the conflict between Israelis and Palestinians as a national conflict, a territorial conflict. The first stage is called a civil war or a national war. It doesn't matter. But there are many conflicts like this, and I believe strongly that this is a conflict soluble through understanding and compromise on both sides.

The Jews who died in the Holocaust were citizens of many different countries. They were not Germany's enemy. It was a genocide, and different from Rwanda and Cambodia and others that developed into genocide. The only thing similar is the genocide of the Armenians. There are historical differences, but this is the only viable comparison. And, of course, the gypsy tribes were certainly victims of genocide during the Nazi period. These are the two cases in which a group of people, because they belong to this group, were designated to be murdered. There are some differences in the case of the gypsies because it was connected to their way of life, unlike the Jews. But essentially because of racial ideology these were the two groups that were designated to be murdered.

175

In that respect, it's easier in a way to see the Jewish-Palestinian or the Israeli-Palestinian conflict as a soluble one. The Israelis bear responsibility and the Palestinians and the Arab states bear responsibility. It's not one-sided.

And we still don't have a social history of the Yishuv in the beginning. If we are able to construct a history of this land, a mutual social history of both communities with respect to the other, this will be a great achievement. If we could take away the political aspect - which of course we can't because it is a political conflict - we could really make some strides forward in describing the life of the communities so that they will somehow come together. I'm not a neo-Canaanite, although I was born in the land of Israel or Palestine. And I'm not a Holocaust survivor and my parents were not survivors. Part of my family was destroyed. Nevertheless, it was not my direct experience. I think the attachment to the land is important, but also the attachment to the history of both communities which goes beyond the land. It's important to understand Islamic and Arabic culture, not only Palestinian. In this respect, I don't agree with narrowing it down the way Meron did, although the taxonomy project you mentioned is a wonderful one.

ATA QAYMARI: This discussion was illuminating and inspiring. The emphasis is on how to deal with the catastrophe of the Nakba. The Holocaust is a general historic problem, while the Nakba is still going on. We have to address it in a practical and political manner, not only educationally or historically.

When I talked about forgetting, what I meant is that, if you don't forget, then you will also not forgive. They go together. I think even the Jews need to neutralize the strong impact this has had on their lives in order to become normal human beings. You need to live and continue to live in the future, not in the past. Fifty years is a long time.

I liked the way Meron introduced the subject by talking about what we have to share. We have to share the land, and we can share also the history and experiences of this land. If the Nakba still exists, then we have a shared responsibility to overcome it. And then we will have to learn how to stop talking about the Nakba in the same way as I call upon you to stop talking about the Holocaust. I don't want children to feel anything similar to what was described about not being able to get off the plane in Germany, or going to Yad Vashem and refusing to go in. It's good for Palestinians to go to Yad Vashem, and it's good for Israelis to address the Nakba, or to let Palestinians in freely to see their lands, maybe even to buy them, rebuy them, settle them sometimes.

BURCKHARD BLANKE: I have learned that historians as agents of memory have also to be the builders of bridges in a certain sense. Common history is not shared history necessarily, but we have to find a way to understand each other's narratives. In that way we will increase our own empathy about the other side, something that is greatly needed now in this conflict.

RUTH KARK: At the entrance to the United States National Archive in Washington DC there is a sentence engraved in the stone that I like very much, and I think we should adopt it for this book. It says, "Past is prologue."

THE U.N. PARTITION RESOLUTION OF 1947: WHY WASN'T IT IMPLEMENTED?

Moshe Ma'oz

THE United Nations plan in November 1947 to divide Palestine into independent Arab and Jewish states and a Special International Regime for Jerusalem had been preceded by a somewhat similar design in July 1937. The British Peel Commission recommended that Mandatory Palestine be partioned into a small Jewish state, comprising the Galilee, the Yezreal Valley and the coastal plain, and a large Arab state, comprising the rest of Palestine and united with Transjordan. Jerusalem, Bethlehem and a few other areas would remain a British Mandatory zone. [1]

The major cause for the 1937 partition proposal - that Arab and Jewish interests could not be reconciled - was aggravated in 1947, after both parties rejected the1946 recommendation by an Anglo-American committee to establish a bi-national state in Palestine under UN trusteeship. While the Jewish community accepted the 1937 and 1947 partition plans, the Palestinian Arab leadership, dominated by the Husseini family, rejected both plans categorically. Indeed, most Palestinians had turned down the 1937 design even though it designated only 20 percent of Palestine to the proposed Jewish state. Furthermore, the Palestinian leadership even rejected the 1939 British White Paper which had promised them an independent state within ten years while limiting Jewish immigration and turning the Jews into a minority in an Arab Palestinian state. [2]

Why, then, did the Palestinian Arab reject these schemes, in particular the UN 1947 partition plan? Undoubtedly, some moderate or pragmatic Palestinians were prepared to accept a small Jewish state in part of Palestine.[3] But the Husseinis' leadership — not democratically elected but backed by the Arab League — continued to intimidate their moderate brethren and to maintain its uncompromising position against the Jews. Even according to a moderate Palestinian intellectual, this leadership adopted an extreme policy vis-a-vis the idea of two states, thus grossly ignoring the will of the UN and the Great Powers, and leading the Palestinians into war and tragedy.[4]

Indeed, this militant syndrome of the Palestinian leadership significantly contributed to preventing a political solution to the Arab-Jewish dispute over Palestine in 1947, as in 1937. This syndrome was inspired by an intense Islamic and nationalist ideology, dominated by the Husseini family and for a long time by

Hajj Amin Al Husseini, the charismatic Grand Mufti of Jerusalem and Head of the Supreme Muslim Council. Denying the right of the Jewish-Zionist community to national self-determination even in part of Palestine, the Husseinis periodically used violence and terror against Jews as well as against the moderate Palestinian Nashashibi faction that for many years cooperated with the Jewish community and acknowledged its national aspirations. But this moderate faction, although supported by many families and notables throughout the country, was not as organized, armed, motivated and influential among the younger generation as the Husseinis. Consequently, the moderate/pragmatic Palestinians were unable to neutralize the powerful militant Palestinian nationalist leadership or induce it to accept a political settlement.

The Nashashibis were politically supported by King Abdullah of Transjordan and, for a period, also by his patron — the British government in Palestine. But neither the British government nor King Abdullah helped the Palestinian moderates; in 1947, both objected to the UN partition resolution, while Abdullah also sought to annex Arab Palestine to his kingdom. As for all leaders of the neighboring Arab nations, they shared, indeed molded and reinforced, the Palestinian militant-negative attitude to the 1947 resolution as well as to the Jewish-Zionist national movement and political aspirations.

The uncompromising Palestinian-Arab and all-Arab positions toward Zionist aspirations and the partition of Palestine had derived predominantly from fundamental Arab nationalist and Islamic religious concepts, namely, rejection of a Jewish national/political presence in Islamic and Arab Palestine. Muslim Arabs were ready to acknowledge a small apolitical Jewish religious community in Palestine — "a small community gently serving the Arabs and getting along with them beautifully,"[5] but not a motivated, vigorous, fast-growing, European-oriented nationalist-Zionist community. By purchasing large tracts of land, building villages and towns, and establishing autonomous and effective institutions — this community posed an increasing threat to Arab control over and the character of Palestine. Numbering, in November 1917 (the Balfour Declaration) only about 10 percent of the total population (60,000 out of 650,000), the Jewish community in Palestine increased to some one-third by November 1947 (600,000 out of about two million). Nevertheless, it was granted more than 50 percent of Palestine (a large part of it was the Negev desert).

From the Jewish-Zionist viewpoint, it was vital to create a "national home" (initially with British help) and subsequently a state in part of Palestine, letting the Palestinian Arabs possess its other part. Driven by newly emerging nationalist aspirations to return to biblical Zion, on the one hand, and by European anti-Semitism on the other, Zionist Jews had emigrated from Europe to Palestine since the early 1880s, either ignoring the Arab presence or trusting that there was room for both of them in Eretz Israel. As Nazism ascended in Europe and the terrible Holocaust occurred, hundreds of thousands more Jews found refuge in Palestine, integrating into the Zionist Yishuv, and determined to be masters of their own destiny.

Already in May 1942 the Zionist movement issued the Biltmore Program which, *inter alia*, mentioned the 1917 Balfour Declaration's reference to the "historical connection of the Jewish people to Palestine" and demanded "that Palestine be established as a Jewish commonwealth" which would absorb Jewish survivors of "the ghettos and concentration camps of Hitler-dominated Europe." The program also expressed "the readiness and the desire of the Jewish people for full cooperation with their Arab neighbors."[6]

Yet, unlike the Biltmore suggestion and contrary to the uncompromising Palestinian Arab position (and that of Jewish revisionists), the Jewish Yishuv, led by David Ben Gurion, agreed in 1947 to create a Jewish state in part of Palestine. This pragmatic position, coupled with international sympathy for the Jewish plight and the backing of the two new superpowers — the United States and the Soviet Union — procured the historic UN resolution to establish a Jewish state and an Arab state in Palestine.

Even though the Jewish community in Palestine, not just its right-wing faction, aspired to obtain a larger share of the country, if not the whole of it, it realistically considered partition as a minimal or tolerable solution. Given the demographic advantage of the Arabs vis-a-vis Jewish national aspirations, the Yishuv mainstream rejected the bi-national solution. Adding to these factors, Palestinian and inter-Arab hostility on the one hand, and the plight of Jewish refugees on the other, partition was the only option, particularly since it was approved by the international community through the UN. To be sure, the Jewish Yishuv had been fairly prepared to establish a state in part of Palestine, having created a solid infrastructure of political, social, economic and educational institutions, as well as a well-trained paramilitary organization, the Haganah. Although the Palestinian Arab community was not as well organized as the Jewish-Zionist Yishuv, it would have been capable of creating its own state in part of Palestine, in coexistence with a Jewish state.

But, as already indicated, not only did the Palestinian leadership reject the partition plan, the Arab states and Britain also objected to it, although they were certainly capable of inducing the Palestinian Arabs to accept it. Britain not only objected to the UN partition resolution but, rejecting official UN requests[7], refused to help implement it or even to permit UN observers to prepare the ground for the partition.

This British refusal was largely motivated by a major interest — to avoid damaging Britain's relations with the Arab states that had overwhelmingly rejected the 1947 partition. Furthermore, the Arab states — and the Arab League — had, in early 1947, already started military preparations to prevent the creation of a Jewish state in Palestine. In late 1947, a pan-Arab "Liberation Army," composed of volunteers from several Arab nations and commanded by regular Arab military officers, invaded Palestine in order "to nullify the UN partition resolution, to eliminate any remains of Zionism ... and to secure the Arabness of Palestine.[8] "Simultaneously, irregular Palestinian Arab militiamen waged armed attacks on Jewish towns, villages and intercity traffic. The Jewish Haganah and Irgun reacted in kind.

A civil war developed in Palestine, turning into an Arab-Israeli war on 15

May 1948, when the State of Israel was proclaimed and several Arab armies invaded Palestine. Initially, the survival of the newly-born Jewish state was in jeopardy but eventually Israel defeated the Arab armies and the Palestinian militias and occupied more land than had been allocated to it by the 1947 UN resolution. For the Palestinian Arab community this war constituted a grave disaster (Nakba). About half of this community fled or was driven out by Israeli troops and became refugees in the West Bank, the Gaza Strip, Lebanon, Syria and elsewhere.

Conclusions

Could the Nakba and Palestinian dispersion have been prevented in 1948? As may be gathered from the above account, the acceptance of the 1947 partition resolution by the Palestinian Arab leadership could possibly have prevented the armed conflict and its tragic consequences. But only if the leadership had been more pragmatic than ideological, democratically elected, attuned to the political and economic interests of the Palestinian community, and not subjected to the militant dictation of the Arab League and its leaders.

Possibly, the British government could have induced the Arab League and the Palestinian leadership to accept the UN partition resolution and helped both Palestinians and Israelis to implement it, as requested by the UN. Instead, the British backed the premeditated design of King Abdullah and the Jewish-Zionist leadership in early 1947, namely that Abdullah would annex the populated Arab areas of Palestine, designated by the UN to become an independent Arab state, in return for his tacit recognition of the Jewish state.[9] If implemented, such a design could possibly have prevented the 1948 war, but King Abdullah, concerned about alienating his government and people as well as other Arab nations and leaders, withdrew from this tacit understanding with Zionist leaders and played a major role in the 1948 war. Ironically, only after the war, once the Palestinians were vanquished, did Abdullah implement the main part of his previous plan by annexing the West Bank to his kingdom.

Finally, another plan that — if implemented — could have prevented the 1948 war was the UN proposal for a federal state in Palestine, presented to the UN General Assembly as a "minority proposal" (versus the majority proposal, partition). This plan suggested that this "independent federal state would comprise an Arab state and a Jewish state. Jerusalem would be its capital ... Full authority would be vested in the federal government with regard to national defense, foreign relations, immigration ... The Arab and Jewish states would enjoy full powers of local self-government and would have authority over education, taxation ..., police ..., social institutions ... The organs of government would include a head of state, an executive body, a representative federal legislative body composed of two chambers ... Election to one chamber of the federal legislative body would be on the basis of proportional representation of the population as a whole, and to the other, on the basis of equal representation of the Arab and Jewish citizens of Palestine ... "[10]

However, as we know, this proposal was not accepted by the UN, let alone by the Israelis and the Palestinians. They have been engaged since then (and even before) in a bitter and bloody conflict (except for several years of relative calm, notably following the 1993 Oslo Accords). This conflict intensified after September 2000, following collapse of the Camp David negotiations in July 2000 between Israel and the Palestinian Authority. Mutual acts of violence, involving great loss of life, are likely to continue unless a political settlement is achieved.

If Palestinians and Israelis wish to reach a political settlement, they should draw lessons from their history during the pre- and post-1947 periods:

1) Militant positions, derived from extreme religious and/or nationalist ideologies, contribute to undermining mutual coexistence and peace settlements between Arabs and Jews.

2) It is essential to enlist the support of Arab nations, particularly Egypt, for an Arab-Jewish settlement in Palestine.

3) The international community, the UN and the Great Powers should intervene at crucial junctures to suggest peace plans and give legitimacy to political settlements.

4) The principles of the UN partition resolution, or its "Federal State" suggestion, should be the basis of an Israeli-Palestinian settlement which takes into account the new realities, namely: either a two-state solution, as suggested by President Bill Clinton on 23 December 2000, or a confederation between Israel and Palestine, with Jerusalem as capital of this confederation as well as of the two states.

---

[1] For the Peel Commission and the UN partition plans see Walter Laqueur and Barry Rubin, *The Israel-Arab Reader* (New York, Penguin Books, 1995), pp. 48, 97ff (respectively).

[2] *Ibid..* pp. 54-64.

[3] Cf. M.E. Yapp, *The Near East Since the First World War* (Hebrew edition, Jerusalem, The Bialik Institute, 1996), p. 109; Eliahu Elyashar, *To Live with Palestinians* (in Hebrew, Jerusalem, 1975), p. 1210.

[4] Muhammad Abu-Shilbaya, *No Peace Without an Independent Palestinian State* (Jerusalem, 1971), pp. 12-15 (in Arabic).

[5] Shukri al-Quwwatli, a Syrian leader, to Elias Sasson, a Jewish official, quoted to Moshe Ma'oz, *Syria and Israel: From War to Peacemaking* (Oxford, Oxford University Press, 1995), p. 35.

[6] Laqueur and Rubin, *op. cit.*, pp. 66-67.

[7] Yapp, *op. cit.*, pp. 114-115; cf. Laqueur, *op. cit.*, pp. 97-98.

[8] Quoted in Ma'oz, op. cit., p. 18.

[9] Cf. Ilan Pappe *The Making of the Arab-Israeli Conflict* (London, Tauris, 1992), p. 119.

[10] Laqueur and Rubin, *op. cit.*, pp. 94-95.

PARADOXES OF THE U.N. 1947 PARTITION PLAN

Walid Salem

SOME historical studies of the 1947 partition plan overwhelmingly demonstrate that the plan was accepted by the Zionist movement, while it was rejected by the Palestinians and the Arab countries. But is this the real story? Aren't there other narratives? What does a re-examination of the historical reality reveal? On another level: was Palestinian and Arab rejection of the plan really the primary reason for failing to implement it? Or were there are other critical factors?

A general problem with the dominant historical narratives is that they either put the events and arguments of 1947 outside their historical context, and outside their relationship to previous events, or they connect these events and arguments only with what fits the writers' biases and inclinations.

The Zionist movement's position on the partition plan

The historical evidence shows that the Zionist movement's position vis-a-vis the partition plan was two-sided. On the one hand, it accepted the plan because it legitimized the Zionist goal of establishing a Jewish state in Palestine. At the same time, leading Zionists wished to use legitimization as a basis to acquire more land than was provided for in the partition plan, and to expel the Palestinians from the Jewish state.

The decision to accept the plan stemmed from two realities. In addition to international legitimization, it awarded the Jewish state 15 million dunams of land, while Jewish land ownership at that time did not exceed 1,678,000 dunams (11.8 percent). On the other hand, the Zionists sought more than was awarded to the Jewish state and this meant that the partition plan "announcement about the establishment of two states in Palestine gave the Zionists the judicial and materialistic basis which will enable them to cancel both states and to establish a third one."[1] This quotation shows how the Zionist movement accepted the partition plan, and also clarifies what happened later - the implementation of Plan Dalet from the beginning of February 1948, to expel the majority of Palestinians from their homeland. Plan Dalet's aim was to obtain control of the area of the Jewish state as set out in the partition plan, and in addition, occupation of other areas including a corridor from the coastal plain to Jerusalem, Tulkarem, Qalqilia, Acre, Hebron, Bethlehem, Beit Jala and Jaffa. In other words, although the Zionist movement formally accepted the UN partition, it had no intention of accepting its limits. Acceptance was the formal cosmetic position, while the real intention was to try to take over most of Palestinian land.

There were three main aspects to Zionist violations of the partition plan:

First, the plan, in its written version, set up a Jewish state that would be bi-national in structure, with Palestinians forming 46 percent of its population[2]; The projected population was to be 498,000 Jews and 407,000 Palestinians[3]. In reality, however, Plan Dalet contemplated removal of the Palestinians.

Second, while the plan talked about two states, the Zionist leadership worked, with British support, to divide Palestine between Israel and Jordan and to prevent the establishment of a Palestinian state, as discussed below.

Third, Jerusalem, according to the partition plan, was to be governed as an international city (*Corpus Separatum*), whereas Plan Dalet set out operational plans for occupying half of it by Zionist forces. For example, in December 1947, a few days after UN approval of the partition plan, David Ben Gurion told a meeting of the executive committee of the *Histadrut*, the General Federation of Jewish Labour in Palestine, that even though Jerusalem under the partition plan was not designated "as the capital of the Jewish Nation" ... "It must be, not only a great and expanding center of the Jewish settlement, but also the center of all Jewish national and international institutions, the center of the Zionist movement, the center of Knesset Israel, which will embrace every Jew in the land of Israel, as well as those residing outside the Jewish state, the center of world Jewry". He added "And finally, ... we know there are no final settlements in history, there are no eternal boundaries, and there are no final political claims and undoubtedly many changes and revisions will yet occur in the world."[4]

Another part of the partition plan that did not accord with Zionist interests spoke of economic unity between the Jewish and Palestinian states. Instead, Zionism looked for economic cooperation with the Arab countries and for projects in those countries. Palestinians viewed the manner in which Zionism dealt with the partition plan as a continuation of the Zionist strategy which had begun in the 1920s with dominance over land and evacuation of its inhabitants. That was followed by Jewish immigration, the establishment of a strong Jewish military power, and then expulsion of Palestinians.

The Palestinian and Arab positions

Western and Israeli historians have interpreted the Palestinian leadership's official rejection of the partition plan as based on either political and cultural rejection of any Jewish rights in Palestine, or on the undemocratic structure of the Palestinian leadership, which considered only its own interests, and not those of the Palestinian people as a whole.

In fact, with the exception of the Communists, who accepted the plan, there was a clear gap between the official and real positions of all other Palestinian groups. There was much more willingness to deal with Israel's existence than official statements would make it appear.

Palestinian official rejection of the partition plan was based on these points:

1) Palestinians considered the plan as an attack on their historical rights in all of Palestine during the 6,000 years before the Zionist invasion. Also, they

considered that the Jews could not ask for rights in Palestine because they had been in it for only a short time 3,000 years previously.

2) Palestinians believed that Jews were not a nation because nations cannot be built on religion, but need historical and cultural bases in addition to other factors. Also, the Palestinians viewed Zionism as a racist colonial movement which exploited the anti-Semitism in Europe to achieve its interests, plus British interests, and not as a national movement for the liberation of its people. On this basis Palestinians believed that the Jews had religious and not national rights in Palestine, and that these rights could be fulfilled without the establishment of a Jewish state. Moreover, Jewish freedom of worship was relatively guaranteed in Palestine at that time despite the clashes of 1929 around the Wailing Wall.

3) Palestinians thus considered partition as an illegitimate plan giving the rights of one people to others who had no right to them; the United Nations had no right to give the lands of one people to another because its Charter was built on the idea of respecting the boundaries and lands of its member states. The Palestinians rejected the claim that the UN Charter was invalid for Palestine because it was not a state. They pointed to the 1915-1916 Hussein-MacMahon correspondence, which included British recognition of the independence of the Arab countries[5], plus the Sykes-Picot British-French agreement of 1916 which viewed Palestine as a special unit

4) The Balfour Declaration of 1917 gave a promise to Jews to establish a homeland in Palestine, not a state as the partition plan declared.

5) The partition plan, according to the Palestinians, was a violation of the British White Paper of 1939 which stated that a Palestinian state would be established within 10 years, and would include its Palestinian and Jewish populations.

6)Palestinians considered the partition plan as "inapplicable from a geographical point of view … [Palestine] will be divided into eight parts, with three different systems, and 40 border lines, and ten passages," as Jamal Al Husseini told the United Nations General Assembly on 26 April 1948.[6]

7) The partition plan did not give Palestinians any opportunity to effect changes from inside to regain their historical rights. While Palestinians were to constitute 46 percent of the Jewish state's population, the plan gave the provisional council of government of each state "full authority in the areas under their control including authority over matters of immigration and land regulation."[7] This meant that the Palestinians in the Jewish state would become a minority in the long run.

8) Palestinians stated that they had a better solution for the rights of Jews in Palestine, by giving them representation in the state's democratic institutions according to their percentage in the population, and by arranging some kind of autonomy in their areas. This plan was presented in February 1939 by the Palestinian delegation to the London conference held at that time.[8]

9) Palestinians were sure that the Zionist goal at that time preceded the partition plan and aimed to occupy additional Palestinian lands than that allocated to the Jewish state in the plan and to deport Palestinians.

10) Palestinians also opposed the plan because it gave a state to the Zionist movement which damaged the landscape. This contradicted Zionist claims that, prior to Jewish immigration, Palestine was an underdeveloped area inhabited by underdeveloped and scattered people[9]. The historical facts indicate that "72 persons were living in every mile in Palestine in the year 1922, when the serious Jewish immigration began to Palestine, and this number was considered high in comparison with the countries of the region, and other countries outside it."[10]

11) Palestinians felt that the partition plan was a result of the world balance of power which at that time was working against Arabs and Palestinians. In their opinion, this explained why the UN passed the plan without taking into account Arab and Palestinian rejection of it.

12) Palestinians were aware of earlier Zionist plans to establish a Jewish state in different areas of the world like Argentina, Sinai, Uganda and others. This meant that all the Jewish historical claims to Palestine were false.

Contrary to what is generally believed, the Palestinians asked the Arab League to establish a Palestinian government on 7 October 1947; the League refused. The request was repeated in February 1948 and was again refused.[11] It might be argued that both these requests were made before the establishment of Israel, in order to establish a Palestinian state in all of historical Palestine. However, the Palestinians repeated their request for the establishment of Palestinian government even after Israel came into being. This third request was made in June 1948. Again the Arab League refused and decided to establish a temporary civil administration in Palestine.[12]

Later, the Palestinians were able to convince the Arab League to establish a Palestinian government: a Palestinian National Council meeting was held in Gaza on 30 September 1948. A government was elected, but was not able to extend its authority to the West Bank, then in the hands of the Iraqi and Jordanian military. In addition, the Egyptian government was not happy with the Palestinian government in Gaza, and on 10 July 1948 it decided to deport Hajj Amin Al Husseini, head of the Palestinian National Council, from Gaza to Cairo.[13]

While Gaza was put under Egyptian administration, the West Bank was annexed to Jordan as part of the implementation of the prior British agreement with Tawfiq Abu-Al Huda, Prime Minister of Jordan This agreement had already been concluded at the end of January 1948 during the Prime Minister's visit to Britain, when he met with British Foreign Minister Ernest Bevin.[14]

These events make clear that Palestinians were ready to deal with the results of partition in a realistic way. However, many historians are still concentrating on the Palestinian verbal rejection, denying the real history built on actions.

Although Arab governments harshly denounced the partition plan, in reality they also accepted it. For example: Arab League General Secretary Abd Al-Rahman Azzam, in a meeting with Eliyahu Sasson on 8 September 1946, more than a year before the plan was promulgated, showed interest in dividing Palestine into two states.[15] King Abdullah of Jordan expressed interest in the same idea in meeting with Sasson from 12-19 August 1946, when the King presented a plan to annex the Arab sector of Palestine to Jordan in addition to Syria. He proposed that this entity establish a federation with the Iraqi Hashemite monarchy, with Lebanon given the option of joining.[16]

185

There were other partition plans in addition to that of the UN. These were partly contradictory but, in the end, effectively complementary. For example, the Zionist movement's real partition plan, as implemented in 1948, dovetailed with the Jordanian plan to divide Palestine between Jordan and the Jewish state. Jordan commenced discussions with the Zionist movement about this in about 1935.[17] This Zionist-Jordanian coordination buried any possibility of a Palestinian state and the right of the Palestinian people to self-determination. This also confirms that, in the final analysis, the function of the partition plan was only to legitimize the establishment of a Jewish state and not to fulfill Palestinian aspirations.

It might reasonably be asked: Why did the United Nations accept the partition plan/resolution in the first place? We do not know if the UN realized in advance that the Palestinian section of the plan/resolution would not be implemented, but we can be certain on two points:

First, the United States was pressing strongly to pass this plan/resolution in order to provide international support and legitimacy for a Jewish state in Palestine. The facts show that the fate of the Palestinian people was not an American interest at that time. Although the Americans changed their position in February-March 1948 from supporting partition to calling for putting Palestine under trusteeship[18], they completely supported the plan when it was approved and they played a crucial role in deciding which states would sit on the UNSCOP committee which was to implement the plan.

Second, we also know that Britain abstained from voting at the UN. However, Britain's Peel Commission was the originator of the first partition plan in the 1930s, which would have divided Palestine between the Zionists and the Jordanians. We know that the British used their full resources to damage the Palestinian leadership during the 1936-1939 revolt, in order to prevent the establishment of a Palestinian state. Britain was thus supportive in practical terms of the establishment of the Jewish state, but not of a Palestinian one. This dual position clarifies the British abstention during the UN vote.[19]

In 1948, the British began to withdraw their troops to assist in the establishment of the Jewish state. Moreover, the British did not respond to the attacks against them by the Zionist Revisionists of the Etzel (Irgun) and the Lehi (Stern Gang), because the British were interested only in withdrawal. This clarifies how Britain, even at that point, supported establishment of the Jewish state.[20]

The partition plan was scheduled to be implemented until 1 August 1948 according to its text, but the Zionist movement began its attacks to establish Israel in February 1948 according to Plan Dalet, and previously according to the A, B and C plans (see Elias Sanbar for details of these plans).[21]

It is now clear that the actors on the ground – Britain, Jordan and the Zionist movement - were all against the part of the UN partition plan that provided for a Palestinian state. However, they all accepted the establishment of the Jewish state while simultaneously working for their own private partition plans.

The Jewish state, legitimized by the partition plan and declared on 14 May 1948, was invited by the Arabs to be a member of the Arab League[22]. In the April 1949 Lausanne negotiations, the Arab states negotiated indirectly with Israel, thus providing their own legitimization, while also calling for implementation of the partition plan. The conclusion of this process resulted in a Jewish state being established and, in effect, being accepted by the Arabs, while Israel rejected the Arab initiatives for peace and the Palestinians became refugees without an address and without a homeland. Our duty today is to continue calling for full implementation of the partition plan, through the establishment of the other, unfulfilled and neglected aspect of the plan, namely, the Palestinian state.

[1] Elias Sanbar, Felastain 1948, *Al-Attag'ieeb,* (Beirut, Arabic Association for studies, 1987) p. 140

[2] Ilan Pappe, "Qira'ah fi siyasat Al-transfer, from Haim Weizmann to Rahba'am Ze'eve", *Qadaya Israeliyya, the Palestinian Forum for Israeli Studies (MADAR)* (Winter 2002) Ramallah. p..6

[3] Sanbar 1987, *Op. cit.* p.135

[4] Mahdi Abdul Hadi, *Documents on Jerusalem.,* (PASSIA - Palestinian Academic Society for the Study of International Affairs, Jerusalem, 1996) p.77.

[5] Mahdi Abdul Hadi, *Documents on Palestine, Volume 1, From the Pre-Ottoman/Ottoman Period to the Prelude of the Madrid Middle East Peace Conference,* (PASSIA -Palestinian Academic Society for the Study of International Affairs, Jerusalem, 1997) p.17

[6] Sanbar, 1987. *Op. cit.* p. 183

[7] Abdel Hadi, 1997, *Op. cit.* p.174

[8] Sakhnini Isam, *Felastain Al-Dowla, Gothour AL-Masa'ala fi Attarikh Al-felastaini,* (Acre, Al-Aswar publication house, 1986 p.11

[9] Tuma, Emile (1983), *Felastain Fi Al-Ahd, Al-Uthmani,* (Jerusalem, Al Fajr publication house, 1983)

[10] Edward Sa'id, Ibrahim Abu Lugod, et al, *Al-Wake'a Alfelastaini* (Cairo, Dar Al Fikr, 1986) p.13

[11] Sakhnini, Isam 1986 *Op. cit.* p. 217

[12] Sakhnini, Isam 1986 *Ibid* p. 218

[13] Sakhnini, Isam *Ibid* p.226

[14] Sanbar 1987 *Op. cit.* p.150

[15] Abdel Hadi 1997 *Op. cit.* p. 138

[16] Abdel Hadi 1997 *Ibid* p. 139

[17] Abdel Hadi 1997 *Ibid*

[18] Sanbar 1987 *Op. cit.* p.152-154

[19] Sakhnini 1986 *Op. cit..* p.120

[20] Walid Khalidi, "Bena'a Al-Dawala Al-Yahoudiyyah 1897-1948, Majallat al-Dirasat al-Felastianiyyah" - (Beirut, Summer 1999) p.91

[21] Sanbar 1987 *Op. cit.*

[22] Abdel Hadi (1997: P.141-142) describes a document of the Jewish Agency Political Department about meetings with the Egyptians on 29 August 1946 during which the Egyptians asked the Jewish state to join the Arab League (see point 6.b on page 142)

DISCUSSION 5

Moshe Ma'oz and Walid Salem

MOSHE MA'OZ: We should all be attuned to the serious juncture of 1947 and United Nations partition resolution 181 which produced different narratives in the two national communities. In Israel, there is almost a consensus, to which I object, that the Palestinians missed an opportunity. Former foreign minister Abba Eban used to say the Palestinians never missed an opportunity to miss an opportunity, beginning with 1947. I would rephrase it: Palestinian leaders missed opportunities, but the generalization is extreme.

According to the Israeli narrative, that first missed opportunity was replaced in 2000 by another at Camp David II, which reinforced the thrust of the Israeli narrative. The Palestinians have a different narrative. Walid Salem holds in his paper that all parties involved were wrong - especially the Zionists, but also the British, the Jordanians, the Arabs, the UN, the United States, except for the Palestinians. This is too good to be true or too bad to be true. Then he says that the Palestinians were ready to deal in a realistic way, not only with the results of the partition of Palestine, but also with the establishment of Israel and the establishment of a Palestinian state in the areas not annexed by Israel.

What does he mean? Does he refer to the old Palestine government in Gaza which was not Palestinian initially, but Egyptian, or the annexation of the West Bank which was approved by the Palestinian leaders? The gist of his paper is an explanation why the Palestinians objected to UN resolution 181. According to him, it was illegitimate because of historical and ideological reasons. An example is the history of 6,000 years. I have heard about 3,000 years or 4,000 years, but this goes a bit too far. And the reference to Canaanites is a myth that comes up again and again.

Another argument is the right of self-determination. Palestinians were a majority at that time. And another argument that I and many Israelis don't accept is that Judaism or Jews are not a nation, but a religion, and therefore are not entitled to a state. To this day, many Palestinians cannot grasp the idea that Jews also have a right of self- determination and that they regard themselves as a nation and a culture, not only a religion. I myself am not religious. The notion that Zionism is racism and imperialistic is not nice.

WALID SALEM: This is not what I say. I am reporting what the people are saying.

MOSHE MA'OZ: This argument has been going on for so many years. Another major argument is that the Zionists accepted the 1947 resolution in order to obtain international legitimacy to establish a Jewish state and to use, or misuse, this legitimacy to take over the entire land and deport the Palestinians, the proof being Plan Dalet of the Yishuv and also what David Ben Gurion said about not being satisfied with part of Palestine. He wanted all of it.

Plan Dalet was formulated only in February, March, early April 1948, not before 1947. Its main objective was to confront the Arab armies' intention to invade. The Arabs were already organizing irregular forces. The idea was to defend Palestine against the Arab armies, not to deport Palestinians.

Ben Gurion did have dreams about all of Palestine, including eastern Jordan. The Irgun certainly had those dreams, and some hold to those dreams even today. But Ben Gurion was pragmatic and realistic enough to be content with the 1947 boundaries and to leave the "grand design," so to speak, for the future. This was because of the constraints he was facing as a leader and a politician. First, there was a two-thirds majority of Palestinian Arabs in the country at this point. The land was predominantly Arab. He was very concerned, especially after World War II, with the absorption of refugees from the Holocaust. This was more important even than peace with the Arabs. Ben Gurion's focus was on absorbing survivors and utilizing a unique constellation that existed after the Holocaust, comprising the UN and the two super-powers, the US and USSR, which supported the partition plan. And Ben Gurion was clever enough to use that to establish a state.

There was already a crystallization, among Jewish leadership in 1936, the time of the Arab revolt. This was also expressed by the acceptance of Britain's Peel Commission, which gave the Jews only 20 percent of the land. Britain's White Paper of 1939 was crucial - a Palestinian state, immigration, purchase of land within ten years - but it was rejected. This too contributed to the Jewish narrative because, for Ben Gurion, it was a sign that there could be no compromise. We had to divide the land.

Again according to the Israeli narrative, Hajj Amin Al Husseini, the Palestinian leader and Mufti, had an ideology, a principled attitude, which I respect. It's legitimate: there was a majority in the land which should have sovereignty over the land. This was based on the ideological tenet of Arabism and a feel for the Islamic Arabic culture of the land, and this was a very serious challenge. But unlike Ben Gurion - and of course there were different circumstances - he did not pay attention to the constraints. He just ignored the fact that the Palestinian community was weak and divided, unlike the cohesive and motivated Yishuv.

We need to study what motivated many Palestinians - maybe the majority, I don't know - to accept this partition resolution in 1947. It was not because of love. There is no love in the Middle East. It was because of interests. I am thinking about the economic interests of the Nashashibis and the Husseinis and many others. I have a student doing a PhD on Palestinian "collaborators". He has found some evidence that large sections of the Palestinian community were inclined to accept the partition resolution. Again, it was not a democratic society, so maybe the majority would have accepted it. It's open to question.

Another constraint is that Jordan's King Abdullah had his own initiative, along with the constellation of the UN and the Soviet Union and the United States. Hajj Amin Al Husseini ignored all that. It was a miscalculation which had already started in 1937 with rejection of the Peel Commission which gave Jews only 20 percent, and the White Paper, which again would have met many Palestinian aspirations. Hypothetically, if the Mufti had been a tactician, he could have used the UN's 1947 resolution to the Palestinians' favor, first by securing a Palestinian state, and then the other part would have been a bi-national state because the Arabs in the Jewish part numbered 45 to 50 percent of the population.

According to what people in the Israeli right wing now say, the Palestinians want two states, one in the West Bank and Gaza and one in Israel. And this could have happened at the time. I'm speaking demographically, not conceptually. Again, these are hypotheses about what could have been done. One indication that this was a miscalculation was that, 41 years later, in 1988, UN resolution 181 was accepted by Yasser Arafat and the Palestinian national movement because, at that time, they took the constraints into account - Israeli power and control over the territories. Certainly, circumstances were different. Still, Arafat took a pragmatic approach in 1988, and the PNC accepted resolution 181. This was a big breakthrough, a bit late, but that's what we can expect in the Middle East.

It is also important to highlight the desire of most Palestinians in the territories to accept Israel. The first Intifada - and even the current one - was not aimed at destroying Israel, but at getting rid of the occupation and at co-existence with Israel. The mandate from Arafat to accept resolutions 242 and 338 led to Oslo and the opening of dialogue. But there was a sequence - the United States and the international community, and Egypt and Jordan too.

Here we see the irony of history. Now it's the Jews who didn't want to do it. The revisionist minority became the ruling majority. In 1988, there was a national unity government. But history changed because Prime Minister Yitzhak Shamir adopted the policy of no Palestinian state and no negotiations with Palestinians

ADEL MANNA: The same with the Labour party

MOSHE MA'OZ: I know. I told them to abandon it and they threw me out of the womb. But at the time, Prime Minister Yitzhak Shamir adopted it. Then, only in 1992, when Yitzhak Rabin came to power, was the first time in 100 years that there was symmetry between the two nations - mutual acceptance and two national movements. Two years later it deteriorated. A major factor was that extremists on both sides destroyed the process. Camp David and Taba didn't work, and then the Intifada.

The lesson I want to draw is that a settlement solution should be based on the principle of 181, a two-state solution, a division, although with different parameters, territorial and demographic. An ultimate settlement should be based on that, or on the Clinton-United Nations resolution and the new Saudi-Arab League initiative, a great breakthrough which many Israelis are ignoring. This is the blueprint - a two-state solution, and then maybe a confederation afterwards. The minority suggestion of 1947 spoke about federation. Now it's confederation.

The British are also responsible for the disaster of 1947 because they didn't help. They could perhaps have convinced the sides - certainly the Arab side - and ushered the two sides into it, but they did not.

WALID SALEM: Regarding the Palestinian refusal of the partition plan in 1947, in the first page of your paper you say that the Husseini family, which was not a democratically elected leadership, rejected the plan. Actually, this is not the case. The Palestinian rejection was not just the position of the Husseini family. It was more than that. Some "civil society organizations" opposed the partition plan, including the Palestinian Student Union and the Women's movement and some labor unions. Others supported the Communist party which backed the partition plan. Of course, there was no written Palestinian record. The historical period didn't allow for that. But there is evidence that sectors of the population opposed partition, including the Arabic Club established by the Husseini family, and a Palestinian Arabic party related to the Husseinis.

Second, we should also take the cultural differences into consideration. One of the problems at that period - maybe today as well - is that we have a confrontation between a culture based on pragmatism and tactics, and another based on absolute terms of justice and human rights. The Palestinian position at that time and today - after Ariel Sharon's visit to al Aqsa mosque, and then Barak's offer - illustrate the same confrontation between two cultures. One culture says you must be realistic, and the other culture looks for justice and human rights. .

Third, although the Husseini leadership refused the 1947 partition plan, they did not have the power to demolish the state of Israel after it was established. The Arab League demanded that Palestinians be allowed to allowed to establish a Palestinian state on 7 October 1947, around a month and a half before the partition plan was announced. They repeated this demand in February 1948. The establishment of Israel on 15 May 1948 meant that any state the Palestinians might establish would have to be on the other part of the territory that Israel did not annex. This was due to the *realpolitik* and the abilities of the Palestinians at that moment.

You are right about one point in your paper. You say that the Palestinians were not able to establish a state, not only because of the Zionist movement, but also because of the positions of others in the area, principally King Abdullah and his negotiations with the British. The Jordanians and the British began thinking about this early on, and it seems that the British also approved the idea of giving Jordan the territory that was not annexed to Israel. This is one of the issues in our history. The problem was not only with the Zionist movement establishing a state, but also with the Arab regimes, such as Jordan, which opposed the Palestinian right of self-determination and establishment of a state.

It was not an accident that the Arab League, in June 1948, one month after the establishment of Israel, accepted the establishment of a civil administration in Palestine rather than a Palestinian state. They maintained that position until September 1948, when the League recognized the Palestinians' right to establish a state. And a state was actually established in the Gaza Strip for one week, from 30 September until 7 October 1948 when the Egyptians put Husseini in solitary confinement in Egypt, and that was the end of it.

We could have a long discussion about the role of the British. Walid al Hadi says that, in 1948, after the partition plan, British troops began to withdraw.

191

I don't know if this was coordinated with Ben Gurion but it helped the establishment of the State of Israel. It's clear to us that the British didn't help establish a Palestinian state but instead worked with Jordan to annex this territory.

You mentioned that the British rejected the partition plan. In fact, they abstained from the vote. So it was not rejection, but abstention.

MOSHE MA'OZ: Officially.

WALID SALEM: That was the way they voted.

I agree with your paper completely that the Arabs afterwards called for implementation of the partition plan. But that did not only happen in 1988, by the Palestinians. In April 1949, the Arabs accepted the idea and called for the implementation of the partition plan.

AVRAHAM SELA: Both sides signed a protocol which included a map of 1947 partition borders, but they did not explicitly say they were willing to accept it.

WALID SALEM: By including this map, they said that.

In conclusion, the Israeli state was established and the Palestinian state was not, and we are still looking for the establishment of the Palestinian state on some part of Palestine. This means that the resolution passed, but was not implemented, and this is what we are looking for at the moment.

AVRAHAM SELA: Regardless of how the Husseini leadership was elected or appointed or emerged, one thing is clear from British documents - and also from Jewish intelligence documents - that the rural Palestinian population, by and large, perceived Hajj Amin Al Husseini as their unchallenged leader from the late 1930s. He was less popular among the urban population.

As for the pro-partition Palestinian Arabs, we know that a small part of the National Liberation Front - the Communists - supported it, and even they were only a minority. As a result, the party split and they had little impact on the debate within Palestinian society. The debate was conducted in an atmosphere in which there was no legitimacy for any official open contact with the Jewish side, and no acknowledgment of it as a legitimate partner for discussing the future of Palestine. This was going on from the late 1920s. As a result, there were a number of murders and terrorist attempts and attacks on the lives of Palestinian Arabs who dared go against the consensus within Palestinian society. In 1946 and 1947, it was mainly the Husseini leadership who saw to the elimination of those people who were willing to go along with ideas of co-existence or finding a middle way.

To Walid, I think we have more of a methodological problem than anything else, even though I do disagree with some basic facts. But do we take everything as if what we see at a certain point in history must proceed as if nothing happens along the way? Speaking about the acceptance or rejection of a certain position, we should look at what happened at each junction of history. For example, at some point, acceptance by the Jewish Agency and the Zionist movement of the partition plan was incomplete. But when riots began in early December 1947, everything changed. They introduced violence, and the need to protect or to attack, and to start thinking in a different way. We have to look at how the positions of each side developed, and how each party changed its position in accordance with circumstances, constraints and opportunities.

We are dealing with realistic people who, first of all, looked to protect their own needs and interests, and secondly, to implement certain goals. But even goals develop in accordance with the situation. For example, with regard to Jerusalem, the Jewish Agency initially accepted internationalization. But when the city came under siege the need to maintain a connection dictated new actions. That led to opening what we call the Jerusalem corridor, removing the Palestinian population along that corridor, and eventually the annexation of Jerusalem to the Jewish state.

Let's deal with these questions as historians. I understand that it can be argued that acceptance of partition was nothing but a ploy on the part of the Jewish Yishuv or the Jewish Agency, and then everything developed according to a plan, of which Plan Dalet a part. But Plan Dalet was not for the purpose of capturing Tulkarem or Hebron or Qalqilya. It was meant to guarantee that the Jewish state, according to the partition plan, would be secure. In case of need - when there was no other way - freedom of action was given to commanders, to the level of battalion commanders, even to remove the Palestinian population from those areas, only if it would otherwise be impossible to hold on to that area. Plan Dalet was implemented earlier than planned because of the situation created by the war on transport. In March, Jamal Husseini, the Arab representative at the UN General Assembly, rejected the proposals for a cease-fire because he felt the Arab hand was stronger. This is all documented. We don't need to prove it. The situation that led to implementing Plan Dalet was a state of despair. In March, the Jews lost over 100 people from attacks on convoys. Regardless of the results - and I can feel a lot of empathy to the way you look at it - historically speaking, these things changed along time. We can't put it all together in a box and say this was the plan from the very beginning, that they only said this or that in order to soothe the process.

It's important to agree on the process and how things changed because the period of 1947-1948 is characterized by unexpected events, misinterpretations of the other's intentions and actions, and lack of command or inability to control things by almost every party you can think of - the British, the Jews, the Arabs. The riots that began immediately after the partition plan were a spontaneous eruption of violence. But they triggered a number of actions on each side. Had you asked the British in April 1947 they would have said they were not sure they were going to leave Palestine. They were entirely surprised by Soviet support of the Jewish state. They were not sure how the United States would react. They tried time and again to coordinate policy with United States and failed.

Eventually, the Jews not only succeeded in implementing the partition plan, but went beyond it, and by and large expelled the Palestinian population from those areas. But the question is: Could we think otherwise, had it been different.? Had the Palestinians accepted the partition plan, would the Jews still have expelled them?

PAUL SCHAM: I feel that in this discussion we have moved in certain respects from the realm of history into the realm of theology. I say that because 1948 basically incorporates the doctrine of original sin in both Jewish and Muslim mythologies. The original sin in the minds of Israelis is that the Palestinians did not accept the existence of Israel when they had the chance, thus demonstrating for 50 years - perhaps forever - that they are unwilling to live with Jews. And this

193

was the theology on which the Jewish state was based. For the Palestinians, this was the year that supported the belief that, no matter what the Jews said, they actually wanted to take over the entire land.

What historians can do at - and I think this is a beginning of doing that - is to try to understand the motivations and the ambiguities on both sides. On the Jewish side there was, of course, hope for all of the land of Israel. That was the Zionist dream. But I think it's up to the Palestinians to try to separate the dream from that which was actually accepted in reality. Try to understand what Ben Gurion was actually thinking when he said certain things. Statements can certainly be found in which he expresses a desire not only for the greater land of Israel, but for the other side of Jordan as well. You can even find folks who want southern Lebanon. But to see that as the essence of Zionist ideology both falsifies it and prevents any understanding.

DALIA OFER: It is true that, when we look at the Yishuv in historical perspective, and in particular after its successes, we see a coherent society that knew how to create a reality step by step that would lead it towards achieving its goals. Even so, during 1946, 1947, 1948, it was far from a unified community. Internal conflicts were very sharp. Ben Gurion was not the leader then that he was after 1948. He was never as strong as our image of him.

Not to mention the major opposition of Menachem Begin and the Revisionists and that, within the Labour bloc, we had Mapam, Achdut Ha'avodah* and Avodah. Mapam was formed in January 1948: right from the start, a major section of the Labor party left and established a separate, more leftist party with more inclination towards the Soviet Union. While all this was happening, we were in the midst of the greatest tragedy that ever befell the Jewish people, the catastrophe and destruction of World War II. So all the issues became burning issues, very emotional, and each fight within this "cohesive" group was extremely hot. There was a period during this conflict between the Revisionists and the Labour party and fighting against the British that the Revisionists took actions that the Labour party declared as terrorist. The Labour party felt this approach would undermine their efforts, and they were even handing people over to the British. Even today, this remains a black zone in Jewish imagination and memory.

So we were far from total cohesiveness and unity. It was really a society with deep differences, and differences is even too soft a word. However, in spite of all that, it did succeed in building institutions during the years of the Yishuv, and there were periods of united actions,. But that already collapsed in June 1946.

When we come to 1947, there was a lot of debate about the partition. Ben Gurion was not happy about it, but he had concluded, in 1946, that the only solution to the problem was that partition should be suggested to the Jews. He himself could not suggest partition. It would have been opposed outright.

When we look at the stages of the War of Independence - I'll say the 1948 war in order not to be provocative - we have to look at the changes up until April and the fear of Arab invasion. There was an assessment that the Arabs were stronger than the Jews. I don't say they were. I say they thought so. I'm still relating to the issue of atmosphere and perception. Much of the Jewish population thought the Arabs were stronger, and there was a tremendous feeling of fear among the Jews. This atmosphere is very important to take into account. The impact of fear is extremely important and caused a lot of dynamics later on.

ADEL YAHYA: It's important what the Jews feel, and not what the Palestinians feel?

DALIA OFER: I didn't say that. I said fear is important on both sides.

ADEL YAHYA: That justifies all that the Jews did?

DALIA OFER: Why put words into my mouth? I don't even think that. I think the creation of the state was justified. I don't think it follows that every action that took place was justified. I even agree that a lot of things were justified on the Palestinian side. But I don't agree with the delegitimization of the right of the Jews to have a state. I believe the Jews did have a national movement and did have a right to a state in Palestine.

Now I want to ask Walid Salem to elaborate about what he means by cultural differences. I don't think Jewish culture does not cherish values, justice and human rights, just as I don't think that Arab or Muslim culture does not cherish those values. I think both cultures share these basic values. But here we are dealing with politics, and when you talk politics, you have negotiations, and you have a term of reference for the negotiations. It's not a matter of cultural values. It's a matter of the culture of how you solve problems. And Arab states and Arab cultures knew how to solve problems in different political situations.

ADEL YAHYA: The problem with Avraham Sela and Moshe Ma'oz, as well as with Benny Morris and other "New" historians, is this notion of unintentional Jewish Zionist actions in the 1947-1948 war. That notion overlooks many aspects of the Arab-Israeli conflict and evades responsibility for actions taken by the Jewish army and underground groups, including massacres which led eventually to the expulsion of Palestinians. New historians adopt the official Israeli position excusing the Israeli army and the Israeli defense forces from the guilt of expelling hundreds of thousands of Palestinians, and all the actions taken against the civilian Palestinian population because it's the Arabs' fault in the first place - the Palestinians refused the partition plan, Arabs attacked Jewish convoys on Palestinian roads and so on.

The implied assumption is that the Palestinians were at fault. It was their sin which led to the war and thus the expulsion and so on. The accompanying assumption is that the Palestinians have no rights. This has always been the official Israeli position. It has led nowhere, and will not lead anywhere, because the refugee problem still exists. It has deteriorated now after more than 50 years of expulsion, and that's why neo-historians are more under attack than official Israeli historians lately.

There has not yet been any departure from the official Israeli position of blaming the 1948 war on the Palestinians. This justifies all the actions that took place. Israeli and Jewish actions were just a reaction to Palestinian actions. In fact, the Jews were in a better position to plan things. The Arabs were probably reacting. When we ask Palestinian refugees about this - hundreds of them - they express themselves very openly. They were reacting. They were fearful. All their actions were in reaction to Israeli and Jewish attacks on them. That is the position of the Palestinians, and it even applies to what is happening at present.

Palestinians will tell you that the suicide attacks are reactions to Jewish or Israeli attacks on us.

MOSHE MA'OZ: I said the Palestinian position was legitimate because it was based on self-determination and so on. But I said it was a miscalculation. I didn't say they were at fault. I said this was their position. I also mentioned that this presented a serious challenge for Zionism.

ADEL YAHYA: You insisted on the fact that the Jews did not plan it. It came about unintentionally. That was Avraham's position.

BURKHARD BLANKE: And Dalia's. I understood from this discussion that the majority of it was not planned.

ADEL YAHYA: They didn't plan the war? They didn't plan the massacres? If anybody was planning at the time, it must have been the Zionist movement.

RUTH KARK: Are you speaking out of knowledge or are you guessing?

ADEL YAHYA: The Jews planned it.

PAUL SCHAM: Do you have evidence?

AMNEH BADRAN: A question to Moshe Ma'oz. Looking into the period before 1947 and the relationship between the British and the Zionist movement, can we go back to the question of colonization and colonialism and look into it again, relating to this period? Second, one problem with history and historiography is that they don't look into questions of legality and legitimacy. They don't speak about the rights of a pre-existing nation when, all of a sudden, another group of people and their national movement want to build a state on these people's land.

If I understand correctly, the Palestinians didn't accept partition because they didn't believe it was right. Israel had no right to exist in this land. It was not a matter of Jewishness, of having Jews or not having Jews there. It was a question of having a Jewish state in Palestine, and this is what they thought was not legitimate, not just, and therefore they rejected it. Even today, if you ask Palestinians if Israel has the right to exist, I don't expect that more than two percent will say it has that right. It is a fact, and the Palestinians are dealing with it, but that doesn't mean they have the right to exist. This is the issue. A right is one thing. A fact is something else.

RUTH KARK: So we are back to point zero .

AMNEH BADRAN: There is now a fact and you accept it. You don't want more bloodshed and you don't want to go to war. At least 70 percent of Palestinians in the last poll said they supported a settlement based on 242, which means accepting the fact of a two-state solution. But speaking about the legitimacy of the establishment of the State of Israel, Palestinians wouldn't say this project has legitimacy.

ADEL MANNA: I want to follow up on Paul Scham's comment, but to put it differently. Rather than to speak about sin or guilt, as a secular person with a pragmatic approach, I want to go to the issue of narratives. I think we can accept the narratives of the two sides as the best explanation for why this side or that side agreed or did not agree to this or that suggestion. Without taking the two narratives into account, we will not be able to understand the history. Israeli society in general, including many historians, is trying to explain the behavior of the Palestinians from their own narrative and perspective, without taking into account the other narrative. This is the big mistake. That's why they brainwash the people, and that's why most people don't understand what Palestinians are talking about when they present the Palestinian perspective of history. They are shocked by it because they are ignorant of this narrative.

I don't think we are here to debate the facts. At least the historians here would probably agree on most of the facts. Dalia's intervention may be factual, but I don't think it adds much to the debate on the issue in terms of understanding why the Palestinian side did not agree to the partition plan in 1947.

When the Jews say this is our country because God gave it to us 3,000 years ago, this is the Israeli Jewish narrative. The Palestinians say, "Hey, we have more historical rights in this country than you because we were here before the Jews." "We" means all other ethnic groups, not nations. The Jews also, at that time, were a religion and an ethnic group and not a nation.

All the ethnic groups who preceded the Jews were incorporated into Palestinian society because, when the Palestinians came here in the 7th century, there was a process of Islamization and Arabization. Therefore, we inherit the collective rights of all the ethnic groups, Canaanites and others who lived here before and after the Jews, and including many Jews who became Palestinians. This is historically true. During this period, many Jews became Christians first and then became Muslims, and some Jews became Muslims directly. I know of at least 20 cases during the Ottoman period in Jerusalem of Jewish families converting to Islam. So Palestinians say that we inherit the collective rights of all those people.

MERON BENVENISTI: The irony is that this same argument is used by Zionists to prove the opposite. This is exactly what Itzhak Ben Tzvi and Ben Gurion used to do.

ADEL MANNA: This is totally different. They said all fellahin were once Jews.

MERON BENVENISTI: They were looking for specific families in Dura, in Yata, who were Jews by their own tradition, to show that Jews were there and all the people you mentioned were converts.

ADEL MANNA: This is precisely the difference between the myths. This is the Palestinian narrative. I don't claim that everything is factual and historical, but this is their narrative. You have those two narratives. That's why, when the issue of nations and nation-states and self-determination arose in the late 19th century, and the Jews said, this is our history and we'll solve the Jewish problem by going back to Palestine and establishing a Jewish state there, the Palestinians, later on, in the 1920s, said, "No. This is our country. We have the historical rights in this country, even though you were probably here."

The most important intellectual among the Arabs living in Palestine in the 19th century was Yusuf al Khalili. He said in a letter to Theodor Herzl, "This is certainly your country. The Jewish people were here before us." But there are realities here. This country is important to all Christians and Muslims, so you can't just transform it into a Jewish state. Khalili was a pragmatist. He could acknowledge the Jewish narrative because, at that time, it didn't translate immediately into a national conflict over the same homeland. But later on, those two conflicting narratives led the Israelis and the Palestinians into conflict.

During the Mandatory period, the Jews were the demographic minority. They were weak. That's why they agreed to partition. They wanted a Jewish state first of all, and not because they agreed to the legitimacy of a Palestinian state. This is an important point to make on both sides. The Palestinians, at that time, still thought of themselves as the numerical majority. They also believed that, together with the Arab states, they could prevent the establishment of a Jewish state. This was their principal reason for rejecting the 1947 division.

Intellectually speaking, I don't think that, in order to understand history, we have to write new articles that change history and say, no, the Palestinians didn't reject it. It is true that there were the Communists who didn't reject it, but they were marginal. Probably there were other Palestinians as well who didn't reject it, but they also didn't accept it. We don't know who and how much. Most Palestinians, and the leadership, rejected the 1947 plan. It was not just Hajj Amin Al Husseini. Collaborators are not representative of a people. The principal reason that the Palestinians rejected partition was because they didn't accept the idea that the Jewish side, the Yishuv, had a collective right of self- determination in Palestine, full stop.

We can speak about auxiliary reasons why the Palestinians didn't agree to the specific partition of 1947, about how much territory was given to a third of the population and how much was given to two-thirds of the population, how many Palestinians would be living in a Jewish state and not in a state of all its citizens. Since 1948, Palestinians inside Israel have understood, even when we are only 15 or 16 or 17 percent of the population, what it means to be Palestinian in a Jewish state which also calls itself a democracy.

Why go into these different arguments rather than just tell the truth? First of all, yes, the Palestinians rejected it. They probably had good and justified reasons for that when we take into account the narratives and the focus on justice rather than on pragmatism. The Palestinian leadership was neither pragmatic nor realistic, and made miscalculations, as Professor Ma'oz said. The leadership are not the only ones to blame, but they have to share the blame for the catastrophe that befell the Palestinian people.

We have to say that. If we don't criticize our leadership of 1948, how can we criticize our leadership now? Should we legitimize everything our leadership does and all the decisions they take, following them like blind people and saying nothing about their mistakes?

RAN AARONSOHN: I am confused. I see two separate levels of discussion here. The first is the academic and historical presentation of the papers. I may or may not agree with what I hear, but at least I understand it. But there is another level, mainly expressed through the discussants, which has to do with myths, narratives and feelings. Then I hear things about unintentional or intentional Jewish activities and plans and Jewish blame for everything; the artificial creation of the Jewish body or whatever - creature; the illegitimate Zionist project or, in essence, the State of Israel. That's the underlying theme that I've been hearing. I cannot accept this, logically or emotionally, because from the rational point of view we have no common ground. What are we here for if

198

everything that was done 100 or 60 years ago is to be viewed through the spectacles of Jewish blame and Jewish illegitimacy, and/or the Palestinian disaster and Palestinian claims.

I really don't find any common ground for discussion if the underlying desire of people is to say never mind the facts and never mind the papers, I look at everything through this particular focus.

PAUL SCHAM: You're right. There are two levels of discourse going on. The reason is that we intentionally invited both professional historians and non-historians to participate . We are hearing different ways of thinking about the past by people who are historically trained and by those who are lay people. That is why this is fundamentally different from an academic conference.

RAN AARONSOHN: Then we lose our comparative advantage. Why are we here? You could have taken anybody from the street.

MERON BENVENISTI: Don't patronize. I question your professional input in this discussion more than his or hers.

ADEL YAHYA: You are too objective and you overlook our narrative.

PAUL SCHAM: There are different levels of discourse going on. I think the value of this is that we are hearing not only the academic historians, but also the unmediated views of Palestinians which is closer to the view of the Palestinian street.

MERON BENVENISTI: This is also patronizing.

PAUL SCHAM: I am explaining why there is what you could call a discontinuity in the discourse. These are the people we have deliberately chosen because this is a different kind of a workshop than traditional ones. We are not trying to solve the problem. We are also not simply looking at this in an academic way.

The discourse has to be limited in some way so we can talk to each other and not just past other. At the same time, we are hearing differing ways of understanding these issues. This is why I mentioned theology, not because I think it should be understood in theological terms. We are talking about things that cut to the very essence of why we are here - the difference in perceptions of Jews and Palestinians.

LILY GALILI: I speak as a "man of the street." Although I'm not an historian, I am very much aware of the fact that things are happening on two different levels. That helps me understand something I've been dealing with for a long time - as have all of us - the big question going back about what's going on here, what went wrong. One of the mistakes the Israeli side made - I think it also happened a little on the Palestinian - is that, with the help of the media, and I am part of that media, we created total confusion. We made a mess by creating an equation between a political agreement and settlement and the notion of reconciliation. Oslo was marketed by politicians, through us journalists as agents, as a process of reconciliation. I think that was far from being true, and it was a big mistake. Reconciliation brings with it expectations that do not necessarily follow a political agreement.

In a political agreement I can accept Amneh saying we accept the fact that you are here although we still don't think it's legitimate. And I can accept Israel

saying we don't really like the idea of a Palestinian state, but we don't see any other solution at this point. I think we'll all be very happy to reach a political agreement and settlement at this point. Reconciliation starts with a collision of narratives, which we have been made aware of in the discussions here. This clarifies the issue for me. I am more convinced than ever that we have to divorce the notions of political agreement and reconciliation. Recently I saw a study conducted simultaneously by Khalil Shikaki on the Palestinian side and Yaakov Shamir on the Israeli side. Even now, there is an impressive and surprising number of Israelis and Palestinians who believe that a political agreement can still be reached, but who have lost trust in the idea of reconciliation. For now. Maybe in another 30 years. We should listen to these forces and reorganize our political behavior accordingly. I'm not saying what we're doing is useless. This may set the ground for the next step, which will be reconciliation. But let's not confuse the two.

AZIZ HAIDER: Regarding Moshe's paper, in this kind of discussion, we can try to tell the truth. In your paper you said that one side accepted the partition plan and the other side rejected it, and you don't put the events in historical context. This is only one-half of the truth, not the whole story. The other story is about legitimacy. I think most Israelis, until the 1990s, didn't recognize the very existence of the Palestinians as a people.

MOSHE MA'OZ: During the Mandatory period, they recognized that there was a Palestinian nation.

AZIZ HAIDER: No. They talked about Arab states, not the Palestinian people.

AVRAHAM SELA: Once again, we have to put it into context. From 1924, the Palestinian leadership said the Jews were no partner to anything. Of course, from then on, all contacts were not with Palestinians but with Arab leaders. That was the only option.

ADEL MANNA: You're confusing political attitudes and narratives and the legitimacy of the other side.

AVRAHAM SELA: How do we know the Jewish side or the Zionist movement did not accept the idea of a Palestinian nation?

MERON BENVENISTI: Because they said so. You know who said it. The only one who didn't - and that's the irony of it - was Ze'ev Jabotinsky.

AVRAHAM SELA: He was not in a position to lead anything.

MERON BENVENISTI: That's what I'm saying.

AZIZ HAIDER: The partition plan is only half the story. That's the Zionist narrative, Zionist propaganda. There is another narrative, and we have to tell the people that other side as well. The Zionists did not recognize the very existence of Palestinians as a people.

ADEL MANNA: As a people with the right of self-determination in Palestine, not just as a people.

AZIZ HAIDER: We came to this conference in order to start thinking another way and to tell both stories. This is very important.

BENJAMIN POGRUND: Doesn't Jewish acceptance of the United Nations partition plan imply the acceptance of another state?

AZIZ HAIDER: No. It's pragmatism. What was said about criticizing our leadership is very important here. Ben Gurion was very pragmatic. The other side wasn't pragmatic. This is our problem. We have to say it.

BENJAMIN POGRUND: The Jewish side accepted that there was going to be another state. For the Jews to have said who would run that state would have been patronizing at its worst. But wasn't it implicit that they accepted a Palestinian state?

DALIA OFER: Not in the general perceptions. This is a very important point. Ben Gurion, among all the leaders - and I'm not talking about Jabotinsky who died in 1940 - was the one who was most ready to accept the legitimacy of the Palestinian people and their right to a state. But it is also true that, in the basic perceptions after the failure of 1947, the issue vanished. You can explain it politically by saying that it was because Jordan annexed the West Bank, but it was not only political. There really was a basic perception. I recall, from my parents and my education, that the legitimacy of the Palestinians to their own state was not pursued as a principle of perception.

What made the issue so important - and therefore, also the peace movement in Israel - is that after 1967, and perhaps after 1973, it crystallized in the Israeli perception that we are talking about a people, that emotionally, perceptionally, psychologically, we have to find a way to accept these people. Not pragmatically. From what I remember from my education, pragmatically was something that was always there, but it was not embedded deeply in our perceptions.

Something else that I can only speak about from my personal experience is the educational system. I taught high school for many years in the Hebrew University High School, and one of my subjects was the revolt of 1936. I received Porath's manuscript before his book was published, and I used it in my classroom. It was very innovative at that time. I wrote on the blackboard, the "Palestinian National Movement and its Revolt," and on that day, we were visited by the Knesset Educational Committee. They saw that on the board and listened to what was going on. I was referring to Shimoni and Porath and talking about historiography and history. Afterwards, they had a meeting with me. Geula Cohen was a member of that committee, and she was outraged. I was working on my master's dissertation on the Holocaust at that time, and she said to me, "I don't understand you. How can you present such an interpretation? I would rather have you teach the history of the Jewish people. For example, do you teach the Holocaust?" This was after I had already established a program on the Holocaust in that high school, before it was even taught at that time.

This is an example, and it's important to be aware of this kind of thing. I think we are now far from this, not only for practical reasons, but also in the Israeli mentality. And I also think that the attitude towards the rights of Palestinians and the perception about their identity has changed a lot among Israelis.

AZIZ HAIDER: After the establishment of Israel, the Israelis continued their propaganda by defining the conflict in the Middle East as the Arab-Israeli conflict, as a conflict between states and not between two nations. As historians and academicians, you yourself contributed to this propaganda by writing or saying that it's an Arab-Israeli conflict and not a Palestinian-Israeli conflict.

201

DALIA OFER: But it was both. It was also with Egypt and Jordan . It was also Israeli-Arab, not only Israeli-Palestinian.

ATA QAYMARI: The Palestinian people, not only their leadership, bear a kind of responsibility for what happened in 1948. Whether or not that leadership was elected, there was some kind of mechanism through which that leadership wielded their power. People who came to the leader and said there was no acceptance share some responsibility for the refusal of the plan. Why shouldn't people reject a proposal which is unjust and unacceptable based on their perception of reality? The Palestinians were the majority, they were to receive the minority of the land, and those lands they were to receive were also not the best.

ADEL MANNA: Keep in mind that the Negev was in the Jewish state.

RUTH KARK: We're talking about 11 million versus 16 million dunams.

ATA QAYMARI: The best parts of Palestine went to the Jewish state. The Negev is not the coast.; 44 percent of Palestine at that time went to the Palestinians, and 56 percent to the Israelis. However, the demographics were approximately equal. There were almost half a million in each society. The logic was to give the Jews more space in which to absorb more Jews who would come later.

RUTH KARK: What do you mean by more space? It's not true.

ATA QAYMARI: At that time, demographically speaking, there were almost half a million Palestinians living in the places allotted to Israel.

ADEL MANNA: To be accurate, there were 600,000 Israelis and 407,000 Palestinians.

RUTH KARK: And the amount of area you cited is not correct .

ATA QAYMARI: On the basis of justice and logic, the people could not be persuaded by this plan. It was unjust and unacceptable. That was the feeling at that time. "What are they doing? This is clearly an international plot - the British together with the Israelis and the Zionists - to destroy our land and to completely take it from us on the basis of international legitimacy."

But now, after 40 years, Palestinians can confess that it was a mistake because Britain wouldn't have given us independence even if we were in the majority in Palestine, and internationally we would not have received legitimacy. And afterwards, even if we did get the right to establish a state of our own in Palestine, that state would not have been ours according to our own self-determination, but rather another kind of partition, annexing part of the land to Jordan, which is what happened later on.

We should learn from the lessons of the past. We are still in the conflict, and the same arguments can be raised among historians and people from the street as well. "Why didn't the Palestinians accept Camp David and Clinton's plan? What's happening to them is because they refused the Camp David plan." It's almost the same thing. I reject the premise that refusal of the partition plan is the basis for what happened afterwards.

Ben Gurion was ethnocentric. He had a goal in mind. He wanted independence for Israel, for the Jews in Palestine, even if it could not include the whole of Palestine. When he accepted the partition plan, that was what was in his mind. That does not imply that he accepted or recognized the other's right of self-determination, especially that of the Palestinians, even though, had the partition plan been implemented, it would automatically have resulted in the Palestinians potentially having a state of their own. But they didn't. So what Dalia said is what happened. Now we have something else as the basis, the conflict on the ground, and each side trying to get more and more of this piece of cheese for its side.

As for fear, I think we do have to acknowledge that, till now, there is fear among the Israelis. In spite of their strength and all their weapons, they are still a minority in the region. If they lose their military superiority, their entire existence could be in danger. Among the Israelis, among the Jews of the Yishuv, there was fear. "We're in a war. We're a minority." I can understand that. But on the leadership level, I doubt that was the case. There were 60,000 armed militants in the Yishuv.

AVRAHAM SELA: You are mistaken by far. Ben Gurion writes in his diary that there were something like 37,000 in all, and those who were really armed and ready for action were no more than 7,000. The 60,000 is a legend taken from British documents based on what they thought.

ATA QAYMARI: My point is not the numbers.

AVRAHAM SELA: That's the point. It's not a matter of numbers.

ATA QAYMARI: 50,000, 60,000. But there was the same number on the entire Arab side, and the Yishuv knew that. They also knew that the Yishuv had better weapons. And what about the capital and the economy and the level of development in the Yishuv of that moment? I think, in any balance of forces at that time, those who controlled the situation on the international level, the British, the Zionist movement, could well have known that the Yishuv would beat the armies that allegedly attacked Israel.

PAUL SCHAM: Not at the beginning.

DALIA OFER: Read the British-American document of 1947.

AVRAHAM SELA: Read George Marshall's meeting with Moshe Sharett.

MOSHE MA'OZ: Amneh mentioned relating Britain with colonialism and Zionism. Yes, the British supported Zionism with the Balfour Declaration. They abolished the Balfour Declaration gradually, especially the White Paper The British were anti-Zionist to a great extent. The British also had a role that they were asked to play by the United Nations - to intervene and to prepare the ground for partition. They rejected that and left the country without any preparation. You said they helped the Jews. I doubt that very much.

WALID SALEM: I didn't say the Palestinians accepted the partition plan. I said the Palestinians were ready to accept the idea of dealing with the results of the implementation of the plan. This is different than accepting the plan. I said that, if the plan were implemented from the Israeli side and an Israeli state were to be established, the Palestinians were ready and were accepting of the idea of establishing a Palestinian state in the other area. Moreover, I said the Palestinians were ready to establish a Palestinian state in the area left after the establishment of Israel in 1948. So I didn't say that they accepted it.

About the British, I want to add: Britain was the Mandatory power in Palestine. There was a great need for an international role in solving the Palestinian-Israeli question. Their role was crucial. Taking into consideration that the Palestinians rejected the plan, it was then the role of the United Nations and the British to impose it, if they wanted to implement it in the area on both sides. But what happened? The British refused to implement the plan by abstaining from voting on it in the United Nations, and that led the Israelis to establish their state in a larger area than the partition plan had given them. It also led to the fact that the Palestinian state was not established.

Finally, I cannot rush quickly into criticizing the Palestinian leadership regarding the partition plan. I would guess that, within the historical context of that period, they did what they thought was right, according to their narrative.

AVRAHAM SELA: The rejection of the partition plan by the Palestinian leadership and by the surrounding Arab countries' governments was not only a legitimate decision given the perception of international and regional reality, but it was also perceived as a pragmatically correct decision. Think about the balance of power. Think about the perception that Britain would not let the Arabs down. Think about the lack of information with regard to the strength and depth of contacts between the Zionist movement and the United States.

And probably the most important thing was a misunderstanding of the new actor in the international arena, the Soviet Union, whose aid to the newly-born State of Israel during the first few months in terms of arms deliveries and so on was tremendously important. Of course you want to say that it was wrong pragmatically. But if you really follow the thinking and how the Arab and Palestinian leaders perceived reality, they did think they had a very good cause and a basis for reversing, if not entirely wrecking, the partition plan and the entire United Nations decision.

ISRAELI HISTORIOGRAPHY OF THE 1948 WAR

Avraham Sela

NOT unlike the practice in other nations, Israeli writing of its contemporary history initially focused on what seemed vital for nation- and state-building rather than on meticulous search for the historical truth. Any contemporary historiography, particularly of a national formative significance, tends to be generally uniform and instrumental. It aims at establishing constitutive myths, symbols and values on which a coherent group identity can be based, and to legitimize past actions and policies. As such, collective- and nationally-driven historiography tends to be consensual, creating an agreeable continuity between a formative past and the present and thus serving as an instrument of social and political mobilization.

Israeli historiography of the Palestine conflict as a whole, and the 1948 war in particular, has gone a long way since the foundation of the State of Israel and particularly since the signing of a peace treaty with Egypt in 1979, which triggered a revision of established beliefs and views regarding the history of Israeli-Arab relations. The highly consensual historiography of the 1948 war - perceived as an inseparable chapter of the Jewish people's struggle for survival—has, since the mid-1980s, come under strong criticism by young historians who questioned the basic Zionist assumptions and myths by scrutinizing Israel's early history, particularly in relation to the Palestinians.

In fact, already during the war and shortly afterwards, a number of short stories and memoirs were published by young Israeli writers who had participated in the battles, criticizing the moral conduct of the Israeli soldiers in the war, particularly in regard to the expulsion of the Arab civil population.[1] While this line of self-searching remained low-key, the new trend of critical historiography from the late 1980s on was strongly driven by major political and military events between Israel and the Palestinians namely, the Lebanon war and the Intifada, and was further facilitated by the opening of new official archives. Nonetheless, these developments can hardly provide a sufficient explanation for this trend since even in comparison to developed Western nations, it is indeed unusual that Israeli society has increasingly exposed itself to soul-searching debate over its actions and policies in the 1948 war, within a generational span of time and despite the continued Palestine conflict.

The new revisionist historiography of the 1948 war reflected a thorough change within Israeli society. The late 1980s witnessed a growing tendency of the urban, educated middle class to depart from established national ideologies that had previously underpinned a strong sense of solidarity and collective identity and purposes. Deepening social and ideological cleavages over the State's national agenda, particularly the future of the occupied territories, further eroded the previously unchallenged national consensus on foreign and security issues. In addition, Israeli society had undergone a rapid tranformation toward individualism, consumerism and growing gaps between rich and poor, all of which contributed to the rise of revisionist approaches to Israel's early history and constitutive myths. The questioned common past of the pre-state society (the Yishuv) thus gave way to new manifestations of group and sectorial memory. By the early 1990s this current had already left a discernible imprint on the writing of history of the Israeli-Arab conflict, particularly the Israeli-Palestinian part of it, including among its adversaries and critics.

This paper presents the main characteristics and trends of Israeli historiography of the 1948 war that developed since the early years of the state. More specifically, it aims at contextualizing these developments and explaining the new trends marking this enterprise.

Early historiography

Israel's early historiography was institutionally mobilized, sponsored by official institutions in conjunction with mainstream political movements as well as by opposition movements and sector groups, all of which played the role of "agents of memory." More significantly, the writing of the struggle for national liberation from the British Mandate and the 1948 war became a battleground of conflicting narratives, reflecting the historic political rivalries and competition within the Jewish community. Particularly conspicuous were the conflicting narratives waged by the dominant labor movement and the Revisionist splinter groups—*Irgun Zva'i Leumi* (IZL) and *Lohamei Herut Israel* (LHI), that turned into a political party (*Herut*) after the war.

State-sponsored historiography was particularly necessary because the State of Israel was to become a melting-pot for hundreds of thousands of Jewish migrants who had already begun to pour in during the war, particularly from central Europe and the Arab countries. These fragments of communities, of different languages, cultures and customs, were to be molded into a coherent national community based on a strong link between the Jewish people and its historic Land of Israel.

The post-1948 Zionist narrative represented little change compared to the one that preceded it and served to build the collective identity of the pre-state Jewish society. It focused on the history, literature and poetry of the pioneers and founders of the renewed Jewish community, glorifying the latter's combatant nature and achievements. Underlying this narrative were specific qualitative terms coined by the Mandate Jewish community to describe the main ingredients of the Zionist enterprise, bestowing on them a missionary-activist character, and pointing to them as lofty values that the newcomers were expected to adopt.

Migration to the Land of Israel was termed *Aliyah* (elevation) and illegal immigration *ha`pala* (mountaineering); purchasing land was termed *ge'ulat hakarka`* (redemption of the land); the struggle over the labor market as *kibbush ha`avoda* (the conquest of labor), just as the cultivation of uncultivable land became *kibbush hashmama* (conquest of the wilderness). Finally, the 1948 war, which enabled the birth of the State of Israel and its survival, came to be defined as the War of "independence" (*atzma'ut*), "liberation" (*shihrur*) and "sovereignty", or "upright" (*komemiyut*).

Not coincidentally, the Israeli narrative of the pre-state Zionist enterprise from the late 19th century on, blurred, or entirely ignored, the growing national resistance of the Palestinian Arabs to Zionism and the dispute with them over the same land (historic Palestine-Eretz Yisrael). In particular, Israeli narratives of the 1948 war glossed over the tragedy of the Arab-Palestinian community caused by the 1948 war. The first two decades were marked by an intensified effort of absorption of the newcomers, founding new towns, agricultural villages and paramilitary collective communities (*kibbutzim*) on the wreckage of the Arab-Palestinian population that had exited the country during the war. The new settlements, often based on the same flattened Arab villages, adopted Hebrew names, often biblical ones or phonetically similar to the original Arab names. Typically, this trend is discernible in school textbooks of history and geography.

With the remaining Arab-Palestinian population in Israel held under military government until late 1966, Israeli society remained until 1967 relatively ignorant of the very existence of a large and proliferated Arab-Palestinian society in the country prior to the 1948 war. Indeed, until the occupation of the West Bank and Gaza Strip in 1967, Jewish-Israeli society was not only ignorant of the devastating impact of that war on the Palestinian-Arab society, it had only just begun to be introduced to the latter's national aspirations, hardly grasping that it had in fact indicated the reopening of the pre-1948 conflict. Part of this ignorance was the ostensible absence of any causal connection between the results of this war and the Arab guerrilla warfare waged across the state's borders by Palestinian-Arabs, mostly refugees, under the auspices of neighboring Arab states and with their support.

As is the case with similar historic events of a total war, the earliest accounts of this experience were individual and documented memoirs, published by leading military as well as political Israeli figures from the mainstream Labor movement and the revisionist groups.[2] These publications were supplemented by translated records of the diplomatic struggle and war published originally in European languages by non-Israeli foreign diplomats and politicians, as well as by journalists who covered the war for overseas newspapers.[3] That these books were translated into Hebrew can be explained by their admiring approach to the Zionist enterprise and the State of Israel and unflattering one toward the Arabs.

Israel's official history of the war was produced primarily by the History Department of the Israel Defense Forces (IDF), under the umbrella of the Ministry of Defense. Early versions of the official history of the war had already been prepared for the internal use of the IDF in the mid-1950s, primarily for purposes of indoctrination. It was not until 1959, however, that these sheets of "Chapters in the History of the War of Independence" were gathered and published in a volume as the IDF's official history of the 1948 war.[4] Parallel to this effort, the Israeli Ministry of Defense, together with the Zionist Library, sponsored a huge project of research and documentation entitled "The Hagana History Book," which presented a detailed account of the pre-state organized Jewish self-defense military efforts since the beginning of the Zionist enterprise.[5] The editing board included leading historians, such as Ben-Zion Dinur and Yitzhak Ben Zvi, in addition to senior practitioners and military historians. The first of the three-part (eight-volumes) book was published in 1954 and the project was concluded in 1972. With its wealth of documents and data, the book still remains the most comprehensive source for the study of the Yishuv's security history during the Mandate, including the "unofficial war" (December 1947 - May 1948), which preceded the invasion of Palestine by the Arab armies.

In the early 1960s the IDF's History Department also engaged in a number of studies on the war, which focused on the role of each of the Arab actors in it, including the Army of Salvation[6], the Palestinian-Arab and the British "factors" in the war. These studies were never published and remained virtually unknown until the official opening of the IDF Archive in the mid-1990s. In addition, veterans' associations, in conjunction with the IDF's History Department, also sponsored the publication of books on certain brigades that operated in the war.[7] These books recorded the stories of individual combatants and units, analyzed operations, reproduced documents and commemorated the fallen members of those units.

In the course of the 1950s another type of semi-official narrative of the war also appeared. The first was Netanel Lorch's "History of The War of Independence," the first comprehensive study of the war from an Israeli perspective.[8] The book was originally written by Lorch during his service as chief of the IDF History Department but rejected by the Chief of Staff. It was only after Lorch obtained the censor's approval that his version of the history of the war could be published. The book turned to be a more complete, and apparently more reliable, account than the IDF's book on the war, which itself had been written by Lorch.

The late 1950s and 1960s also witnessed the publication of a growing number of institutionally-based documentary volumes, in addition to individual memoirs and diaries of the war by key Israeli figures, civilian and military alike. Among those sponsoring the new publications were both official institutions and individuals, of both the ruling Labor movement and the former dissident groups, IZL and LHI, effectively representing the heated debate between these two parties concerning their relative contribution to the end of the British Mandate and to the victory in the war. Indeed, the political strife between these two ideological rivals left its imprint on both their institutional efforts at publishing their particular narratives of the 1948 war and the preceding years of struggle against British domination. While the former upheld its historic role in leading the steady and incremental effort of conquering the land "dunam by dunam", building national institutions, settlements and defense capabilities, the latter apologetically insisted on being those who had "forced the British out," presenting their national resistance to the British as the only appropriate strategy and a necessary alternative to the deferential and shameful policy of the mainstream organized Yishuv. Thus, in response to the "others'[9] distorted history" of the battle on Jaffa, which was initiated by the IZL in late April 1948 and resulted in a counter-attack by the British army, the commander of IZL, Menachem Begin, strongly justified the offensive, claiming that it was his organization's offensive that led to the fall of the Arab city and the exodus of its population.[10]

The emergence of a right-wing-led government headed by Menachem Begin in the general elections of May 1977 finally enabled the Revisionist groups to obtain official recognition of their narratives of the 1940s, including the 1948 war. Whether it was an effort to heal the wounds of past bitter rivalries or to legitimize the nationalist narratives by including them in the mainstream version, some of the books previously published by IZL and LHI veterans were reprinted and published by the Ministry of Defense. Moreover, the latter published, for the first time, the stories of the Haganah, IZL and LHI in one book, authored by a former member of the Haganah who had shifted to the IZL and served as its chief-of-staff until 1945.[11] Finally, the years 1990-1998 witnessed the publication of a five-volume "Collection of Archival Sources and Documents of the IZL."[12]

Interestingly enough, in the early 1980s, as the political right seemed to have become entrenched in power, a new research center for commemorating the legacy of the Haganah was launched by *Hakibbutz Hame'uhad* (one of the three currents of the kibbutz movement in Israel), named after Israel Galili, former chief-of-staff of the Haganah (till June 1948). The new center became a major sponsor of the Yishuv's history and memory before and during the 1948 war. It encouraged new studies by veterans and young scholars alike, conducted symposiums and conferences and published books and proceedings of researchers' debates, which turned it into a primary contributor to the study of the 1948 war.[13]

With the incorporation of the right-wing narrative into the official history of the emergence of the State of Israel, the soil apparently seemed ripe for opening the archives. Even before the official opening of the state archives, a number of studies were published on key issues relating to the war.[14] This trend took an upsurge in the early 1980s, following the decision to release the official state archives after 30 years.[15] This coincided with growing interest among Israeli scholars, both Arabs and Jews, in Palestinian society at large, especially the Arab minority in Israel and its complex relations with the Jewish majority.

The release of official archives paved the way for the publication of a number of volumes of official documents, personal diaries, most notably Ben Gurion's war diary, and the ruling party's papers.[16] It also boosted publication of new memoirs and academic studies, the results of which were published towards the late 1980s and in the 1990s. Most of these studies focused on diplomatic or military history and remained faithful to the Israeli constitutive narratives.[17] Nonetheless, some of them focused on new issues, which enabled them to offer new insights into the history of the war in its broader sense. They took an interest in the development of the Jewish military forces during the war,[18] "collective memory,"[19] commemoration of the fallen,[20] and the Israeli finances of the war effort[21] and, following the heated debate on the "few against the many," also on the balance of Jewish and Arab powers during the war.[22]

Constitutive themes/myths

The first two decades of the state thus witnessed the shaping of the Israeli narratives of the war, which had been largely affected by the course of events in the war itself but also by its consequences and the continued state of war with Arab neighboring states. Hence, already in mid-1948, the Israeli government adopted an official policy of preventing the return of Palestinian-Arab refugees to their homes on grounds of their hostile position toward the newly established Jewish state and continued hostilities with the Arabs, of which the refugees were perceived as an inseparable part. A strict refusal to accept the return of the Palestinian refugees to their homes, in spite of various international and Arab pressures, became a cornerstone of Israeli strategy in the Palestine conflict.

Nonetheless, the possibility of partial repatriation of a certain number of Arab Palestinians (in 1949, Israel proposed accepting the return of 100,000 refugees) was repeatedly suggested, but only within the context of a comprehensive settlement of the Israeli-Arab conflict. In the following years Israel's official position regarding the Arab-Palestinian refugees was that they bore full responsibility for their exodus because it was they who had initiated hostilities against the UN Partition Plan which stipulated the establishment of a Jewish State in Palestine. The official narrative, which came to be expressed in various publications, including pseudo-academic books, was that the neighboring Arab governments had called on the Palestinian Arabs to leave, promising them that they would be able to return to their homes after Palestine had been liberated by the Arab armies.[23]

The massive Jewish immigration from the Arab states during the 1950s and 1960s further strengthened the Israeli refusal to allow the return of the Palestinian refugees. Israel adopted the argument that the war had effectively resulted in an exchange of population between Israel and the Arab states. This implied that the Palestinian refugees were to be resettled in their places and that the issue of abandoned Arab property was a compensation for the property left by Jews in the Arab states.

It is noteworthy that, besides the core values underlined by Israeli historiography in regard to the 1948 war, there were also some differences on major issues between the Yishuv's mainstream movement, led by the then ruling party (Mapai, now the Labour Party), and the left- and right-wings of the Israeli political spectrum. One issue that turned into a bone of contention between Jewish right-wing spokesmen and the government concerned the mountainous area from Jenin to Hebron, which had been allotted to the Arabs in the UN Partition Plan. Already during the war, right-wing spokesmen accused the government of striking a deal with Jordan's King Abdullah on partitioning the country although, they argued, the Jewish forces could have captured the areas held by the Jordanian and Iraqi armies. The right-wing perceived this policy as abandoning a significant part of the Land of Israel for the sake of an alliance with Britain and its Hashemite stooge.[24]

Not surprisingly, by the end of the war, both the Jewish and Arab left (Mapam, and the Communist Party, respectively) in Israel adopted an argument, which accused the government of colluding with "Arab reaction" and British imperialism behind the back of the Palestinians and at their expense.[25] The leftist approach toward Israel's compliance with the Jordanian occupation of what came to be known as the "West Bank" was to be revived and become a major revisionist issue in the Israeli historiography debate during the late 1980s.

Apart from the refugee problem, the collective Israeli narrative can be summarized in the main following themes:

I.   Since the collapse of the Ottoman Empire in World War I, the historic right of the Jewish people for the Land of Israel and its aspiration to establish its own "national home" on this land were repeatedly recognized by the international community. The Balfour Declaration (1917), the Mandate Paper by the League of Nations (1922), and the United Nations Partition Plan (1947) - all combined to bestow international legitimacy on the Zionist enterprise and the foundation of a Jewish sovereign state in Palestine.

II. Although the whole Land of Israel, including East Jordan, has been perceived as the historic homeland of the Jewish people, the Zionist movement was willing to accept only part of Palestine west of the River Jordan. Moreover, though Jews constituted a majority of the inhabitants of Jerusalem, the Zionist movement agreed to the internationalization of Jerusalem.

III. The Yishuv was forced by the Arabs to resort to arms and fight the "War of Independence" for its very survival and for the realization of the UN Partition Plan, which the Zionists sought to implement peacefully.

IV. By rejecting the UN Partition Plan, the Arabs lost their right to claim adherence to its lines. Hence, the additional territories captured by Israel during the war should be perceived as legitimately acquired and not be returned to Arab hands.

V.   In the war itself, the Yishuv was numerically outweighed by the Arabs ("the few against the many") and less prepared militarily for war than the Arab regular armies. That the confrontation with well-trained and well-equipped regular Arab armies, supported by Britain, ended with an Israeli triumph, is a clear indication of the righteous and morally-based war waged by the Jews for their homeland.

VI. During the last few months of the Mandate the Arab League's member states, with the backing of Britain, provided the Palestinian-Arabs with financial aid, arms and volunteers in order to eliminate the Yishuv. When this effort failed, seven Arab regular armies invaded the country in order to nip the fledgling Jewish state in the bud.

VII. Britain did not intend to relinquish the Mandate and withdraw its forces from Palestine. Thus, during the last few months it deliberately let the parties fight each other and let widespread chaos develop to force the Jews and Arabs to call it back to reinstate law and order.

VIII. During the last few months of the Mandate, the British government clearly sided with the Arabs. It arrested armed Jews and confiscated their weapons, supported Arab terrorists in their operations against Jews and prevented the Jews from realizing their military achievements. As for the Arabs, their great ally Britain did everything it could, both militarily and diplomatically, to prevent the establishment of the Jewish State and later to help the Arabs fight against it.

IX. The Jews had no intention of driving the Arab population out of their homes and had called on them to remain in their places and live in peace with the Jews. The exodus of the Arabs from their homes during the fighting was voluntary and in response of the Arab rulers' call to leave, promising them that they would return after the Arab armies had liberated the country and defeated the Jewish forces.

X. At the end of the war, Israel approached the Arab governments in an effort to reach peace with them but the Arabs refused and sought revenge and a "second round" to wipe out the shame of their defeat.

The 'New Historians' and the debate on 1948

It was not until the late 1980s that a new Israeli historiography, bereft of a national agenda or commitment to established collective historic myths and conventions, came to be written. The wave of "new historiography" stemmed not only from the release of and access to new official archival documents related to the war; it was also a belated response of a new generation, disillusioned and frustrated by the harsh reality of a relentless violent conflict, especially between Israel and the Palestinians. Already the aftermath of the 1973 war had witnessed the first ruptures in Israeli society's perspective of national security. However, it was the invasion of Lebanon, the long siege of Beirut and the massacre of Palestinian civilians in the Sabra and Shatila refugee camps, that triggered a bitter public soul-searching over the moral boundaries of the employment of military power in unnecessary conditions ("war by choice"), questioning the IDF's sacrosanct principle of "purity of arms," as revealed in the Lebanon war.[26]

The aftermath of the Lebanon war witnessed a growing restlessness of the Palestinian population in the West Bank and Gaza Strip and tense relations with the occupying Israeli forces, which culminated in the eruption of a popular uprising in late 1987. In between, the ideological debate within Israel over the government policy of an intensified effort of settlement in the occupied territories grew tense, and nurtured a process of political polarization within Israeli society. These events were clearly echoed in the series of books published around 1987 by Israeli journalists and academics, with a clear aim of unveiling the "real" history of the 1948 war.

Apart from the book by Simha Flappan, a veteran activist of the leftist Mapam and critic of the government's Arab policies, which was characterized by a strong polemical character,[27] the rest of the authors were young academics, with clear leftist inclinations, if not a political agenda. The essence of the new trend was defined in an article published by Benny Morris in the Jewish liberal magazine *Tikkun* in 1988.[28] In this article, Morris coined the term "New History," referring to newly published critical studies of Israel's early history by Simha Flappan, Ilan Pappe,[29] Avi Shlaim[30] and himself,[31] which represented a new approach, independent of the Zionist founding myths and narratives. In this article Morris questioned the moral character of Israel's very birth, employing the phrase "born in sin."

The new historiography was a typical development in the process of writing a major national event. What enabled the "New Historians" to move away from constructed "collective" memory to professional studies of the 1948 war was the availability of official archives. In terms of intellectual innovation, however, their studies brought no new methodological approach. Their writing remained strictly positivist (with Pappe's work consciously more relativist). Thus, none of them demonstrated concern with domestic issues—public opinion, state-society relations, the legitimacy of the state's ruling elite, etc.—as a causal factor affecting the parties' foreign policies.

In the ensuing public and academic debate in Israel the term "new historians" became a general descriptive term for those criticizing (and condemning) Israeli behavior before, during and after the war of 1948. Opponents of this line, including other young professional historians, were labeled "Old Historians." The fierce debate over the new historiography of the birth of Israel, which was waged against the backdrop of the Palestinian uprising in the West Bank and Gaza Strip, soon exceeded academic scope and assumed a deep ideological tone concerning the historical and moral foundations of Zionism and, consequently, of the State of Israel too.[32] Interestingly enough, the "new history" debate soon came to also include critical publications concerning discrimination and deprivation of the newcomers from the Arab countries by the Ashkenazi elite.[33] Not surprisingly, by the mid-1990s the new wave of critical historiography and sociology had become identified with "post-Zionism" or even "anti-Zionism."[34]

Though generally defined as "new historiography," however, the new publications on the 1948 war were diverse in academic approach, depth and level of analysis. Flappan's book targeted the founding "myths" related to the birth of Israel and attempted to demythologize them by employing primarily newly published works by Israelis. The younger "New Historians" followed up Flappan's lead, though each of them focused on a specific aspect of the war. The main themes discussed by them were the causes of the Palestinian refugee problem; the Israeli-Jordanian "collusion" against the Palestinians; and the "missed opportunity" for peace at the end of the war.

A. The Palestinian refugees

Writing on the causes leading to the exodus and displacement of the Palestinian-Arabs from their villages and towns, Morris ascribed the phenomenon primarily to the circumstances of war. While some of his works revealed brutal use of force against Palestinian civilians and ad-hoc or local orders for their expulsion, he concluded that he could not find a clear political plan, or an overall order, to expel the Arab population. In the following years Morris has increasingly, though not entirely, adopted the Palestinian narrative regarding the origins of the refugee problem, namely, that the Israeli policies and military operations in 1948 assumed the offprint of at least a decade-long Zionist thought of "transfer" of the Palestinian Arabs from those parts of the Land of Israel that were to become a Jewish state.[35]

Morris' study generated frustrated responses on the part of both Palestinian and Israeli scholars. Though the former found his study a major advance compared to the official Israeli attitude, they could not accept his findings that the tragedy of the Palestinian refugees had been a result of war, not of deliberate Zionist plans.[36] On the Israeli side, even though Morris cleared Israel of a premeditated and intentional expulsion of the Palestinians, his conclusions, especially those referring to an established interest to transfer the Arabs of Palestine, were essentially rejected.[37] It is noteworthy that later studies of the causes for the Palestinian refugee problem by other Israelis portrayed a more complex situation and circumstances and pointed to structural and institutional weaknesses of the Arab Palestinian society, which explain its poor performance and rapid collapse in the early stage of the war.[38]

The debate about the causes of the Palestinians' exodus triggered a study of the circumstances and causes that turned a few thousands of Jews who resided in the territory occupied by the Jordanians into refugees, putting the phenomenon in the context of an ethnic war.[39]

Another aspect of the "New Historiography" of the 1948 war has been the effort to reveal the IDF's involvement in brutal massacres of Palestinian civilians, which culminated in the "Tantura massacre affair," ostensibly revealed by Haifa University graduate student Teddi Katz.[40] Previous publications on the massacres were made by Morris in regard to Lydda and the IDF's "Operation Hiram" in the Galilee (October 1948).[41]

B. The Israeli-Jordanian collusion

As noted above, this argument had previously been a theme in the left's critique of the Israeli government's secret diplomacy and collaboration with King Abdullah of Jordan since the late stages of the war. From the mid-1980s, a number of young Israeli historians took up this issue, pointing to a tripartite alliance of Great Britain, King Abdullah and the Jewish Agency/State of Israel, which led to the partition of Palestine between Israel and Jordan.[42] According to these studies—and others—an early secret agreement between King Abdullah of (the then Trans-Jordan) and the Jewish Agency on the partition of the country between them explains the results of the war as a de-facto partition. The bitter battles that the two parties conducted in Gush Etzion, Jerusalem and Latrun were interpreted as extraordinary and unexpected, that is, stemming from the battle over Jerusalem, which had not been included in their early agreement. The argument of "collusion" was effectively disputed by later studies,[43] claiming that the parties had indeed agreed in general on a peaceful partition of Palestine when the Mandate came to an end, hoping to prevent war and refrain from interrupting each other's take-over of the respective areas allotted to the Jewish and Arab states in accordance with the United Nations Partition Plan. However, by mid-April they found themselves unable to fulfil their unwritten agreement following the entanglement of the civil war, the massive exodus of Palestinians from their towns and villages, and the consequent military intervention of other Arab states in the war.

C. Termination of war and 'missed' opportunity for peace

The "New Historians" only partly studied the termination of the 1948 war and the causes for the failure of international as well as regional peace efforts. Employing diplomatic sources, Avi Shlaim referred to the case of Israel-Jordan[44] and Israel-Syria.[45] Pappe lamented the missed opportunities created by the United Nations Mediator P. Bernadotte's proposals (June-July 1948), the Lausanne Conference (April-May 1949) sponsored by the Palestine Conciliation Commission, and Syrian proposals (July 1949).[46] Shlaim, Pappe (and Morris, who accepted their approach, without studying these cases himself) adopted the argument that the Arab states had been willing to reach peace with Israel but the latter failed to respond in kind and in fact preferred to maintain its territorial achievements at the expense of peace.

Other Israeli scholars who dealt with this issue showed that, although secret diplomatic contacts had indeed taken place during and shortly after the war, especially between Israel and King Abdullah and Israel and Egyptian King Farouq's representatives, the prevailing domestic and regional conditions at that time would not have supported such an agreement, especially against the backdrop of a painful Arab defeat.[47]

Conclusion

The fierce debate triggered by the "New Historians" represents a broader social and political phenomenon of disillusionment by young Israeli scholars. It was apparently encouraged by the shaken consensus within Israeli society regarding security and foreign relations with Arab neighbors, especially Israel's policies towards the Palestinians. No less important, it coinsided with the wave of criticism of Israel's domestic social and cultural policies toward the Jews from the Arab states, raising old grievances of discrimination on ethnic grounds. As such, the "New Historians" of 1948 represented one aspect of the post-Zionist trend which, no matter how strongly rejected, has already had an undeniable impact on Israeli perceptions of the past.

Apart from the effect on public discourse, its impact has also been indicated by a growing penetration of some elements of the new historiography into school textbooks. Indeed, if changing of "collective memory" is bound to be a long process it ought to start by questioning established assumptions and ingrained "myths" or "truths" about one's past.

---

[1] Uri Avneri, *bisdot pleshet 1948* (Tel Aviv: Tverski, 1949). A new edition of the book was published by Hakibutz hameuchad, 1998; Smilansky (S.), Yizhar, *sipur hhirbet khiz'a veod shlosha*

sipurey milhama (Tel Aviv: Zmora Bitan, 1989). The story of Khirbet Khiz`a appeared for the first time in a book published by sifriyat hapo`alim, 1949). For another personal account on this issue see Efraim Kleinman, "Khirbat Khiz'a and other Unpleasant Memoirs", *The Jerusalem Quarterly*, 40 (1986), pp. 102-118.

[2] For the mainstream Labor Movement, see Moshe Carmel, *ma`arkhot tzafon* (`Ein Harod: Hakibutz Hameuchd/Ma'arakhot, 1949); Moshe Braslavski, (ed.), *prakim bemilhemet Israel: tashah-tashat* (Tel Aviv: hakibutz hame'uhad, 1949); David Ben Gurion, *behilahem Israel* (Tel Aviv: Mapai, 1951); David Horowitz, *bishlihut medina noledet* (Jerusalem: Shoken 1951); Elie Shiler, (ed.), *haverim mesaprim `al jimi* (Tel Aviv: hakibutz hame'uhad, 1953). For the revisionist movement, see Menachem Begin, *hamered* (Tel Aviv: Ahi'asaf, 1950); Haim Lazar, (Lita'i), *kibush yafo* (Tel Aviv: shelah, 1951). A second edition was published by the Ministry of Defense, 1981.

[3] On the diplomatic struggle, see for example: Richard Crossman, Palestine Mission (London: Hamish Hamilton, 1946), published as *shlihut eretzisraelit* (Merhavia: sifriyat po`alim, 1947); Jorge Garcia-Granados, *The Birth of Israel* (New York: A.A. Knopf, 1948), published as *kakh nolda medinat israel* (Jerusalem: Ahi'asaf, 1949); James G. McDonald, *My Mission in Israel* (Simon and Schuster, New York 1951), published as *shlihuti beisrael 1948-1951* (Jerusalem: Ahi'asaf, 1951); Bartley Crum, *Behind the Silken Curtain* (New York: Simon & Schuster, 1947), published as *me'ahorei pargod hameshi* (Jerusalem: Ahi'asaf, 1951); Polke Bernadotte, *To Jerusalem* ( ), published as *leyerushalayim* (Jerusalem: Ahi'asaf, 1952); Bilby, Kenneth W, *New star in the near East (*New York: Doubleday ,1950); Carlson, J, Roy, *Cairo to Damascus* (New York, A.A Knopf, 1951); For a later example of such translations, see David & John Kimche, *Both Sides of the Hill: Britain and Palestine War* (London: Secher and Warburg,1960).

[4] Israel Defense Forces, History Branch, *toldot milhement hakomemiyut: sipur hama'araka* (Tel Aviv: Ma`arakhot, 1959).

[5] Slutski, Yehuda (et.al), *sefer toldot ha"hagana"* (Tel Aviv : Ma`arakhot, 1972).

[6] A force of 8 battalions comprised of Arab volunteers and sponsored by the Arab League and commanded by fawzi alqawaqji (Arabic: jaish alinqadh, or jaish altahrir al`arabi).

[7] Yoseff Olitzki, *mime'ora`ot lemilhama: prakim betoldot ha"hagana" `al tel aviv* (Tel Aviv: Mifkedet ha"hagana" betel aviv, 1951); Zerubavel Gila`d (ed.), *sefer haPalmach* (Tel aviv: Irgun yotz'ey palmach, Hakibutz hameuchad, 1953); Avraham Ayalon, (ed.), *hativat giv`ati bemilhemet hakomemiyut* (Tel Aviv: Ma`arakhot, 1959); and also his *hativat giv`ati mul hapolesh hamitzri* (Tel Aviv: Ma`arachot, 1963); Tzadok Eshel, (ed.) *hativat Karmeli bemilhemet hakomemiut* (Tel Aviv :Ma`arakhot, 1973).

[8] Netanel Lorch, *korot milhemet ha`atzma'ut* (Tel Aviv: Massada, 1958). An updated edition of this book was published by the same publisher in 1989.

[9] For the revisionist groups, in addition to Begin's and Lazar's books, see also Ya`acov Banai (Mazal), *hayalim almonim: sefer mivtza`ei lehi,* (Tel Aviv: hug yedidim, 1958); *lohamei herut israel: ktavim, Volumes 1-2* (Tel Aviv: Yair, 1959); Nathan Yalin-Mor, *lohamei herut israel: anashim ra`yonot, `alilot* (Jerusalem: Shikmona, 1975). For the mainstream Labor movements, see: Moshe Sharett, *besha`ar ha'umot 1946-1949* (Tel Aviv: `am `oved, 1958); Ze'ev Sharf, *shlosha yamim: vehem: gimel, daled, hei be'iyar tashah-12, 13, 14 bemay, 1948* (Tel Aviv: `am `oved, 1959); Haviv Kna`an, *betzet habritim* (Tel Aviv: Gadish, 1958); Meir (Munya) Mardor, *shlihut `aluma: pirkey mivtza`im meyuhadim bema`arakhot ha"hagana"* (Tel Aviv: Ma`arakhot, 1957); Dov Yossef, *kirya ne'emana: matzor yerushalayim 1948* (Jerusalem: Shocken, 1960); Alon, Ygal. *ma`arkhot palmach: megamot vema`as* (Tel Aviv: hakibutz hameuchad, 1966); David Ben Gurion, *Medinat Israel Hamehudeshet* (Tel Aviv: `am `oved, 1969).

[10] Menachem Begin, "Introduction," in Lazar, *kibush yafo*. See also Shmuel Katz, *yom ha'esh* (Tel Aviv: Karni, 1966), pp. 302, 304-305. Yigael Yadin, "`al hahistoria vesillufei hahistoria," in: *he`arkhut ha"hagana" likrat milhemet ha`atzma'ut* (Ramat Gan: merkaz galili, 76, 1986).

[11] Examples are: H. Lazar, *kibush yafo* (Tel Aviv: misrad habitahon, 1981), 4th edition; Shlomo Lev-Ami (Levi), *bama'avak 'uvamered: "hagana," etzel velehi 1918-1948* (Tel Aviv, misrad habitahon, 1979).

[12] *Ha'irgun hatzva'l hale'umi be'eretz israel, 1937-1948*, Vol. 1-5 (Tel Aviv: makhon jabotinski, 1990). The last volume was published in 1998.

[13] For some of its publications, see for example the proceedings of a symposium: *he`arkhut ha"hagana" likrat milhemet ha`atzma'ut*, no. 76 (Ramat Gan: merkaz galili, 1986). See also studies based on archival documents by David Koren, *hagalil hama`aravi bemilhemet ha`atzma'ut* (Tel Aviv: merkaz galili and the Ministry of Defense, 1988); as well as his *hahagana `al sdom 1934-1948* (Tel Aviv: merkaz galili, 1989), based on both personal memories and archival documents.

[14] Most conspicuous was Rony E. Gabbay, *A Politic al Study of the Arab-Jewish Conflict: The Arab Refugee Problem* (Geneva: E. Droz. ,1959).

[15] The act of releasing official archives was accompanied by a consecutive publication of thematic and annual volumes of selected documents: State of Israel, State Archive, Gedalia Yogev (ed.), *Political and Diplomatic Documents*. The war period, from late 1947 to the Israel-Syria armistice agreement in July 1949, encompassed four volumes, published along the years (1980-1983).

[16] David Ben Gurion, *yoman hamilhama 1948-1949*, Gershon Rivlin & Elhanan Oren (eds.), (Tel Aviv: Misrad habitahon, 1982). See also Meir Avizohar & Avi Bar'eli (eds.), *akhshav o le'olam lo, diyunei mapai bashana ha'aharona lamandat habriti: mevo'ot ute'udot* (Beit Berl: A'yanot, 1989); David Ben Gurion, *pa`amei medina, zikhronot min ha'izavon March-November 1947*, Meir Avizohar (ed.) (Tel Aviv: `Am oved & Ben Gurion University in the Negev, 1993); David She'alti'el, *yerushalayim tashah* (Tel Aviv: misrad habitahon, 1981), based on She'alti'el's (Commander-in-Chief of Jerusalem) personal papers.

[17] For example: Elhanan Oren, *badderekh el ha`ir: mivtza` dani, July 1948* (Tel Aviv: ma`arakhot,1976 ); Yehuda Wallach (ed.), *hayinu keholmim: kovetz mehkarim `al milhemet hakomemiyut* (Giv`atayim: massada, 1985); Yizhak Levi (Levitza), *tish`a kabin: yerushalayim bikravot milhemet ha`atzma'ut* (Tel Aviv: ma`arakhot 1986), combining personal memory and papers with archival documents; Shlomo Shamir, *"…bekhol mehir"-liyerushalaim – hama`arakha belatrun / hakhra`a bederech 7* (Tel Aviv: Ma`arakhot, 1994).

[18] Meir Pa`il, *min ha"hagana" litsva hagana* (Tel Aviv: Zmora Beitan, 1979); Zehava Ostfeld, *tzava nolad* (Tel Aviv: misrad habitahon, 1994).

[19] Shapira, Anita, "historiographya vezikaron: mikre Latrun tashah," *Alpayim*, 10 (1994), pp. 9-41.

[20] Emanuel Sivan, *dor tashah: mitos, diokan vezikaron* (Tel Aviv: Ma`arakhot, 1991).

[21] Greenberg, Yitzhak, "mimun milhemet ha`atzma'ut," *hazionut*, Vol. 13 (1988), pp. 9-26.

[22] Amitzur Ilan, *embargo, otzma vehakhra`a bemilhemet tashah* (Tel Aviv: misrad habitahon, 1995).

[23] On the Israeli attitude, see for example, Sharett, *besha`ar ha'umot*, pp. 328-330. Shmuel Katz, *admat meriva* (Tel Aviv: 1973), pp. 23-38. For responses refuting the Israeli claim, see: Walid Khalidi, "Why did the Palestinians Leave?," *Middle East Forum*, Vol. 35 (1959), p. 7; Erskin Childers, "The Other Exodus," *Spectator*, 12 May 1961.

[24] Israel Eldad, *ma`aser rishon* (Tel Aviv: 1950), pp. 333-334; Menachem Begin, *hashkafat hayim vehashkafa le'umit* (Tel Aviv: 1952), pp. 38-39; A. Golan and S. Nakdimon, *Begin* (Jerusalem: 1978).

[25] M. Bentov, "hareka` hamedinin shel milhemet ha`atzma'ut," in: Z. Ra`anan (ed.), *tzava umilhama beisrael uva`amim* (Tel Aviv: 1955), pp. 832-48, 880; I. Baer, *bitahon israel: etmol, hayom, mahar* (Tel Aviv: 1966), pp. 125-135. For the Communist approach, see report on a leaflet of the party branches in the Middle East, October 1948, the Research Division to Shim'oni, 29 November 1948, Israel State Archive (ISA), 130.15/2569/15. E. Tuma, *yawmiyat sha`b: thalathuna `aaman`ala alittihad* (Haifa: 1974), pp. 59-60, 63-64.

217

[26] Dan Horowitz, "Israel's War in Lebanon: New Patterns of Strategic Thinking and Civilian-Military Relations," *Journal of Strategic Studies*, 6 (September 1983), pp. 83-102.

[27] Simha Flapan, *The Birth of Israel: myths and realties* (London: Croom Helm,1987).

[28] Benny Morris, "The New Historiography: Israel Confronts its Past," *Tikkun*, 4 (November-December 1988), 19-23, 99-102.

[29] Ilan Pappe, *The Making of the Arab-Israeli Conflict 1947-1951* (London: Macmillan, 1988).

[30] Avi Shlaim, *Collusion Across the Jordan: King Abdullah, the Zionist Movement and the Partition of Palestine* (Oxford: Clarendon Press, 1988).

[31] Benny Morris, *The Birth of the Palestinian Refugee Problem 1947-1949* (Cambridge: Cambridge University Press, 1987). See also his *1948 and After, Israel and the Palestinians* (Oxford: Clarendon Press, 1994).

[32] See for example, Anita Shapira, "Politics and Collective Memory: The Debate Over 'New Historians' in Israel," *History and Memory* 7, 1(Spring/Summer 1995, pp. 9-40; Avi Shlaim, "The Debate About 1948," *International Journal of Middle East Studies*, Vol. 27 (1995), pp. 287-304; Shabtai Teveth, "Charging Israel with Original Sin," Commentary (September 1989), pp. 24-33; Mordechai Bar-On, "Historya shelo hayta: havharot nosafot lesugyat ha'historya hahadasha'", *yahadut zemanenu*, 10 (1996), pp. 3-39. See also his *Zikaron Bassefer: Reshita shel Hahistoriographia hay'sraelit shel milhemet haa'tzmaut 1958-1948* (Ramat Efa'l : haa'muta lecheker ko'ah hamagen a'l shem Israel Galili, 2001).

[33] Uri Ram, *The Changing Agenda of Israeli Sociology: Theory, Ideology, and Identity* (Albany: SUNY Press, 1995).

[34] For a comprehensive study of these debates, see Laurence J. Silberstein, *The Postzionism Debates: Knowledge and Power in Israeli Culture* (New York & London: Routledge, 1999).

[35] Benny Morris, *Tikkun Ta`ut* (Tel Aviv: `am `oved, 2000), p. 15.

[36] Walid Khalidi, "Plan Dalet: Master Plan for the Conquest of Palestine," *Journal of Palestine Studies*, 18 (1988) 1, pp. 3-19.

[37] Shabtai Teveth, "The Palestinian Refugee Problem and its Origins," (review article) *Middle Eastern Studies*, Vol. 26, 2 (1990), pp. 214-249; Efraim Karsh, "silluf mittokh pikahon? Silluf mittokh `ivaron? Benny Morris `al sugyat ha"transfer," *Alpayim*, 13 (1990), pp. 212-232; See also his comprehensive criticque of the "New Historians," in: *Fabricating Israel's History: The "New Historians"* (London: Frank Cass, 1997); and "Benny Morris and the Reign of Error," *Middle East Quarterly*, 6, 1 (March 1999), pp. 15-28.

[38] Avraham Sela, "ha`arvim hafalastinim bemilhemet 1948," in: M. Ma`oz and B.Z. Kedar (eds.), hatnu`a hale'umit hafalastinit me`imut lehashlama? (Tel Aviv: misrad habitahon, 1996), pp. 115-202; Yoav Gelber, *Palestine 1948: War, Escape and the Emergence of the Palestinian Refugee Problem* (Brighton: Sussex Academic Press, 2001).

[39] Arnon Golan, "plitim yehudim bemilhemet ha`atzma'ut," *Yahadut Zemanenu*, 8 (1993), pp. 217-191.

[40] "The Tantura Massacre 22-23 May 1948," *Journal of Palestine Studies*, 30, 3 (2001), pp. 5-18.

[41] Benny Morris, "*Operation Dani* and the Palestinian Exodus from Lydda and Ramle in 1948", *Middle East Journal*, Vol. 40, 1 (Winter 1986), pp. 102-106. Morris based his conclusions regarding the massacre on Elhanan Oren, *ba-derekh el ha-`ir: mivtza` dani yuli 1948* (Tel Aviv: Ma'arachot, 1976); B. Morris, *Tikun Ta`ut* (Tel Aviv: `Am `Oved, 2000), pp. 141-149. For a different version on the events in Lydda, see Alon Kadish, Avraham Sela and Arnon Golan, *Kibush Lod, July 1948* (Tel Aviv: Ministry of Defense, 2000).

[42] In addition to Pappe's and Shlaim's books, see also Uri Bar-Joseph, *The Best of Enemies: Israel and Transjordan in the War of 1948* (London: Frank Cass, 1987); Dan Scheuftan, *optzya yardenit: hayishuv hayehudi, 'umedinat Israel el mul hamishtar hahashemi vehatnu`a hale'umit hafalastinit* (Ef`al: hakibbutz hame'uchad, 1986), especially pp. 61-63.

[43] Avraham Sela, "Transjordan, Israel and the 1948 War: Myth, Historiography and Reality," *Middle Eastern Studies*, 28, 4 (October 1992), pp. 623-688. See also Karsh, *Fabricating Israel's History*.

[44] Shlaim, *Collusion*, Ch. 16-17.

[45] Avi Shlaim, "Husni Zaim and the Plan to Resettle Palestinian Refugees in Syria," *Middle East Focus* (Fall 1986), pp. 26-31.

[46] Pappe, The Making of the Arab-Israeli Conflict, pp. 149-153, Ch. 9-10.

[47] Mordechai Gazit, "The Israel-Jordan Peace Negotiations (1949-1951): King Abdullah's Lonely Efforts," *Journal of Contemporary History*, Vol. 23, 3(1988), pp. 409-424; Itamar Rabinovich, *The Road Not Taken: Early Arab-Israeli Negotiations* (New York: Oxford University Press, 1991); Neil Caplan, *The Lausanne Conference, 1949: A Case Study in Middle East Peacemaking* (Tel Aviv: The Moshe Dayan Center for Middle East studies and African Studies, Tel Aviv University, 1993).

THE BIRTH OF THE PALESTINIAN REFUGEE PROBLEM IN 1947-1948[1]

Adel H. Yahya

THE official Israeli position contends that more than half a million[2] Palestinians left their towns and villages in 1947-1948 upon the command of the Arab leaders and armies. The Arabs, however, are adamant that refugees were ousted according to a deliberate, premeditated plan by the Zionist movement. This paper will confront those two positions with the responses of Palestinian refugees, especially those who lived through the war and the expulsion/flight of 1947-1950. It will examine their validity in the light of new oral data from in-depth interviews with the first generation of Palestinian refugees from different parts of the West Bank and the Gaza Strip. It should be borne in mind that the Palestinian refugees did not leave all at once, but rather in several waves, the first of which began in December 1947 and ending in March 1948. There were at least three more waves, the last of which occurred towards the end of 1950 when the Palestinians of al-Majdal were transferred to the Gaza Strip by the Israeli Defense Forces[3].

When refugees were asked why they left, the overwhelming majority of them, more than 92 percent, responded that they left out of fear. A little over 5 percent of the respondents said that they left to allow Arab armies to fight, or because Arab leaders demanded that they do so, while 2 percent stated that they left out of plain ignorance on their part of the stakes involved. In a parallel question addressing what they feared most, the majority of respondents, 58 percent, confirmed that they feared most for their own lives, 30 percent said that they feared for their honor and especially that of their women, daughters and sisters, while 12 percent replied that they feared for the lives of their families and especially their children.

Most respondents denied having heard any calls on the part of the Arab leaders, armies, or the media to leave their homes. Some even said that the Arab armies encouraged, or forced, them to stay. A woman from Bethlehem, and originally from Beit Atab, told us: "I swear to God that the Egyptian army was forcing the people to go back to their villages. They were returning them by the stick. The people would evacuate their villages and the army would send them back, but the people finally managed to flee out of fear." These testimonies of the older refugees, 60 years and above, cast serious doubts on the Israeli claims that the Arab media, armies and leaders encouraged the Palestinians to leave their homes and lands.

A few testimonies by the first generation of refugees, however, suggest that there were at least rumors of Arab encouragement that may have contributed to the flight. A 66- year-old man from Tal al-Turmus, for example, said: "The Arab armies told us, 'Get out of the way of the armies, and go up to the mountains until we have liberated the land ... '. I didn't hear that myself on the radio, but I heard it from the people. I didn't leave out of fear for anything. I just left to allow the Arab armies to fight." It should be remembered that most Palestinians at the time had no access to radios or newspapers; the older interviewees stated that very clearly, and made it clear to us that their knowledge of the war came solely from rumors and word of mouth.

One 67-year-old man from Jaffa, however, did have radio access and recalled hearing calls to leave from Arab media: "There was a radio station in Ramallah headed by a man named Raji Sahyun, who was originally from Haifa. He used to broadcast military statements for Prince Abdullah calling upon the Palestinian Arabs to leave Palestine out of fear for their lives, because they no longer had weapons, and they were alone. They also said that the Arab armies would liberate them [the Palestinians]. Yes, I heard Raji Sahyun say that himself."

As to the other theory postulating that the Palestinian refugees were ousted according to a deliberate plan by the Zionist movement, the respondents fell short of saying that expulsion was the firm policy of the Jews. Although most recalled one massacre or another by the Jews, especially Deir Yasin*, al-Dawaimeh, Abu Shusheh, Kufur Qasem, etc., very few of them talked about that as a part of a coordinated effort on the part of the Jews to expel the Arabs from their homes. They said that they simply left when the war neared their homes and villages out of fear for their lives and honor, expecting that they would return shortly after the war ended. In fact, a significant 2 percent of the respondents explained that if it wasn't for ignorance on their part, they could have stayed. One man from Beit Tima said: "Personal security is important, but people's ignorance of the political situation at the time caused individual fears to overpower the public interest. A man would start to think how he could save his wife and children from death and couldn't think beyond that."

It thus seems that the flight of 1948 was a classic exodus, which occurs all too often in times of war. The real question is why this issue was never resolved, and why refugees were never able to return to their homes after the war ended.

The flight

Judging from our oral interviews, it seems that most Palestinian refugees were taken by surprise when the 1948 war erupted. They didn't know what to do, or where to go. The overwhelming majority of the population (more than 80 percent) decided to get away from the fighting. About 77 percent of those who left had no clue as to where to go, or where they would end up. They simply desired to flee from the fighting as far as possible, while remaining as close as possible to their homes in case the war ended and they were able to return to them.

As is often the case, the refugees took a minimum, if any, of their belongings with them. Some tried to hang on to, or hide, their more valuable possessions, especially their land ownership papers and the keys to their homes. Many families still hold on to those keys and papers as symbols, or as a proof of their ownership, while others gave up. A refugee from Lud told the story of his father: "My father carried the keys of the house away with him. Our story has become like that of 'Joha' (a jester). People said: 'Joha, they stole your trunk'. Joha said, 'But I have the key'. This is the tragedy of the Palestinian people." Another 85-year-old refugee from Anaba concurred: "My mother had the keys to the door, and I took them from her and threw them away, because there were no doors or houses anymore. Nothing was left . The last time I went back to the village, it was destroyed, and all the stones had been removed."

Very few refugees anticipated that their flight would be long-term. The overwhelming majority (73 percent), as indicated by the interviews, expected to be gone for a few days only. A 53-year-old woman from Lifta stated: "We were certain that we would return soon. We didn't know that we were coming here. My late father, mercy be upon his soul, had just built a house right next to the Israeli Knesset ... When they started bombarding our house, and as we were about to leave, carrying a few clothes and some light things, and descending towards Wadi Beit Eksa, close to our village, my father stopped. He removed the glass of the windows, put it on the floor, and put blankets between them so they wouldn't break from the bombs. He also told me, 'Cover the olives well.' It was as if we were leaving for one or two days and coming right back." About half the respondents (48 percent) said that they didn't realize that their state of refuge would be long-term until 1967. One 74-year- old man from Ramallah commented that he had hope until the mid 1950s. "We lost all hope when they built the camps; when projects began to build houses to replace the tent," he said.

Some refugees praised those who were able to foresee the consequences of the flight. One 66-year-old man from Haifa said: "The smart people were the ones who rolled up their sleeves and started working from the very beginning. These persons are rich in their soul. They didn't count on return, they didn't spend their money. They sold vegetables and other things while others spent their money until it was gone." A 74-year-old man from 'Anaba regretted that he was unable to foresee the consequences of his flight: "We lived from day to day, we were hoping to go back tomorrow. If we knew we weren't going back, we might have bought land and established ourselves, but we didn't know."

Hardships

When we asked the refugees about the difficulties they faced when they became refugees, respondents answered with tales of fear, hunger, thirst and death of relatives. A man from Haifa recalled his flight to Tulkarm: "My father and I were in Haifa three or four days after it fell. The British took us to the port of Haifa, close to the railroad station. They prepared a cargo train, and put us in it. I think we were about 100 or 200 people. The trip from Haifa to Tulkarm was like a trip in hell. We'd stop at the Jewish stations – Zichron Yaacov, Atlit, Hayamin, Hadera – these stations are originally Jewish settlements. Every time the train stopped, we were afraid. We were completely devastated by the time we reached Tulkarm. The train stopped in Tulkarm and never went back." Most other refugees, however, had no means of transportation and had to walk to their places of refuge.

Refugees of rural origin seem to have faced more difficulties as a result of their flight. They were hard hit because they lacked the skills to earn a living in the mostly new urban settings. They were simple farmers, sustaining their life from the land, and were completely ruined when they lost it. Furthermore, most Palestinians before 1948 were not mobile people; they rarely traveled or changed their place of residence. It should be noted that until 1951, up to 87 percent of the refugees, almost all of whom lived in camps, were housed in tents. By 1954, that proportion dropped to 32 percent. It was not until the end of 1955 that tents were replaced by prefabricated shelters or cinder-block dwellings in most camps.

Many refugees had either to beg for food from local people or collect it from army dumpsters in order to survive and to feed their children and elders. One 72-year-old woman from Lud recalled the early days of her refuge: "We died of starvation . My father sold his gun and spent the money. We slept on a burlap sack, and covered ourselves with another burlap sack. We had no blankets until UNRWA* gave us blankets and food."

One factor that all old refugees in the West Bank remembered was the change of weather. They experienced harsh weather after leaving their towns and villages on the coast. Further east in the mountains, it became colder, and those who came unprepared did not know what to do. On the coast, they lived in houses, but after their flight many had to live under the trees, in caves or in small tents donated to them by the International Red Cross.

The year 1949 is remembered by many refugees as the "year of the great snow" (*sanat al-thalja al-kabirah*). A 63-year-old man from Lud recalled: "It was the first time we had seen snow, and from that day, we have never seen so much snow – maybe once or twice. The whole camp at the Friends Girls' school was heavy with snow. I went into the tent and it was soaked. One family from Ramallah took pity on us and gave us a room."

Infiltration and return

The years between 1948 and 1953 were the most difficult for Palestinian refugees. The situation was especially desperate during this period, because assistance was minimal. UNRWA did not begin operations until May 1950, so refugees had to struggle to provide basic food for themselves and their families by whatever means at hand. More than one third of the refugees (35 percent) asserted that they had to risk their lives by going back to their original villages or towns after their flight, in order to search for food and other items left behind, such as clothes and furniture. A 67-year-old man from Beit Nabala recalled: "We went back to our village to get our things, and we were met by Jews. They put us in jail for six months. Another 74-year-old man from Annaba stated: "I used to sneak back into the village at night to get stuff. I went in 100 times, like a thief. We had to sneak in. We couldn't go in the open." The men who decided not to go back cited fear for their lives as the reason why they did not attempt to do so. It was usually men rather than women who returned, and several went back more than once.

The Israeli historian, Benny Morris, mentioned this phenomenon in his book, "1948 and After". He notes that Arab refugees were infiltrating back into

Israeli-held territory, mainly to harvest the summer crops rather than to permanently resettle in their former villages. "The refugees were driven by real hunger,"[4] he says. Some refugees, however, did return with the intention of resettling. One 64-year-old man from al-Majdal described his many attempts to return to stay in his village: "We gathered about five or six of us, and we went to al-Majdal, and each one of us went to his house. The houses weren't strictly guarded. I stayed in my house for about four months. While we were there, the Jewish census bureau came back to the house, as if they knew, they opened the wells and took the wheat. We had the wheat in 150 kilo barrels. They took it and put it in the car, and took me as well. Our house was on Majdal Street. There was a coffeehouse and members of the Jewish census were there. They took the wheat and the corn, etc., and started weighing it and marking it down in a notebook. Sometimes the most desperate situations are those that cause you to laugh. I asked them, 'Why did you write that down?' They said, 'Yhis is to protect your rights.' So I signed to receive the amount. Why did I sign? I don't know. This is what happened."

Those who made return trips in the aftermath of the war ended these excursions in the early 1950s, when the borders between Israel and the Gaza Strip (then under Egyptian administration), and Israel and the West Bank (then part of Jordan), became harder to cross. This was due to Israeli, Jordanian and Egyptian security measures. Beyond this was the fact that, after a while, there was nothing to go back to, especially since most of the villages (more than 400)[5] were destroyed by the Israeli army, making it impossible for refugees to return. One 83-year-old man from 'Anaba recalls sneaking back into his village and seeing the demolished homes: "The last time I went back to the village, it was destroyed, and all the stones had been removed."

Responsibility

There was a large degree of unanimity throughout the interviews with regard to holding the Israeli Jews responsible for the exodus of 1948. Almost all 142 refugees who responded to this question blamed the Jews for creating the Palestinian refugee problem. Sixty-four, or 45 percent of the respondents, said that the Jews alone were to blame for the creation of the problem. The British Mandate authorities, the Arab leaders and armies, the Palestinians themselves, and the international community at large, were also at fault from the point of view of the 78 other refugees who responded to this question. The British Mandate authorities were second to blame after the Jews, and third came the Arab leaders or armies, fourth came the Palestinian leadership, and finally the international community at large. The UN was signaled out for its role in the petition, and certain countries such as the United States and the former Soviet Union were also mentioned.

When considering the role of the Jews in the creation of the refugee problem, many interviewees cited, and strongly attacked, the Zionist claim that Palestine was "a land without a people for a people without a land." They considered themselves to have been victimized by this claim which was used to justify Jewish immigration to Palestine and the subsequent confiscation of

Palestinian land, especially farmland, by the Jews. This land was, in their opinion, intensively cultivated and more productive than any land they ever saw after 1948.

The refugees have vivid memories of the role of the British, and stress that they were a major factor behind the creation of the refugee problem. For some, the British role in the plight of the Palestinian people went even beyond the role of the Jewish army. One 74-year-old man from `Anaba commented: "The British bear the biggest responsibility for the flight of the Palestinian people, in addition to the Jews, of course." Another 66-year-old man from Haifa stated this clearly: "The British basically handed the country over to the Jews." In the minds of these interviewees, without British assistance the Jewish army would never have succeeded in uprooting them from their homes in 1948. The Balfour Declaration is seen as yet another example of what they called "an offer by those who do not possess, to those who do not deserve."

Ironically, the first generation of refugees only had negative memories regarding the British Mandate, while several interviewees cherished their memories concerning their relations with their Jewish neighbors before the '48 war. They recalled that their relations with the Jews were actually quite normal or even good. One 65-year-old man, originally from Deir Yasin, recalls: "Believe me, the relationship between the people of the village and the Jews was a good one. There were no problems, and it made no difference to us whether somebody was Jewish or Arab. They would come to our weddings. They would buy from us and we would by from them. I don't recall any kind of conflict between us and them. There was no killing, or beating, or thievery. I don't recall that our relationship with the Jews was ever bad before the events [of '48]."

The Arab governments were to blame, from the point of view of the refugees, for spreading rumors of rapes and killings on the part of the Jews, and thus encouraging people to flee. One 65-year-old man from Deir Yasin said: "The Arab Legion used to come and tell us '[the Jews] are killing and raping your women,' and you know that Arabs are extremely protective of their honor. These things never happened. Yes, men, women, and children were killed, but the rumors that the Arabs spread had more influence on us leaving than those incidents. They were doing the Jews a favor in having the people flee without fighting."

The Palestinian people must have had very high expectations of their Arab brothers and their armies in 1948. Many of the older respondents believed then that the Jews were absolutely no match for the Arab armies. In fact, some Palestinians believed that the Jews and the British together were no match for the Arabs. A 66-year-old man from Tal al-Turmus was adamant that "the people of Palestine were capable of facing the Jews and the British with them. I wonder why seven Arab armies could not deal with a few Jews. A man was able to run after and scare [the Jews] all the way to the middle of Tel Aviv. When a Palestinian walked through one of the small settlements on a camel, the people of the settlement would run away from fear of the camel. It was not the power of the Jews that expelled us. It was the conspiracy of the British and the failure of the Arab armies."

A few refugees blamed the Arab countries for rejecting the UN partition plan and for encouraging the Palestinian leadership to do the same. Had the Palestinians not listened to the Arab governments, and in fact accepted the UN partition, asserted one 66–year–old man from Tal al-Turmus, they would have maintained at least a section of Palestine. "We, the Palestinians, were satisfied with the partition plan," he claimed, and added: "We hoped that the partition would give us a portion and give the Jews a portion, and we would be able to live together. But the Arab countries said that they wanted to fight the partition by force. We know that the partition plan did not give us anything, but the Jews were successful in obtaining legitimacy after May 15th. When the Jewish state was proclaimed, three-quarters of the world recognized it as a legitimate state founded as part of the partition plan. Very few people said, 'Don't fight the partition plan – say that we accept it.'"

Conclusion

The Palestinian exodus of 1948 was a shock which many refugees, especially from the first generation, were never able to cope with. That explains why refugees constituted the main destabilizing factor in the region for over half a century. The issue now is not any more why the Palestinian refugees left, or who was responsible for their expulsion or flight, or even how much they endured. The real question is: Why were they denied the right of return to their homes after the war ended? And the real challenge is to devise a just solution for their problem so that they are not any more a destabilizing factor in the country, the region, and the world at large.

Rationale for using oral data

This paper is mainly based on oral data. It has often been said that history is the property of the winners. The stories of the defeated often are left out of the chronicles of history. This is especially true in the case of Palestinian refugees, who despite the high level of literacy among them, have left no archives to testify to their experience. Due to the dearth of first-hand material available on the subject, especially from the viewpoint of the refugees themselves, this research has concentrated primarily on collecting, transcribing and analyzing oral data as historical evidence. The centerpiece has been the collection of more than 200 in-depth interviews with Palestinians and Israelis.

Reliability of oral data

It is important to bear in mind that the reliability of oral testimony is not complete. Memories are often based on perceptions and expectations and are customarily affected by the state of mind of the narrator at the time. People tend to report what they expect to see more than what they do actually see. Memory, as some say, "selects certain features from the past and interprets them according to expectations, previous knowledge, or the logic of what must have happened, and fills the gaps in perception."[6] This, however, does not mean that oral testimonies, especially of eyewitnesses, should be considered invalid. Witness accounts are, after all, the fountainhead of all history. Furthermore, oral historians have established that oral accounts by "silenced" sectors of society can serve to complement or correct histories based on written documents which reflect the views of the elite who customarily monopolize writing and record-keeping.

---

[1] This paper is based on the research conducted by the author and others published in Adel Yahya, *The Palestinian Refugees: 1948-1998, An Oral History* (Ramallah, The Palestinian Association for Cultural Exchange - Pace, 1999).

[2] Israeli figures put the number at 520.000; Arab sources estimate it at more than 900.000. The UNRWA records put the number at around 726.000. See: Benny Morris. *The Birth of the Palestinian Refugee problem, 1947-1948.* (Cambridge University Press, 1987) p. 279.

[3] Benny Morris, *1948 and After: Israel and the Palestinians,* (Clarendon Press, Oxford 1994) pp. 289-325.

[4] Morris. 1994, p.293.

[5] This number of demolished villages is contested by some sources, especially Israeli sources. See, for example, Morris, 1987, pp. xiv-xx, Morris lists 360 demolished villages in this book.

[6] Jan Vancina. *Oral Tradition as History,* (Madison, University of Wisconsin Press 1985) p.5.

DISCUSSION 6

Avraham Sela and Adel Yahya

AVRAHAM SELA: Basically, I discerned three main phases in the development of Israeli historiography regarding the 1948 war. Of course, I don't mean precisely from a certain year or a certain day. Until the early 1980s, it was mostly a collective mobilized historiography meant to meet the needs of state-building and nation-building, and to address the regional problems of security and defense and so on. The second phase begins with the gradual dismantling of this collectivist approach, and is primarily marked by the appearance of what we call the New Historians. In my view, what is meant by this is New Historians, not new history. The third phase, from approximately the beginning or mid-1990s, is characterized by an attempt to conceptualize a comparative study, including some criticism of the New Historians regarding the war. This includes, for example, new studies now being conducted around ethnic conflicts or civil wars and discussions of issues such as institution-building.

All those have been encouraged by the waves of releases of new documents, mostly by Israeli archives such as the Haganah archive, the State archive and the IDF archive. In 1992, the IDF archive was declared open to the public. This does not mean that it was not open before that, but from then on it became much more used by researchers.

On the whole, Israeli historiography can be described as dynamic, as one that goes through changes in accordance with circumstances and Israeli public discourse, not only with regard to the Israeli-Palestinian or the Israeli-Arab conflict, but also with regard to social issues, such as cultural and ethnic relationships within Israeli society, and criticism of the founding fathers about various manifestations of discrimination or other painful memories of the years of absorption of the newcomers - especially from Arab countries - to Israel. So I can easily locate the discourse with regard to the early years of Israel and its conflict with the Palestinian Arabs or with the Arab countries as part of that whole public discourse that goes back to the early formative years of the state.

A few words about history and memory. We have to differentiate between professional historical research and what we call collective memory. The gap is tremendous, even bringing in the New Historians, although they do go a little further in terms of trying to understand more or criticize more Israeli actions and decisions in those years. The collective memory is one of a community under siege and in existential danger that had been attacked by the Palestinian Arabs and the neighboring Arab countries. As a result, there is a tendency to perceive that whatever happened as a result with regard to the Palestinian refugees or the Palestinian tragedy as a whole was a historical justice.

This sounds quite ironic when we think about the discordance in what resulted for the two communities. I can only tell you that, from endless appearances and talks to Israeli audiences, I find myself again and again unable even to make people willing to listen to another story. The memory is one of tremendous fear, uncertainty, and the feeling that everything could have collapsed at any point along the war. From a religious viewpoint, I've seen many people who could not be satisfied with any explanation for what happened in the war other than Divine Providence. Not bringing Him in is unacceptable. At the same time, this collective memory also contains the element of tremendous coherence and collectivity, a belief in the righteousness of the Jewish Israeli position, and also in the right of the Jewish people to implement its long-delayed hope for statehood and sovereignty.

In general, we had these two elements of fear and uncertainty, together with feelings of heroism and that something great and miraculous happened because of what we did for ourselves or because we were so wonderful in terms of taking care of ourselves and planning everything and so forth, so that we managed not only to pass this test, but also to succeed in all our current achievements.

Of course, historical debate or historical research puts things under a much less glaring light. Yes, there was fear. Yes, there was uncertainty. But there was also a gap between the two societies in terms of institutionalization, organization, international contacts and the ability to manipulate the international community - which later led to all kinds of results in terms of diplomatic, political, military and financial support - and the ability to foresee needs as a result of having a more or less central leadership that could mobilize part, if not most, of the Yishuv's potential. All this makes up one part of the equation.

I'll tell you the other part by way of illustration. In the early 1980s, I was talking to a forum of the veterans of Israeli brigade commanders. Yigal Yadin, who had been Deputy Chief of Staff, and Israel Galili, who had been head of the National Command of the Haganah. were present. I spoke there about the Palestinian Arabs and the problems of the Arab countries. Yadin erupted and said, "What are you saying? We did nothing? We were fighting against wind or what?"

In other words, here we have both parts of the equation. On the one hand was a relatively high level of organization and an institutionalized society. On the other hand, almost all the Arab countries were societies in turmoil. The Palestinian society had not been well organized. In fact, some historians say that the fate of the 1948 war had already been determined in the 1936-1939 rebellion because of the damage and because of the lessons learned by the Palestinian population at that time.

In any case, we, in historical research, try to put things in balance. We are trying to find out how the war could have ended with such results when the majority were Palestinian Arabs and only a minority were Jews.

Israeli historiography is tremendously focused on what the Israelis did, what they wanted to do, what they thought and what affected them in terms of British policy or international powers, and of course, "the Arab side" as well. That's how it's presented in many conferences and panels - "the Arab side" - as if you can put them all together in one basket and say "the Arab side," and usually your humble servant is the one who fills the role of talking about the Arab side. Because of the multiple actors, the "Arab side" is much more difficult to study and becomes much less coherent. Coordination is a tremendous task when you have so many actors, especially given the type of relationships or the nature of the relationships among the Arab countries and between each of them and the Palestinian leadership at that time, which were not entirely amicable or agreeable.

Almost no attention has been paid to the Army of Deliverance*, which appears under various names. This is one of the most crucial elements in the war because they were present for almost an entire year, unlike other forces. Secondly, they were in almost every part of the country. Finally, even Palestinian historiography places a lot of blame on the Army of Deliverance. Much of the hope of the local Arab population rested on them, but at the crucial moment, they almost always disappointed. They easily disintegrated and deserted the war arena.

When the Arab population becomes not just a subject of research, but the object of research, it is usually tackled as a group of individuals without this identity as a nation or as a people. They are not taken seriously as one political community, but rather as a group of people who fight either on the local level or as individuals without a clear agenda.

As a teacher at Hebrew University, I teach students that you cannot do historical research emotionally. We try to keep a distance from the emotional side, and as much as is possible, analyze things on their merits. In my own study - which I've been conducting for a long time - with regard to the Israeli historiography of the Arab side in the war, I have found that not much attention has been paid to the significance of the public arena in the Arab countries and the role it played in the motivation of the governments, the elites, to enter the war, and how to enter the war, under what parameters and when. All these are very important factors.

Basically, the Arab elites were conducting a war of survival vis-a-vis their own publics, and when they entered the war, they knew they had no chance of winning. Look at the Iraqi report about the April 30 meeting of chiefs-of-staff in Amman when they said to the Arab governments, "We need at least five divisions, six squadrons and one unified command if we want to win." And they actually had less than two, even had they mobilized all the forces in the Arab countries, leaving not even minimal forces to provide for public security.

Why did they do it? For one reason alone. In order to survive. They knew they could not win a war. They were hoping the powers would impose an immediate cease-fire. But the stop-gap policy that they had to adopt was mainly in order to survive

RAN AARONSOHN: Politically.

AVRAHAM SELA: Domestically. I'm talking mainly about Egypt, Iraq, Syria and Lebanon. Not Saudi Arabia. Not King Abdullah, who did not have an urban society with a strong public opinion, press and political movement. But the issue was very much alive, especially during the 1940s, in these four countries.

One question I keep asking myself is, could the war have ended differently? I would like to suggest a number of possible events that could have resulted in an entirely different war scenario. The first, that I mentioned earlier, is if the Soviet Union had never supported the partition of Palestine and the establishment of a Jewish state. This was a surprise. And then, of course, if the Soviet Union had also not approved arms supplies to the Jewish state by Czechoslovakia when it could not be done by the Soviet Union. Second is if the Arab states had fulfilled their commitments and promises to Palestinian Arabs at least with regard to financial and military support.

Third is if Britain had not imposed an embargo on the Middle East in terms of arms supplies. This tremendously affected at least three major countries - Iraq, Jordan and Egypt. They were utterly paralyzed during the war because of this embargo. When I came back from England after six months in the Public Records Office, somebody asked me to state my major finding in one sentence. My response was that Israel should plant a tree in the Forest of the Righteous for the British Foreign Minister at that time. Fourth is if the Arab governments had been willing simply to prolong the first truce of June 1948 - just not to renew the war - that could have changed the whole course of the war. They refused to extend it, and that gave Israel a golden opportunity to hit, and hit strongly. Those were the ten days of battles in which Lod and Ramla were captured and over 50,000 refugees were created, if not more.

Finally, back to the previous discussion, is if the Palestinian Arabs had never resorted to violence after the UN resolution. I repeatedly ask this question. Had the Palestinian Arabs accepted the partition plan - even if we agree that it was an injustice to the Palestinian people - but hypothetically, had they accepted, would Israel or would the Jewish state still have expelled the Palestinians?

A question. I'm not sure I have an answer, but we should think about it.

The Palestinian narrative finds a straightforward line from the establishment of the Zionist movement and the definition of its goals to the expulsion of the Palestinian refugees. Look at Walid Khalidi and others. But if you really look at the documents - and I have a few which I would be happy to supply to all of you - until March, there are clear orders by the brigades not to expel. In one letter from the Kiryati Brigade in Tel Aviv, there is even a threat that those who would dare harm Palestinian Arabs and expel them would be punished.

What happened was all a matter of the level of danger. At some point, it seemed so easy to get the Palestinians to leave only by spreading rumors or threats and so on, and I think the appetite came with this growing wave of exodus. I don't see this as an achievement, but I do believe that the Jews found this extremely wonderful. All of a sudden, they had a solution to the problem of that large population of Palestinian Arabs within the Jewish state. And especially because of the circumstances of the war, they thought this was miraculous. At one point, Ben Gurion comes and speaks in Haifa, and he doesn't understand. He asks, "How did they leave? Why did they leave?" He speaks about it as a miracle, something that happened to the Jewish state like the manna that fell from heaven.

From that point, it was a very short distance to the decision to prevent the return of the Palestinian Arabs. This was a political decision. There was no intention, from that moment on, to let the Palestinians come back. The justification was that they fought us and lost. They have to pay the price. Furthermore, we can't count on them, if they do come back, not to start fighting us again. This is exactly what the Israeli leadership told the international mediator when he came in the summer to try to find a way to bring the Palestinian refugees back.

A fact that is not well known to many is that, in that particular month of the truce, Hajj Amin el Husseini was consulted, and he refused to allow Palestinian refugees to come back, saying they would become hostages of the Israeli state. He preferred to continue the fight. That was his preference in the summer of 1948. The decision of the Israeli government was June 14.

Because I dealt with it quite a lot, I would like to say something about the collusion with King Abdullah. I know it's a nasty thing to collude with somebody behind the backs of others, but this is what states do. Realistically speaking, this is what politicians ought to do if they can achieve more by striking such alliances. Regardless, sometimes I really can't understand why this argument has disappeared from the awareness of those who speak about collusion. Yes, it was against the Palestinian people, but the Palestinian people did not exist at that time. There was no leadership for the Israeli side to talk to. On the other hand, if the Palestinians did maintain a significant portion of the land of Palestine as purely Arab until 1967, it was due to that collusion. Without it, they might have lost that as well. Basically, this collusion was meant to reach an agreement that would prevent war. The whole idea was not to go to war, and to divide the land, but to prevent war. And had the war been prevented, we have to ask the question: Could it be that the phenomenon of the Palestinian refugees would not have come into the world?

ADEL YAHYA: I had to revise my paper because I was given Avraham's paper late. So I am also going to talk about Palestinian historiography in order to counter at least some of Avraham's points.

Palestinian historical writing can be characterized as a form of resistance by means of formulating a national Palestinian narrative. This is how most Palestinian historians have seen their mission and their job. This is motivated by a desire to counter Zionist claims and to protect the national narrative and heritage. If you look at any Palestinian history book from the middle of the 20th century until the present, this motivation is present.

Early historical writings look like emotional speeches and direct national propaganda pieces rather than a search for the truth, or even straightforward research based on evidence and citation of sources. In this regard, one may point to some very famous Palestinian works, such as those of the *Balad Falastin* and others. This phenomenon has never died down. These books are still very popular among Palestinian students and academics, and the phenomenon continues in spite of the fact that new developments have been noted in Palestinian historiography in the past 20 or 25 years.

Again, I stress the fact that most Palestinian historical writing has actually been a form of reaction to Israeli Zionist claims and myths. You cannot find one Palestinian history book without reference to Israeli and Zionist myths and conclusions of some kind or another. Popular topics that Palestinian historians and writers have dealt with, and that are of interest to Israelis as well, vary from topics like a land without a people for a people without a land - there are books actually with this title - and the blooming of the desert. These are Zionist claims to which Palestinians have paid a great deal of attention and which they have tried to counter by a new kind of Palestinian narrative of Palestinian refugees and expulsion, emigration versus expulsion, Nakba or the War of Independence, the right of return, the role of the Arabs, the role of the British and so on.

Most Palestinian historical writing is directed to the Palestinians themselves, not to the outside. Most Palestinian historians write for the Palestinians, and that's why their books are more like propaganda pieces than straightforward narratives based on evidence and the citation of various academic sources. There is some justification for this, at least with regard to early Palestinian historical writings. The Israelis have a great advantage over Palestinian historians because they have their own archives. It has often been said that history is the property of the winners, the victors. The defeated and the weak are usually left out of the chronicles of history. That was the case for the Palestinians, and especially the Palestinian refugees who, despite their high level of literacy, have not really left any archives to speak of. So Palestinians are disadvantaged in this regard because they have not formulated archives. To do that, you need to have authority in the state, and the Palestinians did not have that.

Worse than that, the Israelis have constantly confiscated and destroyed Palestinian archives, libraries and museums from 1948 to the present. Israelis continually prevent the formation of any kind of Palestinian archive, whatever its form.

MERON BENVENISTI: Orient House, for instance.

FATMEH QASSEM: I have a Jewish friend, a soldier who served in the army in Jenin. He received a military order to destroy all the hard disks of the computers in the Education Ministry. Even in the schools. Go from school to school. If you find a computer, destroy it.

AVRAHAM SELA: I can give you many examples.

ADEL YAHYA: So it should be no wonder that Palestinian historiography and historical writing lagged behind that of the Israelis. Palestinian historians have been striving for a kind of match with the Israelis that they were unable to achieve. The most significant development in Palestinian historiography began in the late 1970s, early 1980s, characterized by the adoption of oral history, simultaneously with the opening of some Palestinian academic institutions. Bir Zeit University's first BA students graduated in 1976. At around this time, Palestinian historians, together with American historians who were working in these institutions, introduced a new methodology into Palestinian historiography. In this context, one may mention Professor Thomas Ricks, now at Villanova, and Ted Swedenburg and others who have worked for some time at Bir Zeit. Those people were instrumental to introducing some young Palestinian historians, including myself at that time, to oral history.

We thought this was the way to go. If we have no archive of our own and cannot create one, why not create a Palestinian narrative based on oral data? Upon graduation from Bir Zeit, several friends and I were hired by the then Documentation and Research Center of Bir Zeit, and we started a project, in the late 1970s-early 1980s, to document the history of the demolished villages, one of the very first oral history projects, which formed the basis for the famous book, "All That Remains," edited by Professor Walid Khalidi. From that point on, oral history has become instrumental in formulating the Palestinian narrative, particularly of 1948, but also of the 1936 revolt.

In addition, there is now a new class of Palestinian academics who graduated from Western academic institutions - mostly American, but also German, and even Israeli - who are working in Israel or in the Palestinian territories. They have initiated a process of countering the Israeli narrative by formulating the new Palestinian narrative. In the late 1980s and early 1990s, many workshops and seminars were held to train more and more field researchers to conduct field work in Palestinian territories. These researchers came not only from the West Bank, but also from Jordan, Egypt, Lebanon and Gaza.

However, we have not yet been able to establish a unified Palestinian archive. Various ministries and individuals also have collections, some of which have been duplicated and are being kept in safe places in Jordan or Egypt. It is hoped that these will form the nucleus of a Palestinian archive which will eventually be available to Palestinian and international researchers in the future.

Again, the rationale for using oral data as historical evidence is because the Palestinians have not been able to do otherwise. And they have an advantage over the Israelis in this regard because the Israelis cannot, even if they wanted to, interview Palestinians. Some Israelis tried before 1996, with the help of the Israeli military, but without success because the Palestinians were not willing to cooperate. Palestinian academics and researchers can interview Palestinians about the 1936 revolt, and eye-witness narrators about 1948, so Palestinians do now have something with which to counter the Israeli narrative of those events.

Palestinian oral history researchers are interested in the same topics that earlier Palestinian historians were concerned with, such as Jewish and Zionist myths and claims to the land. The article I prepared for this seminar is based mainly on our findings as reported in our book, "The Palestinian Refugees: 1948-1998, An Oral History," published by Pace in 1999. It's a small book that doesn't actually reflect the huge amount of documents we have collected.

One of the most important questions is: Why did the Palestinian refugees leave? Many theories have been introduced by Israelis, but nobody asked the refugees themselves. Many Israeli historians have theories, but they are based on Israeli archives, mainly the Israeli Army's archive and the Haganah archive and so on. Now we have another archive that can be used, and our findings seem to contradict some of the common Israeli myths, and even some of the Palestinian myths, about the war of 1948.

Now that we have published this book, we sometimes have difficulty explaining the position of the refugees even to Palestinian researchers. One of the problems is the issue of whether or not there was a concentrated effort on the part of the Zionist organization to expel refugees. When we asked refugees – 208 of them - this question they said, "No. We were not aware of a plan. We thought we were going away for a couple of days and coming right back." The Palestinians did not believe the Jews were after them. They thought, even with British assistance, that the Jews would not be up to expelling the Palestinians from their homeland. They thought they would be gone for a few days and that they would be coming right back. A few months at the most.

ADEL MANNA: All these are from the West Bank?

ADEL YAHYA: Yes. That's a problem. During this particular project, we were not able to work in any other region. We are now expanding the research, working in Egypt, Lebanon and Jordan. We see this as a rescue operation, interviewing all these refugees who were eye-witnesses during the 1948 war, in order to collect and preserve the data. Again, I do not deny that we are motivated, like all other Palestinian historians, by wanting to formulate a Palestinian narrative of 1948 and beyond.

LILY GALILI: You said some of the findings contradicted Israeli myths and some Palestinian myths. Could you give us examples of each?

ADEL YAHYA: The Israeli official position is that the refugees left their homeland upon the command of Arab leaders and Arab armies. They claim, "The Arabs told them to leave and they left. It's not our fault." We asked the refugees this question. They said, "Absolutely not. This is stupid. The Arab armies were trying to get us to return. They were even hitting us to make us go back to our villages, but we were so afraid. We wanted to leave because we thought it was very dangerous. Jewish Zionist groups were attacking. We thought we'd get away until the war is over and then come back. That's how we thought."

This was not meant to be quantitative research, but when you have 200 interviews, you are motivated to use quantitative data as well, not only qualitative. We looked at the data and the numbers, and the numbers are extremely significant. We cannot say that our sample is representative of all refugees, but 92 percent of those we interviewed said they left out of fear. Only 5 percent said they left to allow the Arab armies to fight or because Arab leaders demanded that they do so; 2 percent stated they left out of ignorance of the stakes that were involved.

When 92 percent of the interviewees say they left out of fear, this is significant because it's such a huge proportion. We can no longer say the people left because the Arab armies and Arab regimes asked them to leave. The people did not hear anything of this kind.

As always, there was one exception, one case where somebody said yes, he heard something on Palestinian radio calling for the Palestinians to leave. But even that was not clear. He said they heard on the radio that they should leave because it was very dangerous, and that can be explained.

Something else that Palestinian historians don't like is the response to questions about a cohesive plan on the part of the Jewish Zionist groups to expel the Palestinians. The Palestinian refugees were clear on this matter. They said "No". They didn't believe it. They didn't think for a minute that the Jews were out to expel the Palestinians. If there was or was not a plan, they didn't know about it .

ADEL MANNA: How would they know, even if there was ?

ADEL YAHYA: Right. Some people say they should have known because it was clear, but that's a reflection of what we know now, what we think now about the past. But the refugees at the time were not aware of any plan of the Jews to expel them. And some Palestinians do not like to hear that. They think we are siding with the Israelis, but that's not true at all.

We also asked about the issue of responsibility, who was responsible for the expulsion of the Palestinian refugees. The response was unanimous. The Jews were blamed, but also the British. Sometimes the role of the British outweighed that of the Jews. In many cases, refugees said, The Jews are nothing. The Zionists are nothing. It's the British who are responsible for our plight.

They blamed the Arab states to a lesser extent. First, the Israelis; second - but at the same level - the British; third, the Arab states; and fourth, the international community, the UN, because it adopted the partition plan. What amazed us was that they didn't blame the Palestinian leadership. They directed hardly any blame toward the Husseinis or any other Palestinian leadership of the time.

AVRAHAM SELA: In Muzal's book, he offers many testimonies blaming the Army of Deliverance. Did you hear anything about that?

ADEL YAHYA: Yes. They actually accused them of disarming the Palestinians. There were clashes between the Palestinian partners. If they saw a Palestinian fighter with a good gun, they would confiscate it and shoot him.

AZIZ HAIDER: What about blaming themselves ?

ADEL YAHYA: Yes. They blamed themselves as well. Something like two percent said their expulsion or their plight was mainly due to their ignorance of the consequences of their flight. "Had we known what was happening, we would not have left. Let the Jews kill us."

BURCKHARD BLANKE: It's quite interesting, that mention of the age of the interviewees. If somebody is 53 years old, as stated in your paper, he could not have been a witness of the events of 1948.

ADEL YAHYA: We interviewed the younger generation for purposes of comparison. We wanted to know what they think about returning to their villages. We asked questions such as, "Did you visit your village when it was possible to do so?" We used them only for purposes of comparison, to see if there was any tendency among the younger generation to depart from their parents' positions. And it seems there are, in fact, major differences between the generations. The younger generation did not express much enthusiasm about visiting their old homes. That is something else that Palestinian critics do not like in our book. They say everybody wants to go visit. But our research revealed that, out of 70 people above the age of 60 or 70, maybe 70 or 80 percent went back to visit after 1967, while among the second generation of refugees – my age and older - only 11 or 12 percent visited.

So our finding was that there has been a decline in attachment to the original home. They still talk about the right of return, but it's a different concept from that of my father's generation.

MERON BENVENISTI: Some things in the narratives are very important

236

for us to raise here, especially because they support what Avraham was saying about what would have happened had it not happened. Resolution 181, chapter 2, article 8, says: "No expropriation of land owned by an Arab in the Jewish state or by a Jew in the Arab states respectively shall be allowed except for public purposes. In all cases of expropriation, full compensation, as fixed by the Supreme Court, shall be paid previous to dispossession.".

I don't know how many Palestinian colleagues know that, until the end of June 1948, this was the official policy of the Israeli government. There was a committee headed by Ranaan Weitz,* the arch expeller-transferist, and Zalman Lipshiz, that devised the plan for bringing back the refugees, or at least for not touching their property. Not a single dunam of absentee property was touched at that time because the Israelis believed that UN resolution 181 would be implemented, and they didn't want to contravene it. That lasted for about six or seven months, until the end of June. If you want, that can be used to show that the issue of absentees was not pre-determined to result it what later developed. It could have been prevented had that decision been implemented in full, including the internationalization of Jerusalem.

I am just adding the sensitive issue of land. And later on, the Mapam party used the same thing in order to create a new plan for the return of the refugees and for intensification of the land in Israel, meaning to take some of the land, but to compensate the Palestinians in the form of irrigation and so on.

In other words, these little things are totally washed away by the waves of history. But if one wants to be generous, they might show that the results we have seen were not necessarily inevitable. That is one of the lessons we should learn.

I became aware of that when I saw how surprised you were when Dalia spoke about the Jewish community. This was a different narrative than you are used to. That is the importance of this kind of sharing. It is very productive. I learned many things from what has been said here. I think that Ran, for example, was surprised that, since 1948, all attempts of Palestinians to create archives were frustrated and seized as a matter of Israeli government policy. If you want Palestinian archives, they're in the Jewish National Archives.

BENJAMIN POGRUND: Who has access to the IDF archives? Could Adel Yahya access them?

AVRAHAM SELA: In principle, everybody can. But let me tell you something. I am Israeli. I once had a research assistant at the Hebrew University, an Israeli Arab. I went there with him to get him started, and the guy at the entrance was shocked even to think that an Arab could get in. He checked his identity card so he saw the name. He said to me, "Can't you find a Jewish one?" So this is my experience. And he did not go in. He was afraid. And we both returned to Jerusalem.

You can appeal to the court, you can use the law, but the approach is very discouraging. Of course, it's not impossible .

RUTH KARK: I have a research assistant working in the State archive without any problem at all.

AVRAHAM SELA: That's an entirely different story.

ATA QAYMARI: First of all, I don't want to misunderstand Avraham. Did

237

you say - and correct me if I'm wrong - that the result of the war represented a kind of justice for the Palestinians because they lost the war? I could hear this kind of thing from somebody in the street and accept it, but not from an academic

AVRAHAM SELA: Because it's such a painful point, I have to answer immediately. I said this is the collective memory - in other words, public opinion - of many. I differentiated between that and what academic study shows.

ATA QAYMARI: The official and traditional Zionist position for dealing with this question is that the Palestinians launched the war by resorting to violence - killing people, attacking the convoys and so on - and that they have done the same throughout history. They say the Arabs launched the war of 1948 and the Arabs launched the war of 1967. There might have been some red lines drawn at that moment by the British or by the international community. There are also the natural historical relations with the Hashemites. In the eyes of the Zionists, the Hashemites should gain something out of this war. The gains will be distributed among both parties.

Another aspect is the fear, I suppose resulting in the flight/expulsion of the Palestinian refugees. I expected you to be more objective and to talk not only about the lack of orders to expel Palestinians, but also about the orders or the policies that were adopted at that time. In his book, Yitzhak Rabin describes asking Ben Gurion what to do with the people of Lod, and Ben Gurion responded with a gesture of his hand - get them out. Yigal Allon* talks about something else, the battle of cleansing.

Since you say you've been to the IDF archives, I would have expected you to bring out these kinds of documents as well, in order to do real justice to the history of the Palestinians and to confirm that what Adel says is correct. These people were expelled.

I would prefer that we leave aside the fact that we are Palestinians or Jews. In the end, we are individuals who will be living in this country and dealing with each other. We will have to look each other in the eyes. You have to be fair to me and to yourself and to history, and bring these documents out and say there was some kind of direction. This is something that has been discussed and thought about. Why did Ben Gurion only make that gesture without saying a word? Why didn't he give an order? Because he had in his mind the responsibility that such an action could inflict upon Israel and the Jews, so he preferred not to say it aloud.

MOSHE MA'OZ: So Ben Gurion was very careful. Maybe Arafat has also been careful that captured documents do not attest to direct orders to Hamas or others.

I am very impressed with your oral history project. Of course, we all know that one has to be very careful with oral history. After 50 years, people can forget things. There is also distortion and wishful thinking and glorification and what have you. So it always has to be compared to other sources.

About the historiography of the Nakba, yes, from what I've read, there was a lot of self-criticism within the Palestinian community about what led up to the Nakba, about the social regime or the weakness of the society's social system, the influence of religion, criticism of Arab countries and regimes, and something else very surprising -- imitation of the Jews. Look at the Jews. Why did they succeed? They were motivated, organized, secular, democratic. We, the Palestinians, have to be like that. There is something of that too. No doubt about it.

About the exodus, so to speak, you didn't mention another fact - and again, I don't know its significance - that, among the Palestinians, the leaders were the first to leave, because of economic reasons and what have you. And that caused a disintegration of the society because of its social composition. This should also be taken into account.

You mentioned the archives, and I'm ashamed to say that there have been a number of cases in which archives have been destroyed, but not always by order. Sometimes it's vandalism. During the 1967 war, one of my assignments was to collect documents in Gaza, not to destroy them, but to collect them for various purposes. But I saw some soldiers who got there first and just set them on fire. They were paper and they wanted to make a bonfire.

RAN AARONSOHN: That's not the claim. The claim I heard was that they were systematically destroyed.

MOSHE MA'OZ: What I am saying is that it was not always deliberate and systematic. In some cases, there were orders to collect documents. But in some cases, there was also vandalism by the soldiers. It's a mixed picture. In addition, for a long time Israel prohibited the sending of books to Palestinians over the bridge. They were confiscated. So I take the blame - or the credit - for smuggling some materials to Palestinian universities. Keep that in mind for future reference.

Avraham mentioned the notion of new and old historians. I think it's less a matter of old and new, and more a matter of good historians and bad historians. Good historians are those who are careful, balanced and empathetic, which is very important in the end. They use sources, oral or otherwise, presenting the positions and narratives of all sides. You don't have to accept it, but you have to present it, and take into account the various forces at work, the changes and the dynamics.

Avraham also mentioned the position of the elite in the Arab countries as a factor resulting in this war. I want to take this opportunity to mention something else which bothers me a great deal, and that is the Arab rhetoric, which wasn't very helpful because of the gap between the rhetoric and the ability to act. This had a big impact, in my opinion element. The rhetoric about throwing the Jews into the sea and so on provided some sort of motivation and enthusiasm and expectations for the Arabs, but frightened the Jews to the extent that we felt we were fighting with our backs to the sea and we have to do our utmost to defend ourselves. This is a very important element in our conflict.

FATMEH QASSEM: Avraham, have you used any Arab archives? And if you did, whose archives and how did you get to them? If Arab countries were involved in this war, they must certainly have their own documentation and archives.

MOSHE MA'OZ: Unfortunately, they are not open.

FATMEH QASSEM: Okay. I just wondered. To Dr. Adel Yahya, have you made any classifications among the refugees by gender or class? I noticed in your book that you indicated education level. I have also been involved a little with this kind of oral history research, and have heard from many old women that they resisted leaving their homes. They were forced to leave by the men. And this was not confined to only certain areas or regions. So was that common?

ADEL YAHYA: I have here our newest version. It's called "The Dynamic of Social Relations as a Result of Expulsion," if you'd like to have a look.

FATMEH QASSEM: Thank you. Avraham, as a historian - and maybe this is for all historians - who wrote the history and the documentation? I will raise it again and again. Who is absent in history, and why? I am not referring only to women. Palestinians, women, minorities. Kurds and Armenians, for example. I don't know if we have their archives, their history. It's a big problem. Why haven't the Palestinians written books and documented their history? Israelis have written a huge amount of books and articles. Very few Palestinians deal with themselves and their history.

RAN AARONSOHN: Adel, you mentioned that many Zionist claims and narratives have been examined by Palestinian scholars and that they are often referred to in Palestinian books. Would you kindly explain a little about what the attitudes are when looking through the eyes of the Palestinians with regard to the two examples you mentioned - a land without people for a people without a land, and the blossoming of the desert - or other examples.

Second, oral evidence, of course, is of great importance and interest, and I thank you very much for it and for your book. But it's known, and we all admit, that, as soft evidence, it has many disadvantages. Did you try to look into cross-evidence? Are there newspapers of the time, including Arabic newspapers? Did you look into the Arab armies' archives, or are they entirely closed and unavailable? What about foreign diplomatic agents or other evidence? It's great to get testimonies from a specific group of people who experienced an awful tragedy on a personal level, but for purposes of historical research, there has to be other evidence as well to confirm it, even if 200 people from within this specific group report similar memories from their own very specific viewpoint.

ADEL YAHYA: Aren't the Jewish army archives also politically motivated?

RAN AARONSOHN: I guess so .

ADEL YAHYA: Every source has its problems. But sure, we have cross-referenced our research with other sources, including published materials such as those of Benny Morris. We have done the research comparing our findings with Israeli assumptions and ideas. We wanted to investigate this issue, and we confronted the interviewees with these Israeli theories, and we got these answers.

AZIZ HAIDER: I will start with what Avraham said, that there were no plans to exile or expel the Palestinians.

AVRAHAM SELA: Pre-plans. I said that with the actions came the opportunity.

AZIZ HAIDER: Yes. This is important, what happened after that. Why was it was so easy? This is a question for the Palestinians. Why was it so easy to expel such a large segment of the population from Palestine?

This raises another question about the purpose of oral history. You are gathering oral data. If you are trying to write an oral history, what is it for? If it is only to repeat the same narrative or to re-emphasize the same history of the

Palestinians, I don't know if that's so important to us. It's much more important to ask the real questions about why it happened and why it was so easy.

The purpose of oral history must be to seek the truth, to try to understand something about Palestinian society, social structure, the characteristics of social relationships, the institutional level within Palestinian society. What happened there? Why was it so easy to expel the Palestinian population? Let's say there were plans. What about the reaction of the Palestinians to those plans? I think the goal and the purpose of oral history must be to answer these questions, and others about collusion and about the role of the Arab armies and the Arab states in 1948. This is much more important for us than to repeat the same narrative all the time.

The only attempt by Palestinians to do what I am talking about was made by Amira Habibi. Her book, "The Second Exodus," reflects the only research that has been done into these questions about 1948. And she tried to answer by means of her research with the refugees in Jordan after 1967. Habibi talks about the panic, about the effects of the rumors spread by the Zionists, about the effects of the decision by the local leaders to leave. If there were rumors, then some mukhtar or sheikh told his family and the population of his village.

LILY GALILI: This exactly reflects his oral research findings of – fear and rumors.

AZIZ HAIDER: If there are rumors and fear, who takes the decisions? This is the problem. Does the mukhtar or some person in this or that village have to take the decision because of the lack of institutions, for example? Are there leaders to tell them what to do? It is very important for the Palestinians to ask themselves these questions, and to find answers, because today or tomorrow, we may have to react to a similar situation again. It's not only for the future. It's also for the past. Why was it so easy to exile this population?

AVRAHAM SELA: It's even more important because of the variations. In some cases, Palestinians did not leave immediately. Sometimes they re-attacked after a village was taken by Israelis. And there are other scenarios. So how do you explain this? It was not a consistent phenomenon of Palestinians everywhere just leaving. Sometimes Jews objected to deporting them.

DALIA OFER: The two presentations were not only interesting, but very well presented and informative. I applaud the oral history project.

Sometimes, with regard to the history of the Holocaust, all we have from the Jewish point of view is perhaps one or two oral testimonies because communities were completely destroyed. People were not expelled. They were killed. And the only sources we may have are German sources. So in spite of our desire to always be critical, we should not - and particularly in these kinds of cases - attack oral history. It is extremely important. Of course, anyone who deals with oral history must be careful and critical.

On the other hand, there is an example of archival material on the Holocaust, a well-known report of General Stroop about the Warsaw Ghetto uprising, which is completely distorted. He had to justify why he couldn't put this rebellion down in a day or two, so he describes the Jewish forces fighting in the ghetto, in numbers and ammunition and everything, way beyond what really existed there.

People have all kinds of motivations to describe things in certain ways in their reports. They want to be promoted or they want this or that. All sources are biased, and as historians, we have to clean out those biases by cross-checking them. What I think is most important in this kind of oral history project - like the one on the Holocaust period - is that it is not only for the historians of this period to read. The hope is that, in the future, the archives of more Arab states will be opened, and then we will have these and other resources to do the cross-checking that is extremely important.

Having said that, I think we still have a lot of documentation in other archives as well. When I worked on the mass immigration to the State of Israel in the first decades of statehood, I sat in the Public Records Office in Washington, and I found, for example, a particular British document. The first order of the transitional government of Israel, in May 1948, was to abolish the immigration clause of the British Mandate. And the British wrote to the Americans that the State of Israel will surely not endure. When they really open their gates to all immigrants, there will be such chaos that the state will simply fall apart. So you can find all kinds of things in other archives.

I also want to ask a question about the sources, and I will relate this again to material I am more familiar with. Among the Jews in Europe, there was a great awareness about the need to document what had happened. We have archives that were composed in the ghettos, oral histories beginning at the time that people who were expelled from smaller to larger ghettoes were asked to tell others what had happened. This is a very important source. When trying to explain why these people did it, we always relate it to a kind of tradition or culture. They themselves wrote about their purpose in documenting things, and they did it even more when they were aware that they were going to be killed. Then they said, "We have to leave it for the future, for the future historians."

Then I have one question for Avraham. I was confused. You talked about the meeting of Arab leaders in April 1948, and that they thought they had no chance to win the war, that it was a war of survival. But when we talked earlier, you mentioned that Hajj Amin Al Husseini, or the Palestinians, was sure they were going to wipe out the Jews. So how do you put these two things together?

PAUL SCHAM: I wonder if Avraham would talk a bit about how, if at all, these new views that are attempting to understand more of the Palestinian position are percolating through Israeli society, the extent to which these are confined to a comparatively small group of academics or whether they're getting into the street.

WALID SALEM: One theory about why Palestinians left was presented by Elias Sanbar, a Palestinian writer working in the PLO. He wrote that when the Zionist groups attacked, the villagers fought for their villages. Then they left for the next village. This continued until the people finally reached the borders. So the Palestinians did not merely leave. They fought for their rights. And I'd like to know what you think about that. Secondly, he talks about the massacres, Deir Yasin and others. What do you think was the influence of such massacres in the villages on the Palestinians leaving?

RUTH KARK: Also relating to the oral history issue, Adel, were your interviews closed or open? I noted that some of the questions - the one about Jewish plans, for example - were sort of leading questions.

AMNEH BADRAN: To Avraham, one question regarding the relation of Britain to the Yishuv and the Zionist movement. You presented a different view than that of Moshe Ma'oz. You said the British played a very big role in defending the interests of the Zionist movement in terms of the embargo and crushing Palestinian leadership .

AVRAHAM SELA: I didn't say they did those things to protect Zionist interests.

AMNEH BADRAN. They did what they did - the embargo, the crushing of the Palestinian revolt in 1936, and the crushing of the grassroots leadership in Palestine at that time - which resulted in the Palestinians not being ready for the second phase. So we have to go back to the role of the British and how much that helped the Yishuv or the Zionist project. My second question is about the plot or the collusion between Transjordan's Hashemite government and the Zionist movement at that time. You said the aim of this collusion was to prevent the war. What if I say this collusion might have been aimed at dissolving the possibility of the establishment of a Palestinian national entity on some part of Palestine? What would you say about that?

BENJAMIN POGRUND: In follow-up to the question about Deir Yasin and other places. As I understand it, the original figure for Deir Yasin was somewhere around 240 or 260 villagers killed?.

AVRAHAM SELA: The final number is 97.

BENJAMIN POGRUND: It was in the interests of the Irgun to boost the figure to show what great fighters they were. The Haganah as well, but to a somewhat lesser extent. On the Arab side, it was also appropriate to make the figures as high as possible to show what terrible people the Jews were. And that turned out to be a factor that helped scare away the Arabs who ran. They heard what had been done at Deir Yasin, and so they left.

ADEL YAHYA: There were also rapes.

BENJAMIN POGRUND: Yes, and whatever else. This is an interesting example of what you've been talking about. It was the appropriate approach, on both sides at the time, to boost the figure, and only in more recent years has there been calmer research.

MERON BENVENISTI: Also double and triple counting.

ADEL MANNA: Avraham, you mentioned that there are New Historians but no new history, and you promised to elaborate on that. I think this is important for people here. However critical we are about those New Historians, they did uncover a lot of things that Israelis didn't speak about before the 1980s.

Adel, the PLO archives and those of the national movement in Beirut are very important. We didn't speak about those.

Concerning Palestinian historians writing or not writing about 1948, to my knowledge, we still don't have one good book in Arabic by Palestinians on the war in 1948. The question is why? There may be no archives, but we also haven't written many autobiographies or memoirs about 1948. There are some, but they are very few.

243

LILY GALILI: In Israel, in the last decade, we have detected a shift in the manner of commemorating, not only the Holocaust, but also these wars, moving from the collective to the individual, some process of the privatization of memory. Since Palestinian commemoration is just now being defined, is it starting with the collective, or is it going directly to the private sphere? Historical definition is more concentrated on the private sphere, but I wonder if there is the concept of collective or private.

What role does Palestinian television play in documenting these things? You mentioned a lack of books and archives. Television sometimes can serve a purpose. If it does, what is its role?

AVRAHAM SELA: I'll start with the issue of expulsion. The story of 1948 with regard to the expulsion and exodus of Palestinians from their village to the next village and on to a third and fourth village is very complicated. It depends on the specific area, the specific time, the specific stage of the war. Sometimes people went away to hide and came back to their village afterwards. It's a very varied phenomenon, and it would be wrong to take these individual testimonies and try to make one story out of them. You cannot apply individual perceptions and memory this way, even ignoring for the moment the weakness of a testimony taken 50 or 55 or even 30 years later. It is simply very complicated.

The argument of the call from Arab governments or Arab countries to the Palestinians to leave has been refuted by at least two scholars. One is Walid Khalidi, who already wrote about it in the late 1950s. The other is Erskin Childers in 1961. Both of them went through BBC summaries of what was said on Arab radio stations, and they found nothing.

During the last few months of the Mandate, the Palestinians went to King Abdullah or to the Presidents of Syria and of Lebanon and so on, and begged for arms and other assistance. They were told that they could not help them. The only thing they could do was to advise them, if they were afraid for their lives, to leave for a while. Hopefully, when the Arab armies would go in, things would be resolved and they could come back to their homes. I have a number of documents like this. It seems to me that this responds to some extent to the myth that the Arab governments or countries called for the Palestinians to leave.

The irony is that some Palestinians, as well as non-Palestinian Arabs, also support this argument. In the memoirs of the Prime Minister of Syria - and he was not in power or in politics during the war itself - he says, "We Arabs are to blame for the expulsion of the Palestinians because we told them to leave."

Moussa Alamy writes a beautiful phrase that sums up the whole story in one sentence. He says, if the Palestinians left their homes, it was not because they were cowards or unable or unwilling to defend themselves. They were without arms and without leadership. The Arab governments promised them that, in a while, they would be able to come back home. They were hoping that everything would be fine and that that would happen. On the one hand, he and many other Palestinian historians tell individual stories, just like those in your paper. At the same time, they have made up historical explanations that blame the Jews or Britain or all kinds of other powers. I think these two elements go hand in hand in Palestinian historiography. I don't want to go into more detail. I just mention this because it's interesting to see that this is partly collective memory and partly a matter of research. We know for sure, for example, that Kaoukji, during the months of April and May, was threatening to blow up the homes of Palestinians if they left. And even this didn't help because the fear and helplessness and disarray were so tremendous among this population. He was using Ramallah radio, captured from the British after they abandoned it, and he was broadcasting to the whole Palestinian population, not only to the small area around him.

About the question of a plan, we can do all kinds of acrobatics, but I think Benny Morris, so far, is the one who has done the most comprehensive and systematic work on this topic. He comes up with the conclusion that it was the result of war, not the result of a plan. Honestly, when you look at the process of how the Jewish or Israeli or Haganah positions developed during the war, you see there were changes. They didn't start all at once with expulsions. Until March, there was an attempt, even in the case of the notables of Haifa, to beg them not to leave. This was not because of the blue eyes of the Arab Palestinians, but because the Jews really believed that if they could prevent the exodus of the Palestinians, it might prevent the invasion of the country by Arab armies. This was a very important consideration.

I and a colleague have written an article about the case of Lod, responding to the argument that it was sheer expulsion. Yes, it was an expulsion. No question about it. But the circumstances under which this expulsion took place make it a little more understandable historically, though not morally. I emphasize that. There is no question, in the case of Lod, that that hand gesture definitely meant throw them out. Expel them. But in many other instances, that was not the case. There are many examples of Arab villages in which half or most of the population remained. This gives you a sense of reality in that you have to look at each case in its own right. You cannot find consistency in the Israeli policy. In some cases, they gave much more freedom to the local commanders. In other cases, brigade commanders interfered and made clear what they wanted to do.

MERON BENVENISTI: It was divided north and south .

AVRAHAM SELA: The south was a much later phase in the war. In the north, for very good reasons, a large part of the population remained because Operation Hiram, in which the Upper Galilee was captured, was so short. The population was simply caught within the pincer-like movement of the forces. In the south, the Israelis had no hesitation in systematically expelling people. This was later. They were self-confident. They thought it would be fine. They simply did it systematically.

MERON BENVENISTI: Yigal Allon especially.

AVRAHAM SELA: Especially because of him. In every operation of which Yigal Allon was commander, the population was expelled. It started in the northern Hula Valley, went on to Lod and then down into the Negev. This was his policy, his own input. I am not saying that people above him did not agree with him, but this was his contribution. Also in the south, when the Egyptians evacuated the Faluja pocket, they had an agreement with the Israelis that the local population would stay. However, the Israeli commander of the southern sector expelled them. Moshe Sharett* writes about that with anger. He said, "We gave our word and we committed ourselves internationally. How could we do this? The army did one thing and the politicians thought something else."

MOSHE MA'OZ: And that is still going on.

AVRAHAM SELA: Let me say something about the shorthandedness of the Palestinian academic community. Yes, you lack documents and archives. But I think - and I am saying this as a critique of my colleagues here - that even with minimal effort, you could go to the Public Records Office or to the National Archive in Washington and use what is available to everybody. You don't have to go to the IDF archive and be humiliated by the guy at the gate.

Why was it so easy either for the Palestinians to leave or to be expelled? In 1946, the idea of evacuating children and women and the elderly had already been spread generally among Palestinians. This was following the publication of the conclusions of the Anglo-American Committee of Inquiry. Because the Arab governments wanted to make a big noise, they published the idea that they would help the Palestinians send their children and women away as part of the preparations for war. This was in 1946. I can show you.

Here there are two theories. One says that, when you evacuate your children and women, you feel easier and freer to fight. On the other hand, what about the longing for one's family and worrying about what is happening to them? Sometimes they were hidden in the groves or in a cave or someplace. What is happening to them? I came to accept more the second view, which is actually perceiving it as a serious weakness. When you send your family away, there is little to defend.

ADEL YAHYA: Send them where?

AVRAHAM SELA: Even to the neighboring village. Sometimes members of wealthier families were sent to Beirut. I am talking about 1948 now.

I am presenting these two approaches or two views because I myself have no answer. In any case, I think the problem was with the atomistic structure of society, and all the evidence and documents support this very strongly. They were not fighting as a community. They were fighting as villages, sometimes as clans, as *hamoulas*, and in many cases, there was no cooperation between villages.

The cases in which people left were so different one from the other. And if you add to that the early departure of the elite in December-January, remember that that was not just a matter of leadership, but also of economics. They closed their stores and working places, and it was a problem for many people to stay on without work.

So it was not only the lack of leadership, but also the decreasing options for making a living under these circumstances. Add to that the fear and the clashes and the on-going fighting among between Jews and Arabs in neighborhoods, in towns, in villages. I think it was mainly a phenomenon deriving from the lack of authority and the lack of a central address. For example, when the people of Romema in Jerusalem, a Jewish minority within an Arab neighborhood, wanted to evacuate the neighborhood because it was too dangerous, the Haganah told them, "You are staying and we will take care of you." But when Arabs faced such problems, they had almost no one to turn to or to consult with. If anyone, it was the Arab Liberation Army or the Army of Deliverance, and they were

246

irresponsible. Many times you find testimonies saying that when they were approached, they would say it wasn't their job to defend you. They came for other purposes.

With regard to the question on the differing perspectives of the Mufti and the generals, it is important to remember that we are dealing with different times of the war and different people. The politicians who gathered in Amman on 30 April heard it from their chiefs of staff. The chiefs of staff are the professionals. They were supposed to know something about their capability, and this is what they told the politicians. They might have been wrong or anything else, but that's what they told the politicians. And the politicians decided regardless, for other reasons, to go to war. Whether the Mufti believed the Arab armies could do more or less is irrelevant. He was an interested party in this process, not someone who could deliver anything more than a few hundred warriors, mainly in the area of Jerusalem and its surroundings.

Paul, I think these perceptions of historians have very little influence on public opinion and public perception about what happened in 1948. I speak about it again and again. I say again and again that most of the Palestinians did not take part in the war, were not interested in the war, and were unable even to express their capability or anything else in the war. People are not willing to accept it. Remember that we are dealing here with politics. Accepting some of these arguments would mean not only that the Israeli achievement in the war is dwarfed, but would also support the Palestinians claiming they were actually victims in that war. I can understand the Israelis. Often I'm attacked for saying these things. They say it's still a problem and we have to keep our mouths shut about it. We have to keep the secret. It's a very serious thing.

To Walid, yes, there were many cases in which villagers fought, or without fighting, moved from one place to another according to circumstances. I don't think there is anything new about that.

To Amneh, at first the British government loved the Zionists. I agree with you. They supported the Zionist project and everything. But from 1939 on, Britain became perfidious towards the Jewish Yishuv. Britain was accused of betraying its own commitments and its own promises to the Jewish nation.

RAN AARONSOHN: Only in 1939? Not earlier?

ADEL MANNA: Only after the White Paper.

AVRAHAM SELA: Things went from bad to worse during the war, and especially after the war when the Labour government replaced the Conservatives. Then they started to show a clear tendency to lean towards the Arab side in order to maintain the good will of the Arab world. This was a very clear principle in British policy. We don't have to dig far in order to find it. It's public and well-documented. Already during the war, the Zionist movement shifted its main efforts to the United States. Britain was no longer their main basis for support.

With regard to collusion, I did not try to say that the collusion or the agreement with Abdullah was only to achieve this or that. But I disagree that, within the considerations of the Zionist movement, there was this call to prevent a Palestinian state. I say that because it was irrelevant. It was not realistic. The Palestinians had already said hundreds of times that they would not accept anything other than a unified Palestine with no Jews in the country. This is why they rejected all the British offers from 1946 on.

This went on and on. The Palestinians were very clear about it. I'm not blaming them. That was their view. But to say that the Zionist movement had to work hard in order to prevent the establishment of a Palestinian state is quite irrelevant because it was not in the cards, as they say. It was not at all an available option.

To Adel, why is there not new history. This is a big question. I use "the New Historians" in quotation marks because this is how they call themselves. But when we look for new history, we look for new methodology, a new way of looking at things. Had they been doing anything like what Aziz previously mentioned, I would say yes, there is something new about it. But the New Historians are using exactly the same old historical methodology. I don't see them doing anything like trying to see things from below or trying to look at the situation from a conceptual or comparative viewpoint. That would be new history. But they contribute nothing in this respect, I'm sorry to say .

ADEL YAHYA: Let me start with the questions that were asked about the issue of criticism of the local Palestinian leadership in 1948. I heard from an Israeli colleague that Israelis were even less critical of their leadership during the first days of state. Ben Gurion and others were not criticized publicly in the Israeli media .

RAN AARONSOHN: They did, but much less.

ADEL YAHYA: It was marginal. So I can understand why the Palestinians, including the refugees, did not blame the leadership. They were defeated, weak, unsure, without confidence. So they did not blame their leadership. They united with it rather than criticize it. What proves this is that, when the Palestinians became more self-confident, then they began criticizing their leaders. Nowadays, Palestinians criticize Arafat, even *Fatah* members.

ADEL MANNA: Can we speak about historical studies?

ADEL YAHYA: I am talking about this research. When we asked the refugees about leadership, they immediately jumped from 1948 to criticize the present leadership. This is very strange. And we reminded them that we were talking about 1948, not about the present. But they always jumped from 1948 to talk about Arafat and the PLO.

This was in the late 1990s, 1997-1998. They would leave everything and go on to talk about the Palestinian Authority. We were not asking them about that, but they were always willing to criticize the Palestinian Authority, but not the Palestinian leadership in 1948. It was strange.

About the destruction of archives, some people attempt to show it was not systematic. If we had one hundred archives in the Palestinian areas and the Israelis destroyed ten and left ninety, maybe then we could say it was not systematic and not intentional. But we don't have anything. They destroyed everything that could be found, even the Ministries' archives. They intentionally took them and destroyed them, or took them I don't know where.

RUTH KARK: We didn't destroy them. We preserved them in the Israeli archives.

BURCKHARD BLANKE: Hopefully.

ADEL MANNA: Knowledge is power.

ADEL YAHYA: It was done intentionally. It was not vandalism. If they had left one single library or museum - they even took all the artifacts from the Hebron Municipal Museum and several other local museums. They took everything.

PAUL SCHAM: You're talking about when?

ADEL YAHYA: 1967. Jericho and Hebron. They took them to the Palestine Museum, the Rockefeller Museum. Now they have possession of its library and documentation and everything.

RUTH KARK: It will go back.

ADEL YAHYA: It's very hard to believe it was individual vandalism. So they are responsible for this situation we're in.

PAUL SCHAM: Are those available to Palestinian researchers?

ADEL YAHYA: No. When we need documentation, we have to hire Israelis to do the work for us, and we pay them a lot of money. Even the Arab Jerusalemites cannot go into Israeli libraries and do their work.

RUTH KARK: I have news for you. They can.

ADEL MANNA: If they have an Israeli professor from Hebrew University, but not from Bir Zeit. We're talking about sensitive archives.

ADEL YAHYA: Palestinians are always careful about presenting the views of the other side. The Israeli views are always present. Palestinians have no problem with that because the Israeli views are always in their minds. That is the starting point for any Palestinian research. They start where the Israelis leave off and try to confront it.

I think Palestinians are at an advantage when it comes to that. It's the Israelis who refuse to take the Palestinian narrative into account. The new Israeli historians sit facing the mirror even more than the traditional ones. They look more and more into the Israeli picture. They never look through the window to see their neighbors. And I believe it's about time that Israelis start looking through that window.

As to Ran's question with regard to the Palestinian position on Jewish claims and narratives, there is lots of unanimity. Palestinians believe the opposite. The underlying assumption of any Palestinian research is that whatever the Israelis say, the opposite must be true. New academics in the Palestinian areas do try to investigate these positions, but there is a great deal of skepticism about Israeli history. We doubt it very much, and we don't take it for granted.

Reading Benny Morris actually opened our eyes. Every Palestinian academic reads him. But we study him critically, and he is also attacked by Palestinians. In Palestinian academic and non-academic works, there are more attacks on Benny Morris than on any other Israeli historian. He is politically and ideologically motivated like all the other Israelis. He does not take the Palestinian position into consideration. So the Palestinians have many doubts.

RAN AARONSOHN: What about a land without people and the revival of the desert? I asked for more details.

ADEL YAHYA: We ask these questions, at least in our small research. A

249

lot of work has been done by Sheikh Tamani He wrote something about this. It's usually the opposite position. Whatever the Israelis say, the Palestinians start from the opposite viewpoint.

RAN AARONSOHN: Revival of the desert, you say Palestinians think the opposite way based upon …

ADEL YAHYA: Some refugees told us, "The Israelis took our land because they were so envious of our houses and lands. We were better off than they were, so they envied us. They coveted it. They wanted to take the land because we were much better off than they were in 1948." This is an underlying assumption among refugees. We were much better off, especially the people of the towns - Haifa, Jaffa. They were superior to their Jewish neighbors.

MERON BENVENISTI: Even trees. They had about a million dunams of orchards. How much remains now? Nothing. The whole thing of saying we made the desert bloom was for one purpose only - to say that we took Palestine, not from the Arabs, but from nature. That was why that terminology was used, of making the desert bloom. We fought nature, not people.

MOSHE MA'OZ: Also to bring money from the United States.

Finally, I agree with Adel. I also am sorry that we don't have one single Palestinian book like that. I think we should make that a major objective. We need something decent, not only to present to ourselves, but to the world as well.

HOLINESS AND POLITICS IN THE ISRAELI-PALESTINIAN CONFLICT

Moshe Amirav

1. Introduction: Politics of holy places in the 21st century

GENERALLY speaking, holiness and holy places are considered factors in the limited possibility of political compromise in ethnic and national disputes. Holiness cannot be divided, and control by the "other" over a site considered to be holy creates a sense of totality that is likely to serve as a catalyst, intensifying the political dispute.

The growth of secular nationalism during the 19th century replaced the wars of religion in Europe with wars of territorial and national interests. During the 20th century, conflicts over holy sites were very few, and by the beginning of the 21st century, all but two were resolved: that between the Hindus and the Muslims in India, and that between the Israelis and the Palestinians over the Temple Mount in Jerusalem. The dynamics of these struggles are such that their intensity rises and falls in direct relation to political conflicts involving interests that have nothing to do with religion or faith.

In this respect, the holy sites in India and Jerusalem have become powerful tools in the hands of secular political elites, who exploit their respective peoples' historical and religious discourse in the process of national consolidation, for ends related to the struggle over political interests.

In the conflict over Jerusalem's holy sites, the Zionist movement initially agreed to completely forego control over Islam's and Christianity's holy places, in an attempt to avoid having the conflict shift from a political to a religious one. A study of the positions of the Zionist movement and of the State of Israel, however, indicates that, over the course of time, this position changed from complete rejection of domination of the holy places to a position of "compromise" that sought "cooperation" in the control over them, and finally, in the 1990s, to a position that sought formal sovereignty, rather than cooperation, over the Temple Mount. The most extreme expression of this new position was presented at the 2000 Camp David II summit by Prime Minister Ehud Barak, who demanded, within the framework of the permanent settlement, Israeli sovereignty over the Temple Mount as a whole, and not just over the Western Wall.

During the 1980s and 90s, pressure grew from fundamentalist Jewish Israeli groups who demanded not only to "realize sovereignty," but even to build the Third Temple on top of the ruins of the mosques that currently occupy the holy mountain.

In Palestinian political discourse, the Temple Mount/*Haram al Sharif* became a central topic. In contrast to the Israeli interest to separate the religious element from the national one, the Palestinian interest was to not only link the Temple Mount even deeper to the political dispute, but also to place it at its center. The approach expressed by Egyptian President Anwar al Sadat at the first Camp David summit with Menahem Begin in 1977 spoke of a pan-Arab or Muslim presence on the Temple Mount. In the negotiations conducted at the second Camp David summit in 2000, Yasser Arafat pushed his own position to an extreme, and was not satisfied with granting the Arab League or a committee of Islamic nations sovereignty on the mountain, but demanded exclusive Palestinian sovereignty.

The failure of the second Camp David summit is thus largely the result of the substantial gap that was revealed between Arafat and Barak regarding the future of the Temple Mount. While relative flexibility on the other issues – boundaries, security, Jerusalem, and the refugees – and a willingness on both sides to compromise were apparent in the narrowing gap between the positions, with respect to the Temple Mount, both leaders remained captives of their respective religious and historic ethos, denying one another's identity, and bringing the whole negotiations to a total collapse.[1]

2. The Holy Places: From the Western Wall riots of 1929 to Intifadat al Aqsa of 2000

The 1929 prayers held by members of the Betar movement at the Western Wall, and the 2000 visit by then-opposition leader Ariel Sharon to the Temple Mount, both served as a pretext for the most serious outbreaks of violence in the Israeli-Palestinian conflict. That the Palestinians used both these incidents to organize popular opposition and violent struggle surprised the Israeli-Jewish public, and in both cases led to an historical soul-searching.

Many scholars see the 1929 riots as a watershed event in the Israeli-Zionist dispute with the Palestinian national movement. Avraham Sela describes them as "the first threat to the very existence of the Jewish Yishuv," since the beginning of the Zionist enterprise.[2] The threat came not only from the severity of the riots and their tragic results (133 killed, 330 injured), but also from the sudden realization that the Zionist movement's basic concepts concerning the very possibility of Jewish-Arab co-existence had collapsed.

These riots caused the Jewish Yishuv to undertake military preparations for a confrontation with the Palestinian national movement. Ben Gurion realized that from then on, it was necessary to prepare for a military struggle, alongside the political struggle with the British. For their part, the Palestinians saw the 1929 uprising as the beginning of a violent struggle against what they perceived as the Zionist movement's demographic and political threat. Many scholars have noted the Palestinians' own disillusionment with the possibility of co-existence with the Jews. The Mufti, Hajj Amin Al Husseini, saw his power grow as one of the staunchest leaders of an uncompromising struggle against Zionism. At the 1931 Jerusalem Conference, in which representatives of 30 Arab and Muslim countries participated, the Mufti garnered Arab and Muslim support for the protection of "the Arab character of Palestine," for the first time linked with the "protection of the holy places of Islam."[3]

Arafat's rejection of what the Israeli public saw as Prime Minister Barak's far-reaching concessions at Camp David II, and the ensuing uprising which came to be known as *Intifadat al Aqsa*, were seen by the Israeli public as a "continuation of the historic Arab refusal to recognize the State of Israel." A sense of "disillusionment" with Oslo was no longer confined to the right-wing alone, but now also plagued broad elements within the Jewish public. The left's or the Israeli peace camp's ideological crisis was expressed in public opinion polls which showed a sharp drop in support for, or even belief in the possibility of peace with the Palestinians. The right-wing and the West Bank settlers expressed their joy that Arafat had finally "removed the mask." Former Prime Minister Barak and former Foreign Minister Shlomo Ben Ami were no longer leaders of the peace camp, but rather leaders of the "disillusioned." Sharon's position that "there is no one to talk to" was supported by a large majority within the Israeli public. Political and religious radicalism on both sides grew during the years of the Intifada, making the possibility of a political settlement even more remote. In the Palestinian camp, the strength of Hamas and Islamic Jihad grew, as did support among Palestinians for their claim that there was no one to talk to on the Israeli side, and that Arafat had made an historic error in agreeing to Oslo.

The Western Wall/*Al Burak* and the Temple Mount/*Haram al Sharif* were thus transformed into powerful unifying religious and historical symbols, which were once again marshaled, as they had been at the end of the 1920s, to create a national identity and to give legitimacy to a political struggle.

3. The theoretical aspect: The Temple Mount as a changing paradigm for policy

The central thesis of this paper is that the use of religious and historical symbols increases, as the gap between the two sides grows, making their positions more extreme. The political conclusion to be drawn from this is that both Israelis and Palestinians need to detach the question of the holy places from the political conflict, remove them from the realm of public discourse and political negotiations between the two sides, and turn them over to such interested groups as religious leaders, the Arab League, the Organization of Islamic States, the Jewish Agency, the Vatican, and the United Nations.

In recent years, public policy research has emphasized the importance of examining problems from the viewpoint of defining the ensuing political problems. Scholars claim that events and circumstances only become political problems once they are defined by policy makers as relevant to policy. This theoretical framework explains the significance of problems, not necessarily in terms of their objective importance, but rather in terms of the weight of the players who succeed in bringing about their redefinition.[4]

With this approach, one may understand the shifts in the prioritization of problems on the national agenda in terms of the interests of policy makers. The secular leaders' use of holiness themes is usually more frequent than that of religious leaders and believers. And the degree of this frequency may indicate the extent to which the political leaders may have succeeded or failed in attaining their political goals. The case of the holy places as a changing paradigm in Zionist and Israeli policy may help in examining the state of the secular and national goals, and their order of priority in historical policy.

4. Jerusalem and the holy sites: Three paradigms

The first paradigm drawn by the Zionist movement is the **paradigm of "conflicting interests"** between national goals and the holy sites and Jerusalem. Established in the early 1880s by such Zionist leaders as Levanton, Feinberg, and Lilienblum, among the earliest *Hovvei Zion*, and Baron de Rothschild and Theodore Herzl, this paradigm continued until the 1920s, and was expressed in both Zionist policy and national priorities, and in its influence on Jewish public opinion in Israel and the world. For the proponents of this paradigm, the importance of Jerusalem as the holy city and as the historical capital of the nation did not hold its own against the arguments of the majority of the directors of *Hovvei Zion*, who decided on Jaffa as the political and administrative center of the country.

The second is the **paradigm of exchange**, in which the Zionist movement was willing to trade off Jerusalem, and later the Temple Mount, as marginal assets in terms of their importance to Jews, but important in their value to others, in exchange for other, more substantial and central political assets. This paradigm was constructed in the 1930s and 40s primarily by David Ben Gurion who, until 1947, continued to support the exclusion of Jerusalem and the holy places from the territory of the State to be established.

The 1948 division of Jerusalem, however, caused Ben Gurion to alter his position, and instead to annex West Jerusalem and declare it the capital of Israel. As far as the Old City, no Zionist leader ever even suggested conquering it, let alone annexing it, until after the Six Day War in 1967. But even then, the Eshkol government was prepared to give up the holy places of Islam and Christianity, as evidenced in Foreign Minister Abba Eban's speech at the United Nations in July 1967, immediately following the annexation of East Jerusalem. He proposed, in the name of the Israeli government, that in exchange for peace and recognition of Israel's sovereignty in Jerusalem, the holy places, including the Temple Mount, be removed from its hands and given to the UN or some other authorized body.[5]

Even Menahem Begin, at Camp David I in the late 1970s, was initially willing to agree to foreign administration over the Temple Mount in exchange for recognition of united Jerusalem as the capital of Israel.[6]

The third is the **paradigm of identity**, which led Israel to see the Temple Mount as its main asset in reshaping the new Israeli identity. The resumption of the conflict between Israel and the Palestinians specifically over the Temple Mount, in the 1980s and 90s, put it right back at the center of the political conflict between the two sides. In tandem with ongoing Israeli attempts to separate the issue of holy sites from the political dispute, and to preserve the status quo, attempts were made by the Palestinians to link the issue of the Temple Mount to the dispute, and to alter the status quo.

From the Israeli point of view, this paradigm required that the Temple Mount be defined as marginal to Muslims, and that its centrality and importance to Israel be strengthened. Prime Ministers Menahem Begin, Benjamin Netanyahu and Ehud Barak all brought this paradigm to an extreme, using various phrases with deep historical and religious implications so as to identify their political goals within an historical and religious context.

Unlike Rabin, Eshkol and others, who were willing to relinquish control over the Temple Mount in exchange for preserving the integrity of Jerusalem, Barak broke the taboo and agreed to the city's division, and in exchange promised Israelis that he would assure sovereignty over what he regarded as the very heart of the city, "the Holy of Holies" (in Hebrew, *kodesh hakodashim*). Thus identifying the Temple Mount as the central asset of a secular, modern Israel unavoidably led to a confrontation at Camp David II, and was in effect the stumbling block that caused the summit's failure.

5. Separation of holiness from politics: new paradigm

At one of many conferences held on the subject of Jerusalem several years ago, Dr Sari Nusseibeh and I presented a joint theoretical model for a solution to the problem of Jerusalem. In this model, the Palestinians would announce their new capital—Gaza—and leave *al Quds* (Jerusalem) as their holy city, and the Israelis would announce their new capital—Tel Aviv—and leave Jerusalem as a holy city.

This theoretical proposal was unique in that it was impossible to realistically implement. But for two academics somewhat involved in the politics of Jerusalem, this theoretical model represented an important foresight for resolving the problem of Jerusalem by separating holiness from politics.

In this paper I have surveyed the development of the status of the holy places and Jerusalem in Zionist thought, from its inception until Camp David II. Changes in the status of the holy places may also be seen in Palestinian thought throughout the century-long dispute. From a religious paradigm associating *Haram al Sharif* with Islam, the Palestinians turned to a national paradigm, connecting the site to a Palestinian state.

The changing definitions of the "Jerusalem problem," on the part of both Palestinians and Israelis, and the changing weight of its importance during the last one hundred years, allows for a new paradigm, provided that both Israelis and Palestinians agree on it. This paradigm relates to components of identity and of memory. Is it possible to forget the past and isolate it from the public discourse that seeks a solution? Can the Temple Mount be separated from the political discourse that seeks a pragmatic solution, in the here and now, for the two nations? Can one separate politicians from past myths, and force them to speak in the present, for the sake of the future?

The role played by the Temple Mount at Camp David II, like that of the Western Wall during the riots of 1929, exemplifies the manner in which policy makers defined the problem to their colleagues. Would the Palestinian ethos truly be harmed if they could not have full sovereignty over the *Haram al Sharif*? Would the Israeli ethos be damaged if Israel does not have sovereignty over the Temple Mount? The answers, in the affirmative, given at Camp David II, by both Arafat and Barak, more than being indicative of the problems, say something about those who defined them as such.

[1] On the role of the Temple Mount in this failure, see Sher, *Just Beyond Reach; the Israeli-Palestinian Peace Negotiations, 1999-2001* [Hebrew]. Tel Aviv: Yedi'ot Aharonot, 2001, and Klein, *Shattering a Taboo: The Contacts Toward a Permanent Status Agreement in Jerusalem, 1994-2001* [Hebrew]. Jerusalem: Jerusalem Institute for Israel Studies, 2001.

[2] A. Sela, 1972, "Jerusalem in Zionist Vision and Realization" [Hebrew], in Lavsky 1989: 261.

[3] Ibid. 261, n. 1.

[4] See Stone, "Causal Stories and the Affirmation of Policy Agendas." *Political Science Quarterly*, 104 (2), 1989: pp. 281-301, and Dery, *Problem Definition in Policy Analysis*. Lawrence, KS: University Press of Kansas 1984.

[5] See Berkovits, *The Battle for the Holy Places* [Hebrew]. Or Yehuda: Hed Artzi. 2000, p. 59.

[6] See Ben-Elisar, *No More War* [Hebrew], 1995. Tel Aviv: Ma'ariv, pp. 40-41.

Selected Bibliography

Ben Elissar, Eliyahu, *No More War* [Hebrew]. Tel Aviv: Ma'ariv, 1995.

Berkovits, Shmuel, *The Battle for the Holy Places* [Hebrew]. Or Yehuda: Hed Artzi.

Dery, David, *Problem Definition in Policy Analysis*. Lawrence, KS: University Press of Kansas, 2000.

Klein, Menahem, *Shattering a Taboo: The Contacts toward a Permanent Status Agreement in Jerusalem, 1994-2001* [Hebrew]. Jerusalem: Jerusalem Institute for Israel Studies, 2001.

Lavsky, Hagit, ed. *Jerusalem in Zionist Vision and Realization* [Hebrew]. Jerusalem: Zalman Shazar Center for Jewish History, 1989.

Reiter, Yitzhak, ed. *Sovereignty of God and Man: Sanctity and Political Centrality on the Temple Mount* [Hebrew]. Jerusalem: Jerusalem Institute for Israel Studies, 2000.

Shaltiel, Eli, Jerusalem in the Modern Period [Hebrew]. Jerusalem: Yad Ben-Zvi, 1981.

Sher, Gilead, *Just Beyond Reach: The Israeli-Palestinian Peace Negotiations, 1999-2001* [Hebrew]. Tel Aviv: Yedi'ot Aharonot, 2001.

Stone, Deborah, "Causal Stories and the Affirmation of Policy Agendas." *Political Science Quarterly* 104 (2), 1989: 281-301.

JERUSALEM REFUGEES AND PROPERTY CLAIMS SINCE THE 1948 WAR

Salim Tamari

THE start of Final Status Negotiations at Camp David in the summer of 2000 raised a number of issues concerning the future status of Jerusalem, the refugees and settlements. Recent works on negotiating the future of Jerusalem, however, based on a reading of the protocols of Final Status Negotiations, have focused on the charting of boundaries, zoning rights, planning mechanisms, and municipal control and regulations.[1]

What is relevant, for the purposes of this essay, is the manner in which deliberations over the future of the city bring together all final status issues in one package: the presence of a large number of settlements built on confiscated property from West Bank territory (Gilo, Ramot, Giv'at Ze'ev, Ma'aleh Adumim, and others); the presence in Jerusalem of a large number of refugees from the war of 1948; and these refugees' unsettled property claims in areas which have since become the western part of the city and its suburbs. The terms of these claims will have to be dealt with—on both sides—through the mechanisms of documentation, and then the dispensation of rights through restitution or compensation of claimants.

In what follows, I will trace the historical origins of these property claims and examine their consequences in the current dispute over rights. The material here is based on recent research which has emerged in the last five years.[2]

At the heart of the dispute over territory in Jerusalem was the issue of zoning laws and the definition of the municipal boundaries which originated in the Mandate period.[3] While Palestinian Arabs constituted a majority of the population in the Jerusalem District, they were outnumbered by Jews within the municipal boundaries (in 1947, there were 99,400 Jews and 65,100 Arabs).[4] Reviewing the literature on the selective demographics of Mandate Jerusalem, British historian Michael Dumper suggests two main reasons for these population discrepancies: first, estimates counted Jewish migrants who arrived before 1946 in Jerusalem and later moved to Tel Aviv and other localities; and second, while these estimates, on the one hand, excluded Palestinians who were working in the city, but lived in the city's rural periphery (the daytime population, like the commuting workers from Lifta and Deir Yasin), they included, on the other hand, those Jewish residents living on the city's periphery, but who were incorporated into the municipal population (e.g. Beit Vegan, Ramat Rahel, Meqor Hayim) through a process he calls "demographic gerrymandering".[5]

Administrative incorporation within the metropolitan area was not, however, the determining factor differentiating Arab and Jewish communities. Organizations of the Jewish Yishuv chose to establish some of their new Jerusalem suburbs within the western and north-western hinterlands within the expanded boundaries of the city, as was the case with the "garden suburbs" of Talpiot and Rehavia. Rochelle Davis, in her analysis of the evolution of these communities, discusses the organized character of the Jewish communities, in contrast to the unplanned and familial nature of Arab suburbs.[6]

Several studies have narrated the course of the war that led to the tragedy of displacement, both from a Zionist perspective, and – to a far lesser extent – from the Palestinian Arab perspective. The publication of Bahjat Abu Gharbiyyeh's war memoirs a few years ago has contributed, in a modest way, to redressing this imbalance.[7] Also, Nathan Krystall described the military conquest of West Jerusalem and the consequences of war, in terms of the de-Arabization of these communities and the subsequent dispersal of their inhabitants.[8] In his war diaries, which include entries from 14 May to 30 December 1948, and provide a unique "third party" perspective, Constantine Mavrides, a Greek resident of the city, described his eye-witness account of the massive relocation of Arab refugees from the Qatamon and Baq'a neighborhoods, and the counter-relocation of Jewish refugees from the old city.[9]

One major conceptual problem that has confronted writers is how to avoid anachronistic and therefore potentially misleading terminology in designating the nature of the Arab communities being examined here with historical hindsight. The term "West Jerusalem" itself is very problematic since it uses a designation that was the result of border delineation based on 1948 war conditions. The suburban communities that were built west of the city in the 1920s and 30s, like the Ain Karim, Lifta, or Malha villages, had no particular corporate existence outside their relationship to both the Jerusalem urban administrative nexus at large, and to the economic network that linked the city to Jaffa, Haifa and the rest of the country. Since we are dealing here primarily with the fate of these communities and their inhabitants, we decided to use the now common term, West Jerusalem, in its current, i.e. post-1948 boundaries, to reconstruct these lost communities and assess the fate of their refugees and their properties.

A similar problem arises with terms of ethnic identification: "Palestinians" in the Mandate period included both Jews and Arab natives of the city. "Arab" was a designation that increasingly came to mean Christians and Muslims together, as opposed to Jewish Palestinians who - especially after the 1936 rebellion and the massive migration from Europe - identified, consciously or unconsciously, with the Zionist movement. To further complicate matters, there were a substantial number of Arabic-speaking native Palestinian Jews - particularly in Tiberius, Safad, Hebron, and also in smaller numbers in Jaffa, Haifa and Jerusalem. There were also quite a few native Jerusalemites who were neither Jews nor Arabs, but definitely Palestinian, including the Armenians, Greeks, Syriacs and Ethiopians of the old city, and the German Templars of the new city. All were Jerusalemites and Palestinians, in identity if not in citizenship, and therefore it would not do to use the term in its exclusive contemporary connotation of "Palestinian Arab." The solution to this dilemma has been to use the term "Arab" to mean Christian and Muslim Jerusalemites who were Arabic-speaking, and to use denominational terms (Orthodox, Catholic, Muslim, Jewish etc.) when applicable. Since confessional associations played a critical role in the expansion of the western suburbs of the city, it made sense to use these functional designations, although they might seem politically incorrect in today's jargon. The main victims of these approximations are the non-Arab Palestinian minorities (such as Greeks and Armenians) who were sometimes subsumed in these ethnic categories.

The fiftieth anniversary of the state of Israel and of the dispersal of Palestinians from their homeland has raised anew the debate about the causes and conditions of their exile. This paper addresses the atmosphere that preceded the war, and the military operations that accompanied the dislocation of the Palestinian Arab communities from the Western suburbs and villages, as well as the relocation of the inhabitants of the Jewish Quarter to Israeli-held territory. It also addresses the question of land loss and property claims in light of the findings of the Palestine Conciliation Commission.[10] Many problems haunt any attempt at a systematic assessment of these property claims. West Jerusalem's land titles were only partly recorded in the land registry since they were not all part of the land settlement survey which was initiated by the Ottomans in 1858, and which were continued (but not completed) by British Mandate authorities. But virtually all of these land claims can be documented from land tax records, and these records can act as the basis for establishing the authenticity of these claims, where *tabu** records are unavailable.[11]

The process of tracing the fate of Jerusalem refugees and their location is more difficult. The UNRWA (United Nations Relief and Works Agency)* Registry has records on all refugees from Palestine who were eligible for relief services and who sought shelter in one of UNRWA's five field areas (the West Bank, the Gaza Strip, Lebanon, Jordan, or Syria). Since a substantial number of West Jerusalem exiles were middle-class refugees, many of them were not included in UNRWA's records, and their totals are thus always underestimated.

UNRWA's Unified Registration System (URS), this vast database of refugee registration, uses four categories for urban Jerusalem refugees, and a fifth category for Jerusalem District refugees, by village.[12] The urban categories are: Jerusalem - New City; Jerusalem - General (i.e., unspecified); Jerusalem – Poor; and Jerusalem - Old City. The last two categories are those Jerusalem residents whose livelihoods were affected by the war, but who were not displaced from Israeli territories. For the purpose of tracing the fate of Jerusalem refugees, the first two categories are the most crucial.

UNRWA's 1997 URS data, with all their limitations, show that of the total 84,268 urban refugees from Jerusalem and their descendants, the West Bank hosted 53,653, most of whom have taken residence in East Jerusalem (and its suburbs), in Ramallah, and in Bethlehem.[13] Jordan hosted another 26,497 urban Jerusalem refugees, with the Gaza Strip hosting 811, Syria hosting 1,897 and Lebanon hosting 1,410. These patterns, while expected, are drastically reversed for rural refugees. URS data show that while the worldwide figure of UNRWA-registered Jerusalem rural refugees (and their descendants) is 110,439, more than two-thirds, or 73,908 of them live today in Jordan, and only 36,130 live in the West Bank.[14] What does this mean?

First, it means that all UNRWA-registered Jerusalem refugees stayed in the vicinity of their old homes. Particularly, most urban refugees, who tend to be better off and who have substantial documentation on their lost property, stayed within eyesight of their West Jerusalem properties.[15]

Second, it indicates that the poorer refugees, from the villages in the Western environs of Jerusalem - most of whom live in camps - followed UNRWA services to Jordan both before 1967, when employment possibilities were more available in Amman, Irbid and Zarqa, and after the war of 1967, when many Jerusalem refugees were afraid that the Agency would cease to provide its services in areas that came under Israeli occupation.

These figures have great relevance and implication for the Jerusalem refugees' future claims to their properties seized by Israel in the western suburbs and villages. Since many exiles continue to live either in the annexed eastern part of the city, or in its immediate vicinity, their claims for the return of their property (and residence) are particularly poignant since Israel has already established (and expanded several fold) Jewish private residences in the Old City's Jewish Quarter, in Silwan, Ras al-'Amud, Neve Ya'coub, 'Atarot, Abu Tor, in all areas in which Jews had *some property and residence claims before 1948,* and in more than a dozen newly established colonies in areas where no Jewish claims existed prior to 1948. Palestinian property claims in the western part of the city (and its rural environs) are fully substantiated, both in records derived from the land registry (whether in *tabo* or land tax records), as well as in the above-mentioned records of the Palestine Conciliation Commission. The fact that Israel continues to claim that the city is united and indivisible, and is subject to the same administrative laws of the state, makes these claims all the more obvious, and their denial all the more ludicrous.

Final status negotiations over the future of the city have created the atmosphere and the conditions for pushing the historical rights of Arab Jerusalemites to the forefront. The fact that most of these internal exiles are either still alive, or have immediate descendants who are, makes their patrimony more in the here and now, rather than past history.

---

[1] For a discussion of these issues see Menachem Klein,, *Jerusalem: The Contested City,* Hurst and Company, London, 2001, pp. 294-327.

[2] See *Reinterpreting the Historical Record: The Uses of Palestinian Refugee Archives for Social Science Research and Policy Analysis,* Salim Tamari and Elia Zureik, eds, IPS, 2001, and *Jerusalem 1948: The Arab Neighborhoods and their fate in the War,* IJS and Badil, Jerusalem 1999.

[3] The material for this section is based on my essay "The Phantom City," published in the *Jerusalem Quarterly File,* No, 3, Winter 1999.

[4] Walid Mustafa, *Al Quds, Imran wa Sukkan,* JMCC, Jerusalem, 1997.

[5] Michael Dumper, *The Politics of Jerusalem,* New York, 1997, pp. 61-62. On the so-called birth registration see Justin McCarthy, *The Population of Palestine,* New York 1990, p. 165 (note to table A8-14). Dumper claims that these Jewish neighborhoods were excluded from municipal boundaries. Sami Hadawi however includes them as part of the municipal boundaries during the mid-1940s in his survey of the city's property distribution.

[6] Rochelle Davis, "The Evolution of West Jerusalem Communities", in *Jerusalem 1948,* Op. cit.

[7] Bahjat Abu Gharbiyyeh, *Fi Khidamm an Nidal al Arabi al Filastini* (Memoirs of Bahjat Abu Gharbiyyeh 1916-1949), Institute for Palestine Studies, Beirut, 1993.

[8] Nathan Krystall, *"The Fall of the New City",* in *Jerusalem 1948,* IJS and Badil, Jerusalem 1999.

[9] Constantine Mavrides, "Jerusalem Diaries: Old City May14th-December 30, 1948," *Nes Ziona* (1948) Mimeographed bulletin published by the Greek Orthodox Patriarchate in Jerusalem (in Greek).

[10] See Adnan Abdulrazek, "Modernizing the Refugee Land Records: Advantages and Pitfalls," and Michael Fischbach, "UN Conciliation Commission on Palestine: Land Records," both in *Reinterpreting the Record,* Op. Cit; and Salman Abu Sitta, "Notes on UNCCP Records on Land and Landowners", in *Jerusalem 1948,* Op. Cit.

[11] Salman Abu Sitta, in his meticulous research on this issue, is working to provide a preliminary tabulation of these properties in his forthcoming book, Palestinian Property in West Jerusalem.

[12] *UNRWA Registration Manual (Codes);* 95.10 Place of Origin in Palestine/Jerusalem Subdistrict. The manual contains a list of towns, villages, and tribes. Amman HQ, no date.

[13] *URS-Amman;* May 1997. I have excluded from these figures the "Jerusalem Poor" and "Old Jerusalem" categories, so that the data corresponds to urban refugees who actually were evicted from Israeli-held territory.

[14] *URS-Amman;* May 1997. For a discussion of these figures see Chapter 3 in *Jerusalem 1948.* op. cit. I have excluded all data for Jerusalem villages that were not held by Israel after the war of 1948, but included refugees from Abu Ghosh and Beit Naquba.

[15] For data on East Jerusalem residents who are refugees from West Jerusalem, and other areas occupied by Israel in 1948 see Israel Central Bureau of Statistics, *Census of Population and Housing 1967,* East Jerusalem; Jerusalem, 1968, Tables 17 and 18 ("Population Aged 15+, by Place of Personal Residence before the 1948 War").

DISCUSSION 7

Moshe Amirav and Bernard Sabella/Salim Tamari

Note: Because of Israeli travel restrictions, Salim Tamari and others living in the Palestinian Authority were unable to get to Jerusalem where this discussion was held. Salim Tamari's paper was therefore presented by Bernard Sabella.

MOSHE AMIRAV: Holiness and politics are actually sub-issues of the main issue which, in my opinion, is how the two peoples describe the problem. At least in my field of public policy, the trend in the last few years has been to try to see problems through their definition, and there is a whole body of scholarship about defining problems. Sometimes we have a solution, and then we look for the problem, and we define the problem according to that solution. This is true in politics as well, and I have chosen holiness and the Temple Mount as a case study to explain how, from the way you describe the problem, you seek its solution. In other words, if we have a solution for something - let's say the Temple Mount - we have to define the problem according to that solution and not the other way around.

When you look at religion and holiness in the Israeli-Palestinian or the Israeli-Arab conflict, the issue is basically the Holy Land and the holy sites, especially the *Haram al Sharif* and the Temple Mount - *Har HaBait* in Hebrew.

My starting point will be the Camp David II Summit, and while I wouldn't say this was the only problem then, it was definitely the most crucial. Because of the issue of the Temple Mount, we couldn't bridge any other issues. At Camp David II, the question was whether to define the Temple Mount as a political issue or as a religious one. And when it was defined as a political problem, it was then considered as one among all the other territorial issues. We have to find a compromise on the West Bank, on Jerusalem, and also on the Temple Mount.

This was a mistake because you can't deal with an issue like the Temple Mount, which has to do with narratives, stories, ethos, symbols and religion, in the political context.

Before Camp David, I was serving as advisor to Prime Minister Barak on the issue of Jerusalem. While there were those who preferred that Barak not deal with Jerusalem at all, I thought that we couldn't avoid the issue of Jerusalem, but we could avoid the question of the Temple Mount. I had the feeling that we would not reach a solution on the Temple Mount, and that's why I tried to convince the Prime Minister not to deal with it on the political negotiations table, but to leave it for another negotiations table. There are many tables, and we should define this as belonging to the religion table, not the political one.

This would make it much easier for us, because neither Arafat nor Barak were qualified, in my opinion, to deal with the Temple Mount. They did not represent God. They represented political constituencies. Of course, Barak didn't accept my advice. He went to Camp David and he failed to bring peace. One of the reasons was that the problem of the Temple Mount was defined politically, implying that we have to find a compromise. But what compromise? Everybody has their own ideas on a compromise about this very tiny area. The most popular was President Bill Clinton's idea of dividing it on two levels, but it was clear that neither side would be able to accept it. Definitely not Arafat. And that is very understandable. How do you share or how do you divide holy places?

In the early 1920s, the Israeli Zionist point of view defined the Temple Mount in religious terms, rather than political, thus allowing the Zionists to accept giving it up. I would say it was actually a policy of exchange. Many Israelis don't believe me when I say that Zionist and Israeli leaders, from Theodor Herzl through Ussishkin to Ben Gurion, Levi Eshkol and finally Menahem Begin, were all ready to give up Israeli political sovereignty over the Temple Mount. At Camp David I, Begin was even ready to accept six Arab countries' authority over the Temple Mount. He was, of course, insisting on an undivided Jerusalem, a greater Jerusalem, but he was ready - and we have proof - to give up on sole Israeli sovereignty over the Temple Mount.

The first Zionists were always trying to take Jerusalem out of the political context because they understood the problem it created in the exchange of a capital for a state. The idea was that we can give up Jerusalem - definitely the Temple Mount at least - in order to gain something very important to us - a state. This was actually the essence of the Peel Commission's* report in 1937 and of United Nations Resolution 181* in 1947.

Generally, the Arabs looked upon the Temple Mount not as a political issue, but as a religious one. And the first time the Palestinians put the Temple Mount in a political context was in 1929, when the Mufti of Jerusalem, Hajj Amin Al Husseini, used the provocation of the Betar Youth Movement at the Wailing Wall on the eve of Yom Kippur to start what we, in Israel, call the riots of 1929.

There were far fewer victims at that time than there has been in this last Intifada, but the riots were a traumatic shock for both Palestinians and Jews because this was the first confrontation, the first conflict which caused the Zionists to wonder if peace could really be achieved with the Palestinians after such violence. In a very peculiar way, and similar to what happened after Camp David and after this Intifada, it brought about a kind of soul-searching. Where are we going?

But the Mufti was the only one who tried to put the Temple Mount in a political context to help the Palestinians in their national liberation struggle for a state against the Jews, and the Zionists. Later on, when you read statements made by Arab leaders, including Palestinian leaders, they were trying to avoid putting the Temple Mount into the political context. For years, both before and after 1947, Arab leaders from Syria, Jordan, and Lebanon considered the Temple Mount as a

263

Muslim holy site, which should preferably be under Arab sovereignty - they didn't say Palestinian – which, at that time, could have been pan-Arab; or, as an alternative, internationalized.

Actually, Arab leaders understood Resolution 181's clause for the internationalization of Jerusalem to include also the Temple Mount. But when the holy sites came under the authority of a Muslim ruler, King Hussein of Jordan, you notice that the Arab League's position throughout those years was not in favor of the internationalization of holy sites, because this meant removing them from Muslim rule, and turning them over to an international body.

In the Jordanian-Israeli coalition over the Temple Mount, after 1967 - what I call the unholy coalition - the mutual interest was to try and keep the Temple Mount out of the political context and to leave it as a religious issue. This had been King Hussein's interest for years. The Muslim authorities in Jerusalem, the *Waqf,* executed this policy, and managed the Temple Mount. They were loyal to the Jordanian regime of course, and kept, or at least tried to keep the issue out of politics. But all that changed in the 1990s, when we see what I would call a politicization process of the Temple Mount on both sides. Both Palestinians and Israelis began to increasingly speak of the Temple Mount not in religious terms, but in political terms.

In Israel, in the 1970s and 80s, there was a trend among very small groups of 20 or 30 people - like Gershon Solomon and others - who wanted to rebuild the Temple. In the 1990s, that trend grew into a large-scale movement, and steadily increased its membership to include Knesset parties and government ministers who began defining the Temple Mount as a political issue – "We have to reclaim our sovereignty over the Temple Mount." This is something you didn't hear in the 1960s, 70s, or even 80s.

We see the same process among the Palestinians. The PLO, and especially Arafat, were very much interested in politicizing the Temple Mount, beginning at the international level, when Arafat went to the Arab League, the Organization of Islamic States, and to other international bodies, and claimed Palestinian sovereignty over the *Haram.* This was something new for many Arab countries who, for generations, regarded the Haram as a Muslim place that should be run by a Waqf. From a political point of view, they had in mind perhaps pan-Arab or pan-Islamic sovereignty, but certainly not Palestinian sovereignty.

So in the 1990s, we see both Palestinians and Israelis beginning to redefine this holy site within a national political context which, at the end of the day, and by the time the two sides met at Camp David II, had become the most political issue.

To sum up, and looking to the future, the only way we can reach a solution for the Temple Mount is by means of a new definition - or if you like, the old definition - the religious definition that says that the *hajjis* and the rabbis are the ones who should deal with it and resolve it. Leave it out of politics. Leave it out of sovereignty issues. Because Israeli sovereignty would be a disaster, and because Palestinian sovereignty would never be accepted by either the Jews or the Israelis, the only solution then, is to avoid placing it under any one party's political control or sovereignty, and instead putting it under a kind of international umbrella, or some kind of combination. These are ideas that were raised at Camp David II, but Arafat rejected all of them, insisting instead on sole Palestinian sovereignty over the mount.

The only way to solve the problem of the Temple Mount is to bring it back to the religious definition, and to take holiness out of the conflict. Take religion out of politics. We have enough problems at the political level, and if we add the Temple Mount and other religious issues and sites into the conflict, it would make it even more complicated.

ANNE KOEHLER: Salim Tamari could not attend today so Bernard Sabella will offer comments on his paper.

BERNARD SABELLA: I really have a problem with Salim's paper, and usually I don't have this problem because Salim is an excellent academic. In his paper, Salim tried to demonstrate the systematic Israeli gerrymandering that was geared at lowering, as much as possible, the total of Jerusalem's Arab population. Then he documents where "West Jerusalem" refugees ended up. He notes that the richer people with more property ended up closer to their homes, ready with their deeds and keys to go back within a couple of weeks, while the poorer people ended up going east, eventually to Jordan.

It is a good paper in terms of documentation because often, on the Palestinian side, we are worried that the Israelis have more documentation and archives to prove their point of view. What Salim and some others have done - and it is a really good thing - is to go back to and study UNRWA's archives and other documents in order to prove the Palestinian point of view.

I don't have a problem with Salim's approach, but I personally have a problem with this notion of documentation. I like documentation on both sides. There's nothing wrong with that. But it brings us back to the fact that we cannot reconcile our story with yours.

The PLO and Palestinian academics, especially in the United States and North America, and in Beirut, were once obsessed with this notion of coming up with documentation centers, like the Americans are now obsessed with democracy centers in Palestine, because they wanted to prove that we could document every little thing about Palestine in order not to forget, and in order to be able to go to international courts and processes, once the eventual political solution of the conflict had been reached, and prove that this is our property, not yours.

But what I have concluded from these papers is that we really do not have a common ground. It doesn't exist. In a sense, that has been reinforced through the second-track diplomacy, from Common Ground in Washington to IPCRI and the Truman Institute and others here. It's very difficult to differentiate between the personal, emotive, gut-level feeling that there is a need somehow to create common ground, and reality. But I don't see it. Even when I read the papers, I don't see it. It doesn't exist.

I'm not saying we should not document. I think we should. But this is also a reflection of the inability of both sides, at least on an academic, intellectual level, to find that common ground. In one way, this is our common tragedy. Even today, we simply refuse to see the other side. In a sense, by being so self-engrossed, especially in these times, we just forget that there is pain and suffering

265

and horror on the other side, whether caused by us, by them, or caused by both of us together – that's a different question. But as an introduction to the book on Jerusalem neighborhoods and properties and refugees, Salim, as always, does a wonderful job.

WALID SALEM: Do you have any comments about what Moshe said?

BERNARD SABELLA: While I like the idea of going back to the religious dimension of the Haram al Sharif, I don't think, without a clear structure that is agreed upon among the various key religious parties, that you are really going to solve the problem by stressing the religious dimension. Therefore, I'm more comfortable with the political dimension. At least, if Arafat and whoever on the Israeli side strike a deal on the Haram al Sharif, I'm sure that the good majority of the people would go along with it, and then the parties to the agreement would have the power to enforce that agreement.

This is not so with the religious side. They don't have the executive power, so to speak, or the implementing power. You will end up with different interpretations, not only between the different sides, but even sometimes within the Palestinian side. One idea that came out in another discussion, which I liked a lot, was to have a religious council for Jerusalem.

MOSHE AMIRAV: Or the Temple Mount.

DALIA OFER: All the holy sites. It makes it easier if it's not just the one.

BERNARD SABELLA: Why not? The more the merrier. I approached some people on the Christian side with this idea and they said that they have been ready all along to do this. So where is the problem? The problem is with both the Jewish and the Muslim religious authorities. Some Jewish authorities would not be caught dead with Christian religious people. They would work hand in hand with Muslim clergy, no problem, but not with Christians.

Suppose we take the Christian clergy out. Then we come back to the Muslims and the Jews. But here the problem is political. So then both sides will tell you "no". Sometimes, even if the politicians tell the Mufti or whoever to go, he says, "No, I'm not going." It's exactly like what happened when the Pope came here. To my understanding, Arafat wanted the Mufti to go, but the Mufti, who is on his own ground, said no. He did not want to participate in a dialogue with the Pope. But why? Because, again, you have this perception that this is religious, but it is expressed in really political terms.

DALIA OFER: First, Moshe, your suggestion is very logical. You started with wanting to find a solution, and then defining the problem. On a practical level, I can see that working very well. If I think about education, for example, I can see how this could work.

But I think the last thing that Bernard said is really the crux of the matter. In the Muslim perception, and certainly in the Jewish perception today - and I will refer to Zionism in a moment - there is such a close connection between the political and the religious that I'm not sure we can go back to the 1920s, and to the notions of the founders of Zionism who were really political and even anti-religious or, at least neutral with regard to religion. Religious Zionism, which was a very important part of the movement, provided the political ground to the other forces. In this respect, it was the romantic and emotional, not necessarily the

266

religious attitudes in Jabotinsky's* movement that gave rise to Betar's role in the *Kotel** riots and others.

MOSHE AMIRAV: That was actually not Jabotinsky. He was preaching for *Tel Hai**. Betar was pushing for the Kotel. There was a big conflict within his movement.

DALIA OFER: There were big conflicts in the Revisionist movement, in democracy and liberalism, and many other things, but I didn't want to get into that right now. Essentially, either since 1967, or more since 1973, we have this kind of domineering messianic movement within religious Zionism which prevents the separation that you suggest.

For me, it would be very easy. During or right after Camp David II, there was a big Peace Now demonstration at Jaffa Gate, and the slogan there was: "The conflict will end in Jerusalem." We were very optimistic, despite the failure at that point. Many Palestinians spoke at that demonstration, and the feeling was that, thinking politically, we can either divide or share. You know, there was talk then about the bottom and the top.

MOSHE AMIRAV: Jerusalem was solved at Camp David. The *Haram* was the only problem left.

DALIA OFER: So I'm not sure we can separate it today the way you suggest. I wish we could. I'm afraid that Bernard is right in his uneasiness about it, and I think it's true for both Jews and Muslims. There is something basic here in the connection between religion and nationalism. Of course, if we could do something to convince people, that would be very nice. I'm all for it.

One more thing about documentation. We talked a lot [at our earlier meetings] in Cyprus about not really having a shared history. We don't have a common ground. We talked about it in the sessions and outside of the sessions. And I don't think the issue is that we'll find common ground, but that we'll find a way to do at least two things that historians are always doing - understand intellectually, and then create historical empathy so that one can stand in the other side's shoes when one describes historical events.

I must say that my feeling was that this process is possible. That it is possible in this group is not so surprising because the people who come to such dialogues are people who are open and who have the will and so on. But it's a long process. When I came back from Cyprus, I talked with the students in my seminars about the need to see the other side in the academic context, not in the context of a political discourse, but in a discourse where you want to speak to people who will understand in a more neutral way. Of course, we are never neutral because it's our lives, but in our effort to be neutral, we do need this documentation.

I was born in Jerusalem. I was very young during the War of Independence, and by the time I became aware, Katamon and Baq'a were already Jewish neighborhoods, as was Talbiyeh. But I knew that they were not always Jewish neighborhoods. So it's not a matter of knowledge.

I sat in the library this morning and read these papers, and I don't know if the documentation is accurate or not. But I live in Ramot, and it is important for me to understand the connection between the 1948 and 1967 areas. When I say that we have to go back to the 1967 borders, it's important for me to understand what this statement means and what its implications are. We will not take this directly to the negotiation table; and as historians, we have no advantage over politicians, because they also know history. The only advantage one can have is some kind of insight into the long historical processes or conflicts. In that respect, I very much appreciate this documentation, not because of the common ground, but because of the process and the evolution that is taking place. Even within myself, I am certainly left of center. And if it did this to me, it is certainly important to others.

BERNARD SABELLA: Your point is very well taken. It's an excellent point. And it's because you care, and that's why you do what you do. But the majority on both sides doesn't care, especially now, and especially the younger generation.

DALIA OFER: But we cannot look at now. We have a role. What can we take from this? We are not sitting at the negotiations table. We have very little influence on politicians. I'm not a member of a party. What can I do? I can only work in my small corner, and I think I have an important corner in the university.

I'll give you an example. I have many graduate students from West Bank settlements at Hebrew University, and I taught a seminar on memory, history and education, and started with the refugee issue. One of my students came to me and told me that, because of what she studied with me for two years, she wants to invite me to come and speak about the refugee issue. I told her I would come, but I also suggested that she invite Adel Manna to speak as well. She hasn't yet agreed, but I think she will. She wasn't sure she could get the consent of their leadership to bring Adel Manna.

So we have to spread these things. Of course, we don't have time. We have to come to a political agreement as quickly as possible, but this is beyond our capabilities. But what we can do is to gradually bring the message to those who are not at the other extreme. It's a continuum. We are talking to those who are a few millimeters from us, but it's important to do it. Also on your side. I don't think there are angels and villains. I think there are human beings tragically involved in a conflict.

PAUL SCHAM: I very much appreciate the contributions, and I think the discussions and papers are fascinating, but the focus here is on the history up to 1948. So we do not have to focus on the relevance to the current situation.

Your insights are particularly valuable. Both of you have been involved in real-life negotiations dealing with the present situation. I am particularly following the Camp David debate, and we are even talking about possibly having a follow-up seminar on that, although we are clearly not the only ones looking at that. But I think our role here can be most valuable in looking at these issues in a historical framework and with the passage of time. Obviously, we are looking from a very specific political context. We are dealing again with some of the same issues that came up in 1948, and have been coming up in different ways ever since then.

The way you [Moshe Amirav] present perceptions and changes of perception is fascinating. I had never seen that until I read your paper. Your perceptions and Salim Tamari's both provide new insight, but I would hope we would be able to focus our discussion on how this was understood at the time, in the historical perspective. In a sense, that makes our lives easier because of your point about how difficult it is for the two sides. And with regard to Dalia's point, I think the more documentation the better when looking at history. The role of historians is fundamentally different from the role of policy people, even though you two demonstrate that they are sometimes the same people.

WALID SALEM: I noticed from Moshe's presentation that the de-politicization of the question of Jerusalem between King Hussein and the Israeli government during the occupation was, itself, actually a political decision.

MOSHE AMIRAV: For stability.

WALID SALEM: And the consequences were also political. The Jordanians decided to deal with the Israeli occupation as the status quo, as a fact on the ground that they wouldn't fight against, but at the same time agreed to make arrangements only at the religious level. So dealing with the question of Jerusalem at the religious level still led to political consequences, as evidenced by how Jordan and Israel dealt with the question after 1967. I feel your approach might be very relevant if political decision-makers had agreed that the religious personalities from the three faiths would decide this matter. There would be a political decision giving authority to the religious leaders from the three faiths to decide, and the idea of the council that Dr Sabella mentioned might be a solution.

Why do we continue talking about political sovereignty over religious sites? Let's talk about the sovereignty of God, and let's say that this can be decided by the three faiths by means of such a council. And it will still be a political decision in the end, not just a religious one. When you looked to Barak to make a decision, you were looking to a politician to decide whether religious personalities should deal with this question.

BERNARD SABELLA: I agree with Paul. But these two papers also indicate that the Israeli and Palestinian narratives are a mirror image of each other. We see what you do with documentation, and we do it. And sometimes you see what we are doing and you try to improvise and do it on your side. It's a two-way street. But I agree with you. There's nothing wrong with that if it's used to sensitize the other side. But often it's not.

DALIA OFER: It's used to justify.

BERNARD SABELLA: It's often used to justify one side. Moshe said something in the beginning which I think we better pay attention to - how do we define the problem. Sometimes we define the problem not according to the historical narrative, but in terms of the solution we want. It depends on what kind of historical narrative we want. The definition of the problem influences the method of our historical narrative.

Unfortunately it's not essential that we have common ground. I'm not optimistic. I was optimistic ten or eleven years ago. Now I'm not optimistic at all, and not simply because of what happened during the Intifada. I think pessimism began among people like me after Oslo, really, on both sides, every side. Therefore, instead of coming out with fantastic projects about common ground, maybe we would do better by defining our problem with the Zionist movement, rather than saying we have to look at it in an all-encompassing historical narrative.

What are the things that we defined in the Zionist movement? For example, in today's talk, and even in the 1930s and 40s, people spoke about "them" and "us." But isn't there anything in "them" that you can at least identify with, even though you might not agree with it? And the same with Jewish Zionist ideas. Can you find anything with which you can identify with the Palestinians? And how do you define your problem with them?

If you talk to an Israeli today, most likely he'll tell you that all Palestinians are bad. The other day I was talking to some young people at the university, and I was shocked because they told me there is no way we can reach a compromise with the Zionist entity. One of them told me it's an on-going conflict.

We are defining the problem in such all-encompassing terms that we are losing track of the smaller definitions. Maybe we should go back and look historically at those smaller definitions. I think it is important, at least on an academic level, as intellectuals, academics, people who look at the whole process and distance themselves a little from what is going on now, to find these definitions and put them to use in order to have some input, even though I'm not optimistic about the impact of that input.

BENJAMIN POGRUND: As a non-historian, I think the points you raise are enormously important. We cannot reconcile our story with your story. We don't have common ground. And sitting in Cyprus, reading these papers, as you've done, that certainly was the perception.

When I read the papers in advance, I thought, we're over here and they're over there, and there's a huge gap between us. But what I found, and what impressed me was that as people talked, there was an element of surprise at the end of each session about the extent to which people found agreement on some basic acceptance of what had occurred in the past. The gaps were not so big after all, and people had been able to agree on some basic elements. I found this exciting, and this is what Dalia was saying. What I found exciting also was the extent to which people were crossing the boundary in those meetings. Israelis were chiding their fellow Israelis for not listening, and not understanding; and the same from the Palestinian side.

So it's interesting that you have that reaction because it was also mine when I first read the papers. The organizers went to Cyprus with great anxiety. We thought we were in big trouble. But to our astonishment, somehow there was greater accord than anyone had anticipated, and that was marvelous. Paul said we are dealing with history, but some things here are very much in the present and future. I just bought an apartment in Katamon in Jerusalem.

BERNARD SABELLA: I am a refugee from Katamon.

BENJAMIN POGRUND: So we are all in the same basket after all. The building was built in the 1950s by the Jewish Agency or *Keren Hayesod*.* I have a friend who's been saying for years that the question of property in the Katamon area is a ticking time-bomb. People left under whatever circumstances and it was taken over by the custodian - whoever that was - and then sold off at cheap rates. This is going to come back to haunt us. And the last paragraph of Salim Tamari's statement is what interests me, because it seems to go beyond the general refugee issues, talking about people who left this village or that village. This is really a ticking-bomb because it seems to be more blunt and direct than almost any other refugee issue, unless I am just taking it personally because I live in Katamon.

BERNARD SABELLA: Don't worry about it. The Palestinian National Authority will make a deal and all our rights will go out the window. We are accustomed to that already.

BENJAMIN POGRUND: So Salim was overstating this?

BERNARD SABELLA: I think so. Our politicians have disappointed us more than they have disappointed you.

DALIA OFER: The direction that Salim takes is really that these issues have to be settled in some economic way. Jerusalem is part of the story.

MOSHE AMIRAV: I would like to comment on Salim's paper on this very point, the houses in Katamon. The problem of reconciliation in terms of a common narrative is, again, the political implications. If you take out the political implications, we can come together and write the story, and I tried that many years ago.

I have lived in an Arab house in Ein Kerem for many years, and I wrote a book about this village, which started with a small story about a trip I took to Bethlehem to find a Palestinian refugee from the village. I brought him back with me, along with his son, his grandson and his great-grandson, so he could tell me his story of Ein Kerem. When we went to see his house, we knocked on the door and Victoria Cohn, a Moroccan woman, opened it. She recognized me, and I explained to her that I was writing a book and that this Palestinian man used to live here. I told her that he wants to see his house, that he wants to tell the story of the house to his son, grandson and great-grandson, and that I am giving him the opportunity. I asked her if she would agree.

She was white-faced, but told us to come in. And then this old guy started telling the story about the trees and the house, and this was where he was born, and he talked on and on. And when he ended his story, we could all feel the tension in the air. He thanked me, we left, I told him I would write his story, and I took him back to Bethlehem. Then I asked him where he came from before Ein Kerem, and he told me that he was one of the village's four sheikhs, and that his family originated in Granada, Spain, in the 16th century, moved from there to North Africa, and then to Ein Kerem. I wrote his story, and then I went back to Victoria and apologized and asked her to tell me her story. She said: "We are a Moroccan family from Fez. We came here in 1951, and were put in this house in Ein Kerem. I didn't know who had been here before." Then I asked her where she came from before Fez? She told that they had come from Granada in 1492. Maybe her ancestors and the old man's were even on the same ship that sailed to North Africa.

This was a book about the house, not the two families. When I tell this story to Israelis, or when they read the book, they can sympathize with the story of the house, with the story of the two refugees. They have a common ground, you see. But if I ask somebody in Ein Kerem about the political implications, he will immediately say: "Oh, so he wants my house. No, no, no." Forget about the common ground. Forget the story. It is the political implication that scares us Israelis, admitting that this house belonged to a Palestinian. After I wrote this book, there was a program on television about it, and I suggested that we put a sign on each Arab house that gives you the name of the Arab family who had lived there. Palestinians were excited about the idea because, for them, the main thing was to preserve the memory, not to get the house back. They know they won't get the house in Ein Kerem back, but at least this way the memory will be kept alive.

BERNARD SABELLA: But it's a ticking-bomb.

MOSHE AMIRAV: Yes. But you have to deal with it. The Israelis will say: "You want just a sign? I'll put a sign. No problem." This is what I call defining the problem. The problem is not getting the house back. It's keeping the memory alive. This is my comment on what Salim says. The story is how we define the solution. The political solution is, of course, a bomb. But if we don't get into the political context, if we just speak about 1947 and what happened with this guy who left that house, we can find common ground, a common story and a common narrative, because it's a human narrative.

BERNARD SABELLA: You mentioned Katamon. My mother always talked about her need to go back to our home in Katamon. One day, when my mother was dying, my sister persuaded me that we have to go see the house and tell our mother about it. Finally, I agreed. I went with her. And we were shocked because the house was being destroyed and replaced by apartments. I said to my sister: "What do you want now? The house is gone. That's it." But she knew somebody in the Arab Affairs Department, and wanted to at least check with him to see what could be done. I was sure we would get nowhere, but she insisted. It was very painful. We went and spoke to that guy. He looked into it and told us that our home and property had been bought by a Jewish religious organization, and will be used only for religious Jews. We hid this information from our mother. She passed away still clinging to the hope that one day she would go back home.

The experience was so painful to me, and influenced me so much, that I rarely mention the house to my children so as to forget the pain. It was in order to say that we have to go on with the future rather than the past. But it's painful.

I agree that it's not simply the story of the house. But if you talk to my brothers and sisters today, they will tell you they at least want compensation for the property. In a famous interview in Time magazine, Teddy Kollek said: "We Israelis are very smart. We have established a fund to which the people of East Jerusalem can apply for reparations for their homes and property. These reparations will be paid out over 15 years. In this way, we maintain the fund and, at the same time, pay out the money. In the end, the fund will be greater than the money we paid out to the East Jerusalemites, and we will solve the Jerusalem property issue once and for all." To his surprise and shock - and that of others in the Israeli establishment - not one single Palestinian came forward to apply to that fund, because it wasn't fair. They wanted to pay the 1948 rate. Even the most stupid people would never accept that.

DALIA OFER: What if they would have paid the right rate? Twenty times more, fifty times more. I have no idea.

BERNARD SABELLA: No. It wasn't a question of money. It was a political question.

BENJAMIN POGRUND: What you're saying is that what Moshe said about it being only the memory is not true. It's a living pain.

BERNARD SABELLA: Right. I think the Israelis read us very well when they say the Palestinians want the 1948 property back. Last weekend, a young taxi driver took me from the bridge to Amman. I asked him where he was from. He told me he's from a small village in the Jerusalem area. When I asked why he wanted to return to a village that no longer exists, he told me because "it's my home. And if I were given the chance, I would go back."

We cannot wipe out the memory. It's the task of the politicians to find a way to make the memory of both sides accommodate one another. Unfortunately, we don't have politicians who are able to do that.

MOSHE AMIRAV: The memory I am speaking about is something that the Israelis deny. The acknowledgment by Israelis symbolized by putting these signs up on the houses would be revolutionary.

ANNE KOEHLER: Maybe there's another question to be put to that young taxi driver. If his right to come back would be acknowledged, then maybe he might be willing to accept compensation instead. He might think: "What does it mean for me to go back there? It means I have to live in Israel, start looking for a job … "

MOSHE AMIRAV: In talks I had with many Palestinian leaders before Camp David, they all insisted that 80 percent of the Palestinians don't want to go back physically. They want to go back in a symbolic way.

BERNARD SABELLA: I agree.

MOSHE AMIRAV: So you have to agree to the key, and the key is to acknowledge the memory, to say "Yes, this is your house in Jaffa, this is your house in Haifa." I had so many talks with Palestinians about this. When it comes to compensation - not money, but the memory - they say, "I'm not going back. Am I crazy? Go back to Haifa to live with Israelis, get Israeli citizenship and have all my neighbors be Jews? Of course not."

BERNARD SABELLA: And people who are doing well in Amman, Damascus, Beirut and elsewhere would not want to come here.

DALIA OFER: Adel Yahya talked about this at the conference on refugees in October. He didn't agree with your perception at all. He said people do want to go back. It doesn't matter what the leaders decide or what kind of agreement is signed, people really want to go back. The interviews he's conducting in his oral history project testify to that.

ANNE KOEHLER: He said they're insisting on the right of return. When asked what they mean by the right of return, in the end they say that it can also be symbolic, like the return of a contingent of Palestinian refugees, and the rest would receive compensation. But the first thing would be acknowledgment. Unless there is acknowledgment, they won't give up insisting on the right of return. It's also important to really acknowledge the sorrow and the tragedy of the other side. This is a start. I often have the feeling that Palestinians or Israelis are afraid to acknowledge each other as victims because that may then seem to minimize their own victimization.

BERNARD SABELLA: Acknowledgment is intellectual. I'm not

273

convinced that acknowledgment by itself is sufficient. I can acknowledge the pain of Israelis when some stupid suicide bomber blows himself up. And I'm sure there are many Israelis who acknowledge our pain when the soldiers at the checkpoints do not allow someone through and then he dies from the complications of a heart attack, or a pregnant woman doesn't make it to the hospital and so on.

Mutual acknowledgment would be fantastic. But my sense is that eventually it is the framework that can extricate us from the problem.

PAUL SCHAM: The two are not mutually exclusive. Acknowledgment can be expressed in political and social terms. You're right when you say those things to us, or when Israelis say: "He's a nice Palestinian, and he understands our pain." But I don't think that will change the situation. However, there are political means for expressing acknowledgment, and which we have not yet found. Camp David symbolized the peak of our ignoring that issue in certain respects, and look what came out of it.

BERNARD SABELLA: When I first read Moshe's paper, I realized that secular Zionists were not as interested in the Haram al Sharif then as they are now. Not the secular ones. They don't care about anything religious.

MOSHE AMIRAV: It was the consensus of the Zionist political leadership that they be not interested. They saw it as a bother, not as an asset.

BERNARD SABELLA: But now, no Israeli leader can give it away.

MOSHE AMIRAV: Today it is considered a big asset, the most important issue.

BENJAMIN POGRUND: Moshe, when you speak to religious Zionists today, or religious Jews, and talk about this veneration of the Temple Mount as something relatively new, how do they react? Do they call you a liar? Do they say: "Nonsense! It's always been ours"?

MOSHE AMIRAV: I spoke with former Minister Roni Milo about this. He is not at all religious. I asked him: "What's this thing about the Temple Mount? Is it historical? Is it religious? Is it sentimental?" He told me that it is the essence of Zionism. So then I told him the facts about how Zionism rejected the Temple Mount in the beginning. But he didn't believe me. He didn't know these things, not to mention that Herzl and Ussishkin and Ben Gurion and Levi Eshkol, all also rejected it. Eshkol sent his Foreign Minister, Abba Eban, to the United Nations a few weeks after the liberation of the Temple Mount, and there he said that Israel was ready to give up sovereignty over the Temple Mount. These were the Israeli Foreign Minister's words a few weeks after the big euphoria, and Roni didn't know about it.

So it's a matter of providing the information, putting it in context, and showing how things are changing.

BENJAMIN POGRUND: It's astonishing how history has been rewritten so rapidly and on such a scale. The clarity in which you set it out was also fascinating.

DALIA OFER: If you read Zionist textbooks - even new ones - you never find that the Temple Mount is so important.

MOSHE AMIRAV: It only began to be seen as the essence of Zionism in the 1980s and 90s. Before that it was peripheral.

WALID SALEM: Will the Israeli government accept solving the issue of religious sites using the religious approach?

MOSHE AMIRAV: Definitely. I'll tell you about a talk I had with Minister Dan Meridor at Camp David. He was telling me how he would not accept having the Temple Mount under Palestinian sovereignty, but that he would accept a joint Saudi-Jordanian-Egyptian condominium arrangement. When I asked him what the difference was he said that if it can be Palestinian sovereignty, then why not Israeli? So Dan Meridor's acceptance - and he comes from the right wing - means there is something to putting a new religious formula on it. Even Begin was ready for that. We can't find a more patriotic leader than Begin, and he was ready to give up sovereignty over the Temple Mount to an Arab League council or some other body.

WALID SALEM: There is the danger that this will be done without a formal political solution for all the questions of Jerusalem. Palestinians are sometimes worried about the Arab countries.

BERNARD SABELLA: Get ready because they're coming back.

WALID SALEM: We're afraid that the arrangement made between King Hussein and the Israeli government for that long period after 1967 will be repeated in such a way that Israeli sovereignty will continue at the political level, along with a religious arrangement between the Arab governments and Israel.

MOSHE AMIRAV: Moroccan leaders are asking why we are discussing the Temple Mount with the Palestinians. They don't see it as being our or the Palestinians' business, but rather theirs or the Egyptians. Of course, you can find some kind of a coalition between Israel and Egypt to screw the Palestinians on this issue. But that is not the question. The question is how we define the problem of the Temple Mount.

WALID SALEM: To what extent do you personally accept religious arrangements being made for the holy sites in Jerusalem prior to the overall resolution of all Jerusalem-related issues?

MOSHE AMIRAV: I don't believe in partial agreements. I don't believe in interim agreements. I believe in a solution which has to do with everything. Before Camp David II, I was advocating ideas that included every aspect of the conflict, even psychological problems. I was even talking about building a Nakba museum in Jaffa. This has something to do with the memory, and it goes along with the political aspect of the solution.

The religious aspect can be dealt with separately. Let's have a religious solution to the Temple Mount tomorrow. Of course, it's not fair if it will be partial. It will immediately be used politically. But if we take the context of a permanent solution between us and the Arab world - not only the Palestinians - we have to find a solution to the Temple Mount. It's not a problem only between the Palestinians and Israel, but among Muslims and Jews and Christians.

WALID SALEM: Archeological studies don't prove that the Temple Mount is what the Israelis claim it is.

PAUL SCHAM: You cannot prove something when all the material is removed. There is also nothing in the archeological studies that gives any indication that it may have been any other place. In the Christian Bible, Christians are told that not one stone shall be left standing on another. Then the Muslims came to rebuild the Haram six centuries after the destruction of the Temple, and there is every reason to believe that everything was systematically destroyed and used for other things. As far as I know, there is no archeological evidence whatsoever showing that it's located any place else.

MOSHE AMIRAV: The historical proof is in the Arabic term of *Beit al Maqdas*. This is the old name for Jerusalem given by the Arabs. But it's not important. They also didn't find archeological proof of Muhammad ever being in Jerusalem. It doesn't matter.

WALID SALEM: I raise it not because it's important, but only to say that religious legends are powerful.

MOSHE AMIRAV: The Wailing Wall is not part of the Temple. It has nothing to do with the Temple. These are archeological facts.

GLOSSARY

(* refers to an additional glossary entry)

Achdut Ha'avodah: (Hebrew) Literally, "The Unity of Labor." Israeli left-wing party in the 1940s, but generally with a more hard-line stance than the *Labour Party*.* Its best-known leaders were Yisrael Tabenkin and *Yigal Allon*.* Merged with *Mapai*.* and another Labour Zionist Party, Rafi, in 1968 to form the *Labour Party*.*

Ahad Ha'am: (Hebrew) "One of the people." Pen name of Asher Ginzberg (1856-1927), an early Zionist, who advocated a Jewish cultural center in Palestine.

Ali, Mohammed: (d. 1848) Ottoman Viceroy of Egypt who revolted against Ottoman rule and, in 1831, conquered Palestine. The Ottomans recovered it in 1840.

Aliyah: (Hebrew, pl. aliyot) To ascend. Traditionally used to describe the act of a Jew moving to the Land of Israel (see *Eretz Yisrael*.*). In modern Israeli history, the various waves of immigration to Israel, beginning with the First Aliyah of 1882.

Allon, Yigal: (1918-80) Commander of the *Palmach*.* in the 1948 War and later an Israeli government minister and leader of the *Achdut Ha'avodah*.* Party.

Army of Deliverance: A volunteer irregular force led by *Fawzi Al Kawukji*,* a Syrian guerrilla leader, in the North of Palestine during the 1948 War.

Balfour Declaration: A British government decision on 29 November 1917 which stated in part: "His Majesty's Government views with favor the establishment in Palestine of a national home for the Jewish people . . . it being clearly understood that nothing shall be done which may prejudice the civil and religious rights of existing non-Jewish communities in Palestine."

Ben Tzvi, Yitzhak: (1884-1963) A prominent Zionist leader who became the second President of Israel.

Betar: The youth movement of the Zionist right-wing *Revisionist movement*.* An acronym for "*Brit Yosef Trumpeldor*"* and also the place of an ancient Jewish battle against the Romans.

Bilad al Sham: (Arabic) Literally, the Land of Syria. Usually includes Lebanon, Jordan, and Palestine as well as the modern borders of Syria.

Biltmore Program: Resolutions by the Zionist leadership meeting in 1942 at the Biltmore Hotel in New York, calling for a Jewish Commonwealth in the postwar world.

Bund: Anti-Zionist Jewish socialists in Europe, advocating the use of Yiddish, not Hebrew.

Burak, Al: (Arabic) The wall where the Prophet Mohammed was believed to have tethered his horse (named Burak) before his ascent to Heaven. Known to Jews as the *Kotel* or *Western Wall*.*

Camp David II: The summit hosted by President Bill Clinton in July 2000, at which

Israeli and Palestinian leaders failed to make peace. Contrasted with Camp David I, in 1978, when President Jimmy Carter brokered a peace between Egypt and Israel.

Canaanites: Original inhabitants of Palestine, according to the Bible. Also a movement in Israel in the 1950s calling for solidarity between Israeli Jews and Palestinian Arabs and rejecting the Diaspora.

Circassian: A Muslim tribe from the Caucasus known for its fierce fighters. The Ottoman government sent large numbers into the Levant in the 19th century, and their descendants are still active in community life in Jordan, Palestine, and Israel. In Israel, they are among the few Muslims who serve in the army.

Dabkeh: (also *debkeh*) A traditional Middle Eastern dance that has become one of the best-known Palestinian cultural symbols.

Deir Yasin: A Palestinian village near Jerusalem (now within the city) that was the scene of a battle and of a massacre of Palestinians carried out by the *Etzel** and the *Lehi** on 9 April 1948.

Dunam: A land measure used in Palestine, Jordan, and Israel equal to 1,000 square meters, or about one-quarter of an acre.

Emir: (Arabic) Prince or ruler.

Eretz Yisrael: (Hebrew) Literally, the "Land of Israel." Traditionally, it included all of Palestine west of the Jordan River plus a portion of Jordan. However, the biblical references are in dispute, and some claim that it includes the land "from the Nile to the Euphrates."

Etzel: (Hebrew) Acronym for "National Military Organization," the pre-state underground military organization led by Menahem Begin and affiliated with the *Revisionist** movement. It is generally referred to outside Israel as the *"Irgun."*

Fatah: The organization founded by Yasir Arafat in 1959 and which he led until his death, whose name forms a reverse acronym for "the movement for liberation of the Palestinian homeland," and which became the major component of the Palestine Liberation Organization (PLO) when it was founded in 1965.

Fellah: (Arabic, pl. fellahin) Palestinian peasant.

Gordon, Aaron David: (1856-1922) Early Zionist figure who helped develop the *Labor Zionist** philosophy linking the land, Zionism, and culture.

Haganah: (Hebrew) Literally, "self-defense." The military wing of the Zionist community in Palestine from 1920 to 1948, which became the Israeli Army (*Tzahal**) in 1948.

Hajj: (Arabic) The pilgrimage to Mecca is one of the five pillars of Islam. Often used in the name of a person who has made the pilgrimage.

Hajji: (Arabic) One who has made the pilgrimage to Mecca.

Haram al Sharif: (Arabic) "The Noble Sanctuary," referring to the Dome of the Rock, the Al-Aqsa Mosque, and the entire Muslim religious space on the area that Jews refer to as the *Temple Mount.**

Hashemite: The royal family of Jordan, which traces its ancestry back to the Prophet Mohammed.

Hassid: (Hebrew, pl. Hassidim) Ultra-Orthodox Jews whose practices emphasize spirituality and joy, and who are usually part of a particular community following a specific "*rebbe.*"

Herzl, Theodor: (1860-1904) A Viennese journalist who founded the Zionist movement, and the author of *The Jewish State.*

Histadrut: Israel's General Federation of Labor, founded in 1923. Founded many early Zionist enterprises; closely associated with Labour parties.

Hourani: Native of the Houran region of southern Syria and northern Jordan.

Hussein, Sharif: (1853-1931) The patriarch of the Hashemite family during World War I, whose sons became rulers of Iraq and Transjordan. See also *Sharif.**

Husseini Family: One of the most prominent Palestinian families of Jerusalem, whose most famous member was Hajj Amin Al Husseini.

Jabotinsky, Ze'ev (Vladimir): (1880-1940) A prominent Zionist leader who founded the "*Revisionist*"* (right-wing) movement within Zionism and led it until his death.

Jazzar, Ahmed Pasha Al: Ottoman ruler of Acre (Akko) in the late 18th century; defended the city against Napoleon's attack.

Jewish National Fund: (Hebrew: *Keren Kayemet l'Yisrael*) Founded in 1901, it was the principal land-buying institution of the Zionist movement.

Kaoukji, Fawzi Al: (also Kawukji) Syrian leader of Palestinian *Army of Deliverance** in the 1948 War.

Kastner affair: A political uproar in Israel in the 1950s, based on allegations that Rudolf Kastner, a leader of the Hungarian Jewish community and later a *Mapai** official in Israel, had cooperated with the Nazis during the Holocaust.

Kibbush adamah: (Hebrew) Conquest of soil: Refers to the *Labour Zionist** ideology of redeeming the Land of Israel through work on the soil.

Kibbush avodah: (Hebrew) Conquest of work: Refers to the *Labour Zionist** ideology of redeeming the land through work, as opposed to hiring others.

Kibbutz: (Hebrew) Communal settlement, based on the ideals of *Labour Zionism,** used for settling the land. The first was founded in 1913.

Kufeyeh: (Arabic; also *kaffiyeh*) The checkered headdress for men that has become a Palestinian national symbol.

Labour Party: The official name of the main *Labour Zionist** Party after 1968, but often used, especially in foreign languages, for *Mapai** for many years before that.

Labour Zionism: The socialist wing of Zionism that was dominant from the 1920s until 1977, headed for much of that time by David Ben Gurion. It emphasized, especially during its early years, rural communal settlements such as *kibbutzim** and *moshavim.** It was usually divided into a number of different parties, of which the largest was *Mapai.**

Land of Israel: See *Eretz Yisrael.**

Lehi: (Hebrew) Acronym for "Fighters for the Freedom of Israel," the most radical of the pre-State Zionist underground military organizations.

MacDonald Letter: Written in 1931 by British Prime Minister Ramsay MacDonald, effectively reversing the Passfield White Paper of 1930, which had limited Zionist immigration and other activities in Palestine.

Mameluke: Egyptian rulers who conquered Palestine in 1250 and held it until it was taken by the Ottoman Turks in 1517.

Mapai: (Hebrew) Acronym for "The Party of the Workers of the Land of Israel," which was the dominant political party in the Yishuv* from 1930 until it merged with two other Labour-oriented parties in 1968 to form the *Labour Party*.*

Mapam: (Hebrew) Acronym for "The United Workers Party," a left-wing socialist-Zionist party that often opposed David Ben Gurion from the Left in the 1940s, '50s, and '60s. In 1992 it joined the "Meretz" bloc.

Mizrachi: (Hebrew, pl mizrachim) "Those from the East," usually referring to Jews of the Middle East and North Africa, many of whom came to Israel in the fifteen years after the 1948 War.

Moshav: (Hebrew, pl. moshavim) Cooperative settlements in Israel of various types, where families usually owned and farmed their own plots individually, rather than communally.

Mughrab: (Arabic) North Africa.

Mughrabi: (Arabic) One who comes from North Africa.

Mukhtar: (Arabic) The mayor, or traditional leader, of an Arab village.

Nakba: (Arabic) literally, "catastrophe." The word generally used in Arabic for the events of 1948 in Palestine and their aftermath.

Nashashibi Family: One of the most prominent Arab Jerusalem families, which was often more conciliatory on Arab-Jewish relations and frequently found itself in opposition to the *Husseinis*.*

Palmach: (Hebrew) Acronym for "Strike Companies," the strike force of the *Yishuv** in Palestine in the 1940s.

Peel Commission: British body that investigated the Arab Revolt of 1936-39 and, in its report, set out the first major Partition plan (1937).

Revisionism: The right-wing Zionist movement that eventually became the Herut Party and later the Likud.

Sanjak: (Turkish) District of the Ottoman Empire. In the last years of the Empire, Palestine was composed of the sanjaks of Jerusalem, Balka and Acre.

Sephardim: Jews whose ancestors lived in Spain and Portugal before 1492. Sometimes used to refer to Jews from North Africa and Asia, generally now called *Mizrachim*.

Shamir, Yitzhak: (1915-) Leader of the *Lehi** (Stern Gang) in the 1940s and Prime Minister of Israel 1983-84 and 1986-92.

Sharett, Moshe: (1894-1965) Zionist leader and Prime Minister of Israel from 1953-55. Before 1948, he used the last name Shertok.

Sharif: (Arabic) Noble. Used to refer to any descendant of the Prophet Mohammed.

Shari'a: (Arabic) Muslim (Koranic) law.

Shura: (Arabic) Consultation. Usually used to describe an Islamic alternative to formal democracy, implying consultation between government and people in the spirit of Islam.

Tabu: (Turkish) The Ottoman land registry; still the name for the land registry in the State of Israel.

Tanzimat: (Turkish) Literally "reorganization." Used for the reform program implemented in the Ottoman Empire between 1839 and 1876.

Tel Hai: Village in northern Palestine where *Yosef Trumpeldor** was killed in 1920. Used as a symbol of militant Zionism.

Templars: A group of devout German Christians who established a number of settlements in Palestine in the late 19th century. They were expelled by the British after the outbreak of World War II.

Temple Mount: The area in Jerusalem where the first and second Jewish Temples are believed to have stood. It is essentially the same area as the *Haram al-Sharif.**

Transjordan: Created in 1922 in the portion of the British Mandate east of the Jordan River. Became independent in 1946 and adopted the name "Jordan" in 1949.

Trumpeldor, Yosef: (1880-1920) Early Zionist military leader who was killed at the *Battle of Tel Hai.**

Tzahal: (Hebrew) An acronym for "Army for the Defense of Israel." The usual Hebrew expression for the Israeli Army.

Umma: (Arabic) The community of all Muslims.

UNRWA: (United Nations Relief and Works Agency) The United Nations Agency that has had the principal responsibility for providing care for the Palestinian refugees of 1948 and 1967 and their descendants.

Waqf: (Arabic) The charitable trust in a Muslim community that often owns and cares for religious buildings and institutions, such as the *Haram al Sharif** in Jerusalem.

Wattan: (Arabic) Homeland.

Weizmann, Chaim: (1874-1952) Leader of the Zionist movement from World War I until the 1940s. Instrumental in obtaining the Balfour Declaration. First President of the State of Israel.

Western Wall: Believed to be the only standing remnant of the Second Temple complex in Jerusalem built by King Herod. The focus of Jewish prayer and lamentation since its destruction in 70 CE. Also known as the Wailing Wall or the *Kotel.** Muslims know it as *Al Burak.**

Yishuv: (Hebrew) Literally, settlement. Usually refers to the Jewish community in Israel before 1948. "Old *Yishuv*" designates older, more religious, non-nationalistic Jewish communities; New *Yishuv* refers to the Zionist settlements that began in 1881.

Young Turks: The Turkish army-centered faction that took power in the Ottoman Empire in 1908 and ruled until the end of the Empire.

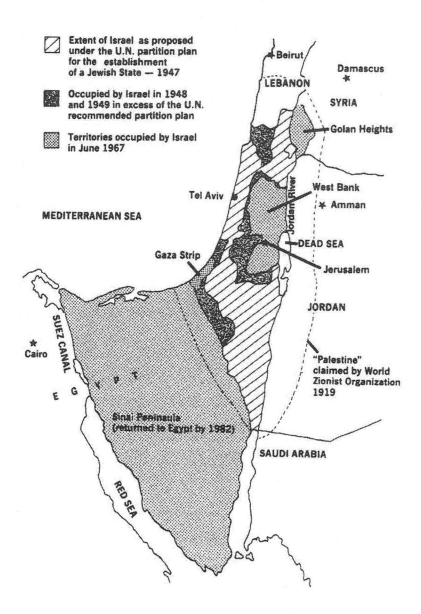

Israel/Palestine, showing 1947 Partition Plan, 1948 Boundaries, and Borders After the 1967 War. Reprinted from *Understanding the Contemporary Middle East*, 2nd edition, edited by Deborah J. Gerner and Jillian Schwedler. Copyright © 2004 by Lynne Rienner Publishers, Inc. Reprinted with permission of the publisher.

FOR FURTHER READING

This makes no pretence to being a comprehensive bibliography of even the most important works illustrating the two narratives. The literature on every aspect of the Israeli-Palestinian conflict is huge, and growing daily. However, this bibliography is intended to be used to locate works that give either a joint or separate perspective on the conflict, and would be particularly useful for classes or for discussion groups on the subject.

Avineri, Shlomo. *The Making of Modern Zionism: The Intellectual Origins of the Jewish State.* New York: Basic Books, 1981. A classic from a prominent Israeli professor writing within the Israeli tradition.

Benvenisti, Meron. *Sacred Landscape: The Buried History of the Holy Land since 1948.* Berkeley, Calif.: University of California Press, 2000. A fascinating analysis of how Israeli geographers transformed the landscape of Palestine, by an Israeli geographer and project participant.

Bregman, Ahron. *A History of Israel.* New York: Macmillan, Palgrave, 2002. A new, brief history of Israel with an eclectic perspective.

Enderlin, Charles. *Shattered Dreams: The Failure of the Peace Process in the Middle East, 1995-2002.* New York: Other Press, 2003. A French journalist's history of the peace process, and especially Camp David, in the words of the participants.

Ezrahi, Yaron. *Rubber Bullets: Power and Conscience in Modern Israel.* Berkeley: University of California Press, 1997. A well-known dovish Israeli professor reflects on the history and culture of Israel through the prism of his own life and experiences.

Farsoun, Samih. *Palestine and the Palestinians.* Boulder, Colo.: Westview, 1997. A Palestinian sociologist writes about his people.

Gelber, Yoav. *Palestine 1948: War, Escape and the Emergence of the Palestinian Refugee Problem.* Brighton, England: Sussex Academic Press, 2001. A prominent and highly respected right-wing Israeli professor discusses the 1948 War.

Grossman, David. *The Yellow Wind.* New York: Farrar, Strauss, 1988. An extraordinary and unique account of Palestinians and Israelis in the West Bank by an Israeli, written on the eve of the first Intifada.

Hadawi, Sami. *Bitter Harvest: A Modern History of Palestine.* Ithaca, N.Y.: Olive Branch Press, 1989. A classic history of Palestine by a Palestinian scholar who lived through the Nakba.

Hertzberg, Arthur, ed. *The Zionist Idea.* Philadelphia: The Jewish Publication Society, Rev. ed., 1997. An important collection of documents with analysis by a liberal Zionist rabbi and scholar.

Khalidi, R. *Palestinian Identity: The Construction of Modern National Consciousness.* New

York: Columbia University Press, 1997. A discussion of Palestinian identity through his own family history by a prominent Palestinian-American historian who is the scion of a famous old Jerusalem family.

Kimmerling, Baruch and Joel Migdal. *The Palestinian People: A History*. Cambridge, Mass.: Harvard University Press, 2003. A sympathetic and important treatment of Palestinian history by a left-wing Israeli scholar and an American professor.

Laqueur, Walter, *A History of Zionism*. New York: any ed. A general history of the Zionist movement from the beginnings of the movement to 1948 from a traditional Zionist perspective.

Mattar, P. *The Mufti of Jerusalem: Muhammad Amin al-Husayni, a Founder of Palestinian Nationalism*. New York: Columbia University Press, Rev. ed., 1985. A biography of a major figure in Palestinian history by a Palestinian-American scholar who has taken significant account of both narratives in his work.

Morris, Benny. *The Birth of the Palestinian Refugee Problem, 1947-1949*. Cambridge, UK: Cambridge University Press, 1989. A study using new Israeli archival research that contains some of the seminal research contradicting the traditional Israeli narrative of 1948. A new edition was published in 2004.

Morris, Benny. *Righteous Victims: A History of the Zionist-Arab Conflict, 1881-1999*. London: John Murray, 2000. One of the best general histories of the conflict by a controversial Israeli "New" historian.

Muslih, Muhammad. *The Origins of Palestinian Nationalism*. New York: Columbia University Press, 1988. A Palestinian scholar looks at the PLO and its beginnings.

Oren, Michael B. *Six Days of War: June 1967 and the Making of the Modern Middle East*. New York: Oxford University Press, 2002. A highly respected recent history of the 1967 War by a mainstream Israeli historian.

Pappe, Ilan. *The Making of the Arab Israeli Conflict 1947-51*. New York: St. Martin's Press, 1992. A significant work by a highly controversial Israeli scholar who generally supports the Palestinian cause.

Rogan, Eugene L. and Shlaim, Avi, eds. *The War for Palestine: Rewriting the History of 1948*. Cambridge, UK: Cambridge University Press, 2001. A collection of essays giving new interpretations to aspects of the 1948 conflict.

Said, Edward. *The Question of Palestine*. New York: Vintage, 1980. A classic by the best-known post-modernist Palestinian scholar.

Segev, Tom. *One Palestine Complete: Jews and Arabs under the British Mandate*. New York: Henry Holt, 1999. A very readable social history of the mandate period by a non-academic Israeli often identified as a revisionist historian.

Shapira, Avraham, ed. *The Seventh Day: Soldiers Talk about the Six Day War*. London: Andre Deutch, 1970. An unusual collection of memories of and feelings about the war by Israeli soldiers, given shortly after its conclusion.

Shlaim, Avi. *The Iron Wall: Israel and the Arab World*. New York: Norton, 2000. A prominent Israeli historian gives a revisionist perspective on Israeli foreign policy.

Silberstein, L. *The Postzionism Debates: Knowledge and Power in Israeli Culture*. London:

Routledge, 1999. A discussion of the post-Zionist movement in Israeli scholarship by an American scholar sympathetic to it.

Smith, Charles. *Palestine and the Arab-Israeli Conflict: A History with Documents*. New York: St. Martin's Press, 2001. The most-assigned text on the conflict by an American historian.

Sprinzak, Ehud. *The Ascendance of Israel's Radical Right*. New York, Oxford, 1991. A discussion of the religious right and the settler movement by a noted Israeli political scientist.

Tessler, M. *History of the Israeli-Palestinian Conflict*. Bloomington: Indiana University Press, 1994. A comprehensive, though slightly dated, history of the conflict, attempting to give the perspective of both sides.

INDEX

(prepared for American publication)

ABOUT THE CONTRIBUTORS

Dr. Ran Aaronsohn is a historical geographer of the modern Middle East. He is a Senior Lecturer in the Hebrew University's Geography Department, and has published extensively on the late nineteenth and early twentieth centuries and on problems of modernization and colonization with regard to Jewish immigration to Eretz Yisrael/Palestine in that period. He is still red-headed.

Moshe Amirav is Director of the Department for Public Policy, Beit Berl College, and Associate Professor of Political Science and Public Policy, Haifa University. He was Advisor on Jerusalem Affairs to Prime Minister Ehud Barak during peace talks with Palestinians and has written or edited six books about Jerusalem.

Amneh Badran is Director of the Jerusalem Center for Women (JCW), an NGO committed to protection of human rights, advancement of women's rights, and realization of a Middle East peace based on justice. As coordinator of the Jerusalem Unit of JCW, Ms. Badran directs projects and activities that focus on conflict resolution, coalition building, human rights, and nonviolent resistance.

Dr. Meron Benvenisti is a historian, former Deputy Mayor of Jerusalem, and author of books on Jerusalem, the Israeli-Arab conflict, cemeteries and the Crusader Period in Palestine. In the 1980s he initiated the West Bank Data Project, which recorded and analyzed conditions in the occupied territories and established a basis for future studies. Dr. Benvenisti is currently editing his autobiography for publication.

Dr. Michael Burckhard Blanke was resident representative of the Friedrich Naumann Foundation in Jerusalem from 1999 to 2002 and served as chairman of this conference. A historian and political scientist, he has had extensive experience in development projects, in adult education, and in dialogue activities, mainly in Latin America. Dr. Blanke is now retired and living in Germany.

Lily Galili is a senior writer with the Israeli newspaper *Ha'aretz*. For over twenty years she has followed the changing face of Israeli society and its schisms, including those between Sephardi and Ashkenazi, religious and secular, veteran Israelis and new immigrants, Jews and Arabs. She also focuses on extra-parliamentary protest movement and the Israeli peace camp.

Aziz Haidar is a Palestinian/Israeli sociologist and graduate of the Hebrew University of Jerusalem. He is Professor at the Center for Regional Studies at Al Quds University in East Jerusalem.

Manuel Hassassian is Professor of International Politics and Relations and Executive Vice President of Bethlehem University. His field is comparative politics, emphasizing Middle East politics, Armenian nationalist movements, and political theory. He has published extensively in these areas, and also written numerous articles on the PLO, the peace process, democracy and elections, refugees, and civil society in Palestine.

Ruth Kark is Professor of Geography at the Hebrew University, Jerusalem. She has written and edited twenty books and over 150 articles on the history and historical geography of Palestine and Israel. Her research interests include concepts of land, land use, and patterns of land ownership globally, with special emphasis on the Middle East.

Anne Koehler is Project Coordinator on the Israel Desk of the Friedrich Naumann Foundation, Jerusalem, with emphasis on Israeli-Palestinian dialogue projects. She is an M.A. student in Yiddish Literature.

Dr. Adel H. Manna is Director of The Institute for Israeli Arab Studies of the Van Leer Jerusalem Institute and Research Fellow at the Truman Institute, Hebrew University. He has authored more than twenty-three publications.

Moshe Ma'oz is Professor Emeritus of Islamic and Middle Eastern Studies and former Director of the Truman Institute for the Advancement of Peace at Hebrew University. He has published a number of works on Syrian and Palestinian history and politics, Arab-Israeli relations, and Middle Eastern minorities. He has also organized and participated in numerous projects and workshops with Palestinian scholars.

Issam Nassar is Assistant Professor in the Department of History, Bradley University in Peoria, Illinois. He is also Associate Director, Institute of Jerusalem Studies in Jerusalem, and is affiliated with the Institute for Palestine Studies of Washington, Beirut, and Paris. He lectures and has written numerous books and articles.

Dalia Ofer is Professor of Holocaust Studies at the Avraham Harman Institute of Contemporary Jewry, Hebrew University. She was formerly head of the Vidal Sassoon International Center for the Study of Anti-Semitism. The six books she has written and edited include *Escaping the Holocaust* and *Illegal Immigration to the Land of Israel 1939-1944*.

Benjamin Pogrund is founder and Director of Yakar's Center for Social Concern, Jerusalem. South African born, he was formerly deputy editor of the *Rand Daily Mail*, Johannesburg, and also worked on newspapers in Britain and the United States. He is the author of books on Robert Mangaliso Sobukwe, Nelson Mandela, and the press under apartheid.

Fatmeh Qassem is a Ph.D. student in the Department of Behavior Sciences at Ben Gurion University, Beersheba. She was previously a Lecturer/Facilitator in the department's Coexistence Through Life Stories project. She was founder and director of The Association to Promote Negev Bedouin Women's Education.

Ata Qaymari is a Jerusalem journalist. He works in writing, consulting, evaluating, and facilitating projects in media, translation, peace, and conflict resolution. He is General Director of Almasdar Translation and Press Services; a columnist for *Al-Quds* newspaper, assistant correspondent of the Japanese newspaper *Asahi*, and project evaluator and workshop facilitator at the Panorama Center.

Norman Rose is a historian and graduate of the London School of Economics. He is a Professor and holds the Chair of International Relations at the Hebrew University, Jerusalem. A Fellow of the Royal Historical Society, his books include biographies of Winston Churchill and Chaim Weizmann, and a study of the Cliveden Set.

Bernard Sabella is Professor of Sociology at Bethlehem University, co-author of numerous academic articles and books, and Executive Secretary of the Department of Services to Palestinian Refugees in the Middle East Council of Churches. Publications include *A Date with Democracy—Palestinians on Politics, Economy and Society* (1983) as well as publications on the emigration of Christian Arabs from the Middle East.

Walid Salem is Director of Panorama Center (The Palestinian Center for Dissemination of Democracy and Community Development), Jerusalem Branch. He is also a journalist, and is active in writing, consulting on, evaluating, and facilitating projects. He has trained 25,000 people, including 15,000 young people throughout the West Bank in democracy and human rights.

Trained as a lawyer, **Paul Scham** has worked in universities and NGOs on Israeli-Palestinian reconciliation issues since 1989. During 1996-2002, he coordinated joint academic projects with Palestinians and Jordanians at the Truman Institute. He is currently a Scholar at the Middle East Institute and a Visiting Scholar at George Washington University, both in Washington, D.C.

Avraham Sela is Professor of Middle East studies in the Department of International Relations at the Hebrew University of Jerusalem. He specializes on the history of Arab-Israeli relations and Palestinian politics and society. His most recent book (with Shaul Mishal), is *The Palestinian Hamas: Vision, Violence and Adjustment* (New York: Columbia University Press, 2000).

Professor Salim Tamari is Director of the Institute of Jerusalem Studies (Jerusalem) and a Professor in the Department of Sociology and Anthropology of Birzeit University.

He edits the *Jerusalem Quarterly File* for the Institute of Jerusalem Studies and serves as a consultant on socioeconomic surveys, project assessments, and rural and community projects. He is the author of more than fourteen books.

Dr. Adel Husein Yahya is Director of the Palestinian Association for Cultural Exchange (PACE) in Ramallah, with a Ph.D. in Near Eastern History and Archaeology from the Free University of Berlin. Besides numerous articles, his books include *The Origin of the Philistines, An Oral History Manual for Field Workers, The Pace Tour Guide of the West Bank and the Gaza Strip*, and *The Palestinian Refugees in 1948-1998 (An Oral History)*.